Between Community and Collaboration

This is the first comprehensive, comparative study of the 'Jewish Councils' in the Netherlands, Belgium and France during Nazi rule. In the post-war period, there was extensive focus on these organisations' controversial role as facilitators of the Holocaust. They were seen as instruments of Nazi oppression, aiding the process of isolating and deporting the Jews they were ostensibly representing. As a result, they have chiefly been remembered as forms of collaboration. Using a wide range of sources including personal testimonies, diaries, administrative documents and trial records, Laurien Vastenhout demonstrates that the nature of the Nazi regime, and its outlook on these bodies, was far more complex. She sets the conduct of the Councils' leaders in their pre-war and wartime social and situational contexts and provides a thorough understanding of their personal contacts with the Germans and clandestine organisations. *Between Community and Collaboration* reveals what German intentions with these organisations were during the course of the occupation and allows for a deeper understanding of the different ways in which the Holocaust unfolded in each of these countries.

Laurien Vastenhout is researcher and lecturer at the NIOD Institute for War, Holocaust and Genocide Studies in Amsterdam. She received her doctorate in History at the University of Sheffield and was awarded various scholarships and prizes, including the Claims Conference Saul Kagan Fellowship in Advanced Shoah Studies and a Yad Vashem research fellowship.

T0382279

Studies in the Social and Cultural History of Modern Warfare

In recent years the field of modern history has been enriched by the exploration of two parallel histories. These are the social and cultural history of armed conflict, and the impact of military events on social and cultural history.

Studies in the Social and Cultural History of Modern Warfare presents the fruits of this growing area of research, reflecting both the colonization of military history by cultural historians and the reciprocal interest of military historians in social and cultural history, to the benefit of both. The series offers the latest scholarship in European and non-European events from the 1850s to the present day.

A full list of titles in the series can be found at: www.cambridge.org/modernwarfare

Between Community and Collaboration

'Jewish Councils' in Western Europe under Nazi Occupation

Laurien Vastenhout

NIOD Institute for War, Holocaust and Genocide Studies, Amsterdam

CAMBRIDGE
UNIVERSITY PRESS

Shaftesbury Road, Cambridge CB2 8EA, United Kingdom

One Liberty Plaza, 20th Floor, New York, NY 10006, USA

477 Williamstown Road, Port Melbourne, VIC 3207, Australia

314–321, 3rd Floor, Plot 3, Splendor Forum, Jasola District Centre, New Delhi – 110025, India

103 Penang Road, #05–06/07, Visioncrest Commercial, Singapore 238467

Cambridge University Press is part of Cambridge University Press & Assessment, a department of the University of Cambridge.

We share the University's mission to contribute to society through the pursuit of education, learning and research at the highest international levels of excellence.

www.cambridge.org
Information on this title: www.cambridge.org/9781009054416

DOI: 10.1017/9781009053532

First published 2022
First paperback edition 2024

A catalogue record for this publication is available from the British Library

Library of Congress Cataloging-in-Publication data
Names: Vastenhout, Laurien, author.
Title: Between community and collaboration : 'Jewish Councils' in Western
Europe under Nazi Occupation / Laurien Vastenhout, NIOD Institute for
War, Holocaust and Genocide Studies, Amsterdam.
Description: Cambridge, United Kingdom ; New York, NY : Cambridge
University Press, 2023. | Based on author's thesis (doctoral –
University of Sheffield, 2020) issued under title: The 'Jewish Councils'
of Western Europe : a comparative analysis. | Includes bibliographical
references and index.
Identifiers: LCCN 2022009575 | ISBN 9781316511688 (hardback) |
ISBN 9781009053532 (ebook)
Subjects: LCSH: Jewish councils – Europe, Western – History – 20th century. |
Jews – Europe, Western – Politics and government – 20th century. |
Holocaust, Jewish (1939–1945) – Belgium. | Holocaust, Jewish
(1939–1945) – France. | Holocaust, Jewish (1939–1945) – Netherlands.
Classification: LCC KBM2612.J83 V37 2023 | DDC 940.53/18–dc23/eng/20220729
LC record available at https://lccn.loc.gov/2022009575

ISBN   978-1-316-51168-8   Hardback
ISBN   978-1-009-05441-6   Paperback

To Mark, light of my life

Contents

Illustrations

Preface

This book has been written to understand the circumstances and mindset that shaped Jewish leaders' choices and behaviour in Nazi-occupied Western Europe. The controversy still surrounding the 'Jewish Councils',[1] and the supposed collaboration with German authorities of their chairmen, stimulated my desire to provide a comprehensive understanding of these organisations in Western Europe (the Netherlands, Belgium and France). During the course of this research, I realised that a comparative approach is crucial if we want to fully grasp the histories of these organisations, because such an approach enables a more thorough understanding of how local conditions shaped German rule in the occupied territories and, in turn, how differences in local conditions affected the form and function of the 'Jewish Councils' as well as the choices of their leaders.

The image on the cover of this book depicts one of the administrative departments of the Jewish Council in the Netherlands (De Joodsche Raad voor Amsterdam), situated in Amsterdam. It is symbolic of the organisation's day-to-day reality. During the course of this investigation, reading through numerous personal testimonies, meeting reports and other administrative sources, it was striking to see how quickly the 'Jewish Councils' in Western Europe turned into expansive bureaucratic apparatuses. On a daily basis, employees of the administrative offices dealt with numerous letters of Jewish individuals who needed (social or financial) support, or material resources, while they also facilitated

---

[1] As will be further explained in the introduction of this book, the term 'Jewish Councils' (the literal translation of the term *Judenräte*) is not an entirely accurate term for all representative organisations the German authorities imposed upon the Jewish communities across Europe. For example, in Belgium and France respectively, the Association des Juifs en Belgique (AJB) and the Union Générale des Israélites de France (UGIF) were referred to as Associations. Yet because 'Jewish Councils' is a widely used and understood concept, it was considered most straightforward to use the term, between quotation marks, in certain instances when general references are made to these organisations (including those in Belgium and France).

communication between the organisation's numerous departments and sub-departments. The piles of paper on the desk in this photograph are illustrative of the bureaucracy involved.

The cover image is part of a series of more than 100 photographs in which the work of the Jewish Council in the Netherlands is visually recorded. The photographer Johan de Haas produced the images on the occasion of the sixtieth birthday of the chairman of the Dutch Council, David Cohen, on 31 December 1942. It was a period in which there was little to celebrate. Between summer and winter 1942, conditions for Jews in the Netherlands, and Western Europe more broadly, had drastically deteriorated. As decreed by the German authorities, summer 1942 marked the start of the mass deportations of Jews to Eastern Europe and there was uncertainty about the fate of those deported. Jews were increasingly deprived of their basic human rights. Moreover, German pressure on the 'Jewish Councils' to facilitate the removal of Jews from society grew. In this atmosphere of distress and anxiety, the Dutch Council's functionaries wondered whether it was appropriate to celebrate Cohen's anniversary. In the end, they decided they *had* to. On the day of the celebration, Meyer de Vries (general advisor to the Jewish Council), Henri Eitje (who chaired the Council's Aid to Non-Dutch Jews department) as well as Chief Rabbi Simon Dasberg, all emphasised in their speeches for Cohen that they wished to honour him because, for years, he had tirelessly dedicated himself to the plight of the Jews.[2]

Surrounded by his closest colleagues and representatives of the Jewish communities throughout the Netherlands, David Cohen (Illustration P.1) received a photo-album that captured the social work in which the Council's functionaries were engaged.[3] While many images were taken at the organisation's main office at the Nieuwe Keizersgracht in Amsterdam, the work of other departments is also shown, including that of the so-called Expositur, where exemptions from deportation to Eastern Europe for Jewish individuals were arranged, as well as that of the office for Help for the Departing (Illustration P.2). The so-called *Gids voor den Joodschen Raad* (Guide to the Jewish Council), published in March 1943, shows that the Dutch Council consisted of more than 150 departments, sub-departments and commissions. These included the bureau for Extracurricular Youth

---

[2] Speeches of Meyer de Vries, Henri Eitje and Simon Dasberg in honour of David Cohen, Doc I 248-0294, Prof. D. Cohen, Inv. No. 2, NIOD Institute for War, Holocaust and Genocide Studies, Amsterdam.

[3] René Kok, 'Het fotoalbum van de Joodsche Raad voor Amsterdam', in Willy Lindwer (ed.), *Het fatale dilemma: De Joodsche Raad voor Amsterdam 1941–1943* (The Hague: SDU Uitgeverij Koninginnegracht, 1995), 173. There exist photos and photo-albums that capture the work of other Jewish Councils in Nazi-occupied Europe as well. A notable example is that of the Judenrat in Łódź. For further reading on this, see Tanja Kinzel, *Im Fokus der Kamera. Fotografien aus dem ghetto Lodz* (Berlin: Metropol, 2021), 127–369; Paweł

Illustration P.1 Chairman of the Joodsche Raad voor Amsterdam
(JR), David Cohen (centre), at Olympia Square in Amsterdam during
a raid, 20 June 1943. Photograph by Herman Heukels. Reproduced by
kind permission of the NIOD, Amsterdam.

Care (Illustration P.3), a sub-department at Tehuis Oosteinde that was
responsible for sewing and mending (Illustration P.4), and a commission
that administered the distribution of vegetables (see Illustration P.5).

Fifty years later, De Haas reflected on his visit to the organisation's
offices. He was struck by the fact that the employees were eager to be
portrayed.[4] Perhaps, having witnessed the deportation of thousands of
Jews from the Netherlands at this point, and unsure about their own
future, they wanted to leave a visual trace of themselves, and their work,
behind. Today, the whereabouts of the album, if it still exists, remains
unknown. Fortunately, De Haas preserved the negatives.

In addition to the photographs, numerous other sources bear witness
to the untiring efforts the Council's employees and its leaders to provide

Michna, 'Visual Representations of modernity in documents from the Łódź Ghetto' in
Jack Dominic Palmer and Dariusz Brzeziński (eds), *Revisiting Modernity and the Holocaust:
Heritage, Dilemmas, Extensions* (Abingdon, Oxon; New York, NY: Routledge, 2022)
88–107; and 'Modernism in the Lodz Ghetto. A Tentative Interpretation of Forgotten
Holocaust Documents', *Miejsce (Place)*, Vol. 6 (2020), 81–111; Andrea Löw, 'Documenting
as a "Passion and Obsession": Photographs from the Lodz (Litzmannstadt) Ghetto',
Central European History, Vol. 48, No. 3 (2015), 387–404.
[4] Statement of Johan de Haas in Lindwer, *Het fatale dilemma*, 170.

Illustration P.2 Employees of the Help for the Departing department in front of the JR office at Oudeschans 74 in Amsterdam, late 1942. Photograph by Johan de Haas. Reproduced by kind permission of the De Haas family and the NIOD.

assistance to the Jews in the Netherlands. In Belgium and France, the situation was similar. The Union Générale des Israélites de France Nord (UGIF-Nord) and the UGIF-Sud administered a wide range of social aid activities in France, including the provision of juridical aid to Jews, schooling and the supply of food through canteens. Numerous departments and sub-departments of the UGIF were scattered across both occupied and unoccupied France. The Association des Juifs en Belgique (AJB) in Belgium similarly provided care to the Jewish communities. In June 1942, a representative of the AJB Brussels branch (and member of the central board), Salomon van den Berg, wrote that the organisation sought to help the poor, assisted in emigration efforts and provided schooling, adding that the organisation 'has done a good job in social matters, not caring in the least about political issues'.[5] In February 1943, the former secretary of

---

[5] Salomon van den Berg, Journal de guerre, p. 37, A006685, Joods Museum van Deportatie en Verzet (JMDV), Centre National des Hautes Études Juives (CNHEJ), Buber Collection, Kazerne Dossin, Mechelen.

Illustration P.3 Children celebrating Chanukah, organised by the Extra-curricular Youth Care department of the JR, late 1942. Photograph by Johan de Haas. Reproduced by kind permission of the De Haas family and the NIOD.

the AJB central board likewise indicated that the organisation's sole aim was to provide for the social and legal needs of the Jewish communities in Belgium.[6]

Most Jewish leaders under Nazi rule were first and foremost interested in alleviating the suffering of their communities. In doing so, they faced a dilemma: they could only provide social assistance if they cooperated with the Germans. Their intention to do so was increasingly frustrated as they were forced to deal with and abide by increasing anti-Jewish legislation. As a result, Jewish leaders had to perform a balancing act, assisting their communities while giving in to German demands, simultaneously trying to minimise their level of cooperation. To them, cooperation with

[6] Maurice Benedictus, 'Historique du problème Juif en Belgique depuis le 10 Mai 1940 jusqu'au 21 Décembre 1942', 18 February 1943, A006683, JMDV, CNHEJ, Buber Collection, Kazerne Dossin.

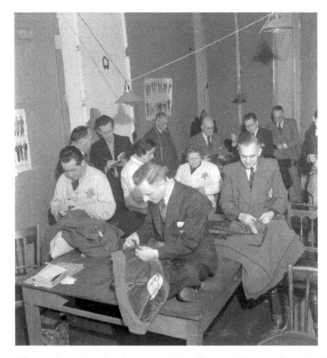

Illustration P.4 Sewing and Mending at Tehuis Oosteinde, a sub-department of the JR, late 1942. Photograph by Johan de Haas. Reproduced by kind permission of the De Haas family and the NIOD.

the Germans and assisting Jewish communities were two sides of the same coin.

As the deportation process accelerated, the line between cooperation and collaboration became thinner. Contemporaries as well as scholars have labelled the Jewish leaders' wartime behaviour as collaboration or have used the terms 'collaboration' and 'cooperation' interchangeably. Yet, in line with what the historian and political scientist Evgeny Finkel has argued, I believe we should make a distinction between the two concepts in the context of the 'Jewish Councils'. Those Jews who *cooperated* with the Germans first and foremost set out to safeguard and help the wider community; those who *collaborated* were motivated by personal gain and were not aiming to serve the interests of their communities at large. From the German viewpoint, Jews' collaboration was most desirable and effective since it merely involved placating the Jewish leaders and (pretending to) acquiesce to their individual interests. Caught between their own wish to help the communities on the one hand, and

Illustration P.5 Vegetable Distribution department of the JR, late 1942. Photograph by Johan de Haas. Reproduced by kind permission of the De Haas family and the NIOD.

increasing German pressure to collaborate on the other, Jewish leaders in Western Europe, whether successfully or not, continued to make their decisions according to the perceived interests of the community at large.

The foundations of this book were laid in January 2013, when I wrote a comparative research paper on the 'Jewish Councils' of the Netherlands and Belgium. I am grateful beyond measure to the teachers who then encouraged me to develop this project further and who have now become my close colleagues at the NIOD Institute for War, Holocaust and Genocide Studies in Amsterdam. Specifically, I want to thank Nanci Adler, Thijs Bouwknegt and Uğur Ümit Üngör for their invaluable support, and for being an inspiration.

I owe a great debt to the large number of scholars who were willing to exchange thoughts on this subject, and who, during various stages, shaped this project. First and foremost, I had the great fortune of having two exceptional supervisors at the University of Sheffield, where I completed my doctoral studies. Bob Moore and Daniel Lee offered indispensable guidance and advice, both during and after my studies. Their knowledge and zeal have been nothing if not inspiring. The generous comments and suggestions on the manuscript provided by Dan Michman, whose contribution to the historiography of Jewish Councils is indispensable, have been of considerable support. Likewise, I have greatly appreciated the feedback from Dan Stone and Benjamin Ziemann. I would furthermore like to thank Jean-Marc Dreyfus, Jean Laloum, Michel Laffitte and Jacques Sémelin for their time and consideration whilst I was doing research in France. During my stay in Belgium, commentaries from Rudi van Doorslaer, Nico Wouters, Lieven Saerens and others guided me through the very early stages of this project. I am also very grateful for the support and advice of Richard Cohen. At the University of Oxford, Martin Conway's insightful comments stimulated me to rethink my research within the broader context of the nature of the National Socialist regime. Vicki Caron not only shared her thoughts on my work, but also kindly sent me one of her earlier articles on the UGIF. In addition, I am greatly indebted to the extraordinary individuals at Ohio State University. Their reflections on the transnational perspectives of my work were of immense help.

This book would not exist were it not for the help of the many archivists and librarians who guided me through the archives and who made my numerous trips abroad so valuable and so pleasant. At the Yad Vashem research centre in Israel, the aid of Eliot Nidam was especially useful. The staff of the Mémorial de la Shoah and the Archives Nationales in Paris were patient and helpful in showing me how to navigate through their collections. In Belgium, the archivists of the Centre for Historical Research and Documentation on War and Society (CEGESOMA), Documentatie Oorlogsslachtoffers (DOS), Krijgsauditoraat Brussel and the Algemeen Rijksarchief (ARA) were endlessly supportive. A few individuals went above and beyond the call of duty in sharing their archival knowledge and expertise. In particular, my gratitude is owed to Laurence Schram and Dorien Styven, who quickly responded to my requests and generously led me through the extensive archives of the Belgian Jewish Association at Kazerne Dossin in Mechelen.

Ariel Sion's kind welcome to the Mémorial de la Shoah, combined with her insurmountable knowledge of the library's collection, made my stay in Paris enormously memorable. I am grateful to Karen Taieb and Veerle Vanden Daelen for their time and generous assistance at the Mémorial de la Shoah and CEGESOMA archives during my European Holocaust Research Infrastructure (EHRI) fellowship. To the staff of the Nationaal Archief (NA) in the Netherlands, I extend my appreciation. The NIOD staff members have likewise been exceedingly helpful and supportive. In particular, I am thankful for the ongoing support and interest of Hubert Berkhout and René van Heijningen, who repeatedly aided me in my search for documents. To Erik Somers and René Kok, I am hugely grateful, not least for asking me to take part in their important (photography) projects. Their confidence and support have been truly remarkable. I would furthermore like to express my gratitude to Esmeralda Böhm and Melinde Kassens for their trust during the preparations for the 2021 documentary on the Dutch Jewish Council.

This project would not have been possible without the generous support of various organisations, including the White Rose College of Arts and Humanities (WroCAH), the Arts and Humanities Research Council (AHRC), the Prins Bernhard Cultuurfonds, the EHRI and the Conference on Jewish Material Claims Against Germany (the Saul Kagan Fellowship in Advanced Shoah Studies). The feedback I received from other fellows, alumni and affiliated faculty during the annual Kagan Fellowship summer workshops greatly helped me in refining my arguments. Specifically, the encouragement of Karel Berkhoff, Steven Katz, David Silberklang and Dalia Ofer, gave me the confidence to continue my work. It is with great pleasure and with gratitude that I look back on those stimulating weeks in Jerusalem and Washington and on the friendships I built there. I would furthermore like to thank the editors at Cambridge University Press for their confidence and support.

My heartfelt gratitude to Yonathan Barzilay for introducing me to Mirjam Bolle-Levie, a remarkable and inspiring woman who generously invited me to her house in Jerusalem several times. The ways in which she shared with me her memories of working for the Dutch Jewish Council, paired with her kindness, courage and strength, have left an indelible impact on me.

Finally, the support of my dear friends and family has been indispensable. They were always there with words of encouragement and a listening ear. Froukje, whom I love more than I can say, has been my sunshine and I cherish every minute of seeing her grow up. Above all, I am intensely grateful to Mark for his unconditional support, love and understanding. There are no words to describe the incredible journey we share.

Abbreviations

ACIP	Association Consistoriale Israélite de Paris
AIU	Alliance Israélite Universelle
AJ	Armée Juive
AJB/VJB	Association des Juifs en Belgique/Vereniging der Joden in België
ANDB	Algemene Nederlandse Diamantbewerkers Bond
ARA	Algemeen Rijksarchief
ASG	Amsterdamse Studenten Groep
CA	Contact Afdeling
CAR	Comité d'Assistance aux Réfugiés
CEGESOMA	Centre for Historical Research and Documentation on War and Society
CBIP	Comité de Bienfaisance Israélite de Paris
CBJB	Comité voor Bijzondere Joodsche Belangen
CC	Consistoire Central des Israélites de France
CCOJA	Commission Central des Organisations Juives d'Assistance
CDJ	Comité de Défense des Juifs
CDJC	Centre de Documentation Juive Contemporaine
CGQJ	Commissariat Général aux Questions Juives
CJV	Comité voor Joodsche Vluchtelingen
CNHEJ	Centre National des Hautes Études Juives
CRIF	Conseil Représentatif des Israélites de France
CUDJF	Comité d'Unité et de Défense des Juifs de France
DOS	Documentatie Oorlogsslachtoffers
EHRI	European Holocaust Research Infrastructure
EIF	Éclaireurs Israélites de France
FI/OF	Front d'Indépendance/Onafhankelijkheidsfront
FSJF	Fédération des Sociétés Juives de France
FTP-MOI	Francs-Tireurs et Partisans - Main d'Oeuvre Immigrée
JCC	Joodse Coördinatie Commissie

IKG	Israelitische Kultusgemeinde
JMDV	Joods Museum van Deportatie en Verzet
JR	Joodsche Raad voor Amsterdam
LiRo	Lippmann, Rosenthal & Co.
LO	Landelijke Organisatie voor Hulp aan Onderduikers
KD	Kazerne Dossin
MJS	Mouvement de Jeunesse Sioniste
MNR	Musée National de la Résistance (also see : NWM)
MOE	Main d'Oeuvre Étrangère
MOI	Main d'Oeuvre Immigrée
NA	Nationaal Archief
NIK	Nederlands Israëlitisch Kerkgenootschap
NIOD	Institute for War, Holocaust and Genocide Studies
NIW	*Nieuw Israëlietisch Weekblad*
NSB	Nationaal Socialistische Beweging
NSDAP	Nationalsozialistische Deutsche Arbeiterpartei
NWM	Nationaal Museum van de Weerstand (also see: MNR)
NZB	Nederlandse Zionistenbond
OCIS	Oeuvre Centrale Israélite de Secours
ONE	Oeuvre National d'Enfance
ORT	Organisation Reconstruction Travail
OSE	l'Oeuvre de Secours aux Enfants
OT	Organisation Todt
RSHA	Reichssicherheitshauptamt
SDAP	Sociaal-Democratische Arbeiderspartij
SDB	Sociaal-Democratische Bond
SiPo-SD	Sicherheitspolizei und Sicherheitsdienst
SS	Schutzstaffel
SA	Sturmabteilung
SSJ	Service Sociale des Jeunes
STO	Service du Travail Obligatoire
UGIA	Union Générale des Israélites d'Algérie
UGIF	Union Générale des Israélites de France
ULB	Université Libre de Bruxelles

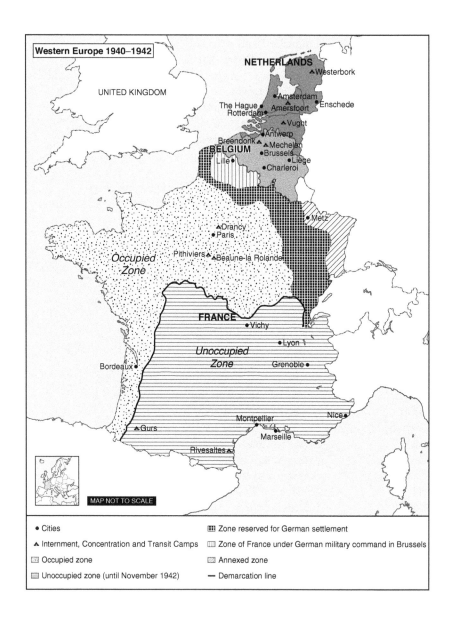

Western Europe 1940–1942

UNITED KINGDOM

NETHERLANDS
▲Westerbork

▲Amsterdam
The Hague● ▲●Enschede
Rotterdam● Amersfoort
▲Vught
●Antwerp
Breendonk▲ ▲Mechelen
BELGIUM ●Brussels
Lille● ●Liège
●Charleroi

Metz

▲Drancy
●Paris

Occupied Pithiviers▲ ▲Beaune-la-Rolande
Zone

FRANCE
●Vichy

●Lyon
Unoccupied
Bordeaux● *Zone* Grenoble●

Nice●
Montpellier●
▲Gurs
Marseille●
Rivesaltes▲

MAP NOT TO SCALE

- ● Cities
- ▲ Internment, Concentration and Transit Camps
- ▦ Occupied zone
- ▤ Unoccupied zone (until November 1942)
- ▦ Zone reserved for German settlement
- ▥ Zone of France under German military command in Brussels
- ▨ Annexed zone
- — Demarcation line

Introduction

The Holocaust in Western Europe is a story of identification, registration, despoliation and deportation. Few Jewish victims were killed by their German persecutors in France, Belgium or the Netherlands. Instead, they were transported to concentration and extermination camps in Eastern Europe. Understanding how that process was facilitated and enacted has therefore been central to the national Holocaust historiographies of all three countries albeit in different ways. Analyses of the perpetrators and of the economic, sociocultural and political circumstances, both regional and national, have played their role in the debate, but perhaps the most contentious issue has been the contribution made by the victims themselves; unwittingly through their social and economic position within society, or wittingly through either resistance or cooperation. Of prime concern have been the roles played by the 'Jewish Councils' in the three countries – all created in 1941 and at the behest of the Germans, but different in form and function: the Joodsche Raad voor Amsterdam (JR) in the Netherlands, the Assocation des Juifs en Belgique (AJB) in Belgium (in Dutch referred to as Vereniging der Joden in België, VJB) and the Union Générale des Israélites de France (UGIF) in France.

These organisations were intended to serve as intermediaries between the Jewish communities and the German authorities. Among other things, their functionaries communicated anti-Jewish decrees and regulations, and were held responsible for tasks that had previously been carried out by local government organisations. These included the provision of education, health care and social welfare to Jews, who were increasingly suffering under the yoke of the occupation. As the war unfolded, new responsibilities were imposed on the JR, the AJB and the UGIF. German authorities employed the organisations to expedite the isolation of Jews from society and to facilitate their deportation from Western Europe. For example, in the Netherlands and Belgium, the organisations' functionaries assisted with the registration of Jews and they were engaged in the production of summonses to report for 'police-supervised

1

work in the East' (*polizeilicher Arbeitseinsatz*).[1] The JR, the AJB and the UGIF also provided necessities to Jews who were interned, and who were soon to be deported. During the course of the occupation, various German (and, in the case of France, Vichy) departments attempted to use the organisations to serve their own interests.

The actions of these Jewish organisations and the choices of their leaders,[2] in both academic and public spheres, have been dominated by moral condemnation. The predominant focus on these organisations as instruments in the hands of the German occupier in carrying out the so-called Final Solution to the Jewish Question has oversimplified our understanding of these bodies.[3] Owing to a significant lack of comparative studies on the JR, the AJB and the UGIF, there is little understanding of their precise nature and function in a wider (Western) European context. Their histories were far more complex, and local conditions were more decisive in shaping their form and function, than has hitherto been recognised.

The purpose of this book is to gain a comprehensive understanding of the controversial 'Jewish Councils' of the Netherlands, Belgium and France. It should be noted that the term 'Jewish Councils' (the literal translation of the term *Judenräte*) is not entirely accurate in the context of the Jewish representative bodies of Belgium (the AJB) and France (the UGIF). While the Dutch Jewish Council was officially referred to as a *Judenrat*, the AJB and the UGIF were *Vereinigungen* (Associations). This

---

[1] This was a euphemistic term that concealed the German authorities' true intentions: the mass destruction of the Jews.

[2] The term 'leaders' or 'leadership' will be used to address those who stood at the helm of the Jewish organisations in Western Europe. Dan Michman proposed the term 'headship' as an alternative in the context of the Jewish organisations. However, despite the objections raised by Michman to the use of the term 'leadership', the central board members of these organisations did fulfil a leadership function. The tasks they took on and the decisions they were forced to make can in my opinion best be understood through this term. See Dan Michman, 'Jewish Leadership in Extremis', in Dan Stone, *The Historiography of the Holocaust* (New York: Palgrave: Macmillan, 2004), 319–340; and '"Judenräte" und "Judenvereinigungen" unter nationalsozialistischer Herrschaft: Aufbau und Anwendung eines verwaltungsmäßigen Kozepts', *Zeitschrift für* Geschichtswissenschaft, Vol. 46, No. 4 (1998), 293–304.

[3] See, for example, Nanda van der Zee, *Om erger te voorkomen: de voorgeschiedenis en uitvoering van de vernietiging van het Nederlandse jodendom tijdens de Tweede Wereldoorlog* (Amsterdam: Meulenhoff, 1997), 97–139; Hans Blom, 'The Persecution of the Jews in the Netherlands: A Comparative Western European Perspective', *European History Quarterly*, Vol. 19 (1989), 347–349; Loe de Jong, *Het Koninkrijk der Nederlanden in de Tweede Wereldoorlog* ('s Gravenhage: Martinus Nijhoff, 1976), Part 7, Vol. 1, 252; Part 5, Vol. 2, 1045.

study highlights the institutional (dis)similarities between these organisations, and, therefore, terminologically differentiates between the JR on the one hand and the AJB and the UGIF on the other. The JR will be referred to as a Jewish Council, and the AJB and the UGIF, are referred to as Associations. For general claims on the organisations, the terms 'Jewish Councils' (between quotation marks) or 'Jewish (representative) organisations' are used. Even though the organisations were not always considered as representative by a (substantial) part of the Jewish communities, this was essentially what both their leaders and the Germans aimed for.

As Dan Michman has pointed out, the common tendency to put the Netherlands, Belgium and France 'in one bag' has obscured the unique aspects in each of these countries, including the dissimilar compositions of their Jewish communities, and the fact that German policies were characterised by varying forces and aims.[4] A comparative approach allows for a better understanding of the Jewish organisations' distinctive characteristics and the unique national contexts in which they operated. It shows, for example, that the socio-historical premises on which these organisations were built were very different across Western Europe. This affected their acceptance by the Jewish communities, and in turn the choices the Jewish leaders made. By taking a wider comparative view, this study identifies the major differences and similarities between Jewish representative bodies across Western Europe, revealing what German intentions with these organisations were during the course of the occupation and how Jewish leaders used their positions to assist their communities. This in turn allows for an integrative understanding of the different ways in which the Holocaust unfolded in each of these countries.

The 'Jewish Councils' in Western Europe: An Overview

The Western European 'Jewish Councils' were different from their Eastern European counterparts in form and function. The main differences are the scope of their power and the nature of their function. Eastern European *Judenräte*, officially established in November 1939 by Governor General Hans Frank, had only local authority, while the JR, the AJB and the UGIF

---

[4] Dan Michman, 'Comparative Research on the Holocaust in Western Europe: Its Achievements, its Limits and a Plea for a More Integrative Approach', *Moreshet Journal for the Study of the Holocaust and Antisemitism*, Vol. 17 (2020), 290–291.

were (eventually) national bodies. The case of France is distinctive because of the Franco-German armistice of 22 June 1940, which culminated in the physical occupation of only the northern half and the western coastal areas of the country until November 1942. As a result, the UGIF was split into an UGIF-Nord, overseeing the Jews in the occupied (later northern) zone, and an UGIF-Sud, overseeing the Jews in the unoccupied (later southern) zone. The organisational and functional divergence between the UGIF-Nord and the UGIF-Sud, even after the German invasion of the southern zone in November 1942, necessitates an approach that considers the UGIF-Nord and the UGIF-Sud as two separate organisations. The two central UGIF boards, one for each zone, did not meet in common session until 15 February 1943, when plans for a reorganisation of the UGIF into a centralised body in Paris were discussed.[5]

Another difference between the Western and Eastern European bodies is that even though the *Judenräte* in Eastern Europe used different models of governance, many were held directly responsible for organising deportations.[6] Unlike the situation in Western Europe, failure to abide by German regulations could lead to severe punishment, including deportation and murder. The chairman of the first Jewish Council in Lwòw (Ukraine), Dr Joseph Parnas, for example, was arrested in October 1941 and apparently killed shortly thereafter for refusing to hand over several thousand Jews to German authorities for forced labour.[7] Despite these differences, Eastern European *Judenräte* unquestionably served as blueprints for the Western European Jewish organisations and there are parallels between some of their functions and leaders.

---

[5] Because it was established by the collaborationist Vichy government, the presidency of the UGIF and the office of the general-secretary were situated in the unoccupied (later southern) zone. For the meeting on 15 February, see Jacques Adler, *The Jews of Paris and the Final Solution: Communal Response and Internal Conflicts, 1940–1944*, transl. from the French (New York/Oxford: Oxford University Press, 1987; first ed. 1985 [French]), 140; Michel Laffitte, 'Between Memory and Lapse of Memory: The First UGIF Board of Directors', in John K. Roth and Elisabeth Maxwell (eds.), *Remembering for the Future: The Holocaust in an Age of Genocide* (Basingstoke: Palgrave, 2001), 674.

[6] Isaiah Trunk, *Judenrat: The Jewish Councils in Eastern Europe under Nazi Occupation* (Lincoln: University of Nebraska Press, 1996; first ed. 1972), 413–436; Andrea Löw and Agnieszka Zajaczkowska-Drozdz, 'Leadership in the Jewish Councils as a Social Process. The Example of Cracow', in Andrea Löw and Frank Bajohr (eds.), *The Holocaust and European Societies: Social Processes and Social Dynamics* (London: Palgrave Macmillan, 2016), 196–203; Barbara Engelking and Jacek Leociak, *The Warsaw Ghetto: A Guide to A Perished City*, transl. Emma Harris (New Haven/London: Yale University Press, 2009), 145–147.

[7] Trunk, *Judenrat,* 437.

As its name suggests, the Joodsche Raad voor Amsterdam (the Jewish Council for Amsterdam) was in fact directly modelled after the local *Judenrat* model that existed in Eastern Europe, and its authority was initially limited to the city of Amsterdam. As Michman has convincingly shown, wherever the Schutzstaffel (SS) and police were strongly represented, as was the case in the Netherlands, the local model was applied.[8] The two highest ranking Nazis in the Netherlands, Reich Commissioner (Reichskommissar) Arthur Seyss-Inquart and the Highest SS and Police Leader (Höhere SS- und Polizeiführer) Hanns Albin Rauter, both Austrian born, had previously observed the establishment of *Judenräte* with only local authority in Eastern Europe. They had also witnessed the transformation of the Jewish Community of Vienna (Israelitische Kultusgemeinde, IKG) into a Council of Elders (*Ältestenrat*) directly overseen by SS-Obersturmbannführer Adolf Eichmann, regrouping all existing Jewish organisations in 1938.[9] Most likely inspired by these examples, a similar organisation, with initially only local authority, was established in the Netherlands.[10]

The use of the term *Judenrat* was a literal copy of the wording used by Heydrich in his so-called *Schnellbrief* (urgent letter) of 21 September 1939. In this letter, sent to all *Einsatzgruppen* (special police units) commanders and department heads in the SiPo-SD, Heydrich detailed the form and function of the Jewish Councils in the occupied Polish territories.[11] Combined with the fact that the Dutch Council, contrary to the AJB and the UGIF, was not anchored in law, these factors all demonstrate how

---

[8] Dan Michman, 'Judenräte, Ghettos, Endlösung: Drei Komponenten einer antijüdischen Politik oder Separate Faktoren?', in Jacek Andrzej Mlynarczyk and Jochen Böhler (eds.), *Der Judenmord in den eingegliederten polnischen Gebieten 1939–1945* (Osnabrück: Fibre Verlag, 2010), 167–176; and 'On the Historical Interpretation of the Judenräte Issue between Intentionalism, Functionalism and the Integrationist Approach of the 1990s', in Moshe Zimmerman (ed.), *On Germans and Jews under de Nazi Regime: Essays by Three Generations of Historians* (Jerusalem: Magness Press, 2006), 395.

[9] From 1939 until December 1942, the IKG functioned as a Jewish Council, serving as an intermediary between the Germans and the Jews. After December 1942, the IKG was transformed into a Council of Elders. See Bernard Klein, 'The Judenrat', *Jewish Social Studies*, Vol. 22, No. 1 (1960), 27; Doron Rabinovici, *Instanzen der Ohnmacht. Wien 1938–1945. Der Weg zum Judenrat* (Frankfurt am Main: Jüdischer Verlag, 2000), passim. On the role of the IKG in the emigration and deportation of Jews, see Lisa Hauff, *Zur politischen Rolle von Judenräten, Benjamin Murmelstein in Wien, 1938–1942* (Göttingen: Wallstein Verlag, 2014), 99–283.

[10] Dan Michman, 'De oprichting van de "Joodsche Raad voor Amsterdam" vanuit een vergelijkend perspectief', in Madelon de Keizer and David Barnouw (eds.), *Derde Jaarboek van het Rijksinstituut voor Oorlogsdocumentatie* (Zutphen: Walburg Pers, 1992), 87.

[11] For further reading on Heydrich's *Schnellbrief*, see Dan Michman, 'Why did Heydrich Write "the Schnellbrief"? A Remark on the Reason and on its Significance', *Yad Vashem Studies*, No. 32 (2004), 433–447; and 'Jewish Leadership in Extremis', 328.

its inception was based on that of the Eastern European *Judenräte*. Even the personal order of Hans Böhmcker, the representative (Beauftragte) of Reichskommissar Seyss-Inquart for the city of Amsterdam, to institute the JR resembled that of the Eastern European Councils, which were usually established on a private basis (a town commander, for example, would appoint a prominent Jew). By contrast, the AJB and the UGIF were established on the basis of official decrees and were anchored in their local legal systems.[12] This difference is significant, because as Michman has demonstrated, the 'Jewish Councils' with only local authority, not anchored in official law, provided controlling German authorities (the local German police apparatus) more direct control over these bodies.[13]

In Belgium and France, where the Military Administration had a strong presence and the SS was less prominently represented at first, *Judenvereinigungen*, inspired by the German Reichsvereinigung model that had nationwide authority, were established. In both countries, the Military Administration was initially reluctant to force a Jewish representative body on the Jewish societies, in part because it feared the responses of non-Jews to this measure, a theme we will explore later. Partly as a result of the Military Administration's reluctance, the AJB, the UGIF-Nord and the UGIF-Sud were established, under pressure from the SS authorities, only in November 1941. Documents suggest that the 'Jewish experts' of the SS in Belgium preferred the Eastern European *Judenrat* organisation to the *Judenvereinigung* type. However, their limited power meant that they had to compromise with the Military Administration who favoured a different model.[14] In France, the collaborationist Vichy regime commanded the establishment of the UGIF after prolonged negotiations with the Germans.

The fact that the AJB in Belgium and the UGIF in France were both organisations with a nationwide authority, while the JR was initially meant to have authority only over the Jewish community in Amsterdam, was the main functional difference between these bodies.[15] On 27 October

---

[12] Michman, 'De oprichting van de "Joodsche Raad voor Amsterdam"', 88; Dan Michman, 'Research on the Holocaust in Belgium and in General: History and Context', in Dan Michman (ed.), *Belgium and the Holocaust: Jews, Belgians, Germans* (Jerusalem: Yad Vashem Studies, 1998), 33–34. Also see Maxime Steinberg, 'The Trap of Legality: The Belgium Jewish Association', in Michael Marrus (ed.), *The Nazi Holocaust: The Victims of the Holocaust* (Toronto: Mecklermedia, 1989), 798.

[13] Michman, 'Jewish Leadership in Extremis', 328–329. In the Netherlands, the Council chairmen attempted to negotiate a juridical status for the JR, but this attempt failed. See: Pim Griffioen and Ron Zeller, *Jodenvervolging in Nederland, Frankrijk en België, 1940–1945: Overeenkomsten, Verschillen, Oorzaken* (Amsterdam: Boom, 2011), 382.

[14] Michman, 'Research on the Holocaust in Belgium and in General', 35–36.

[15] Jozeph Michman, 'The Controversial Stand of the Joodse Raad in the Netherlands: Lodewijk E. Visser's Struggle', *Yad Vashem Studies*, Vol. X (1994), 18; Rudi van

1941, for reasons that will be examined later, the Amsterdam Jewish Council officially extended its influence to the entire country. Despite these differences in organisational structures, the outlook of Jewish leaders was similar. All Jewish leaders were primarily invested in providing social welfare to their communities through these bodies. As the war progressed, the pressure on these institutions increased, and, as we will see in Chapter 4, they were used to varying degrees of success (from the German perspective) to carry out German demands.

In other Western European countries or colonies and overseas territories of these countries, similar organisations were either not imposed, or the nature of the organisations was essentially different from that of the JR, the AJB and the UGIF. In Algeria (under the rule of Vichy France), for example, a Jewish representative organisation was established by decree on 14 February 1942: the Union Générale des Israélites d'Algérie (UGIA), modelled after the UGIF.[16] Like the UGIF, the UGIA was officially intended to replace all existing Jewish organisations and its board members were chosen from among the Jewish leadership.[17] After the Allied landings in North Africa in November 1942, the organisation was disbanded.

In Tunisia, occupied by the Germans from November 1942 until May 1943, when the British army captured Tunis and the Axis powers surrendered, SS-Obersturmführer Walther Rauff ordered the establishment of a Jewish Council in the country's capital, Tunis.[18] Jewish leaders who chaired this organisation continued to hold responsibility in much the same way as they had done before the Germans arrived.[19] As Friedl has

Doorslaer and Jean-Philippe Schreiber, 'Inleiding', in Rudi van Doorslaer and Jean-Philippe Schreiber (eds.), *De curatoren van het getto: De vereniging van de joden in België tijdens de nazi-bezetting* (Tielt: Lannoo, 2004), 9. Also see Michman, 'Judenräte, Ghettos, Endlösung', 167–176; 'On the Historical Interpretation of the Judenräte Issue', 395; and 'Research on the Holocaust in Belgium and in General', 35–36.

[16] Yves C. Aouate, 'La place de l'Algérie dans le projet antijuif de Vichy (octobre 1940–novembre 1942)', *Revue française d'histoire d'outre-mer,* Vol. 80, No. 301 (1993), 605; Valérie Assan, 'Israël William Oualid, juriste, économiste, professeur des universités', *Archives Juives,* Vol. 46, No. 1 (2013), 140. It should be noted that Richard Ayoun has inaccurately claimed that the UGIA was instituted by decree on 31 March 1942. See Richard Ayoun, 'Les Juifs d'Algérie dans la Tourmente Antisémite du XXe siècle', *Revue Européenne des Études Hébraïques,* No. 1 (1996), 77.

[17] Ayoun, 'Les Juifs d'Algérie', 77–78. For further reading on the UGIA and its distinct position in relation to the UGIF, see Aouate, 'La place de l'Algérie', 605–607.

[18] For the biography of Walther Rauff, see Martin Cüppers, *Walther Rauff: In deutschen Diensten: Vom Naziverbrecher zum BND-Spion* (Darmstadt: WBG Academic, 2013).

[19] Sophie Friedl, 'Negotiating and Compromising Jewish Leaders' Scope of Action in Tunisia during Nazi Rule (November 1942–May 1943)', in Frank Bajohr and Andrea Löw (eds.), *Holocaust and European Societies: Social Processes and Social Dynamics* (London: Palgrave Macmillan, 2016), 228.

pointed out, the brevity of direct German rule in Tunis (six months) limited the destructive effect on the Jewish community.[20] As a result, the Jewish Council never faced the same pressure as its counterparts in German-occupied Europe. In Morocco, no traces can be found of a similar Jewish organisation.[21] Since the Jewish Councils in Algeria and Tunis were hardly functional and operated in a different (colonial) context than the Jewish organisations in the Netherlands, Belgium and France, there was insufficient common ground to include these case studies in the present study.

In the case of Luxembourg, the Jewish Consistory, chaired by Alfred Oppenheimer since October 1941, was renamed the Jewish Council of Elders in April 1942.[22] The fact that the country had a very small Jewish community made the existence of this organisation different from its counterparts in neighbouring countries. Over 3,000 Jews fled the country immediately after the beginning of the military campaign in the West in May 1940, or left before October 1941 for France or Belgium. Around 816 Jews remained, of whom 664 were deported in a total of seven transports – the first in October 1941 and the last in June 1943.[23] In Norway and Denmark, Jewish organisations modelled after the *Judenräte* were never established for various reasons, including the fact that relatively few Jews lived in these countries.[24]

Perspectives on Jewish Leaders' Cooperation

Discussions on whether Jewish leaders should cooperate with the Germans, in an attempt to (temporarily) delay, or influence, the decision-making process, or to serve as a buffer between the Jewish

---

[20] Friedl also highlighted other factors that limited the destructive effect of German policies in Tunisia, including the lack of resources to deport Tunisian Jews en masse, and the military charges faced by the Germans. Ibid., 227.

[21] For further reading on the Jews in North Africa specifically during Nazism, see Filippo Petrucci, *Gli ebrei in Algeria e in Tunisia, 1940–1943* (Florence: Giuntina, 2011); Christine Levisse-Touzé, *L'Afrique du Nord dans la guerre 1939–1945* (Paris: Albin Michel, 1998); Michel Abitbol, *The Jews of North Africa during the Second World War*, transl. from the French by Catherine Tihanyi Zentelis (Detroit, MI: Wayne State University Press, 1989); the contributions of various authors in *Revue d'Histoire de la Shoah: Les Juifs d'Orient face au nazisme et à la Shoah, 1930–1945*, Vol. 205 (2016).

[22] Marc Schoentgen, 'Luxembourg', in Wolf Gruner and Jörg Osterloh (eds.), *The Greater German Reich and the Jews: Nazi Persecution Policies in the Annexed Territories 1935–1945* (New York/Oxford: Berghahn, 2015), n.50; Ruth Zariz, 'The Jews of Luxembourg during the Second World War', *Holocaust and Genocide Studies*, Vol. 7, No. 1 (1993), 56–57.

[23] Schoentgen, 'Luxembourg', 307–311.

[24] For an overview of the persecution of Jews in Norway, see Bjarte Bruland, 'Norway's Role in the Holocaust: The Destruction of Norway's Jews', in Jonathan Friedman

communities and the German authorities, were prevalent within all the Jewish communities as soon as plans for the establishment of representative bodies were first mentioned. Some Jews openly refused to support such institutions early on, fearing they would become tools in the hands of the Germans. In the French unoccupied zone, for example, Jews initially refused to accept their nomination at the helm of the umbrella organisation, the UGIF-Sud, because they feared its activities would stretch beyond the provision of social welfare.[25] In the Netherlands, the former president of the Dutch Supreme Court, Lodewijk Ernst Visser, was critical of the JR leaders' strategy of obedience and submissiveness towards German authorities: 'As Dutch Jews, it is our plight to do everything in our power to obstruct him [the German occupier] in achieving his goal [.] That is not what you are currently doing!'[26] Some became more critical of the 'Jewish Councils' during the course of the war, when leaders were increasingly forced to abide by German regulations. As Isaiah Trunk indicated in the context of Poland: 'Opposition to the Jewish Councils emerged as soon as they came into being and became even stronger when, as a result of their activities, much of people's initial suspicion was confirmed.'[27]

After the war, disapproval of Jewish leaders' wartime choices was reinforced, when Jewish courts of honour and state courts across Europe formally assessed their cooperation with the German occupying authorities. These courts were established in various countries across Europe, including Germany, Poland, France and the Netherlands. Even though the honour courts were of limited punitive power, they are symbolic of the urge that was felt in post-war Jewish society to address supposed Jewish collaboration. State courts investigated the wartime behaviour of Jewish leaders in several countries, including France, Belgium, the Netherlands, Austria, Poland, Czechoslovakia, Hungary and the Soviet Union.[28] In the immediate post-war period, many were unable to make a

(ed.), *The Routledge History of the Holocaust* (London: Routledge, 2011), 232–247. For Denmark, see Mette Bastholm Hensen and Steven Jensen, *Denmark and the Holocaust* (Copenhagen: Institute for International Studies, Department for Holocaust and Genocide Studies, 2003).

[25] Letter of Gamzon, Mayer, Lambert, Millner, Jarblum, Oualid, Olmer and Lévy to Xavier Vallat, 24 December 1941, XXVIIIa-13, CDJC, Mémorial de la Shoah.

[26] Letter of Visser to Cohen, 18 November 1941, 248–179A (mr. Lodewijk Ernst Visser), Inv. No. 14, NIOD.

[27] Trunk, *Judenrat*, 528.

[28] Laura Jokusch and Gabriel N. Finder, *Jewish Honor Courts: Revenge, Retribution and Reconciliation in Europe and Israel after the Holocaust* (Detroit, MI: Wayne State University Press, 2015), 4. Also see Dan Michman, 'Kontroversen über die Judenräte in der Jüdischen Welt, 1945–2005. Das Ineinandergreifen von öffentlichem Gedächtnis und Geschichtsschreibung', in Freia Anders, Katrin Stoll and Kartsen

distinction between the actual perpetrators (the Germans and their non-Jewish accomplices) and the few Jewish victims who, for various reasons, had cooperated with the Germans. Across Europe, Jewish leaders were often called 'traitors to the Jewish nation'.[29]

Historians have contributed to this moral condemnation of Jewish Councils, and similar organisations, starting in the immediate post-war period with understandably personal and emotional responses.[30] In his 1954 publication *Harvest of Hate: The Nazi Program for the Destruction of the Jews of Europe*, Léon Poliakov, for example, claimed that 'many out-right scoundrels insinuated themselves into the councils'.[31] Criticisms of these bodies, and the choices of their leaders, continued in the 1960s, epitomised by Hilberg's *The Destruction of the European Jews*, in which he stated that not only perpetrators play a role in a destruction process: 'the process is shaped by the victims, too'.[32] Hilberg claimed that the traditional pattern of Jewish leadership over centuries of persecution and expulsion was characterised by compliance, acquiescence and negotiations with their oppressors in order to preserve the communities. This proved self-destructive during Nazi rule because the Jewish leadership had been unable to switch to resistance.[33] Two years later, Hannah Arendt assessed the role of Jewish leaders in the destruction of their own people, and (in)famously claimed that if the Jewish people had really been unorganised and leaderless, 'there would have been chaos and plenty of misery, but the total number of victims would hardly have been

---

Wilke (eds.), *Der Judenrat von Białystok. Dokumente aus dem Archiv des Białystoker Ghettos 1941–1943* (Paderborn/Munich/Vienna/Zürich: Ferdinand Schöningh, 2010), 309–317.

[29] Jokusch and Finder, 'Revenge, Retribution, and Reconciliation', 11–12.

[30] Whereas in Belgium it almost took almost twenty years before scholars started paying attention to the history of the AJB, historiography on the JR, the UGIF and similar Jewish organisations was scrutinised from early on. See, for example, Heinz Wielek, *De oorlog die Hitler won* (Amsterdam: Amsterdamsche Boek- en Courantmij, 1947), 108; Léon Poliakov, *Harvest of Hate. The Nazi Program for the Destruction of the Jews of Europe* (New York: Syracuse University Press, 1954), 88–89. In Eastern Europe, ghetto writers and chroniclers regarded Judenräte leaders, including Chaim Rumkowski in Lodz, Jacob Gens in Vilna, Moses Merin in Sosnowiec-Bedzin and Joseph Diamond in Radom, as collaborators, villains and enemies of the people. See Philip Friedman, *Roads to Extinction: Essays on the Holocaust* (New York: Conference on Jewish Social Studies, 1980), 353.

[31] Poliakov, *Harvest of Hate*, 88–89. This statement is remarkable in light of his earlier claim that he mistrusted any moral judgement of the past; see *Le Monde Juif*, August–September 1949, Mémorial de la Shoah, Paris.

[32] Raul Hilberg, *The Destruction of the European Jews* (London: W.H. Allen, 1961; a revised edition of this work was published in 1985), 662.

[33] Ibid., 666.

between four and a half and six million people'.[34] In different ways, both prominent scholars blamed Jewish leaders for their role in the destruction of European Jewry and seemed to attribute more agency to these leaders than they had had in reality.

Some scholars in Western Europe shared their belief that a refusal of Jewish leaders to cooperate would have been of benefit to the Jewish communities.[35] In doing so, they ignored the fact that if individuals had refused to cooperate, the Germans would simply have appointed a new leadership. Moreover, it has been demonstrated that there is no causal relation between the presence of a Jewish Council in a particular locality, or a similar representative organisation enforced by the Germans, and the losses suffered by its communities.[36]

In the 1980s, historians such as Maurice Rajsfus, Cynthia Haft, Maxime Steinberg and Hans Knoop continued to accuse Jewish leaders of having aided the Germans in carrying out the Holocaust in Western Europe.[37] The title of Rajsfus' work – Jews in collaboration – is indicative

---

[34] Hannah Arendt, *Eichmann in Jerusalem: A Report on the Banality of Evil* (New York: The Viking Press, 1963), 111.

[35] See, for example, Jacques Presser, *Ondergang: de vervolging en verdelging van het Nederlandse Jodendom, 1940–1945*, Vol. 1 (The Hague: Staatsuitgeverij Martinus Nijhoff, 1965), 507–509; Lucien Steinberg, *Le comité de défense des Juifs en Belgique, 1942–1944* (Brussels: Éditions de l'Université, 1973); Loe de Jong, *Het Koninkrijk der Nederlanden tijdens de Tweede Wereldoorlog*, Part VII, Vol. 1 (The Hague: SDU Uitgeverij Koninginnegracht, 1976), 352.

[36] Dan Michman, 'Reevaluating the Emergence, Function, and Form of the Jewish Councils Phenomenon', in *Ghettos 1939–1945: New Research and Perspectives on Definition, Daily Life, and Survival: Symposium Presentations*, Center for Advanced Holocaust Studies, USHMM (Washington, DC: USHMM, 2015), 79–80.

[37] Maurice Rajsfus, *Des Juifs dans la collaboration: l'UGIF 1941–1944* (Paris: Études et Documentation Internationales, 1980), 131. Cynthia Haft uncritically referred to the UGIF as a *Judenrat* and states it was an institutional trap, claiming that it was an impeccable machine that could be equally efficient in any country in which it was established. Haft did not make a distinction between the French Jewish organisation and its Eastern European counterparts, and the work lacked a thorough understanding of the essentially different natures of the UGIF from Eastern European *Judenräte*. Cynthia J. Haft, *The Bargain and the Bridle. The General Union of the Israélites of France, 1941–1944* (Chicago: Dialog Press, 1983). Hans Knoop contended that the Dutch chairmen had been well aware of where their actions might lead. He considered their decision to take the lead over the Jewish community as an act of arrogance by the Jewish bourgeoisie at the cost of poor and working-class Jews. He thereby dismissed the idea that some members of the Amsterdam Jewish community genuinely saw it as their task to take up a leading role under increasingly threatening circumstances. Hans Knoop, *De Joodsche Raad: Het drama van Abraham Asscher en David Cohen* (Amsterdam/Brussels: Elsevier, 1983). Maxime Steinberg positioned the actions of the AJB directly in opposition to the attitude of resistance organisations and argued that the AJB had remained in control of the 'legal ghetto' during the first period of occupation, informing their fellow Jews that they should obey German demands up

of its content. Rajsfus was himself the son of immigrant Jews from Eastern Europe, and he indicated that in France established Jewry had sacrificed foreign Jews while pursuing their own, class-based, interests. He held UGIF leaders responsible for their failure to reflect upon their own decisions: '[they are convinced] that they have rendered an invaluable service to their Jewish community and pursue their actions without departing from this certainty'.[38]

There were also attempts for less emotional approaches towards Jewish wartime leadership and (supposed) Jewish collaboration.[39] In the 1950s, Polish Jewish historian Philip Friedman advocated in-depth inquiries into individual Jewish leaders, their aims, choices (and mistakes) rather than a collective condemnation of Jewish leadership.[40] Highly critical of the Jewish Council leaders, whom he called 'ghetto dictators', he identified a lack of nuanced and scholarly investigations into Jewish collaboration. In his view, these leaders 'were not simple brutes or tyrants, nor were they traitors in the ordinary sense of the word'.[41] It was the task of historians to examine the 'profound complex of internal and external contradictions' with which leaders were faced.[42] Friedman was ahead of his time yet his ideas failed to reach an international audience.

Twenty years later, Trunk's comparative study on the Jewish communities in Poland and the Baltic states, which, contrary to what the subtitle suggests, does not cover all of Eastern Europe,[43] marked a turning point in international approaches towards Jewish Councils. Above all, Trunk emphasised the enormous pressure placed on Jewish leaders by

---

to the very limits of the politics of 'the lesser evil'. Maxime Steinberg, *L'étoile et le fusil: La traque des juifs 1942–1944*, Vol. 2 (Brussels: Vie ouvrière, 1986), 248. This work was published in three parts. Part 1: *La question juive 1940–1942*, Part 2: *1942. Les cent jours de la déportation des juifs de Belgique*. Part 3 (2 volumes): *La traque des juifs 1942–1944*.

[38] Rajsfus, *Des Juifs dans la collaboration*, 131.

[39] See, for example, Zosa Szajkowski, 'The Organization of the "UGIF" in Nazi-Occupied France', *Jewish Social Studies*, Vol. 9 No. 3 (1947), 254.

[40] Philip Friedman, 'Aspects of the Jewish Communal Crisis in Germany, Austria and Czechoslovakia during the Nazi Period'; 'Pseudo-Saviors in the Polish Ghettos: Mordechai Chaim Rumkowski of Lodz'; 'The Messianic Complex of a Nazi Collaborator in a Ghetto: Moses Merin of Sosnowiec'; 'Jacob Gens: "Commandant" of the Vilna Ghetto'; 'Preliminary and Methodological Aspects of Research on the Judenrat', in Philip Friedman, *Roads to Extinction: Essays on the Holocaust* (New York: Conference on Jewish Social Studies, 1980).

[41] Friedman, 'Pseudo-Saviors in the Polish Ghetto', 334. This article was first published in 1954.

[42] Ibid.

[43] This has been pointed out by Dan Michman in *The Emergence of Jewish Ghettos during the Holocaust* (Cambridge: Cambridge University Press, 2011), 12–13.

the Germans to cooperate with their demands.[44] Throughout the 1970s, prominent Holocaust historians such as Yehuda Bauer, Yitzak Arad, Israel Gutman, Aharon Weiss and Dan Michman fostered new insights into the broader theme of Jewish leadership during Nazi occupation. By underlining the particular circumstances of the ghettos in which the *Judenräte* were forced to operate, their analyses resulted in the gradual loosening of the more generalised, stigmatising approach to the study of Jewish organisations.[45] Increasingly, *Judenräte* came to be regarded as an 'expression of the Jewish community's desire to conduct its affairs within the framework of a hostile regime whose exact intentions were unknown'.[46]

While some historians, despite these historiographical developments, continued to accuse Jewish leaders of having aided the Germans in implementing anti-Jewish measures, others instead built on the more nuanced analyses of Trunk, Friedman and others, and adopted a distanced perspective, positioning the activities of the Jewish Councils and the decisions of its leadership in the broader context of German coercion.[47] Michman proposed a balanced perspective, rejecting the notion that the actions of Jewish leaders should be exclusively regarded in the

---

[44] Trunk, *Judenrat,* 570–575.
[45] See the various articles in Yisrael Gutman and Cynthia Haft (eds.), *Patterns of Jewish Leadership in Nazi Europe, 1933–1945: Proceedings of the Third Yad Vashem International Historical Conference – April 1977* (Jerusalem: Yad Vashem, 1979).
[46] Yehuda Bauer, 'The Judenräte: Some Conclusions', in Gutman and Haft, *Patterns of Jewish Leadership*, 397.
[47] In the context of Western Europe, Annette Wieviorka made an important contribution to the debate by making a solid distinction between the Eastern European *Judenräte* and the UGIF in France. She highlighted that in contrast to Councils in Eastern Europe, the UGIF had never been used to directly organise deportations and thus was never as instrumental to the aims of the German occupier as were the Eastern European *Judenräte*. Annette Wieviorka, 'l'UGIF n'a jamais été un Judenrat', *Pardès*, No. 2 (1985), 191–209. In an attempt to give an overall evaluation of the actions and decisions of UGIF functionaries, Richard Cohen argued that its leaders were forced to operate in an impossible situation, but that they were also guilty of wishful thinking, exaggerated legalism and an unfounded confidence in the robustness of French liberal traditions. Richard Cohen, *The Burden of Conscience: French Jewish Leadership during the Holocaust* (Bloomington/Indianapolis: Indiana University Press, 1987). In Belgium, Lucien Steinberg proposed a balanced perspective on the AJB's functions. In his view, it had played a detrimental role as an intermediary in the deportation of Belgian Jews to death camps in Eastern Europe. At the same time, he acknowledged that the AJB had become a cloak for clandestine activities at a later stage, impeding the very regime that had created the instrument in the first place. By doing this, Steinberg made an important step in acknowledging that the nature of this Jewish body had changed over time and that it had fulfilled various – apparently contradictory – roles simultaneously. Steinberg, *Le comité de défense des Juifs en Belgique,* 64.

context of the so-called Final Solution to the Jewish Question.[48] He furthermore highlighted the importance of a comparative understanding of these Jewish organisations across Western Europe.[49] Yet subsequent historians have generally failed to satisfy Michman's demands for more comparative analyses.[50] In this respect, Western European historiography has lagged behind its Eastern European counterpart. Even though Trunk's comparative work on *Judenräte* in Poland and the Baltic states, dating back to 1972, has highlighted the importance of a comparative examination of these bodies, showing that each Council has to be evaluated on its own merits, most of the literature on the Jewish organisations in Western Europe remains marginal, hidden in more general works on the histories of these countries during the Nazi occupation. In the last two decades, attempts to bridge this gap have produced monographs on the Jewish organisations of Belgium, France and the Netherlands.[51] These works have expanded our understanding of the structure and function of these organisations. Yet their analyses remain within national frontiers.

A Reinterpretation of the Role of 'Jewish Councils' in Western Europe

Restricting historical examination to the nation-state makes it difficult to contextualise the choices made by these organisations' leaderships, and we have seen that this risks fostering moral judgements. The behaviour of Jewish leaders is often analysed on an individual basis and proper attention is not paid to the larger situational circumstances from which these leaders emerged. With the exception of some studies, little overall attention is given to the position of those who chaired the Jewish organisations in the pre-war Jewish communities in Western Europe, or

---

[48] Michman, 'Reevaluating the Emergence, Function, and Form of the Jewish Councils Phenomenon', 77–78; and 'Research on the Holocaust in Belgium and in General', 33.
[49] Michman, 'De oprichting van de "Joodsche Raad voor Amsterdam"', 75–100.
[50] An exception in this regard is the comparative study on the persecution of the Jews in the Netherlands, France and Belgium by Griffioen and Zeller, titled *Jodenvervolging in Nederland, Frankrijk en België*, published in 2011. Even though the 'Jewish Councils' are not central to their study, the authors do examine these organisations as part of their larger, comparative, framework.
[51] Michel Laffitte, *Un engrenage fatal: l'UGIF face aux réalités de la Shoah 1941–1944* (Paris: Liana Levy, 2003); van Doorslaer and Schreiber, *De curatoren van het getto*. In the Netherlands, after almost forty years since the last monograph on the Dutch Jewish Council by Hans Knoop (1983), a study on the Jewish Council was published in April 2022. It was not possible to include the findings of this author in the present study. See: Bart van der Boom, *De politiek van het kleinste kwaad: een geschiedenis van de Joodse Raad voor Amsterdam, 1941-1943* (Amsterdam: Boom, 2022).

to how the nature of particular Jewish communities affected their leadership.[52] Indeed, the organisations' general operations depended upon the decisions and actions of central board members. At the same time, these decisions relied strongly on larger (socio-) historical developments where these leaders generally had little influence. Moreover, forced to respond to changing realities, Jewish leaders wavered between various modes of behaviour that cannot exclusively be defined by concepts as collaboration, cooperation or resistance. In an inherently complex situation, Jewish leaders could simultaneously cooperate and resist.

The terminology traditionally used in the context of Jewish Councils, and similar representative bodies, has been widely discussed. Raul Hilberg used 'collaboration' to describe the behaviour of Jewish leaders in the first edition of *The Destruction of the European Jews*, yet, as Finkel has pointed out, he opted for 'compliance' in subsequent editions.[53] There exists a conceptual difference between the various terms that have been employed, and it is important to make a distinction between the often used concepts of 'cooperation' and 'collaboration'. One could argue that the difference lies in the intended goal of the actions taken. As Yehuda Bauer has pointed out, collaboration implies some form of ideological identification with the enemy's goals, in this case those of the German occupier. If we follow this line of argument, Jewish leaders did not collaborate. Instead, Bauer used 'cooperation', which he defined as the 'unwilling yielding to superior force'.[54]

More recently, Finkel has pointed out that Bauer's understanding of these concepts is problematic since there were Judenrat leaders who, to the detriment of their communities, were 'driven by desires for personal enrichment and survival' and, as a result, were 'utterly corrupt, despotic and abusive toward ghetto populations'.[55] In Finkel's view, therefore, while some leaders indeed cooperated, others collaborated, or could adopt both types of behaviour over the course of time. Taken into consideration that the Jewish leaders in Western Europe first and foremost

---

[52] For France, Vicki Caron provided a thorough overview of the impact of the pre-war refugee stream on the leadership of the Jewish community. However, she did not examine how the pre-war structures affected the nature of the UGIF's leadership specifically; see Vicki Caron, *Uneasy Asylum: France and the Jewish Refugee Crisis, 1933–1942* (Stanford, CA: Stanford University Press, 1999). Michel Laffitte has examined the pre-war status and social position of the UGIF leadership, see, for example: Laffitte, 'Between Memory and Lapse of Memory', 674–687. For the Netherlands and Belgium, such analyses are conspicuously absent.

[53] Evgeny Finkel, *Ordinary Jews: Choice and Survival during the Holocaust* (Princeton/ Oxford: Princeton University Press), 72.

[54] Yehuda Bauer, *Rethinking the Holocaust* (New Haven: Yale University Press, 2001), 148.

[55] Finkel, *Ordinary Jews*, 69–97.

acted to preserve the communities in their respective countries, cooperation is considered the more accurate term to use in the context of present
study.

In addition to the fact that there has been hardly any attention paid
to the socio-historical context from which the Jewish leaders emerged,
little research has been done on the workings of these 'Jewish Councils'
within the broader context of German persecution of the Jews in Western Europe. As a result, the depiction of German attitudes towards the
organisations has been oversimplified. The institutions have traditionally
been seen as instruments of German oppression, effectively aiding the
process of identifying, registering, isolating and deporting the Jews they
were ostensibly representing. Accordingly, they have been assessed as
part of debates about the mortality rates of the Jews in individual countries (25 per cent, 40 per cent and 75 per cent in France, Belgium and
the Netherlands respectively).[56]

As a result, the Dutch Jewish Council, which functioned more effectively, is considered to have played a more pivotal role than its Western
European counterparts.[57] The problem with this approach is that it is
based on the highly contested intentionalist perspective that the 'road
to Auschwitz' was carefully planned and premeditated. It is built on the
idea that the 'Jewish Councils' were an integral part of German anti-
Jewish policies that led to extermination. If we accept this viewpoint,
then we also have to accept that Jewish organisations were established
primarily in order to carry out the orchestrated process of removing Jews
from occupied countries.

However, this approach has long been challenged, first and most
notably in the early 1960s by Raul Hilberg, who suggested that an
order for the so-called Final Solution might not have existed. Instead,
he proposed that the genocide of the Jews resulted from a sequence of
decisions. To him, the annihilation of European Jewry was above all
'functionalist', a bureaucratic process of destruction.[58] Rather than trying

---

[56] Scholars have different perspectives on the precise percentages of Jews murdered
in each country, yet there exists a consensus on these approximate numbers. See,
for example, Griffioen and Zeller, *Jodenvervolging in Nederland, Frankrijk en België*,
17; Maxime Steinberg, *Un pays occupé et ses Juifs: Belgique entre France et Pays-Bas*
(Gerpinnes: Éditions Quorum, 1998), 16; Wolfgang Benz (ed.), *Dimension des
Völkermords: die Zahl der jüdischen Opfer des Nationalsozialismus* (Munich: Oldenbourg,
1991), 15–16.

[57] See, for example, Pim Griffioen and Ron Zeller, 'Jodenvervolging in Nederland
en België tijdens de Tweede Wereldoorlog: Een Vergelijkende Analyse',
Oorlogsdocumentatie '40–'45, Vol. 8 (1997), 38–49; Blom, 'The Persecution of the
Jews in the Netherlands', 347–349.

[58] Hilberg, *The Destruction of the European Jews*, passim.

to pinpoint the precise course of events that would explain German policies in terms of continuity, historians have increasingly become convinced of the Holocaust's unplanned nature and of the reduced role of Hitler in the decision-making process.[59] It is clear that historiography has evolved during recent decades so that we can no longer understand the nature of these Jewish organisations in the context of the intentionalist perspective.[60] We will see that a comparative approach allows for a more nuanced perspective, which highlights the importance of local conditions and local actors for the form and function of the JR, the AJB, the UGIF-Nord and the UGIF-Sud.

The sources used in this book uncover the heterogeneous nature of the Jewish organisations and show that their function changed over the course of time. Correspondingly, the (self-) perception of their leaders and their intentions altered and were by no means consistent. It should be noted that only a handful of the JR, the AJB, the UGIF-Nord and the UGIF-Sud employees kept diaries or reported on the course of events during the war. Those who survived gave relatively few testimonies after the war. It is therefore necessary to combine a wide range of sources, including administrative documents, trial records, personal testimonies (wartime and post-war) and biographical documents, to reach an understanding of personal motives and experiences, and of the choices made by the Jewish leaders. The sources used fall broadly into four categories: 1) pre-war immigration and naturalisation reports; 2) administrative documents; 3) wartime reports written by the Jewish leaders; 4) post-war (honour) trial reports and accounts of Jewish, German or Vichy individuals who were involved in the affairs of the Jewish organisations.

These sources are for the most part stored in national archives across Western Europe, the United States and Israel. These archives include the Centre de Documentation Juive Contemporaine (CDJC), Mémorial de la Shoah and the National Archives in Paris, France. Here, the papers of the Vichy-led General Commissariat for Jewish Affairs (Commissariat Général aux Questions Juives, CGQJ), which directly oversaw the UGIF, provided insight into how Vichy officials as well as Jewish leaders, reflected upon the interactions between the UGIF and the CGQJ.

---

[59] See, for example, Uwe Adam, *Judenpolitik im Dritten Reich* (Düsseldorf: Droste, 1972); Karl Schleunes, *The Twisted Road to Auschwitz: Nazi Policy Toward German Jews* (Urbana/Chicago: University of Illinois Press, 1970); Peter Longerich, *Politik der Vernichtung: Eine Gesamtdarstellung der nationalsozialistische Judenverfolgung* (München: Piper, 1998); Ian Kershaw, *Hitler 1889–1936: Hubris* (London: Allen Lane, 1998); and *Hitler 1936–1945: Nemesis* (London: Allen Lane, 2000).
[60] Also see Michman, 'On the Historical Interpretation of the Judenräte Issue', 385–397.

In Belgium, the Centre for Historical Research and Documentation on War and Contemporary Society (CEGESOMA) and Kazerne Dossin in Mechelen, where the entire body of AJB administrative documentation is stored, was of crucial value. At the Belgian Military Krijgsauditoraat, testimonies that were conducted in preparation for the post-war trial of the AJB leaders, in combination with the as yet little explored trial documentation against members of local AJB branches show how ambiguously Jewish society reflected upon the function of the AJB.

The quantity of material available in Belgium and, especially, France is immense compared with that in the Netherlands, where substantial parts of the JR archive are missing (with much destroyed during the war). The remaining material, including the administrative documents, is mainly stored at the NIOD Institute for War, Holocaust and Genocides Studies in Amsterdam. At the National Archives in The Hague, the legal documents of the proceedings against the JR leadership and against Nazi officials highlight the views of both the organisation's leaders and their German overseers about the course of events. Apart from these archives, various interview collections, including the Visual History Archive of the USC Shoah Foundation, have greatly added to an in-depth understanding of the ways in which Jews experienced Nazi occupation and perceived the role of Jewish leaders. The conversations with Mirjam Bolle, a secretary in the bureaucracy of the Dutch Joodsche Raad, have similarly proven invaluable.

All of these sources have their limitations. Administrative documents, for example, rarely show the doubts, fears and reluctance of the Jewish organisations' leaders. Trial documents often contradict one another because people largely tried to depict their actions in a positive light. Post-war memories and testimonies are coloured by information received after the events. Individuals' recollection of events often changes over the course of time. Nevertheless, when analysed together, it is possible to overcome most of these limitations.

This book is organised thematically and is based on a series of case studies. Three major themes – the Jewish bodies' socio-historical nature, their organisational structures and their connections to clandestine operations – are examined through a combined bottom-up and top-down analysis. Chapter 1 explores the socio-historical contexts in the Netherlands, Belgium and France. It shows that the pre-war nature of Jewish communities, as well as the forms of the Nazi occupation in each country, need to be considered when explaining the nature of the Jewish organisations' function. The chapter demonstrates that stability and structures of the pre-war communities in Belgium and France were strongly affected by the influx of refugees and immigrants, whereas this was not the case in the Netherlands. An examination of the positions of those who would later lead the Jewish bodies in these pre-war societies illustrates that the premises on which the JR, the AJB and the UGIF were built were very different. It furthermore considers the nature of the German occupation and its impact on Jewish representation, reflecting on the different forms of occupation in the Netherlands, Belgium and France.

Chapter 2 examines the establishment history of the Jewish organisations in the broader context of Nazi rule and ideology. It shows that Eastern European *Judenräte* served as blueprints for the Western European Jewish organisations to varying degrees, and that there are parallels between some of their functions and leaders. It furthermore explains why the Dutch Council was operative as early as February 1941 while its Belgian and French counterparts were established only nine months later. In doing so, it argues that the form and function of these bodies were inherently dependent upon the nature of German rule, which was itself epitomised by contradictions. With the absence of a clearly defined plan for how the Greater German Reich would be governed, there were competing interests, and different initiatives on a local level. Since there was no clear understanding about what the (long-term) remit of these organisations would be, this chapter shows that the Jewish representative bodies were used by rival German (and Vichy) institutions, often to effect their own intentions. The improvised decisions that followed on a local level were decisive in shaping the Jewish bodies, and institutional rivalry inevitably affected their form and function.

Chapter 3 expands upon the findings of Chapter 1 by examining whether those who were appointed at the helm of these organisations constituted a continuation or discontinuation of pre-war structures. It demonstrates the wide social variation in the organisations' central board membership, showing how far the central board members of the JR, the AJB, the UGIF-Nord in the northern zone and the UGIF-Sud in the southern zone (felt they) represented the Jewish communities. It also contextualises their acceptance by these communities. It furthermore contrasts those chairmen who exhibited a confident belief that there was no one else who could better take up the leadership of such an important organisation, such as David Cohen in the Netherlands, with those who felt uncertainty and discontent about having been forced into such a situation, including Salomon Ullmann in Belgium. These differences not only help to explain their choices at later stages, but also elucidate organisational divergences, including why some of the leaders of the AJB and the UGIF-Nord and the UGIF-Sud were replaced, while the Dutch leadership remained in place until the JR was dismantled in 1943.

In light of how vaguely the responsibilities of the Jewish organisations had been set out, Chapter 4 explores how the Germans judged the organisations' effectiveness throughout the course of the war. German satisfaction with the effectiveness of the JR is contrasted with the discontent about the form and function of the AJB, the UGIF-Nord and especially the UGIF-Sud. It seeks to understand the interaction of the Jewish leaders with their German (or Vichy) overseers, including the SiPo-SD, the General Commissariat for Jewish Affairs (in France), the Military Administration (in Belgium and France) and the Civil Administration (in the Netherlands). The chapter explains why the Germans perceived the success and effectiveness of these bodies so differently, examining both factors inherent to the Jewish communities and the nature of their leaderships as well as the nature of the German occupation.

Chapter 5 deals with how the 'Jewish Councils' were connected to organised resistance groups and other forms of opposition. Whereas their leaders have often been condemned for their failure to resist any form of cooperation with the Germans, this chapter shows that the reality was far more complex. It assesses two central themes. The first explores the ways in which the JR, the AJB, the UGIF-Nord and the UGIF-Sud were wittingly and unwittingly used by others as cloaks for clandestine activities. Overall, the very presence of these bodies in all three countries facilitated, to varying degrees, clandestine activities that would never have been possible without their existence. The connections between official Jewish bodies and illegal subversive groups in Belgium and France were complex, manifold and fluid. Secondly, the chapter examines the active engagement of the organisations' leadership and membership in these activities, and explains why the JR's leadership's absence of engagement in such activities is distinct from the situation in Belgium and France. Existing scholarship has focussed primarily on individuals who crossed the line between legality and illegality, outwardly conforming while also working outside the legal organisations. This chapter takes the analysis one step further and investigates whether and how the Jewish representative organisations in Western Europe were used for clandestine activities in ways that extended beyond this individual level.

1   Disrupted Communities?
Jewish Leadership and Communal Representation to 1941

On the eve of the German occupation, the Jewish communities in the Netherlands, Belgium and France were entirely different in terms of their composition and organisation.[1] During the previous decades, a large number of Jewish immigrants from Central and Eastern Europe had settled in Western Europe. In total, around 95 per cent, 45 per cent and 15 per cent of the Jews in Belgium, France and the Netherlands respectively were immigrants.[2] They had mainly settled either at the turn of the century or during the 1930s, when anti-Jewish hostilities grew in their home countries.

    The presence of immigrants affected the nature of the Belgian and French Jewish communities to a large degree. The large majority of immigrants did not assimilate into the long-standing Jewish population. Instead, they organised themselves in so-called *Landsmannschaften* (homeland organisations), mutual aid organisations in which immigrants from a particular local community in Eastern Europe were united, and whose members shared the same religious beliefs and traditions. Partly because of this, traditional representative organisations in Belgium and France, such as the Consistories, the bodies governing the Jewish Congregations, were under pressure. The lack of unity ensured that they could no longer represent the Jewish communities in the way they had done for centuries. In the Netherlands, by contrast, the vast majority of Jews belonged to families who had been living in the country for at least a

---

[1] For the discussion of Jewish communities in Belgium, France and the Netherlands, the plural *communities* rather than the singular *community* will be used in order to underline the diverse nature of these populations. Using the term community would imply a form of coherence that was absent in these countries. This chapter shows that, in the cases of Belgium and France, the influx of sizeable numbers of immigrants in the pre-war period further contributed to the diversified nature of the Jewish communities in both countries.

[2] For an overview of the estimated number of Jews in each country at the outbreak of the war and their composition see Pim Griffioen and Ron Zeller, *Jodenvervolging in Nederland, Frankrijk en België 1940–1945: overeenkomsten, verschillen, oorzaken* (Amsterdam: Boom, 2011), 170.

hundred years. Since the number of immigrants, mostly from Germany, was relatively low, the refugee crisis had less impact on the nature of the communities. As a result, the Jewish leaders were better able to keep existing structures in place throughout the 1930s.

Various other factors contributed to differences in the fabric of the pre-war Jewish communities in the Netherlands, Belgium and France, including the level of Jewish integration into non-Jewish society, the position of immigrant Jews vis-à-vis the long-standing Jewish population, the level of religious adherence, the influence of Zionist thinking and the traditional organisation of the Jewish communities. The nature of the pre-war (Jewish) communities and the position of Jewish leadership in these communities were decisive in shaping the self-perception of the leaders of the Joodsche Raad voor Amsterdam (JR), the Association des Juifs en Belgique (AJB), the Union Générale des Israélites de France (UGIF)-Nord and the UGIF-Sud during the war. Moreover, pre-war social structures largely determined the level of acceptance of these organisations by Jewish communities. We will see that the variations in social structures that predated the establishment of the 'Jewish Councils' proved important for the position of wartime Jewish leaders and their level of representation. Throughout 1941, German officials intended the Jewish organisations in the Netherlands, Belgium and France to represent and coordinate all Jews in each country respectively; whether or not this was a viable idea will be examined in this chapter.

Traditional Communal Organisation and Zionism in the Early Twentieth Century

Between 1870 and 1920, the Netherlands underwent a process of accelerated change, expansion and prosperity that was felt by almost all sections of society, including Jews.[3] In 1889, 98,000 Jews lived in the country. They were mostly concentrated in the major cities (Amsterdam, Rotterdam and The Hague) with the largest percentage in Amsterdam (56 per cent). In terms of religious orientation, the 1848 declaration of a separation of Church and State resulted in a remodelling of the Portuguese–Israelite (Sephardi) and Dutch–Israelite (Ashkenazi) denominations

---

[3] Hans Blom and Joel J. Cahen, 'Dutch Jews, the Jewish Dutch, and Jews in the Netherlands, 1870–1940', in Hans Blom, David Wertheim, Hetty Berg et al. (eds.), *Reappraising the History of the Jews in the Netherlands,* transl. from the Dutch by David McKay (London: The Littman Library of Jewish Civilization in association with Liverpool University Press, 2021; revised and updated version of *The History of the Jews in the Netherlands*, published in 2002), 251.

in 1870. Elected in 1874, the Chief Rabbi of the Dutch–Israelite Synagogue (Nederlands–Israëlitische Hoofdsynagoge), Joseph Hirsch Dünner (1833–1911) and the wardens of the Sephardic Jewish community (*parnassim*) left their imprint on Jewish religious life for years. Under their leadership, religious life became a remarkable combination of 'tightly organized' Orthodox religious services and 'the acceptance of looser observance of Jewish precepts by many people affiliated with the denomination'.[4]

Apart from major celebrations, a decline in regular synagogue attendance and observance was visible in this period, exemplifying the increasing secularisation of Dutch Jews.[5] The country's economic, social and cultural circumstances ensured emancipation, assimilation and acculturation as well as integration. At the same time, there was still a group that maintained Orthodoxy in their own circle. Between full absorption in the national community on the one hand, and the adherence to orthodox traditions and beliefs on the other, there existed a wide variation of approaches to being Jewish in the Netherlands. Above all, '[i]t became increasingly clear that any talk of *the* Jewish community [...] was an oversimplification'.[6]

In the period between the late nineteenth and early twentieth centuries, the social and political orientation of Dutch Jews, specifically in Amsterdam, changed. Jewish labour organisations were founded and a few pioneer Jewish workers entered the socialist movement. While the anti-authoritarian disposition of the Social Democratic Union (Sociaal-Democratische Bond, SDB) as well as its anti-clericalism, had previously fitted ill with the traditions and convictions of Jewish workers, Jews now became integrated into the labour movement and were 'conscious of being a worker and socialist in the first place and a Jew second (if at all)'.[7] This development was partly caused by the general economic decline in the late 1880s. The decline strongly affected the diamond industry and spawned unemployment and poverty among the Jewish diamond workers, who were traditionally well represented in this industry. Combined with the fact that the socialists had become more moderate and were no longer as unpopular as in the early 1880s, this was a major catalyst for the shift of Jewish workers to the socialist movement.[8]

Jews also worked in other areas, including the cigar industry and the garment sector, where they entered the respective unions. Through the

---

[4] Ibid., 252.
[5] Ibid., 252–253; Bob Moore, *Victims and Survivors: The Nazi Persecution of the Jews in the Netherlands* (London: Arnold, 1997), 25.
[6] Blom and Cahen, 'Dutch Jews', 253.
[7] Karin Hofmeester, 'Image and Self-Image of the Jewish Workers in the Labour Movements in Amsterdam, 1800–1914', in Chaya Brasz and Yosef Kaplan (eds.), *Dutch Jews as Perceived by Themselves and by Others* (Leiden: Brill, 2001), 187–190.
[8] Ibid., 195–197.

socialist movement, Jews became involved in the Sociaal–Democratische Arbeiderspartij (SDAP), the Dutch Socialist Party in which Henri Polak, head of the Dutch Diamond Workers' Union (Algemene Nederlandse Diamantbewerkers Bond, ANDB), played a leading role.[9] Overall, Jewish participation in trade unions meant relative integration into Dutch (working-class) society even though inside the SDAP Jewish members were occasionally still seen primarily as Jews rather than socialists.[10]

Between 1813 and 1940, positions that officially represented the state, such as those of mayor, commissioner of the king, governor or ambassador, generally remained inaccessible to Jews. Only two Jewish ministers were appointed in this period and only a few Jews served in the First Chamber, the Second Chamber (which, together with the First Chamber, form the Dutch parliament), the Provincial Councils or Municipal Councils.[11] In 1940, 8 out of 100 members of the Second Chamber were Jews: four socialists, two progressive liberals, one liberal and one communist. It should be noted that these members of the Dutch parliament had Jewish origins but did not necessary feel connected to Jewish life and culture; they included, for example, converted Jews. It is indicative of pre-war anti-Jewish sentiment that those in Dutch society generally believed that Jews ought not to fulfil political representative functions. In 1933, for example, strong criticisms were voiced when four Jews (of different political parties) were simultaneously elected as aldermen in the municipality of Amsterdam.[12]

The relatively high level of Jewish social and cultural integration and assimilation meant that Zionist ideas initially did not flourish in the Netherlands. For various reasons, including the Chief Rabbis' wishes to combine Orthodox Judaism in the religious sphere with the integration of Jews into the national culture, the socialist and Orthodox movements were hostile to Zionism.[13] The neutral position of the Netherlands

---

[9] Jozeph Michman, Hartog Beem and Dan Michman, *Pinkas: Geschiedenis van de joodse gemeenschap in Nederland* (Amsterdam/Antwerp: Uitgeverij Contact, 1999; first ed. 1992), 110.

[10] Hofmeester, 'Image and Self-Image', 199.

[11] Michman, Beem and Michman, *Pinkas*, 107; Henri Polak, 'Het wetenschappelijk antisemitisme: weerlegging en vertoog', in *Volksdagblad voor Gelderland*, 27 December 1938.

[12] Hans Daalder, *Politiek en historie. Opstellen over Nederlandse politiek en vergelijkende politieke wetenschap* (Amsterdam: Bert Bakker, 2011; first ed. 1990), 105–106.

[13] Michman, Beem and Michman, *Pinkas*, 119–120; Blom and Cahen, 'Jewish Netherlanders', 254–255. It should be noted that in contrast to Belgium and France, there was no Chief Rabbinate for the Netherlands as a whole. Nevertheless, the Chief Rabbis of the provinces would meet occasionally. During these meetings, the Chief Rabbi of Amsterdam played a leading role.

during the First World War resulted in an increase of Zionist activity in the country in this period. Germany's invasion of Belgium in August 1914 prompted the exodus of thousands of Belgian citizens who had been predominantly dispersed among France, the United Kingdom and the Netherlands. In the following months, 'all the frontier communities in the Netherlands were invaded by a continual flood of refugees'.[14] On 1 November 1914, as many as 320,000 Belgian refugees resided in the country.[15] Among them were thousands of Jewish refugees, almost all of them originally from Eastern Europe, which caused a stronger impulse of organised Zionist activity. The fact that the Belgian Zionist Federation transferred its office to the Dutch capital city of Amsterdam contributed to this development.

There remains disagreement among historians as to the exact impact of Zionist ideas on the Jewish communities in the Netherlands in the early twentieth century. Whereas some scholars, including Hans Blom and Joel Cahen, have suggested that the role of Zionism was marginal, others such as Chaya Brasz underlined its importance in strengthening Jewish identity and in preventing further assimilation into non-Jewish society.[16] Despite these differences in opinion, we can definitively say that from the 1930s onwards, Zionist activity was stimulated in the Netherlands.

By 1936, the earlier rejection of Zionism by the Dutch Rabbis had radically changed: Lodewijk Hartog Sarlouis could only be appointed Chief Rabbi of Amsterdam because he agreed not to oppose Zionism.[17] In this period, the Dutch Zionist Union (Nederlandse Zionistenbond, NZB) noted a strong increase in members: from 2,094 in 1931 to 4,246 in 1939. This can mainly be explained by the fact that in this period the Zionist movement's sense of national solidarity was turned, in part, towards matters of social welfare rather than politics; many were concerned for those Jews being persecuted abroad.[18]

Despite the blurring of distinctions between separate Jewish communities, Jews could nonetheless not be considered a homogeneous group

---

[14] Peter Gatrell and Philippe Nivet, 'Refugees and Exiles', in Jay Winter (ed.), *The Cambridge History of the First World War*, Vol. 3 (New York/Cambridge: Cambridge University Press, 2014), 190.

[15] Ibid. At the end of 1914, refugees came under pressure to return home, which resulted in a decrease of the number of refugees to 85,000 in 1915. Mainly as a result of the evacuation of several thousand children, the number increased again to 100,000 in early 1918.

[16] Blom and Cahen, 'Dutch Jews', 308; Chaya Brasz, 'Dutch Jews as Zionists and Israeli Citizens', in Brasz and Kaplan (eds.), *Dutch Jews as Perceived by Themselves and by Others*, 223.

[17] Blom and Cahen, 'Dutch Jews', 309.

[18] Michman, Beem and Michman, *Pinkas*, 122, 152.

in the interwar period. Conflicts regarding religious and economic divisions encouraged some to move away from religious observance and from regarding themselves as Jewish at all.[19] The organised Jewish congregations in Amsterdam, both the Portuguese–Israelite (Sephardi) and Dutch–Israelite (Ashkenazi), lost their central function in Jewish social life. Instead, they focussed on Jewish religious affairs exclusively.[20]

Many Jews felt a stronger connection to their Dutch, rather than their Jewish, roots. However, despite Jewish integration into socialist circles and other forms of non-Jewish life, Jewishness continued to remain an important distinctive feature. This was in large part the result of the nature of the Dutch society, which was structured according to so-called *zuilen* (pillars), in which groups were linked by religion and associated political beliefs. Protestants, Catholics, socialists and liberals each had their pillar. Even though Jews did not officially have their own pillar, they still occupied a distinct position.[21]

Relatively little has been written about the nature of Belgian Jewry at the beginning of the twentieth century and in the interwar period.[22] After Belgian independence in 1830, Jews from the Netherlands and France (mostly from Alsace-Lorraine) settled in the country. Increasing poverty in the Dutch countryside and discrimination against Jews in Germany and France fuelled this immigration into Belgium, which was the pioneer country in terms of industrialisation on the continent and provided an open political climate. As in other Western European countries, the history of the small group of Jews in Belgium can be characterised by increasing emancipation and assimilation from the end of the eighteenth century onwards.

From the 1880s, there was a significant influx into Belgium of Eastern European Jews from Poland, Russia and Austrian Galicia (among other places) who were fleeing antisemitism and poverty. As a result, the

---

[19] Moore, *Victims and Survivors*, 24.

[20] Michman, Beem and Michman, *Pinkas*, 130.

[21] Ernst Heinrich Kossmann, *The Low Countries, 1780–1940* (Oxford: Clarendon Press, 1978), 348. Integrated subcultures (*zuilen*) cut across class lines, uniting disparate economic and social groups on the basis of their religious affiliation. The four pillars encompassed a large proportion of the Dutch population and were bound together by a common adherence to bourgeois precepts and beliefs.

[22] In his unpublished PhD thesis, Janiv Stamberger has recently made an important contribution to a better understanding of Jewish life in Belgium before the outbreak of the Second World War. See Janiv Stamberger, 'Jewish Migration and the Making of a Belgian Jewry: Immigration, Consolidation, and Transformation of Jewish Life in Belgium before 1940' (unpublished PhD thesis, University of Antwerp, 2020). Apart from this work, there have only been fragmentary discussions of the subject in book chapters and articles.

Belgian Jewish community, which had been very small at the beginning of the nineteenth century, increased ten times in size in the second half of the nineteenth century to around 20,000 in total.[23] The presence of these newcomers, who settled mainly in the cities of Brussels, Antwerp, Arlon, Ghent and Liège, radically changed the nature of Jewish society in Belgium. This was particularly visible in terms of demography and in the socio-political and religious outlook of Jews. At the beginning of the 1920s, various groups on the Jewish left emerged, including the socialist Bund, various Zionist groups and the communists.[24] The latter group consisted mostly of young men who were strongly committed to Bolshevism and who, hardened by the struggle in their homelands, were hostile towards Bundists and Zionists.[25]

Throughout the 1920s, the Zionist movement grew in size and diversity, varying from the leftist Linke Poale-Zion, which adopted a radical revolutionary position, to supporters of Jabotinsky's revisionist Zionist ideas and from the Orthodox Zionist Mizrachie to the atheist and Marxist Hashomer Hatsaïr.[26] Zionist ideas had a larger scope and impact than in the Netherlands and France at this stage. Although at first a movement of opposition against the status quo, the movement underwent a process of accelerated change and after the First World War even became part of the Jewish establishment in Belgium – unlike the situation in the Netherlands and France.[27] Even in the more traditional

---

[23] Ludo Abicht, *De Joden van België* (Amsterdam/Antwerp: Atlas, 1994), 44. For further reading on the influx of Jews from Eastern Europe in Belgium between 1880 and 1914, see Stamberger, 'Jewish Migration and the Making of a Belgian Jewry', 45–84.

[24] The Bund, established in Vilna in 1897, was the oldest Jewish socialist party, and the first left-wing Jewish political party to come into existence in Belgium after the First World War. The movement initially played an important political role in the Russian Empire and, in the decades that followed, (ideologically) underwent a significant transformation. During the interwar period, the Bundist ideology was characterised by its strong support for a class struggle and its advocacy for Jewish national and cultural autonomy in their lands of residence. See Stamberger, 'Jewish Migration and the Making of a Belgian Jewry', 178–179.

[25] Rudi van Doorslaer, 'Jewish Immigration and Communism in Belgium, 1925–1939', in Dan Michman (ed.), *Belgium and the Holocaust: Jews, Belgians, Germans* (Jerusalem: Yad Vashem, (1998), 65–66, 68.

[26] Ludo Abicht, *Geschiedenis van de Joden van de Lage Landen* (Antwerp: Meulenhoff and Manteau, 2006), 258–263. Also see Rudi van Doorslaer, 'Het Belgische Jiddischland. Een politieke geschiedenis van de joodse gemeenschappen in België tussen de twee wereldoorlogen', *Les Cahiers de la Mémoire Contemporaine*, Vol. 11 (2014), 43–66. For further reading on the Poale-Zion and the difference between its Left and Right factions, see Stamberger, 'Jewish Migration and the Making of a Belgian Jewry', 180–182.

[27] Daniel Dratwa, 'The Zionist Kaleidoscope in Belgium', in Michman (ed.), *Belgium and the Holocaust*, 34. Janiv Stamberger has highlighted that the impact of the Zionist movement was different across Belgium, emphasising that the Zionist movement

Consistory circles, pro-Zionist views were introduced as early as 1926. The historian Daniel Dratwa has convincingly argued that this continued to be the case throughout the 1930s with the nomination of Rabbi Joseph Wiener, an adherent of Zionist ideology for the post of Chief Rabbi in 1932.[28]

As in France, immigrants to Belgium from Central and Eastern Europe remained wedded to their political and religious traditions. They distinguished themselves from the long-standing Jewish population, and even more so from Belgian non-Jewish society, despite the fact that there was a wish to integrate into Belgian society in exchange for 'a decent existence'.[29] As a result, Jews rarely fulfilled representative political functions for the Belgian state.[30] There were a few exceptions, including Léon Sasserath and Herbert Speyer. Sasserath was mayor of Dinant and senator of the Liberal Party in the Namur-Dinant-Philippeville department from 1935 but he had no ties to the Jewish community.[31] Speyer was, among other things, senator of the Liberal Party in the Arlon-Marche-Bastogne-Neufchâteau-Virton department between 1912 and 1925.[32]

In addition to the increase in Zionist activity, religious orthodoxy became stronger with the influx of Eastern European immigrants in Belgium. The traditional Jewish leadership of the Consistory was forced to respond to these transformations. Aware of the increasing Jewish Orthodox presence in the country, it aimed to safeguard the position of this group in Belgian society. It successfully ensured that the renewed influence of Orthodoxy was acknowledged by the Belgian state and this included the recognition of the Orthodox Machsike Hadass communities

became a dominant ideological current in some cities (including, and most strongly, in Antwerp), while it remained an opposition movement in others. For an in-depth analysis of the Belgian Zionist movement during the interwar period, see Stamberger, 'Jewish Migration and the Making of a Belgian Jewry', 277–382.

[28] Dratwa, 'The Zionist Kaleidoscope', 53. Dratwa argued against the idea that the role of Zionists was marginal. Contrary to what historians have often assumed, he believes there was no unbridgeable distinction between immigrants and native-born Jews. Stamberger has highlighted that the Zionist movement, paradoxically, even served to facilitate the integration of Jewish immigrants into Belgian society, see Stamberger, 'Jewish migration and the making of a Belgian Jewry', 381.

[29] Rudi van Doorslaer, *Kinderen van het getto: Joodse revolutionairen in België, 1925–1940* (Antwerp/Baarn: Hadewijch, 1995), 40.

[30] For a biographical overview of Jews in Belgium in the nineteenth and twentieth centuries, see Jean-Philippe Schreiber, *Dictionnaire Biographique des Juifs de Belgique: Figures du judaïsme belge XIXe-XXe siècles* (Brussels: Éditions De Boeck Université, 2002).

[31] Schreiber, *Dictionnaire Biographique*, 306; Paul van Molle, *Het Belgisch parlement: 1894–1972* (Antwerp: Standaard, 1972), 294.

[32] Schreiber, *Dictionnaire Biographique*, 322–323; van Molle, *Het Belgisch parlement*, 306.

of Brussels and Antwerp.[33] These communities also participated in the Consistory and, in doing so, played a role in the spiritual development of Belgian Judaism.[34] The liberalism that was an essential feature of the Jewish Central Consistory encouraged this broadening spectrum of ideological diversity and pluralism among Jews. In a Jewish society that was increasingly changing, the Consistory managed to remain the central religious representative organisation of Jews in Belgium. Combined with top-down governance of Jewish communities under the umbrella of the Consistory, this created a form of stability.[35] As we shall see, this was about to change in the 1930s, after the second influx of Eastern European Jews into the country.

In France, by the end of the nineteenth century, around 72,000 Jews resided in the country. Outside Alsace-Lorraine, Jews were traditionally heavily concentrated in towns, but with the exception of a few cases, no place 'seems to have boasted more than a thousand Jews'.[36] In Paris, by contrast, the Jewish population had grown exponentially throughout the nineteenth century. By 1900, 50–60 per cent of the Jews in France lived in the capital city, in part because of the influx of many Jewish refugees from Alsace-Lorraine (annexed by the Germans in 1871). During a period in which cultural integration was running its course, Jews increasingly integrated in French society and competed with other Frenchmen on all professional levels. By the end of the nineteenth century, as in other Western European Jewish communities, the self-definition of Jews in France was expressed 'more consistently within the acceptable framework of a religious rather than an ethnic subculture'.[37]

---

[33] Machsike Hadass is a Haredi Jewish community that rejects modern secular culture and can be considered strictly, or even ultra, Orthodox. Machsike Hadass literally means 'Adherents to the divine Law'. On the early history of Machsike Hadass, see Rachel Manekin, 'The Growth and Development of Jewish Orthodoxy in Galicia: The 'Machsike Hadas' Society 1867–1883' (unpublished dissertation [Hebrew], Hebrew University, 2000); Rachel Manekin, 'Orthodox Jewry in Kraków at the Turn of the Twentieth Century', *Polin: Studies in Polish Jewry*, Vol. 23 (2011), 165–198. For further reading on Machsike Hadass in Belgium, see Stamberger, 'Jewish Migration and the Making of a Belgian Jewry', 67–69, 324–326, 333–352.

[34] Willy Bok, 'Vie juive et communauté, une esquisse de leur histoire au vingtième siècle', in *La Grande Synagogue de Bruxelles: Contributions à l'histoire des Juifs de Bruxelles, 1878–1978* (Brussels: Communauté Israélite de Bruxelles, 1978), 153–154.

[35] Jean-Philippe Schreiber, *Politique et Religion: le consistoire central israélite de Belgique au XIXe siècle* (Brussels: Editions de l'Université de Bruxelles), 398.

[36] Eugen Weber, 'Reflections on the Jews in France', in Frances Malino and Bernard Wasserstein (eds.), *The Jews in Modern France* (Hanover/London: University Press of New England, 1985), 9–10.

[37] Paula Hyman, *From Dreyfus to Vichy: The Remaking of French Jewry 1906–1939* (New York: Columbia University Press, 1979), 7.

The leadership of French Jewry was traditionally in the hands of the Central Israelite Consistory of France (Consistoire Central des Israélites de France, CC), which not only enjoyed a monopoly of Jewish religious association, but also spoke for French Jewry at large, thereby wielding enormous power. As well as the religious appointment of Rabbis, it made all policy decisions affecting Jewry as a whole. Throughout the nineteenth century, the Consistory conservatively asserted that the ideological and institutional structure of Jewish society, in which it played a vital role, had proven itself. Consequently, newcomers were expected to adapt to the existing institutional framework. This resulted in a relatively homogeneous Jewish community in France in terms of class, ethnicity and ideology by the end of the nineteenth century.

Having benefited from the economic development of French society, Jewish occupations varied from clerks and small tradesmen to financial occupations. All were part of the petite or haute bourgeoise.[38] Some 90,000 French Israelites belonged to families that had long been established in France and were well integrated into French society. Up until almost the end of the nineteenth century, French Jewry enjoyed the reputation of being the most successfully assimilated and stable Jewish society in Western Europe.[39] However, even though earlier historiography has argued that French Jews sought to negate Jewish particularity by embracing a politics of assimilation, other studies have shown that acculturation was an inconsistent process and that French Jews never intended to fundamentally integrate into French society.[40] As Pierre Birnbaum has shown, even at the highest levels of the French state, Jews actively continued to operate in their Jewish circles.[41] Through institutions such as the Universal Israelite Alliance (Alliance

---

[38] Ibid., 26–27.

[39] Ibid., 1.

[40] For the earlier historiography, see Michael Marrus, *The Politics of Assimilation: A Study of the French Jewish Community at the Time of the Dreyfus Affair* (New York: Oxford University Press, 1971); David Weinberg, *A Community on Trial: The Jews of Paris in the 1930s* (Chicago: University of Chicago Press, 1977). For those who have argued that Jews deliberately maintained aspects of their minority culture, see Hyman, *From Dreyfus to Vichy*; Jay Berkovitz, *The Shaping of Jewish Identity in Nineteenth-Century France* (Detroit, MI: Wayne State University Press, 1989); Phyllis Cohen Albert, *The Modernization of French Jewry: Consistory and Community in the Nineteenth Century* (Hanover, NH: Brandeis University Press, 1977).

[41] Pierre Birnbaum, *The Jews of the Republic: A Political History of State Jews in France from Gambetta to Vichy* (Stanford, CA: Stanford University Press, 1996). This work was first published in French as *Les Fous de la République: histoire politique des Juifs d'état, de Gambetta à Vichy* (Paris: Fayard, 1992). For further (recent) literature on French Jewry at the (late) nineteenth century, see Lisa Moses Leff, *Sacred Bonds of Solidarity: The Rise of Jewish Internationalism in Nineteenth-Century France* (Stanford,

Israélite Universelle, AIU), founded in 1860 by a group of French intellectual Jews dedicated to their emancipation in the territories under French control and to the provision of aid to persecuted Jews elsewhere, the continued ties of French Jews to their ethnic background were accentuated.[42]

The Dreyfus Affair (1894–1906) was emblematic of the changing perspectives towards Jews in the late nineteenth century. On 15 October 1894, Captain Alfred Dreyfus, an officer attached to the 39th Infantry regiment of the French Army, was arrested and accused of high treason, namely, spying for the Germans. The media, including the antisemitic *La Libre Parole*, were quick to seize on the fact that Dreyfus was a Jew. The evidence presented during his trial in December of that year was far from convincing. A secret dossier, not shown to the defence, in the end convinced the judges of Dreyfus' guilt, but this was only the beginning of the Dreyfus Affair, which attracted widespread public attention. By the time Émile Zola published his famous letter *J'Accuse*, in which he criticised the army for covering the errors that had led to Dreyfus' conviction, France was split into two opposing camps: the anti-Dreyfusards, who were against moves to reopen the case and considered these an attempt of the enemy to discredit the army; and the Dreyfusards, who sought to exonerate Dreyfus. Even though Zola did not risk alienating potential support by reflecting on antisemitism as a motivating force for Dreyfus' conviction, it had undoubtedly played a role.[43]

Antisemitism was pervasive in France in the late nineteenth and early twentieth centuries following the influx of large numbers of Jews from Alsace-Lorraine, Germany and Austria, which nourished hostile feelings among French workers who accused the Jews of taking their jobs.[44]

CA: Stanford University Press, 2006); Nadia Malinovich, *French and Jewish: Culture and the Politics of Identity in Early Twentieth-Century France* (Oxford/Portland, OR: The Littman Library of Jewish Civilization, 2008).

[42] For more information on the AIU, see André Chouraqui, *Cent Ans D'Histoire: L'Alliance Israélite Universelle et la Renaissance Juive Contemporaine, 1860–1960* (Paris: Presses Universitaires de France, 1965); Aron Rodrigue, *French Jews, Turkish Jews: The Alliance Israélite Universelle and the Politics of Jewish Schooling in Turkey, 1860–1945* (Bloomington: Indiana University Press, 1990); Laurent Grison, 'L'Alliance israélite universelle dans les années noires', *Archives Juives*, Vol. 34, No. 1 (2001), 9–22; André Kaspi (ed.), *Histoire de l'Alliance israélite universelle de 1860 à nos jours* (Paris: Armand Collin, 2010).

[43] David Drake, *French Intellectuals and Politics from the Dreyfus Affair to the Occupation* (Basingstoke: Palgrave Macmillan, 2005), 20.

[44] Doris Bensimon-Donath, *Socio-démographie des juifs de France et d'Algérie 1867–1907* (Paris: Publications Orientalistes de France, 1976), 96–97; Nancy Green, *The Pletzl of Paris: Jewish Immigrant Workers in the Belle Époque* (New York: Holmes and Meier, 1986), 206. The exact figures for Jewish immigration in the late nineteenth and early

These feelings increased after the Russian Revolution of 1905 and the Bolshevik Revolution of 1917, when French Jewry had to contend with substantial further immigration by Eastern European Jews.[45]

In 1906, when the separation of Church and State (which in the Netherlands had been introduced as early as 1848) came into effect, the position of the Consistory was undermined. Jewish institutions and organisations were now able to function independent of the Consistorial framework. This heralded a period of time in which the disaffected members of the upper class, who had turned away from the Consistory, could make their voice heard. They were encouraged to establish their own religious associations and they challenged the notion that Consistorial circles could speak for all of French Jewry.[46]

The Consistory also found its authority constrained by the immigrant communities that were growing in size and self-confidence. Whereas previously immigrants had not been allowed to serve on the Consistory's council, this decision had to be repealed in 1919 because of the ever-growing number of immigrants. The Consistory recognised that a policy of exclusion would eventually lead to its own marginalisation since newcomers could organise themselves into separate communities and would by far outnumber Consistory circles. The acceptance of immigrant Jews into their council therefore seems to have been driven more by self-protectionism than by goodwill towards the immigrants in question.[47] There were those, including William Oualid, a prominent jurist of Algerian birth and a member of the Paris Consistory, who publicly criticised the organisation for not having allowed immigrant Jews to be part of the organisation's leadership earlier on.[48]

As in the Netherlands, but in contrast to Belgium, Zionist ideas were relatively weak in France in the early twentieth century. For the majority of assimilated Jews in Western Europe, Zionism was considered to be contradictory, and even a threat to their position as relatively well-assimilated citizens. Traditional institutions such as the AIU and the Consistory publicly displayed their anti-Zionist stance, claiming that the longing for a Jewish nation obstructed emancipation and would have

---

twentieth centuries vary considerably. There seems to be a consensus that their number was more than 35,000.

[45] Hyman, *From Dreyfus to Vichy*, 27–29.

[46] Ibid., 28–30.

[47] There were restrictions as to who was eligible for a position in the council: only immigrant Jews who were resident in Paris for ten years and had been members of the Consistory for five years, were allowed to apply. Hyman, *From Dreyfus to Vichy*, 145.

[48] For further reading on the personal history of Oualid, see Assan, 'Israël William Oualid, juriste, économiste, professeur des universités', passim.

severe consequences for Jews in the diaspora.[49] However, throughout the 1920s, and prompted by French Jewry's contribution to the First World War, Zionism began to leave its imprint on French society.[50] This was reinforced by the arrival of Jews from Central and Eastern Europe in the 1930s, when increasing anti-Jewish persecution led to a growing interest in Zionist activity and its ideas began to spread among existing institutions. Some people became convinced that Zionism was the only solution to the refugee problem and committees were instituted in order to support Jews, including, most importantly, the Committee for Assistance to Refugees (Comité d'Assistance aux Réfugiés, CAR). Its secretary-general was Raymond-Raoul Lambert (1894–1943), who would later play a crucial role in the institution of the UGIF.[51]

Interest in a Jewish Palestine in the 1920s and 1930s is now recognised to have been more widespread in France than was initially thought.[52] The movement even began to prevail among the Consistory.[53] Above all, as Lee has shown, it was the youth who felt a growing affinity with Zionism in this period. Zionism and Jewish culture influenced, for example, the Jewish scout movement (Éclaireurs Israélites de France, EIF) which by the 1930s had reshaped its focus from traditional religious Judaism into a more plural understanding of Judaism in which Jews from a range of social, political and religious backgrounds were welcomed. This new understanding of Jewish identity and its accompanying support for the Zionist cause did not contradict the youth's commitment to France, however. Instead, Zionism was woven into the identities of Franco-Jewish EIF members.[54]

---

[49] Cathérine Nicault, 'Face au Sionisme, 1887–1940', in André Kaspi (ed.), *Histoire de l'Alliance Israélite Universelle de 1860 à nos jours* (Paris: Armand Colin, 2010), 189–226; Hyman, *From Dreyfus to Vichy*, 163–165.

[50] Hyman, *From Dreyfus to Vichy*, 154; Cathérine Nicault, 'L'Acculturation des Israélites Français au Sionisme après la Grande Guerre', *Archives Juives*, Vol. 39. No. 1 (2006), 14. As Aron Rodrigue has shown, the development of Zionist ideas in France was a complex process that took shape in the aftermath of the Dreyfus Affair. Aron Rodrigue, 'Rearticulations of French Jewish Identities after the Dreyfus Affair' *Jewish Social Studies*, Vol. 3, No. 2 (1996), 1–24.

[51] Vicki Caron, *Uneasy Asylum: France and the Jewish Refugee Crisis 1933–1942* (Stanford, CA: Stanford University Press, 1999), 105.

[52] See, for example, Cathérine Nicault, *La France et le sionisme, 1897–1948. Une rencontre manquée?* (Paris: Calmann-Lévy, 1992); and 'L'Acculturation des Israélites Français au Sionisme après la Grande Guerre', 9–28.

[53] Hyman, *From Dreyfus to Vichy*, 176. Also see Michel Abitbol, *Les deux terres promises: les Juifs de France et le sionisme, 1897–1945* (Paris: Perrin, 2010; first ed. 1989), 146–158.

[54] Daniel Lee, *Pétain's Jewish Children: French Jewish Youth and the Vichy Regime, 1940–1942* (Oxford: Oxford University Press, 2014), 34–43.

The Impact of Refugees and Immigrants
in the Interwar Period

European Jews who sought refuge elsewhere after the First World War were primarily driven by economic stagnation and antisemitism in their home countries. With the imposition of immigration quotas by the United States, South American countries, Canada, Australia and South Africa, Western Europe became the only alternative. We have seen that the influx of Jewish immigrants in the 1920s and 1930s, to various degrees, resulted in an increase of Zionist activity; yet their presence affected the nature of the Jewish communities in the Netherlands, Belgium and France in other ways as well. The French and Belgian Jewish communities in particular were greatly destabilised in this period because both the absolute and relative numbers of immigrants in Belgium and France were large. Since the immigrant communities struggled to integrate well into the long-standing Jewish population, a great variety of parallel Jewish communities lived alongside each other. In the Netherlands, the number of immigrants, mainly from Germany, was smaller and their composition more uniform compared with neighbouring countries.

The small group of Jews from Eastern Europe who settled in the Netherlands after the First World War drew attention to a more traditional Jewish way of life. Among Dutch Jewry, this led to a greater sensitivity to Jewish origins. Many spoke Yiddish among themselves and kept their old traditions alive. We have seen that not all Jews, incidentally, were Orthodox; their number also included socialists and Zionists. Throughout the 1920s, Jewish emigrants from Germany, mostly affluent, also arrived in the Netherlands, fleeing the country's economic and political crises as well as the mounting anti-Semitism.[55]

In 1930, the Jewish population numbered almost 112,000 – 77.4 per cent lived in one of the three major cities, with 65,523 Jews residing in Amsterdam (58,6 per cent).[56] This number would increase in the following years. Hitler's assumption of power on 30 January 1933, and the subsequent anti-Jewish legislations in Germany created a stream of German refugees. Estimates of the number of German refugees in the Netherlands in the period between 1933 and 1940 vary from 35,000 to

[55] For further reading on the distinctive nature of this group of Jews, see Dan Michman, 'Migration versus "Species Hollandia Judaica". The Role of Migration in the Nineteenth and Twentieth Centuries in Preserving Ties between Dutch and World Jewry', *Studia Rosenthaliana*, Vol. 23 (1989), 66–68.
[56] Michman, Beem and Michman, *Pinkas*, 91–92, 125–126.

50,000.[57] These numbers include transmigrants who managed to move on to other countries overseas and those who only stayed in the country for a short period of time, and therefore do not represent the number of refugees in the country at any given moment.

At the time of the German invasion in May 1940, around 140,000 Jews resided in the country, including around 22,000 Jewish immigrants, in some cases because they had not been able to leave the country in time.[58] The refugees comprised both Germans (15,000) and a substantial number of Eastern European nationals and stateless Jews (7,000), 'primarily so-called Ost-Juden, who had been resident in Germany but had lost their former nationality and now sought to acquire a new one'.[59] They came from a wide range of classes and occupational backgrounds, 'from left-wing working-class activists to the highest echelons of the German Jewish bourgeoisie'.[60] Overall, 60 per cent of the Jews were concentrated in Amsterdam, 10 per cent in The Hague and 8 per cent in Rotterdam.[61] The Dutch Jews 'had little in common either with the German-speaking westernised, liberal Jews from metropolitan Germany, or with the Yiddish speaking, Central European Ost-Juden'.[62] As was the case in all three countries, albeit to differing degrees, there were tensions and disputes between immigrants and the long-standing Jewish population, and these affected the stability of the Jewish communities in the Netherlands.

In Belgium and France, the situation was different and more complicated. Here, the immigrants deeply affected the nature of the established Jewish communities and the ways in which they were represented.[63] Between 1925 and the beginning of 1940, a wave of immigrants entered Belgium including refugees from Poland (responsible for almost half of the total number of immigrants), Romania, Yugoslavia, Hungary Austria,

---

[57] Daan Bronkhorst, *Een tijd van komen. De geschiedenis van vluchtelingen in Nederland* (Amsterdam: Mets, 1990); Corrie K. Berghuis, *Joodse Vluchtelingen in Nederland 1938–1940. Documenten betreffende toelating, uitleiding en kampopname* (Kampen: Kok, 1990); Michman, Beem and Michman, *Pinkas*, 149.

[58] Griffioen and Zeller, *Jodenvervolging in Nederland, Frankrijk en België*, 169–170.

[59] Moore, *Victims and Survivors*, 32. Also see Bob Moore, *Refugees from Nazi Germany in the Netherlands, 1933–1940* (Dordrecht/Boston/Lancaster: Martinus Nijhoff Publishers, 1986), 17–27.

[60] Moore, *Victims and Survivors*, 32.

[61] Griffioen and Zeller, *Jodenvervolging in Nederland, Frankrijk en België*, 170.

[62] Moore, *Victims and Survivors*, 32. Also see Dan Michman, 'Die jüdische Emigration und die niederländische Reaktion zwischen 1933 und 1940', in Katharina Dittrich and Max Würzner (eds.), *Die Niederlande und das Deutsche Exil, 1933–1940* (Königstein: Athanäum Verlag, 1982), 82–85.

[63] Moore, *Victims and Survivors*, 40.

Czechoslovakia, the Baltic states and the Netherlands.[64] After the German annexation of Austria in March 1938, around 10,000 German refugees also sought refuge in the country. The influx of these immigrants, who were motivated by social, economic and political push factors, caused national political unrest in Belgium and in Western Europe more broadly. In light of economic depression and high unemployment rates, these individuals were considered a threat.[65] Legal refugees were housed in centres throughout Belgium. Around a thousand Jews obtained asylum in the Belgian colony of Congo, where their arrival was heavily contested by the white colonists.[66]

Thousands of poor immigrant Jews did not integrate in Belgian society the way their predecessors had. Antwerp became an important city for Orthodox Jews to settle in, and this was a unique phenomenon in the mostly liberal-oriented cities of Western Europe.[67] As a result, the social and political fabric of the Jewish population in Antwerp changed even more than that in Brussels.[68] Liberal, religious and socialist Zionism and especially Communism, which had a breakthrough in the 1930s with its political utopia of equality and ideological rigidity, all struggled to find their place in the increasing antisemitic climate of Belgium.[69] Although the Council of Jewish Associations in Brussels and the Central Council of Jewish organisations in Antwerp tried to unite the Jews living in Belgium, the politically and socially distinctive elements remained deliberately aloof from one another. As historian Lieven Saerens has indicated in the case of Antwerp, there existed a mosaic of different communities and individuals, all with their own convictions and behaviour.[70]

As immigrants remained wedded to the political and social beliefs that had characterised the communities they had left behind, a single 'Jewish leadership' cannot be identified at the outbreak of the war in Belgium. As in France, several Jewish administrations headed different Jewish communities, often with distinctive religious, social and political

[64] Bok, 'Vie juive et communauté', 161; van Doorslaer, *Kinderen van het getto*, 25.
[65] Frank Caestecker, *Ongewenste Gasten: Joodse vluchtelingen en migranten in de dertiger jaren* (Brussels: VUB Press, 1993), 144–174.
[66] Abicht, *Geschiedenis van de Joden van de Lage Landen*, 281–282.
[67] Veerle Vanden Daelen, *Laten we hun lied verder zingen: de heropbouw van de joodse gemeenschap in Antwerp na de Tweede Wereldoorlog, 1944–1960* (Amsterdam: Aksant, 2008), 166.
[68] Ibid. Initially, the growth of the population was mainly visible in the port city of Antwerp, but in the 1930s in particular it also spread to Brussels where many German and Austrian refugees had been stranded.
[69] Dratwa, 'The Zionist Kaleidoscope', 81.
[70] Lieven Saerens, *Vreemdelingen in een wereldstad: een geschiedenis van Antwerpen en zijn joodse bevolking, 1880–1944* (Tielt: Uitgeverij Lannoo, 2000), 27; Also see Steinberg, *L'étoile et le fusil. La question juive*, 75–78.

backgrounds.[71] Whereas the Jewish communities had traditionally been mostly governed top-down and served under the umbrella of the Consistory throughout the nineteenth century, there was now a de facto grassroots community, composed of a large variety of religious, political, cultural, professional and charitable institutions.[72] Symptomatic of this is the fact that more than 100 different periodicals appeared between 1930 and 1940, including 6 daily newspapers in Yiddish.[73]

Both Antwerp and Brussels were economically attractive for Jewish migrants: Antwerp for its diamond industry and Brussels for its leather industry.[74] The immigrants were therefore primarily concentrated in the agglomerations of these cities.[75] There was a specific concentration of Jewish immigrants in the small-scale semi-industrialised production of luxury goods: in textile, diamond and leather trade companies.[76] This threw many Jewish migrants during the economic crisis of the 1930s back into the hopeless situation they had hoped to leave behind in Eastern Europe.[77] By contrast, the Belgian Jewish minority (6.6 per cent of the total Jewish population) formed the social elite in trade and industry. They occupied important positions in banking, financing and the diamond industry. This Belgian Jewish bourgeoise, small in number, had been living in Belgium from the beginning of the nineteenth century and earlier. They were relatively well integrated into Belgian non-Jewish society, particularly in the capital city Brussels.[78]

---

[71] Dan Michman, 'De oprichting van de VJB in internationaal perspectief', in van Doorslaer and Schreiber, *De curatoren van het getto*, 28.

[72] Jean-Philippe Schreiber, 'Les Juifs en Belgique: une présence continue depuis le XIIIe siècle', *Cahiers de la Mémoire contemporaine – Bijdragen tot de eigentijdse Herinnering*, Vol. 2 (2000), 13–37. For an overview of the nature of the Jewish communities in Belgium in the interwar period, including their political composition, see van Doorslaer, *De kinderen van het getto: Joodse immigratie en communisme in België, 1925–1940*, band 1, Proefschrift Rijksuniversiteit Gent, Faculteit Letteren en Wijsbegeerte (c. 1990), 11–61; Stamberger, 'Jewish Migration and the Making of a Belgian Jewry', 107ff.

[73] Schreiber, 'Les Juifs en Belgique', passim. For an overview of the Jewish press in Antwerp until May 1940, see Ephraim Schmidt, *Geschiedenis van de Joden in Antwerp* (Antwerp: Uitgeverij S.M. Ontwikkeling, 1963), 253–255.

[74] Frank Caestecker, *Alien Policy in Belgium, 1840–1940: The Creation of Guest Workers, Refugees and Illegal Aliens* (New York/Oxford: Berghahn Books, 2000), 104–105.

[75] For an overview of where exactly Jews of specific origin (Poles, Romanians, Hungarians) resided in these agglomerations, see van Doorslaer, *De kinderen van het getto*, band 1, 20–23.

[76] Israël Shirman, 'Een aspekt van de 'Endlösung'. De ekonomische plundering van de joden in België', *Bijdragen tot de Geschiedenis van de Tweede Wereldoorlog*, Vol. 3 (1974), 174.

[77] Van Doorslaer, *De kinderen van het getto*, band 1, 33.

[78] Griffioen and Zeller, *Jodenvervolging in Nederland, Frankrijk en België*, 163; Vanden Daelen, *Laten we hun lied verder zingen*, 70; van Doorslaer, *Kinderen van het getto*, 27–28.

The figures given for the number of Jews residing in Belgium on the eve of the Nazi occupation vary.[79] There seems to be a consensus that around 66,000 Jews resided in the country in 1940, of whom 45 per cent lived in Brussels and 45 per cent in Antwerp – 9 per cent of the Jews lived in Liège or Charleroi. Out of these 66,000 Jews, around 62,000 were immigrants and refugees from Eastern Europe and Germany without Belgian citizenship.[80] The explanation for the small percentage of Jews in Belgium with Belgian citizenship is twofold. First, these Jews were reluctant to become Belgian citizens because of 'an inherent fear of state bureaucracy, based largely on their experiences in Tsarist Russia'.[81] Second, the Belgian state obstructed an easy naturalisation process by 'insisting upon a "bond" with the country, a ten-year residence period (after 1932), and by making the process increasingly costly'.[82] As a result, the large variety of Jewish communities in Belgium remained non-integrated.

In France, as in Belgium, there were strong differentiations among the 300,000–330,000 Jews living in the country on the eve of the Second World War – both between foreign and French Jews, but also within both of these groups.[83] In addition to the Jews who had sought refuge in France at the turn of the century and in the early twentieth century, a new wave of immigrants arrived in the 1930s. They formed small organisations, the so-called *Landsmannschaften*, which were brought under one umbrella in the Federation of Jewish Societies of France (Fédération des

---

[79] Maxime Steinberg estimated between 64,000 and 70,000 Jews resided in Belgium in May 1940: *L'étoile et le fusil. La question juive*, 76, 83–85. Dan Michman based his research on data published in 1980, claiming 65,696 Jews lived in the country: 'Belgium', in Israel Gutman (ed.), *Encyclopedia of the Holocaust* (New York: Macmillan, 1990), 161. Lieven Saerens claimed there were 56,000 Jews residing in the country by the end of 1940: 'De Jodenvervolging in België in cijfers', *Bijdragen tot de eigentijdse geschiedenis 30/60*, No. 17 (2006), 200.

[80] Griffioen and Zeller, *Jodenvervolging in Nederland, Frankrijk en België*, 170. For the features of the Jewish population in Brussels and Antwerp specifically, see Saerens, *Vreemdelingen in een wereldstad*, 551–552.

[81] Bob Moore, *Survivors: Jewish Self-Help and Rescue in Nazi-Occupied Europe* (Oxford: Oxford University Press, 2010), 167.

[82] Ibid. Also see Frank Caestecker, 'The Reintegration of Jewish Survivors into Belgian Society, 1943–1947', in David Bankier (ed.), *The Jews are Coming Back: The Return of the Jews to their Countries of Origin after World War II* (New York/Jerusalem: Berghahn/Yad Vashem, 2005), 73–74.

[83] Renée Poznanski, *Jews in France During World War II*, transl. N. Bracher (Waltham, MA: Brandeis University Press, 2001; first ed. 1994 [French]), 1–2; Abitbol, *Les deux terres promises*, 110. It should be noted that historians have used different statistics regarding the number of Jews that resided in France on the eve of German occupation. There is a consensus, however, that this number must have been somewhere between 300,000 and 330,000. Apart from Poznanski and Abitbol, see Cohen, *Burden of Conscience*, 11; Jacques Adler, 'The Jews and Vichy: Reflections on French Historiography', *The Historical Journal*, Vol. 44, No. 4 (2001), 1068.

Sociétés Juives de France, FSJF), established in 1926. This organisation was headed by Marc Jarblum, leader of the Zionist-Socialist Poale-Zion, who later refused to become part of the UGIF-Sud.[84]

When the Germans invaded France in May 1940, around 130,000–140,000 Jews in the country were immigrants from Eastern Europe and Germany (approximately 45 per cent). There were between 190,000–200,000 Jews with French citizenship, of whom around 86,000 lived in the greater Paris region. Overall, 46 per cent of the Jews lived in this region; 24 per cent lived in Lyon, Marseille or Bordeaux. Around 22,000 Jews resided in Alsace-Lorraine and were expelled into the Vichy zone after the German annexation of the region in 1940.[85]

As in Belgium and the Netherlands, the new immigrants distinguished themselves from France's long-standing Jewish population. They spoke Yiddish and generally regarded the government as an entity to be wary of. Their political sensitivity, be they Bundists, Communists, Zionists or militant anti-Fascists, was markedly different from that of the French Jews. Unlike the immigrants, French Jewry was very much wedded to the French state and, after the resolution of the Dreyfus Affair, they believed they had every reason to put their trust in the government. Ironically, the Jews of the Consistory believed the immigrants were not sufficiently French, and the immigrants opposed the French Jews because they believed they were not sufficiently Jewish.

As in both other countries, the immigrant Jews were seen as a threat: French Jews feared for their position in the increasingly antisemitic society. Particularly during the recession of 1926–1927, the newcomers were

---

[84] Leni Yahil, 'The Jewish Leadership of France', in Gutman and Haft, *Patterns of Jewish Leadership*, 318–321. The FSJF was established in 1926, but a predecessor of this organisation was established in 1913; see Hyman, *From Dreyfus to Vichy*, 68–69; Weinberg, *A Community on Trial*, 20.

[85] Serge Klarsfeld, *Vichy-Auschwitz: la 'solution finale' de la question juive en France*, Vol. 1 of *La Shoah en France* (Paris: Fayard, 2001; first published as *Vichy-Auschwitz le rôle de Vichy dans la solution finale de la question Juive en France*. Paris: Fayard, 1983), 359–360; Griffioen and Zeller, *Jodenvervolging in Nederland, Frankrijk en België*, 170; Leni Yahil, *The Holocaust: The Fate of European Jewry, 1932–1945*, transl. from the Hebrew by Ina Friedman and Haya Galai (New York: Oxford University Press, 1990), 177; Doris Bensimon, 'Socio-Demographic Aspects of French Jewry', *European Judaism: A Journal for the New Europe*, Vol. 12, No. 1 (1978), 12. As Sémelin has highlighted, the studies on the waves of Ashkenazi Jewish immigration have neglected the parallel influx of Jews from the Balkans at the end of the nineteenth and the beginning of the twentieth centuries. Around 15,000 so-called Levantine Jews arrived in France during the interwar period. Another little-known migration is that of the Jews from North Africa in this period. See Jacques Sémelin, *The Survival of the Jews in France, 1940–1944* (London: C. Hurst & Co, 2018; revised and updated version of the French *Persécutions et entraides dans la France occupée*, Paris: Éditions les Arènes-le Seuil, 2013), 19–20; Also see Malinovich, *French and Jewish*, 109.

perceived as illegitimate competitors for the limited positions available in the French economy. Whereas immigrant leaders expected to be on an equal footing in the pre-war period, Consistorial circles disregarded the immigrants' culture and ideologies.[86]

A large part of the French Jews rejected the immigrants' leftist political orientation, believing that its revolutionary character was, first, a threat to their own status as Jews and, second, a threat to their wealthy bourgeois material interests.[87] French Jewry's perception of these Jewish immigrants has been a subject of debate for decades. A number of journalists and historians, including Maurice Rajsfus, an immigrant Jew himself, accused French Jews of betraying the refugees in the 1930s, claiming that they failed to offer support to Jewish immigrants and even actively collaborated with the government when it sought to restrict immigration.[88] By contrast, others, including most recently Jacques Sémelin, highlighted that even though there was indeed a fear that these immigrants would threaten their position in society, French Jewry nonetheless did institute several committees to help refugees.[89]

Vicki Caron has persuasively argued that several phases in the approaches to immigrants can be identified, characterised by a wide range of Jewish responses to the new arrivals from Central and Eastern Europe. Rather than a progressive hardening of policy after a brief liberal period in 1933 culminating in the extremely harsh immigrant laws of 1938, as historians have generally posited, Caron demonstrated that there were two major periods in the anti-refugee crackdown of the 1930s; the first in 1934–1935 and the second in 1938. Her work focuses on the fluidity of policy towards refugees and rightly makes a distinction between the government treatment of the problem, the role of public opinion and the role of the long-standing Jewish community.[90]

---

[86] Poznanski, *Jews in France during World War II*, 3–11; Simon Schwarzfuchs, *Aux prises avec Vichy: Histoire politique des Juifs de France, 1940–1944* (Paris: Calmann-Lévy, 1998), 10; Hyman, *From Dreyfus to Vichy*, 128, 148. For a general overview of the history of immigration in France, see Yves Lequin (ed.), *Histoire des étrangers et de l'immigration en France* (Paris: Larousse, 2006).

[87] Hyman, *From Dreyfus to Vichy*, 23.

[88] Rajsfus, *Des Juifs dans la collaboration*, 27–35.

[89] Sémelin, *The Survival of the Jews in France*, 26–27. These committees included the National Aid Committee for German Refugees, Victims of Antisemitism (Comité National de Secours aux Réfugiés Allemands Victimes de l'Anti-Sémitisme), the Committee for the Defence of the Rights of Jews from Central and Western Europe (Comité pour la Défense des Droits des Israélites en Europe Centrale et Occidentale) and the Committee for Assistance to Refugees (Comité d'Assistance aux Réfugiés, CAR). The CAR had been established with Raymond-Raoul Lambert, later chairman of the UGIF-Sud, as its general secretary.

[90] Caron, *Uneasy Asylum*, passim.

Caron underlined that the Consistory, and especially its director Jacques Helbronner, was reluctant to be involved in refugee relief,
believing above all that identifying French Jewry with foreign Jews
would encourage the government to 'lump all Jews, French and foreign, together'.[91] Consistorial leaders also feared that any engagement
in non-religious activities would 'only substantiate the administration's
effort to define Jews on ethnic or racial lines, thus facilitating anti-Jewish
rather than anti-foreign discrimination'.[92] At the same time, there were
also pro-refugee Consistory members. Refugee organisations such as the
CAR, supported by the American Jewish Joint Distribution Committee,
were created by the French Jewish establishment to provide for refugees. The CAR leadership maintained a distance from hardliners such as
Jacques Helbronner and instead adopted a more moderate outlook which
was 'above all represented by Raymond-Raoul Lambert, the CAR's
secretary-general, as well by Albert Lévy, its president and member of
the Central Consistory; William Oualid, a member of the Paris Consistory and vice-president of the AIU; and Louise Weiss, a prominent
journalist and feminist leader'.[93] Lévy and Lambert became directors
of the UGIF (both -Nord and -Sud) and the UGIF-Sud respectively.
Evidently, in a period when the traditional Consistorial rule was being
challenged by a disaffected upper class, differences in perspectives on the
'refugee problem' crystallised.

The Institution of Jewish Refugee Organisations

The influx of large numbers of refugees and the passive attitude of the
local governments vis-à-vis these Jews in terms of providing social welfare
and shelter encouraged, and even necessitated, initiatives from the Jewish communities themselves. In the case of the Netherlands and France,
the later chairmen of the JR, the UGIF-Nord and the UGIF-Sud, along
with other central board members, fulfilled various prominent positions
in Jewish refugee organisations before the war. In Belgium, central board

---

[91] Ibid., 349.
[92] Ibid.
[93] Ibid., 303. Jacques Helbronner was vice-president of the Central Consistory and
became its president in March 1941. Born in 1873, Helbronner was nominated as
auditor at the State Council (Conseil d'État), the highest administrative power in
France, in 1898. In 1917, he was appointed as director of Paul Painlevé's military
cabinet. A decorated First World War veteran, Helbronner became state council-
lor while also fulfilling representative functions in the Jewish community as, among
other things, a member of the central committee of the AIU. See Laffitte, *Juif dans la
France allemande* (Paris: Éditions Tallandier, 2006), 46.

members of the AJB had comparatively little pre-war social welfare leadership experience. Salomon Ullmann (1881–1977), the AJB's first chairman, was active in the Antwerp Committee for the Defence of the Rights of Jews (Comité tot Verdediging der Rechten der Joden), but this organisation neither exclusively controlled the provision of assistance to immigrants, nor operated on a national level. Moreover, Ullmann's role in this organisation was marginal compared with the positions his counterparts in the Netherlands and France fulfilled in their respective refugee aid organisations.[94] We have seen that in France, for example, Raymond-Raoul Lambert was the secretary-general of the CAR; in the Netherlands, as we will see, both JR chairmen, Abraham Asscher (1880–1950) and David Cohen (1882–1967), were prominently involved in the plight of Jewish refugees in the 1930s. By highlighting either the continuation or discontinuation of pre-war structures in this regard, we will see that the nature of the wartime Jewish leadership was crucially different in the three countries.

In the Netherlands, Professor of Classical History David Cohen, who served on the board of the Permanent commission of both the Dutch–Israelite (Ashkenazi) and the Portuguese–Israelite (Sephardi) church congregations, took the initiative to establish the Committee for Special Jewish Affairs (Comité voor Bijzondere Joodse Belangen, CBJB), a committee that would coordinate refugee aid, in March 1933. Cohen was firmly rooted in Dutch social and cultural life and had close bonds with Dutch Jewry. In some respects, he represented the assimilationist form and functioning of the Jewish community of the time. Although discussions have been raised about the exact position he held in the Dutch Zionist movement, we know that he was a convinced Zionist.[95] He initiated the establishment of the CBJB together with Abraham Asscher, an experienced leader who fulfilled dozens of representative functions. Asscher was the owner of the best-known diamond factory in Amsterdam,

---

[94] For further information on the activities of this Antwerp committee, about which little is known because its archives were destroyed on 10 May 1940, see Jean-Philippe Schreiber, 'Belgian Jewry', 97–102.

[95] On the one hand, Cohen has been referred to as a misunderstood (*miskend*) Zionist leader as he never became the clear leader of the NZB. On the other hand, it has been argued that this might never have been his aim in the first place because, as a Zionist propagandist and humanitarian aid-giver, he was more concerned with NZB activities on the periphery. See KBI Inv. No. 1420 Prof. Dr. David Cohen, NIOD; Evelien Gans, 'De generaal en zijn adjudant. Piet Schrijvers' biografie van David Cohen', *Biografie Bulletin*, Vol. 10, No. 2 (2000), 153. For further reading on Cohen and (his relation to) Zionism in the Netherlands, see Piet Schrijvers, *Rome, Athene, Jeruzalem: het leven en werk van prof. dr. David Cohen* (Groningen: Historische Uitgeverij, 2000), 70–86, 191–193.

politically active as the provincial leader of the Liberal party and, above all, president of the Dutch–Israelite church congregation (Nederlands Israëlitisch Kerkgenootschap, NIK), established in 1814.[96] His appointment at the helm of the NIK, combined with the other functions he fulfilled, made him the principal representative of Jews at the time.[97] The central aim of the CBJB was to serve as a non-violent response to the Jewish persecution in Germany and to take care of German Jewish refugees in the country by providing social and financial support.[98] In order to promote this aim, its leadership established the Committee for Jewish Refugees (Comité voor Joodse Vluchtelingen, CJV), as a sub-commission.[99] The CBJB worked closely together with Stichting Joodse Arbeid, a Zionist organisation that aimed to prepare young Jews for their emigration to Palestine.

In a difficult, unstable period in which Dutch Jewry became increasingly secular, Asscher and Cohen ensured there was a close link between refugee work and the Dutch–Israelite church congregation. In addition, they tried to unite the Jewish communities through the CBJB, with the aim of bringing together various Jewish interests groups: Orthodox and Liberal; Ashkenazic and Sephardic; assimilationist and Zionist.[100] The outlook of the CBJB on its future role in Jewish society was therefore more ambitious than merely providing aid to refugees. At the same time, its leadership deliberately excluded the religious leadership as well as socialist and communist Jewish groups.[101]

A 1939 letter from Asscher's hand as head of the NIK sent to the Mayor and Deputy Mayor of Amsterdam, supports the idea that his aims reached higher than merely carrying out the duty of supporting Jewish welfare. Asscher feared the influence of the Liberal Jewish Congregation (Liberaal Joodse Gemeenschap) in the Netherlands. This congregation consisted mostly of German Jews, many of whom had only recently

---

[96] Blom and Cahen, 'Dutch Jews', 317; Michman, Beem and Michman, *Pinkas*, 134.
[97] Michman, Beem and Michman, *Pinkas*, 134.
[98] Ibid., 148. Katja Happe, *Veel valse hoop: de jodenvervolging in Nederland, 1940–1945*, transl. from the German by Fred Reurs (Amsterdam: Uitgeverij Atlas Contact, 2018; first ed. 2017 [German]), 30–32.
[99] In 1955, David Cohen published a monograph on Jewish refugees in the Netherlands between 1933 and 1940, including a description of the activities of the Committee for Jewish Refugees; see David Cohen, *Zwervend en dolend: de Joodse vluchtelingen in Nederland in de jaren 1933–1940, met een inleiding over de jaren 1900–1933* (Haarlem: Bohn, 1955), 60–79.
[100] Moore, *Refugees from Nazi Germany in the Netherlands*, 27.
[101] Michman, Beem and Michman, *Pinkas*, 148; Hans Blom, 'In de ban van de Joodse Raad', in Hans Blom, *In de ban van goed en fout? Wetenschappelijke geschiedschrijving over de bezettingstijd in Nederland* (Bergen: Octavo, 1983), 52.

immigrated into the Netherlands.[102] He considered the fact that its members had to pay dues, that it consisted mostly of Germans and that even non-Jews were accepted in the congregation as 'a threat for the rest and peace' within the Jewish society.[103] The firmness and tone of Asscher's letter marks a line of demarcation between immigrant and Dutch Jewry.

Asscher did not afford the mostly liberal German Jews the same status as Dutch Jews. Although the Dutch–Israelite church congregation (chaired by Asscher) was a cooperation between 'liberal' and orthodox Dutch Jews that aimed to unite Dutch Jewry and to be a universal *volkskerk* (church of the people), the presence of the German liberal congregation was a step too far for him. Above all, the leadership of the CBJB enabled Asscher and Cohen to definitively establish their position as leaders within the community in this period.[104] These two men, as well as Henri Eitje (1889–1943) and Gertrude van Tijn-Cohn (1891–1974), who organised the actual running of the Committee for Jewish Refugees while Cohen served as its chairman, would fulfil (prominent) positions in the Dutch Jewish Council from 1941 onwards.

In France, the influx of refugees, and the criticisms that were voiced from various sides about the way in which the traditional leadership dealt with the problem forced the Consistory to establish aid organisations. In reality, however, Consistorial leaders and members generally continued to regard refugee Jews with suspicion, believing that they constituted a threat to their own position. This mistrustful perspective vis-à-vis immigrant Jews is a tendency that can be identified in the traditional (Jewish) institutions in all three countries.

In some cases, attempts were made to remove refugees from France. For example, throughout the 1930s, the Consistory's president, Jacques Helbronner, ensured that migration and repatriation of refugees (rather than providing social assistance for immigrants to remain in France) became the sole priorities of the National Aid Committee for German Refugees, Victims of Antisemitism (Comité National de Secours aux Réfugiés Allemands, Victimes de l'Anti-Semitisme), an aid organisation that was established to deal with the influx of Jewish refugees from Germany. Together with the Committee for the Defence of the Rights of

[102] Dan Michman, *Het Liberale Jodendom in Nederland, 1929–1943* (Amsterdam: Van Gennep, 1988), 107.
[103] 'Brief gericht aan het college van burgemeester en wethouders van Amsterdam', KBI, Liberaal Joodse Gemeente, A. Asscher, Inv No. 200, NIOD. For an overview of Asscher's openly hostile position towards German Jews who associated themselves with the liberal movement, see Michman, *Het Liberale Jodendom in Nederland*, 107–108.
[104] Blom, 'In de ban van de Joodse Raad', 52.

Jews from Central and Western Europe (Comité pour la Défense des Droits des Israélites en Europe Centrale et Occidentale), this was the among the most important sources of refugee assistance in France in the 1930s.[105] Helbronner's hesitant involvement in refugee aid is indicative of a broader sentiment in which the traditional Jewish leaders carefully measured their own decisions against the possible repercussions in a larger society that increasingly perceived the Jew as a foreign threat.[106]

We have seen that the approach of French Jewry towards refugees was not exclusively negative. A substantial number of French Jews became sympathetic to the achievements of the Zionist movement in Palestine. Refugee organisations, such as the CAR and the Comité National of the Central Consistory, competed with each other to have the upper hand in political influence about Jewish matters, and about the influx of Jewish refugees specifically. Throughout the 1930s, as secretary-general of the CAR, Raymond-Raoul Lambert had taken up a pro-refugee stance after the deteriorating anti-refugee outlook of the Comité National. Increasingly influenced by Zionist ideas, he worked hard to find jobs for refugees between 1933 and 1935, permitting them to stay in France. At the same time, Lambert was not an extreme radical on the matter; he accepted certain government policies, such as isolating Eastern European immigrants and making a distinction between political and economic refugees. Despite this, his opposition to the established Jewish authorities is clear.[107]

The refugee problem of the 1930s therefore altered the power balances within French Jewish communities. With the divisions between immigrant and French Jewry becoming more visible than before in this period of political, economic and social instability, the Consistory lost the last element of its exclusive authority over the Jews. Although a significant degree of consensus was reached by 1939 on the issue of refugees among pro-refugee organisations, namely that France could only function as a transit country under its contemporary economic and political circumstances, there was a range of other issues that divided the communities.[108] This instability encouraged some Jews who had been part of the Jewish establishment for years to publicly voice their discontent with the

---

[105] Caron, *Uneasy Asylum*, 107; Laffitte, *Juif dans la France allemande*, 28–29; Sémelin, *The Survival of the Jews in France*, 27.

[106] Hyman, *From Dreyfus to Vichy*, 23.

[107] Caron, *Uneasy Asylum*, 105–107, 303. Also see Richard Cohen (ed.), 'Introduction', in *Diary of a Witness 1940–1943: Raymond-Raoul Lambert*, transl. from the French by Isabel Best (Chicago: Ivan R. Dee, 2007; first ed. 1985 [French]), xvii–xxxii.

[108] Caron, *Uneasy Asylum*, 319; Weinberg, *A Community on Trial*, 72–211.

way the Consistory ruled Jewish society. The future leader of the UGIF-Sud, Lambert, was among those who did so.

In Belgium, as in the Netherlands and France, the government was reluctant to take care of Jewish refugees. Jewish communities instituted various aid organisations, including, as we have seen, the Antwerp Committee for the Defence of the Rights of Jews, in which Salomon Ullmann (later chairman of the AJB) was involved, and the Brussels Committee for Aid and Assistance to Victims of Antisemitism in Germany (Comité d'Aide et d'Assistance aux Victimes de l'Antisémitisme en Allemagne). Both organisations were established in 1933 as a response to the influx of German Jewish refugees. The Brussels committee functioned under the auspices of the Central Consistory and was supervised by Max Gottschalk, a high ranking international functionary and one of the most important community leaders of Belgian Jewry.[109]

The Jewish Central Consistory encouraged the creation of philanthropic organisations to help immigrants and promoted recognition of the diverse forms of worship they brought with them.[110] However, as in the cases of the Dutch and French traditional leadership, their solidarity with German Jews was not without limits. Assuming that Belgium was only a transit country for immigrants, the humanitarian limits of the Brussels Committee for Aid and Assistance were reached when it turned out that Brazil and Uruguay had closed their borders for immigrants on 26 September 1933: they advised refugee Jews to go back to either Germany or Poland.[111] As we have seen, Belgium faced difficulties in integrating large number of refugees, and the Central Consistory struggled to find a way to substantiate its role as the representative of all Jewish communities.

Many of those who had held leading positions (in refugee aid organisations) before the war, fled abroad when the German invasion was imminent, and did not return after the German occupation. Among them were Chief Rabbi Joseph Wiener, the majority of the Board of Directors of the Israelite community and other prominent members of Belgian Jewish society, including Max Gottschalk who fled to the United States.[112] Consequently, there was a leadership vacuum in what was already a disorganised Belgian Jewish society at the outbreak of the war. This pattern can be seen too in the occupied zone in France, where a

---

[109] Schreiber, *Dictionnaire Biographique*, 139–141.
[110] Dratwa, 'The Zionism Kaleidoscope in Belgium', 46.
[111] Caestecker, *Ongewenste gasten*, 31–33.
[112] Jean-Philippe Schreiber, 'Tussen traditionele en verplichte gemeenschap', in *De curatoren van het getto*, 71–110.

large part of the traditional leadership also fled after the German invasion. In the Netherlands and the French unoccupied zone, the situation was different since many Jews who fulfilled prominent positions in pre-war society, remained in place. We will see that these differences had an impact on the nature of the wartime Jewish leadership.

May 1940: The German Invasion and Its Machinery of Government

In May 1940, the Germans unleashed their forces on France and the Low Countries and their rapid advance resulted in chaos, panic and astonishment. Particularly in the Netherlands, where people had strongly believed in the power of neutrality, the German invasion shocked its citizens and, when it became clear the Dutch army could not resist Germany's advancement, many tried to flee abroad. In Belgium and France, the fear of a German occupation also incited refugee streams to the South, which resulted in some 3 million refugee civilians in West Flanders and a rapid population drain in the towns and cities in the north of France.[113] The responses of the Jewish populations in Western-Europe, which had observed the increasing persecution of Jews in Germany, varied from outright distress and panic to more moderate reactions based on the belief that the situation in the West would be different from that in Germany and Eastern Europe.[114] On 15 and 28 May respectively, the Dutch and Belgian forces surrendered to the Germans. In France, the collaborationist Vichy regime signed an armistice on 22 June 1940, which culminated in the physical occupation of the northern half and the western coastal areas of the country.

The nature of the German occupation differed across the three countries under investigation. Whereas a Civil Administration (*Zivilverwaltung*) was introduced in the Netherlands, a Military Administration (*Militärverwaltung*) governed Belgium and France. This difference is important in terms of understanding the particular contexts in which German and Vichy officials forced the leaders of the 'Jewish Councils' to

---

[113] Moore, *Survivors*, 15–17.
[114] Happe, *Veel valse hoop*, 39–44; Michman, Beem and Michman, *Pinkas*, 164; Wichert ten Have, *1940: Verwarring en Aanpassing* (Houten: Spectrum; Amsterdam: NIOD, 2015), 65–84; Bart van der Boom, *'We leven nog': de stemming in bezet Nederland* (Amsterdam: Boom, 2003), 17–30; Jules Gérard-Libois and José Gotovitch, *L'an 40: La Belgique occupée* (Brussels: CRISP, ca. 1972; first ed. 1971), 90–122; Werner Warmbrunn, *The German Occupation of Belgium, 1940–1944* (New York: Lang, 1993), 43–52; Steinberg, *L'étoile et le fusil: La question juive*, 85–88; Poznanski, *The Jews in France during World War II*, 23–29.

operate. Initially, the plan was to establish a Military Administration in all three countries. According to Kwiet, Hitler's last-minute order to introduce a Civil Administration in the Netherlands on 18 May 1940 exemplifies his impulsivity and the improvised nature of his decisions.[115] Yet the choice for a Civil Administration can be explained by the fact that the Netherlands, in contrast to France and Belgium (Wallonia in particular), was considered a *Germanisches Brudervolk* (Germanic brother people), which at some point ought to be included in the German Reich.

In light of the aim to Nazify the *Brudervolk* in the Netherlands, German leaders with strong ideological backgrounds, led by Reich Commissioner (Reichskommissar) Arthur Seyss-Inquart, were appointed in the country immediately after the occupation.[116] By contrast, the German generals preferred a military occupation in Belgium and France for strategic reasons because they eventually wished to use these countries as a venture point for an invasion of Great Britain.[117] The initially accommodating attitude of King Leopold III of the Belgians and the armistice agreement with France, leaving the south and parts of the east of the country unoccupied until November 1942, also served to help the establishment of a Military Administration in these countries.[118]

There was a strong presence of the SS in the Netherlands. Höhere SS- und Polizeiführer Hanns Albin Rauter was the highest SS representative in the country and stood in direct communication with Reichsführer-SS Heinrich Himmler in Berlin. By contrast, in Belgium and France, the party and the SS were hardly represented at first. In France, only Werner Best (civilian branch of the Military Administration) and Otto Abetz (ambassador) were important ideologists of the occupation regime. The SS established an office of the SiPo-SD in Paris, but its influence was initially restricted because the Military Administration did not allow it any executive role. In

---

[115] Konrad Kwiet, *Reichskommissariat Niederlande: Versuch und Scheitern nationalsozialistischer Neuordnung* (Stuttgart: Deutsche Verlags-Anstalt, 1968), 49–50; 'Erlaß des Führers über Ausübung der Regierungsbefugnisse in den Niederlanden', 18.5.1940 in *Reichsgesetzblatt* part I, 788. Published as 'Erste Verordnung (VO I/1940)' in *Verordnungsblatt für die besetzten niederländischen Gebiete* (VOBL), 1940 (part 1), 4.

[116] For an overview of the history and structure of the Reichskommissariat in the Netherlands, see: Gerhard Hirschfeld, *Nazi Rule and Dutch Collaboration: The Netherlands under German Occupation, 1940–1945*, transl. from the German by Louise Willmot (Oxford/New York/Hamburg: Berg, 1988; first ed. 1984 [German]), 12–54.

[117] Kwiet, *Reichskommissariat Niederlande*, 61–68.

[118] Albert de Jonghe, *Hitler en het politieke lot van België (1940–1944). De vestiging van een Zivilverwaltung in België en Noord-Frankrijk: Koningskwestie en bezettingsregime van de kapitulatie tot Berchtesgaden, 28 mei – 19 november 1940*, Vol. 1 (Antwerp: De Nederlandsche Boekhandel, 1972), 313–323.

Belgium, there were no representatives of the party or SS present within the leadership of the Military Administration. As a result, the SiPo-SD had an even weaker position here than in France and the Netherlands. This continued to be the case even after the head of the Reich Security Main Office Reinhard Heydrich appointed a direct representative for France and Belgium, Max Thomas, Commissioner of the Security Police and Security Service (Beauftragter des Chefs der Sicherheitspolizei und des Sicherheitsdienst für Belgien und Frankreich).[119]

The differences in the nature of occupation found their expression in the implementation of anti-Jewish legislation. Whereas the presence of the Military Administration in Belgium and France resulted in a more gradual introduction of anti-Jewish legislation, the SS in the Netherlands was more radical.[120] This difference can be explained by the fact that the Military Administration took the responses of the non-Jewish populations more carefully into consideration, in part because it was chiefly interested in exploiting resources for the German war effort and limiting the use of German manpower; aims that necessitated stability over disruption.[121] Particularly during the first phase of the occupation, the presence of the Military Administration in Belgium and France served as an inhibiting factor in the process of persecution and in the preparations for the large scale deportation of Jews. This was enabled by the provisional nature of German policy toward the Jews in this period. From the outbreak of the war in Western Europe until the autumn of 1941, the so-called Final Solution to the Jewish Question still vaguely encompassed a 'yet unspecified project of mass emigration'.[122]

During this first phase of the occupation, the various German authorities in Western Europe pursued anti-Jewish objectives primarily by

---

[119] Griffioen and Zeller, *Jodenvervolging in Nederland, Frankrijk en België*, 107–108; Hans Umbreit, *Der Militärbefehlshaber in Frankreich* (Boppard am Rhein: Harald Boldt Verlag, 1968), 107–108; Joseph Billig, *Die 'Endlösung der Judenfrage.' Studie über ihre Grundsätze im III. Reich und in Frankreich während der Besatzung* transl. from the French by Eva Schulz (New York: The Beate Klarsfeld Foundation, 1979; first ed. 1977 [French]), 99; Steinberg, *L'étoile et le fusil. La question juive*, 22.

[120] Griffioen and Zeller, *Jodenvervolging in Nederland, Frankrijk en België*, 233–234.

[121] Marrus and Paxton, *Vichy France and the Jews* (Stanford: Stanford University Press, 2020; this is an updated and revised version of the 1981 publication of this work), 45–48; Steinberg, *L'étoile et le fusil. La question juive*, 19–25; ibid., *La Persécution des Juifs en Belgique* (Brussels: Complexe, 2004), 37.

[122] Michael Marrus and Robert Paxton, 'The Nazis and the Jews in Occupied Western Europe, 1940–1944', in *The Journal of Modern History*, Vol. 54, No. 4 (1982), 687. Also see Saul Friedländer, *The Years of Extermination: Nazi Germany and the Jews, 1939–1945* (New York: HarperCollins, 2007), 3–194; Peter Longerich, *Holocaust: The Nazi Persecution and Murder of the Jews* (Oxford: Oxford University Press, 2010) 123–130, 148–176.

'controlling the movements and organizations of Jews, confiscating their property, enumerating them, and sometimes concentrating them in certain regions'.[123] In Belgium, the head of the Military Administration (Militärverwaltungschef), Eggert Reeder, prevented the SiPo-SD from engaging in a *Judenpolitik* of its own in this period, safeguarding his own position as well as stability and order. In order to do this, Reeder confirmed in January 1941 that the SiPo-SD was only permitted to arrest Jews when instructed or approved to do so by the Military Administration.[124] Only in summer 1942, shortly before the start of the deportations of Jews from Belgium did the SiPo-SD enlarge its influence. As we shall see, this was the result of a dramatic reversal of German policy towards Jews.[125]

In France, the Military Administration, headed by General Otto von Stülpnagel had overall authority. It initially obstructed SS-Hauptsturmführer Theodor Dannecker, who directly served under Adolf Eichmann, in his attempts to concentrate Jews in order to commence their forced deportation as quickly as possible. Von Stülpnagel wished to limit the number of internment camps in the occupied zone and considered the mass arrest of Jews to be a matter for the French. Moreover, he wanted to restrict the power of the SiPo-SD in order to safeguard the position of the Military Administration.[126]

From autumn 1941, the faltering campaign in Russia showed that the war would last longer than Hitler had expected. German policies therefore changed and Jews in Western Europe, no longer allowed to emigrate from occupied countries, were segregated and interned.[127] As a result, the SiPo-SD increased its power at the cost of the Military Administration. However, as we shall see, the continued rivalry between the two institutions continued to exist and, in the case of France, sometimes frustrated Dannecker's radical plans.[128]

The occupation of France had its own peculiarities as the French regime opted for an armistice with the Germans, while the country was officially administered by the collaborationist Vichy regime, headed by

[123] Marrus and Paxton, 'The Nazis and the Jews in Occupied Western Europe', 678.
[124] Steinberg, *L'étoile et le fusil. La question juive*, 25–27.
[125] Albert de Jonghe, 'De strijd Himmler-Reeder om de benoeming van een HSSPF te Brussel (1942–1944)', *Bijdragen tot de Geschiedenis van de Tweede Wereldoorlog*, Vol. 3 (1974), 197–199; Griffioen and Zeller, *Jodenvervolging in Nederland, Frankrijk en België*, 235.
[126] Griffioen and Zeller, *Jodenvervolging in Nederland, Frankrijk en België*, 179–181. Also see Marrus and Paxton, *Vichy France and the Jews*, 45–48.
[127] Marrus and Paxton, 'The Nazi Jews in Occupied Western Europe', 687–688.
[128] Claudia Steur, *Theodor Dannecker: ein Funktionär der 'Endlösung'* (Essen: Klartext Verlag, 1997), 47–91. For an overview of the increasing initiatives taken by the SiPo-SD to gain power over anti-Jewish policies in France, see: Griffioen and Zeller, *Jodenvervolging in Nederland, Frankrijk en België*, 181–192.

Marshal Henri Philippe Pétain. The Vichy regime thus operated along-side the German Military Administration, creating a rivalry between the French and German institutions. For example, Vichy outpaced the Germans by introducing the *Statut des Juifs*, the first widespread anti-Jewish legislation, first in October 1940 and then in June 1941.[129] Above all, when the deportations began in summer 1942, the German SD's Juden-referat had to share its control over the deportations of Jews with both the Military Administration and Vichy.

In the Netherlands, the preparations for the implementation of anti-Jewish measures were initially chiefly administered by General Commissioner for Special Affairs (Generalkommissar zur besonderen Verwendung) Fritz Schmidt (a protégé of the Propaganda Minister Joseph Goebbels and Martin Bormann, head of the Nazi Party Chancellery) and General Commissioner for Administration and Justice (Generalkommissar für Verwaltung und Justiz) Friedrich Wimmer, both of whom officially supported the office of Reichskommissar Arthur Seyss-Inquart (Civil Administration).[130] Until March 1941, Seyss-Inquart successfully kept anti-Jewish policy within the Reichskommissariat's sphere of influence. In this period, the Highest SS and Police Leader (Höhere SS- und Polizeiführer, HSSPF), Hanns Albin Rauter, was not actively involved in the preparation and execution of anti-Jewish policies. However, the SiPo-SD gained increasing operational freedom throughout 1941, restricting the authority of the Reichskommissariat as a result.[131]

From the end of February 1942, the policy of persecution came under the supervision of Eichmann's IV B4 Berlin office, a sub-department of the RSHA that was directly responsible for the implementation of the so-called Final Solution to the Jewish Question. One month later, Rauter informed Karel Johannes Frederiks, Secretary-General of Internal Affairs, that Jews no longer fell under Dutch government

---

[129] Laurent Joly, *Vichy dans la 'solution finale': histoire du commissariat général aux questions juives, 1941–1944* (Paris: Grasset, 2006), 75–100, 190–200; Marrus and Paxton, *Vichy France and the Jews*, 7–9, 60–62.

[130] Griffioen and Zeller, *Jodenvervolging in Nederland, Frankrijk en België*, 208–210, 216.

[131] For an overview of the process in which the SiPo-SD gained increasing power in the Netherlands, which was by no means a linear process, see Griffioen and Zeller, *Jodenvervolging in Nederland, Frankrijk en België*, 216–226; Houwink ten Cate, 'Der Befehlshaber der SiPo-SD in den besetzten niederländischen Gebiete', in Wolfgang Benz, Gerhard Otto and Johannes Houwink ten Cate (eds.), *Die Bürokratie der Okkupation. Strukturen der Herrschaft und Verwaltung im besetzten Europa* (Berlin: Metropol, 1999), 87–133; Hirschfeld, *Nazi Rule and Dutch Collaboration*, 45–54; Frits Boterman, *Duitse daders: de jodenvervolging en de nazificatie van Nederland, 1940–1945* (Amsterdam: Uitgeverij de Arbeiderspers, 2015), 16–19; Johannes Koll, *Arthur Seyss-Inquart und die deutsche Besatzungspolitik in den Niederlanden, 1940–1945* (Vienna/Cologne/Weimar: Böhlau Verlag, 2015), 121–192.

authority.[132] As a consequence, the Germans had more operational freedom to implement anti-Jewish legislation than their counterparts in Belgium and France. After summer 1942, Seyss-Inquart, who was at first directly subordinate to Hitler, was also overseen by Reichsführer-SS Himmler. From this point on, Seyss-Inquart was forced to reach agreements with SS-representatives in the Netherlands, most notably Rauter, even in non-police matters. Seyss-Inquart's generally good relations with Himmler and, as Gruppenführer of the SS, his affinity with the ideas of the SS, combined with the fact that Himmler's agreement had become necessary 'for almost every development in the occupied Netherlands' encouraged him in doing so.[133] As a result, the Reichskommissariat (Civil Administration) and the SS, even though they were rival institutions, acted in liaison in preparing and implementing increasingly radical anti-Jewish policies in the Netherlands.

1940–1941: Restructuring Communal Representation

The flight abroad of some of the pre-war Jewish leaders after the German occupation in May 1940, combined with a feeling that the communities needed to confront the Nazis in a unified way, resulted in the restructuring of communal representation. This materialised differently in each of the countries. In the period between the invasion and the establishment of the JR, the AJB, the UGIF-Nord and the UGIF-Sud in 1941, as a consequence of the German occupation, Jewish representative organisations came into existence. These were either established by German demand or by the initiative of Jewish community members. All were so-called Coordinating Committees, which generally aimed to oversee all Jewish philanthropic work and sought to unite the various Jewish communities.[134] From the German perspective, the existence of these (national) representative Jewish bodies may have decreased the perceived need to institute Jewish Councils, or similar organisations, immediately after the occupation of the Netherlands, Belgium and northern France (in the occupied Polish territories this *did* happen).[135] Furthermore, the absence

---

[132] Griffioen and Zeller, *Jodenvervolging in Nederland, Frankrijk en België*, 222–223; De Jong, *Het Koninkrijk*, Vol. 5, 1031–1035.

[133] Hirschfeld, *Nazi Rule and Dutch Collaboration*, 47–48.

[134] Yahil, 'The Jewish Leadership of France', 320–321; Michman, 'De oprichting van de VJB in internationaal perspectief', 36–37; Jozeph Melkman, 'De briefwisseling tussen Mr. L.E. Visser en Prof. Dr. D. Cohen', *Studia Rosenthaliana*, Vol. 8, No. 1 (1974), 109–114.

[135] Dan Michman has pointed out that, in the occupied Polish territories, SS officials appointed Jewish leaders (*Obmänner*) in various communities, including Piotrków

of a central order to force such institutions upon the communities in Western Europe undoubtedly played a role in delaying their establishment. Heydrich's September 1939 *Schnellbrief*, in which he detailed the establishment of Jewish Councils for occupied Poland, did not apply to countries other than Poland.[136]

Prior to the forced establishment of the AJB in Belgium, the Coordinating Committee of the Jewish Communities (Comité de Coördination des Communautés Israélites, CC) was established in April 1941 at the initiative of the German SS. Similar to its successor the AJB, the CC was established to function as an umbrella organisation for Jewish social and religious life. Initially, Jewish community representatives voiced objections, because they wanted to safeguard the organisational autonomy of religious institutions. However, after careful deliberation, the Chief Rabbi – Salomon Ullmann – was appointed head of the CC.[137] Various social welfare organisations, including the Aid Organisations for Jews from Germany (Hilfswerke für die Juden aus Deutschland), were included in the organisation.[138]

In the French occupied zone, the Coordination Committee of the Israelite Charities of Greater Paris (Comité de Coordination des Oeuvres de Bienfaisance Israélites à Paris) was established by a German order in January 1941; it was made up of the Paris Consistory and various Jewish welfare organisations.[139] These organisations included the Jewish Welfare Committee of Paris (Comité de Bienfaisance Israélite de Paris, CBIP), the Organisation Reconstruction Work (Organisation Reconstruction Travail, ORT), the Children's Aid Society (Oeuvre de Secours aux Enfants, OSE) and the Amelot Committee, a Jewish relief organisation that was founded by Jewish immigrants in Paris in May 1940, and whose members later engaged in clandestine activities to secure their aid to Jews in need.[140]

Trybunalski and Lodz, shortly after the occupation of these territories (and even before Heydrich's *Schnellbrief*). See Michman, 'Why Did Heydrich Write the 'Schnellbrief'?', 434–437.

[136] Michman, 'On the Historical Interpretation of the Judenräte Issue', 392.

[137] Maxime Steinberg, 'The Jews in the Years 1940–1944: Three Strategies for Coping with a Tragedy', in Michman, *Belgium and the Holocaust*, 354; Michman, 'De oprichting van de VJB in internationaal perspectief', 36–37.

[138] 'Betrifft: Organisation der Juden in Belgien', 23 April 1941, *Verwaltungsabteilung/ Gruppe VII: Fürsorge – Juden*. SVG, Marburg Documentation, Film XIV, R.184/ Tr50.077, Documentatie Oorlogsslachtoffers.

[139] Marrus and Paxton, *Vichy France and the Jews*, 108; Adler, *The Jews of Paris*, 63; Laffitte, *Un engrenage fatal*, 27–31; Moore, *Survivors*, 105.

[140] The Amelot Committee was made up from three political groups (the Bund, and the left and right wings of the Poale-Zion), and two other organisations, the FSJF and

In October 1940, the Central Committee for Jewish Aid Organisations (Commission Centrale des Organisations Juives d'Assistance, CCOJA) was created in Marseille, in the unoccupied zone, under the aegis of the Chief Rabbi of France, Isaïe Schwartz. The CCOJA regrouped the nine major welfare organisations that were either still operative, or had moved their offices from the occupied zone to the unoccupied zone. While Lambert's CAR was its chief operating agency, the CCOJA worked closely with the FSJF, one of the major Jewish immigrant aid organisations, and the OSE, a children's welfare organisation that after the armistice focused its efforts on obtaining the release of as many internees as possible, primarily children, from the camps in the unoccupied zone. The CCOJA was disbanded in March 1942, unable to achieve many of its objectives.[141]

In the Netherlands, Lodewijk Ernst Visser, the dismissed president of the Dutch Supreme Court (Hoge Raad), and one of the central figures inside the Jewish community, initiated the establishment of the Jewish Coordinating Committee (Joodsche Coördinatie Commissie, JCC) in December 1940.[142] Established under the auspices of the Dutch Zionists in the commissions of both the Dutch–Israelite (Ashkenazi) and Portuguese–Israelite (Sephardi) Church, the aim of the organisation was to provide a representative organ for Jews in the Netherlands that could provide aid and relief.[143] Visser refused to cooperate with the Germans,

the Colonie Scolaire. See Béatrice le Douarion, 'Le Comité "Rue Amelot", 1940–1944 à Paris. Assistance aux Juifs et Sauvetage des Enfants', master's thesis Paris Sorbonne (1994), 1–2, 8. The (clandestine) activities of the Amelot Committee will be thoroughly examined in Chapter 5.

[141] Poznanski, *Jews in France during World War II*, 132. Raymond-Raoul Lambert held a diary, which covers three years of the war, terminating on the day before his arrest on 21 August 1943. In his diary, Lambert, secretary general of the CAR (which was included in the CCOJA), stated that the authorities did not recognise the CCOJA 'which got no further than its pretensions'. It 'only organised some discussion sessions, and accomplished nothing'. The English translation of this diary was published in 2007, edited and with an introduction by Richard Cohen: Raymond-Raoul Lambert, *Diary of a Witness, 1940–1943: The Ordeal of the Jews of France during the Holocaust*, transl. Isabel Best (Chicago: Ivan R. Dee, 2007; the diary was also published in French by Librairie Arthème Fayard in 1985), 11 December 1941, 80.

[142] For a short biography of Visser, see J. A. Polak, *Leven en werken van mr. L.E. Visser* (Amsterdam: Athenaeum-Polak &Van Gennep, 1997). For the history of the Hoge Raad between 1930 and 1950, see Corjo Jansen and Derk Venema, *De Hoge Raad en Tweede Wereldoorlog: recht en rechtsbeoefening in de jaren 1930–1950* (Amsterdam: Boom, 2011).

[143] Melkman, 'De briefwisseling', 109; Abel Herzberg, *Kroniek der Jodenvervolging* (Arnhem: Van Loghum Slaterus/Amsterdam: Meulenhoff, 1956), 144. This latter book first appeared as a chapter in Johannes Jacobus van Bolhuis, Coenraad Dirk Jan Brandt, Henk van Randwijk et al. (eds.), *Onderdrukking en Verzet, Nederland in Oorlogstijd*, Vol. 3 (Arnhem: Van Loghum Slaterus, 1950). For the archive

and, partly as a result, the JCC was disbanded on 10 November 1941. This is remarkable, because whereas the Coordinating Committees in Belgium and France were largely dysfunctional, the JCC functioned comparatively well. In fact, there was an entire infrastructure in place, with a central committee and local sub-committees in places where Jews lived throughout the Netherlands.

The fact that the Germans refused to make use of an organisation that successfully fulfilled the major social welfare tasks that were later allotted to the JR, in part, was undoubtedly a result of Visser's refusal to cooperate with the Germans. However, rather than disbanding the JCC altogether, from the German perspective, the easiest solution would have been to put the organisation under severe pressure and to nominate a new director who *was* willing to work with them. Instead, an entirely new organisation in the form of a Jewish Council was founded. The classic Nazi policy of what we might call 'institutional Darwinism', that is, superimposing additional organisations rather than rationalising existing policies and institutions, can be clearly seen here. The JR competed with the Coordinating Commission and, in the end, proved to be more useful for German aims. In Belgium and France, neither the Military Administration nor the SiPo-SD believed that the Coordinating Committees had successfully united the Jewish communities.[144] In all three countries, the supposed failures of the committees served as the springboard for establishing alternative representative bodies: the JR, the AJB, the UGIF-Nord and the UGIF-Sud.

---

of the Jewish Coordinating Committee in the Netherlands, see: Coördinatie-Commissie, ingesteld door de Nederlandsch-Israëlitische en Portugees-Israëlitische Kerkgenootschappen, 181d, NIOD.

[144] For France, see Cohen, *The Burden of Conscience*, 30; For Belgium, see Michman, 'De oprichting van de VJB in internationaal perspectief', 37.

2 Institutional Rivalry and Improvisation
The Establishment of 'Jewish Councils' in 1941

In early 1941, the demand to establish 'Jewish Councils' was voiced by leading Nazis in Western Europe in an attempt to marginalise the Jews through these umbrella organisations. This was part of increasing anti-Jewish legislation that aimed to exclude and isolate Jews from the non-Jewish public sphere. The predominant approach towards 'Jewish Councils' as instruments in the hands of the Germans has reinforced the notion that these bodies were established to aid in the process of identi-fying, registering, isolating and deporting the Jews they were ostensibly representing. Yet this approach is too narrow because it fails to address the complex nature of the Nazi regime and the conflicting outlook on these Jewish bodies among the various (German and Vichy) departments involved in their establishment.

A careful examination of the establishment histories of the JR, the AJB, the UGIF-Nord and the UGIF-Sud reveals that the form and function of these bodies was inherently dependent upon the nature of German rule, which was itself epitomised by contradictions. With the absence of a clearly defined plan for how the so-called Greater German Reich would be governed, there were competing interests, and different initiatives on a local level. As a result, the Jewish representative bodies were used by rival German institutions, often to effect their own inten-tions. In terms of the formation of an actual Jewish Council, these factors explain why only in the Netherlands an early decision was made to force this body upon the Jewish communities (in February 1941, nine months before its counterparts in Belgium and France were established).

The establishment histories of the Jewish bodies in Western Europe are characterised by improvisation and the copying of blueprints from else-where. In Belgium, the head of the Brussels office of the SiPo-SD, Ernst Ehlers, confirmed that the AJB was modelled after the Reich Association of Jews in Germany (Reichsvereinigung der Juden in Deutschland).[1]

---

[1] 'Sonderbericht: Das Judentum in Belgien', 31 January 1942, 37–38, SVG-R.184/Tr 50 077, Marburg Documentation, DOS. From February 1942 until March 1943, Ernst

The establishment order of the AJB, issued on 25 November 1941, was an almost exact copy of its German counterpart.[2] Ironically, the objective of the Association was to 'promote emigration of the Jews' while the directive to prohibit emigration of Jews from Belgium was drafted by Chief of the Gestapo Heinrich Müller in the same period (October 1941), on the orders of Reichsführer-SS Heinrich Himmler.[3] In fact, on 23 October 1941 Müller informed Commissioner of the Security Police and SD for Belgium and France Max Thomas of the prohibition on emigration.[4] Since emigration continued to be a task the Germans ascribed to the AJB well into 1942, it has been suggested that this also might have meant the evacuation of Jews to Eastern Europe, a territorial solution to the so-called Jewish Question that was still considered in this period.[5]

If this was the case, one would expect that the establishment order of the UGIF, which was almost simultaneously published in neighbouring France, would also allude to emigration; yet this was not the case.[6] This again shows that there was a lack of clear central directives regarding the remit of these organisations in Western Europe. That the German Reich Association's blueprint was copied, and the precise role of the AJB was not clearly explicated, highlights the fact that German policies were improvised and were not explicitly adapted for the specifics of the Belgian situation. This is especially remarkable when we go on to consider that the AJB, and 'Jewish Councils' in Western Europe

Ehlers headed the Brussels branch of the Dienststelle. In July 1940, Eggert Reeder, head of the Belgian Military Administration, had asked the RSHA for reinforcement of the Secret Field Police (Geheime Feldpolizei), one of the two police forces of the Military Administration. As a result, the Dienststelle for Belgium and the occupied French territories was instituted. The Dienststelle had two branches: one in Brussels and one in Paris.

[2] For the establishment order of the AJB, issued by the German Military Administration, see *Verordnungsblatt des Militärbefehlshabers in Belgien und Nordfrankreich*, No. 63, 2 December 1941.

[3] Johannes Tuchel, 'Heinrich Müller: Prototyp des Schreibtischtäters', in Hans-Christian Jasch and Christoph Kreutzmüller (eds.), *Die Teilnehmer: die Männer der Wannsee-Konferenz* (Berlin: Metropol-Verlag, 2016), 120.

[4] Michman, 'De oprichting van de VJB in internationaal perspectief', 43.

[5] Insa Meinen, *De Shoah in België*, transl. from the German by Iannis Goerlandt (Antwerp: De Bezige Bij, 2011; first ed. 2009 [German]), 84–85; Michman, 'De oprichting van de VJB in internationaal perspectief', 43–44.

[6] For the establishment order of the UGIF, issued by the French government, see Katja Happe, Michael Mayer and Maja Peers (eds.), *Die Verfolgung und Ermordung der europäischen Juden durch das nationalsozialistische Deutschland, 1933–1945*, Vol. 5. *West- und Nordeuropa 1940–Juni 1942* (Munich: Oldenbourg Verlag, 2012), Dokument (DOK) 295, 750–751. For the original (French) text of this order, see Raymond Sarraute and Paul Tager, *Les Juifs sous l'occupation: Recueil de textes français et allemands* (Paris: Éditions du Centre, 1945), 102–103.

more broadly, seemed so important to the various German institutions involved in their establishment.

The notion that the Germans did not carefully think through the establishment of the AJB fits into a broader trend in historiography that highlights the improvised nature of German rule. Rather than assuming that Hitler had given 'the order' for the Final Solution, as was proposed in the earliest studies on the Holocaust,[7] it has gradually become clear that the destruction of European Jewry was the result of improvisation and an interplay between Hitler and the Nazi leadership at the centre and those on the periphery at the local level.[8] In the Netherlands and France, as well as in Belgium, the absence of a clear plan for Jewish representative bodies resulted in improvisation and the borrowing of blueprints from elsewhere. The Nazi leadership in Western Europe used examples from Eastern Europe, Germany and, in the cases of Belgium and France, from the Netherlands as well. In so doing, they often ignored the specific contexts of the countries concerned.

The absence of a clear and carefully thought-out master plan resulted in rivalry between the various German institutions involved in Jewish affairs, and this continued after the JR, the AJB and the UGIF had been officially established. At times, there was uncertainty about the precise role that Jewish organisations were meant to play, and it was not always clear who had final authority over these bodies. We will see that various German institutions interpreted the exact remit of each of the Jewish organisations differently. As a result, the 'Jewish Councils' in Western

---

[7] See the works of Gerald Reitlinger, *The Final Solution: The Attempts to Exterminate the Jews of Europe, 1939–1945* (New York: Beechurst Press, 1953); Poliakov, *Harvest of Hate*; Wolfgang Scheffler, *Judenverfolgung im Dritten Reich 1944 bis 1945* (Frankfurt am Main: Büchergilde Gutenberg, 1961); Helmut Krausnick and Martin Broszat, *Anatomy of the SS State,* transl. from the German by Dorothy Long and Marian Jackson (New York: Walker & Co., 1968; first ed. 1965 [German]).

[8] In the 1960s and 1970s, a few scholars proposed new perspectives on the nature of the National Socialist Regime. See, for example, Hilberg, *The Destruction of the European Jews*; Schleunes, *The Twisted Road to Auschwitz*; Adam, *Judenpolitik im Dritten Reich*. In the late 1990s, Peter Longerich proposed a model in which vaguely worded orders required personal initiative of local authorities who possessed considerable latitude: Longerich, *Politik der Vernichtung*. Ian Kershaw shared this view in his biography on Hitler, where he argued that Hitler approved initiatives of those 'working towards the Führer', which turned into what we now know as the so-called Final Solution to the Jewish Question, without any clear or decisive tuning points: Kershaw, *Hitler 1889–1936*. Mark Mazower, in his 2008 work on Nazi rule in Europe, elaborated on this perspective: *Hitler's Empire: How the Nazis Ruled Europe,* passim. From his point of view, the incredible speed of military expansion outpaced the level of administrative and intellectual preparation by those Nazis who were responsible for the implementation of measures. This explained why Nazi rule in Eastern Europe was unplanned and apparently irrational: there was a need to improvise, particularly at the local level.

Europe were all organised in different ways and all functioned differently, despite the strong German desire to unify anti-Jewish policies.

Attempts to Unify German Policies in Western Europe

The discrepancy between the differences in form and function of the JR, the AJB, the UGIF-Nord and the UGIF-Sud on the one hand, and the desire of German officials in Berlin to unify (the implementation of) anti-Jewish policies in the Netherlands, Belgium and France on the other shows the importance of local actors in determining the level and timing of anti-Jewish policies. The wish to unify approaches towards the so-called Jewish problem in (Western) Europe was expressed by all sides. In February 1941, for example, the Belgian head of the Military Administration, Reeder, indicated that a uniform *Judenbegriff* (understanding of what constitutes a Jew) must be developed throughout Europe, following the laws of the Reich (*Reichsgesetzgebung*).[9]

In a similar vein, there was an attempt to implement antisemitic legislation equally across Western Europe and the 'Jewish Councils' were used, to varying degrees, to try to accomplish this. Reichsführer-SS Heinrich Himmler and Director of the Reich Security Main Office (Reichssicherheitshauptamt, RSHA) Reinhard Heydrich did not want any deviations (in timing) between the countries in the occupied West in terms of the implementation of anti-Jewish legislation, because they believed that any differences would lead to a wave of Jewish refugees. A variable policy might encourage Jews to flee from the country where a particular anti-Jewish law was implemented to a neighbouring country where this was not yet the case. For these reasons, SS-Obersturmbannführer Adolf Eichmann also preferred the simultaneous implementation of legislation in the Netherlands, Belgium and France.[10]

The relative similarities in terms of the nature and timing of the occupation of these three countries, which contrasted with the situation in Eastern Europe, enabled equivalence in this regard. So-called 'experts in Jewish affairs' (*Judenreferenten*), were important in implementing anti-Jewish laws simultaneously in Western Europe. These experts supervised the deportation of Jews from the Netherlands, Belgium and France and

[9] 'Draft, Concerns: Measures Against Jews', Administration Department Group 7: Care, February 1941, SVG-R.184/Tr 50 077, DOS.
[10] Steinberg, *L'étoile et le fusil. La question juive*, 21–22; Griffioen and Zeller, *Jodenvervolging in Nederland, Frankrijk en België*, 395.

served under the direct responsibility of Adolf Eichmann's Referat IV B4 in Berlin. The predecessor of Referat IV B4, Referat IV D 4, had been established by Reinhard Heydrich in order to oversee all matters related to the expulsion and deportation of Jews into the Generalgouvernement (the central zone of Poland that was occupied, but not incorporated into, the German Reich, and which was divided into the districts or Radom, Lublin, Cracow and Warsaw). In March 1941, this Referat was renamed IV B 4, and its tasks expanded from overseeing the expulsion of the Jews to their organised annihilation, as it coordinated the deportation of Jews across Europe to ghettos, concentration camps and extermination camps. Members of Referat IV B4 were assigned to the occupied countries, including the Netherlands, Belgium and France and served as *Judenreferenten*, initially advising local authorities on anti-Jewish measures, and later promoting the deportation of Jews from the countries to which they were assigned.[11]

In the Netherlands, Wilhelm (Willy) Zöpf was the *Judenreferent*. In Belgium and France, Kurt Asche and Theodor Dannecker respectively served in this capacity. Zöpf was born in Munich in 1908, and while studying law he became a member of the Nationalsozialistische Deutsche Arbeiterspartei (NSDAP) in May 1933. Four years after joining the SS in 1937, his close connection to Commander of the SiPo-SD Wilhelm Harster brought Zöpf to the Netherlands, where he served under Harster's authority from March 1941.[12]

Kurt Asche, born in 1909, joined the Nazi party in 1931 and the SD in 1935. From 1936, he became Hilfsreferent, assistant expert, in the Jewish department, where he operated alongside Adolf Eichmann, Theodor Dannecker and Dieter Wisliceny. He was sent as SS-Einsatzkommando member to occupied Poland in 1939, where he served as expert on Jewish affairs under SS-Polizeiführer Odilo Globocnik.[13] At the end of 1940, Asche became *Judenreferent* in Brussels.

Dannecker, born in 1913, was a fanatical antisemite with years of experience in the anti-Jewish bureaucracy of the SS. After subscribing to the NSDAP in 1932, he served the SS in one of the local sections of the SD. In March 1937, he joined the SD in Berlin and worked for Eichmann's

---

[11] For further reading on Eichmann, the history of Referat IV B4 and this section's role in the policies of segregation, despoliation, expulsion and annihilation of Jews, see, for example, Hans Safrian, *Eichmann's Men*, transl. Ute Stargardt (Cambridge: Cambridge University Press, 2010; first ed. 1993 [German]); David Ceserani, *Eichmann: His Life and Crimes* (London: William Heinemann, 2004).

[12] Griffioen and Zeller, *Jodenvervolging in Nederland, Frankrijk en België*, 228–229.

[13] Lutz Hachmeister, *Der Gegnerforscher, Die Karriere des SS-Führers Franz Alfred Six* (Munich: Beck, 1998), 187–198.

Jewish affairs department.[14] In 1938, Dannecker, together with Eichmann and SS-Sturmbannführer Herbert Hagen, went to Vienna in order to establish the Central Office for Jewish Emigration (Zentralstelle für Jüdische Auswanderung), and at the end of the following year, Dannecker was sent to Poland to explore the possibilities for emigration in the region.[15] In summer 1940, he was appointed as Eichmann's representative advisor on Jewish affairs in France and, as *Judenreferent*, headed the IVB4 Paris RSHA office. This was 'the most active of the German agencies involved with long-range planning of Jewish policy in France and with efforts to prod Vichy into more active anti-Jewish measures'.[16] Throughout the course of the war, the *Judenreferenten* of the Netherlands, Belgium and France were in touch with each other to discuss the impact and execution of anti-Jewish measures in their respective countries. For example, a letter to SS-Sturmbannführer Willy Lages (based in Amsterdam) on 16 March 1942 shows that Kurt Asche and Theodor Dannecker wanted to create a uniform policy on the implementation of the yellow star.[17] Asche and Dannecker had already worked together in

---

[14] Steur, *Theodor Dannecker*, 21; Serge Klarsfeld, *Vichy-Auschwitz: la 'solution finale' de la question juive en France*, 38; Joly, *Vichy dans la 'solution finale'*, 110.

[15] Joly, *Vichy dans la 'solution finale'*, 112. For biographical information on Herbert Hagen, see Serge Klarsfeld, *Le livre des otages: la politique des otages menée par les autorités allemandes d'occupation en France de 1941 à 1943* (Paris: Éditeurs français réunis, 1979), 280–288; Ernst Klee, *Das Personenlexikon zum Dritten Reich: wer war was vor und nach 1945* (Frankfurt am Main: Fischer, 2003), 218. For further reading on the Zentralstelle in Vienna, see Gabriele Anderl, Dirk Rupnow and Alexandra-Eileen Wenck, *Die Zentralstelle für Jüdische Auswanderung als Beraubungsinstitution* (Vienna: Oldenbourg, 2004); Gerhard Botz, *Nationalsozialismus in Wien: Machtübernahme, Herrschaftssicherung, Radikalisierung, Kriegsvorbereitung, 1938/1939* (Vienna, Mandelbaum Verlag, 2018), 332–342.

[16] Marrus and Paxton, *Vichy France and the Jews*, 79.

[17] Letter from SS-Sturmbannführer Lischka (Paris) to SS-Sturmbannführer Lages (Amsterdam), 16 March 1942, XLIXa-49, CDJC, Mémorial de la Shoah; Telegram from Zöpf to Knochen and Ehlers, 27 April 1942, XLIXa-50, CDJC, Mémorial de la Shoah. There were numerous other occasions where attempts were made to create uniform policies across occupied Western Europe. See, for example, Letter of the Reichskommissar of the occupied Dutch territories to the Militärbefehlshaber of Belgium and France, 3 December 1940, Marburg Documentation, DOS; Meeting of the *Judenreferenten* at the RSHA – IVB4, 4 March 1942, Berlin, XXVI-18, Centre de Documentation Juive Contemporaine (CDJC), Mémorial de la Shoah; 'Concerning the Identification of Jews', 15 March 1942, in Klarsfeld, *Recueil de documents des dossiers des autorités allemandes concernant la persécution de la population juive en France (1940–1944)*, 1er Janvier 1942 au 31 Mai 1942; Note and letter sent by SS-Hauptsturmführer Dannecker to SS-Sturmbannführer Lischka and to Eichmann's IV B 4 office, 23 May 1942–29 May 1942, XXVb-31, CDJC, Mémorial de la Shoah; Dannecker's report on a meeting between Zöpf, Asche and Dannecker in Berlin, 15 June 1942, Eichmann Trial documents TR.3-585, Yad Vashem; Yaacov Lozowick, *Hitler's Bureaucrats. The Nazi Security Police and the Banality of Evil* (London/New York: Continuum, 2002), 88–92, 100–105, 190–193.

Berlin and they continued to do so in their respective positions as *Juden-referenten* of Belgium and France. They were both directly supervised by the Commissioner of the Security Police and SD, Max Thomas. Both held similar roles in almost identical contexts where the Military Administration operated as their superior. As a result, Asche and Dannecker faced similar procedural and political problems.[18]

Nevertheless, we will see that despite their wish to unify the timing and implementation of anti-Jewish measures across all three countries, there are a number of factors, including institutional rivalry between the various (local) departments involved, that hampered the simultaneous establishment of the JR, the AJB, the UGIF-Nord and the UGIF-Sud. Moreover, once established, these rivalries obstructed the ability of the Jewish organisations (which were held responsible in varying degrees for the communication and execution of these measures) to function in parallel.

The Netherlands: Rivalry between Civil Administration and the SiPo-SD

The formation of a Jewish Council in the Netherlands was ordered after the provocative actions of the National-Socialist Movement (Nationaal-Socialistische Beweging, NSB) against the Jews in Amsterdam resulted in a fight with a Jewish *knokploeg* (action group) in early February 1941. One member of the NSB's paramilitary Weerafdeling, Hendrik Koot, was seriously injured and died three days later.[19] This disruption fostered the idea that a representative Jewish organisation should be established that could be held responsible for maintaining order in the Jewish quarter.[20] The period in which the JR was established was marked by contradictions and by the competing interests of the German institutions involved. Because there is little documentation about the precise establishment history of the JR, historians continue to disagree about exactly how it came to be. Houwink ten Cate claimed that the representative of Reichskommissar Arthur Seyss-Inquart for the city of Amsterdam, Hans Böhmcker, and General Commissioner (Generalkommissar) Schmidt, took advantage of Highest SS and Police Leader in the Netherlands Hanns Albin Rauter's sick leave, and initiated the

---

[18] Griffioen and Zeller, *Jodenvervolging in Nederland, Frankrijk en België*, 206.
[19] Koert Berkley, *Overzicht van het ontstaan, de werkzaamheden en het streven van den Joodsche Raad voor Amsterdam* (Amsterdam: Plastica, 1945), 12; Ben Sijes, *De Februaristaking: 25–26 februari 1941* ('s Gravenhage: Nijhoff, 1954), 100–112.
[20] Michman, 'De oprichting van de "Joodsche Raad voor Amsterdam"', 88.

institution of a Jewish Council in Amsterdam. Neither Schmidt nor Böhmcker was an SS functionary.[21]

Based on extensive research into Jewish Councils across occupied Europe, which showed that the SS was always responsible for the establishment of these institutions, Michman has argued instead that the Commander of the Sipo-SD in the Netherlands, Wilhelm Harster, with the backing of Rauter 'and following the guidelines of the Jewish expert of the SD', proposed the establishment of an Amsterdam Jewish Council of the Polish type. He also claimed that Reichskommissar Seyss-Inquart, who had served as head of the civil section of the Military Administration in Cracow in late 1939, accepted the idea 'because this was the only model he knew from personal experience'.[22] As a result, Michman says, Seyss-Inquart ordered Hans Böhmcker to apply this idea. Therefore, whereas Michman has claimed that Seyss-Inquart played a (passive) role in this process, Houwink ten Cate argued that the Reichskommissar was not involved. Moreover, Houwink ten Cate asserted that the SS was not involved in the establishment of the Council, while Michman has stated that Harster in fact proposed the establishment of the JR. Neither during his post-war trial interrogations, nor during his conversations with Dutch historians Louis (Loe) de Jong and Adolf (Dolf) Cohen in 1949, did Harster describe what his exact role in the establishment of the JR had been.[23]

In light of the absence of documentation, it is impossible to offer a definitive conclusion on the history of the JR's creation or about the specific role of the various German officials and departments involved. Nevertheless, we can establish that the rivalry between, and among, various German offices was an important part of its institution. The wish of prominent SS officials to dominate anti-Jewish policies at the expense of the Civil Administration, headed by Seyss-Inquart, became increasingly visible in the two months following the JR's establishment in February 1941. Rivalries surfaced regarding the supervision of the Council, primarily between Seyss-Inquart, who answered to Hitler directly, and the highest SS representative Rauter, who was subordinate to Heydrich and Himmler.

[21] Johannes Houwink ten Cate, 'Heydrich's Security Police and the Amsterdam Jewish Council, February 1941–October 1942', *Dutch Jewish History*, Vol. 3 (1993), 384.
[22] Michman, 'The Uniqueness of the Joodse Raad', 376.
[23] For Wilhelm Harster, his post-war trials in both the Netherlands and Germany and the post-war statements on his role as Commander of the Security Police and SD (Befehlshaber der SD und Sicherheitsdienst) in the Netherlands, see Louis de Jong and Adolf E. Cohen, 'Twee gesprekken met Dr. W. Harster', 1949, W. Harster, Doc. I, 248–639, NIOD; Dossier W. Harster, CABR, Access No. 2.09.09, Inv. No. 378 I BRvC 292/49, NA; Dick de Mildt, *De rechter en de deporteurs* (Hilversum: Uitgeverij Verloren, 2018); Theo Gerritse, *Rauter: Himmlers vuist in Nederland* (Amsterdam: Boom, 2018), 173–178.

In April 1941, Heydrich had grown increasingly dissatisfied with Seyss-Inquart's policies and he then ordered the establishment of a branch of the Central Office for Jewish Emigration (Zentralstelle für Jüdische Auswanderung) in the Netherlands, perhaps hoping that it would function in a similar way to the Judenreferaten (which oversaw Jewish affairs) in Belgium and France.[24] The Zentralstelle, overseen by the SS and modelled after its namesakes in Vienna, Prague and Berlin, originally founded to promote the expulsion and expropriation of Jews, was intended to work as the body that would oversee the emigration of Jews from the Netherlands. For Heydrich at this time, emigration was to be part of the solution of the so-called Jewish Question in all European countries.[25]

As soon as the Zentralstelle was established, Seyss-Inquart unsurprisingly attempted to decrease its sphere of influence, fearing an expansion of SS authority over Jewish affairs. After continued discussions between Rauter and Seyss-Inquart about who should exercise authority over the Zentralstelle, Wilhelm Zöpf, a protégé of Harster (head of the SiPo-SD) was nominated on 1 April 1941 as its head. The supervision of the Zentralstelle's daily work was transferred to SS-Hauptsurmführer Ferdinand aus der Fünten. In practice, the Zentralstelle never actually assisted in arranging the emigration of Jews. Instead, it took on an executive role in the deportation process while also directly supervising the work of the JR.[26]

---

[24] Griffioen and Zeller, *Jodenvervolging in Nederland, Frankrijk en België*, 216. For Rauter's order for the establishment of a Zentralstelle für jüdische Auswanderung, see Memorandum of Hanns Albin Rauter on the establishment of a Zentralstelle für jüdische Auswanderung in Amsterdam, 18 April 1941, 020 Generalkommissariat für Verwaltung und Justiz, Inv. No. 9137, NIOD; Happe, Mayer and Peers, *Die Verfolgung und Ermordung der europaïschen Juden*, Vol. 5, DOK. 70, 243–244.

[25] Letter from Rauter to Seyss-Inquart, 18 April 1941, 020 Generalkommissariat für Verwaltung und Justiz, Inv. No. 1461, NIOD. Also see Jozeph Michman, 'Planning for the Final Solution against the Background of Developments in Holland in 1941', *Yad Vashem Studies*, Vol. 17 (1986), 150–151; Anna Hájková, 'The Making of a Zentralstelle: Die Eichmann-Männer in Amsterdam', in Jaroslava Milotová, Ulf Rathgeber et al. (eds.), *Theresienstädter Studien und Dokumente* (Prague: Institut Theresienstädter Initiative Academia, 2003), 353–381. For further reading on the histories of the Zentralstelle in Berlin, Prague and Vienna, see Anderl and Rupnow, *Die Zentralstelle für Jüdische Auswanderung als Beraubungsinstitution*; Rabinovici, *Instanzen der Ohnmacht*, 102–114; Wolf Gruner, *Die Judenverfolgung im Protektorat Böhmen und Mähren: lokale Initiativen, zentrale Entscheidungen, jüdische Antworten 1939–1945* (Göttingen: Wallstein Verlag, 2016), 69–70; Beate Meyer, *A Fatal Balancing Act: The Dilemma of the Reich Association of Jews in Germany, 1939–1945*, transl. from the German by William Templer (New York/Oxford: Berghahn Books, 2016; first ed. 2011 [German]), 26–27.

[26] Hájková, 'The Making of a Zentralstelle', 367; Griffioen and Zeller, *Jodenvervolging in Nederland, Frankrijk en België*, 223.

In response to the establishment of the Zentralstelle, Seyss-Inquart, dissatisfied with the control of the SS over this organisation, formulated an alternative plan with the help of jurist Kurt Rabl. In this, the Zentralstelle would be governed by the Reichskommissar (that is, Seyss-Inquart himself). In addition, the Jewish Council would be replaced by the Verband der Juden in die Niederlanden, which, in turn, would be subject to the Zentralstelle. As Michman has indicated, the task of the Verband der Juden would be, among other things, 'to supervise all aspects of Jewish life in the occupied Dutch territories and to give them the necessary instructions' as well as to promote 'the emigration of Jews living in the occupied Dutch territories'.[27] The regulations for the proposed Jewish organisation were very similar to that of the Reich Association of Jews in Germany, which had been established in February 1939.[28]

Clearly, Seyss-Inquart wanted to keep the authority of the Jewish Council within the sphere of the Civil Administration, and, more specifically, his Amsterdam representative Hans Böhmcker. The alternative model he presented indicates that, to him, the JR as it existed at that time was not the definitive version. Owing to the objections of the SS, Seyss-Inquart's proposals were never implemented.[29]

On 27 October 1941, the JR, which until then had only had jurisdiction in the city of Amsterdam, officially extended its influence to the entire country.[30] The local model had proven unrealistic since Jews in the Netherlands, unlike in occupied Eastern Europe, were not concentrated

---

[27] Michman, 'Planning for the Final Solution', 149.
[28] Preliminary draft B, section I, 'Verband der Juden in den Niederlanden', paragraph 1, 21 May 1941, 020 Generalkommissariat für Verwaltung und Justiz, Inv. No. 1461, NIOD. On the history of the Reich Association of the Jews in Germany, see Meyer, *A Fatal Balancing Act*.
[29] Dan Michman, 'Jewish Headships under Nazi Rule: The Evolution and Implementation of an Administrative Concept', in Dan Michman, *Holocaust Historiography: A Jewish Perspective. Conceptualization, Terminology, Approaches and Fundamental Issues* (London: Vallentine Mitchell, 2003), 169.
[30] Report meeting Asscher, Cohen, Lages and Böhmcker, 27 October 1941, 182, Inv. No. 4, NIOD. In March 1941, the first steps towards the extension of the Council's jurisdiction had already been taken. On 18 March 1941, Reichskommissar Seyss-Inquart's representative for the city of Amsterdam, Hans Böhmcker, declared in a letter to the Council that it had to incorporate all non-religious Jewish organisations in the Netherlands. The following months, the Council investigated which organisations would be disbanded. Those that remained were incorporated under the Council's umbrella. See letter Hans Böhmcker to the chairmen of the Jewish Council, 18 March 1941, 182, Inv. No. 26, NIOD; Berkley, *Overzicht van het ontstaan, de werkzaamheden en het streven van den Joodsche Raad voor Amsterdam*, 22.

in local ghettos. From the German viewpoint, there was therefore a need for a Jewish organisation that effectively represented all Jews in the country. The Coordinating Committee, which had nationwide authority, did not serve German interests as its chairman, Lodewijk Ernst Visser, refused to cooperate with the occupying authorities. The extension of the JR's jurisdiction to the entire country solved this problem. As we will see, David Cohen, chairman of the JR, was in favour of an extension the Council's geographic scope of activity, as it enabled him to carry out his work more effectively.

As a result of the extension of the JR's jurisdiction, local branches of the Coordinating Committee, including those in The Hague, Rotterdam and Den Bosch, were taken over and transformed into local branches of the central Amsterdam Jewish Council (the Coordinating Committee was officially dissolved soon thereafter).[31] The local JR branch of Enschede (in the east of the country), whose leaders had provided social welfare to German refugees before the occupation through the Committee for German Refugees, was also created in October 1941, while the Groningen branch (in the north of the country) was established one month later.[32] In a memorandum of May 1941, David Cohen stressed the need to establish local branches of the JR throughout the country. The leaders of these local branches (between three and five in total per branch) 'will be appointed by the Jewish Council of the Netherlands [sic]', he wrote.[33] However, he seemed to have been overly optimistic about the central board's influence on these local branches. Although the local branches were dependent upon Amsterdam, they could be used directly by the SiPO-SD – without the involvement of the Amsterdam central board.[34]

Over time, the SS became increasingly powerful in the Netherlands at the expense of Seyss-Inquart and the Civil Administration. Seyss-Inquart

[31] The enlargement of the Dutch Jewish Council's influence to the entire country and the disbandment of the Coordinating Committee was a subject of controversy between the chairman of the Coordinating Committee (Lodewijk Ernst Visser) and David Cohen, chairman of the JR. See Melkman, 'De briefwisseling', 111–116. For the letters that were exchanged between Cohen and Visser, see: 248-1798A, mr. Lodewijk Ernst Visser, Inv. No. 14, NIOD. For the letter of Asscher and Cohen to former local Coordinating Committee members in the Hague in early November 1941, see M.19, No. 4, pp. 45, 51, Yad Vashem, Jerusalem.

[32] Memorandum David Cohen, Doc. I 248-0294, Prof. D. Cohen, Inv. No. 1, NIOD. For the Enschede branch of the JR, see Marjolein Schenkel, *De Twentse Paradox: De lotgevallen van de joodse bevolking van Hengelo en Enschede tijdens de Tweede Wereldoorlog* (Zutphen: Walburg Pers, 2003), 89–95.

[33] Memorandum David Cohen, Doc. I 248-0294, Prof. D. Cohen, Inv. No. 1, NIOD.

[34] Michman, 'Oprichting van de Joodsche Raad voor Amsterdam in vergelijkend perspectief', 91.

had previously successfully obstructed attempts to establish a separate department responsible for Jewish Affairs that would be overseen by the SS (similar to the Judenreferaten in Belgium and France).[35] However, through the course of 1942, the situation began to change. In February 1942, in response to decisions that were made during the infamous meeting of senior Nazi government officials at Wannsee on 20 January 1942 (which later become known as the 'Wannsee Conference'), Heydrich and Eichmann increased the influence of the RSHA over Jewish affairs in the Netherlands by establishing a Judenreferat. The department was remodelled on the basis of Eichmann's Referat IV B4 in Berlin, and headed by Harster's protégé Zöpf. As a result, Commander of the SiPo-SD in the Netherlands, Harster, became responsible for a framework in which IV B4 was the central organisation in charge of Jewish affairs.[36]

In early 1941, the German authorities involved had no clear idea about what the (long-term) remit of the JR ought to be. While anti-Jewish policies were gradually imposed on the communities in the Netherlands, and on those of Western Europe more broadly, the so-called Final Solution to the Jewish Question encompassed vaguely outlined ideas. In general terms, 'Jewish Councils' in German-occupied Europe were held responsible for maintaining order, for uniting the Jewish communities under their umbrella and for communicating German legislations to the Jewish communities, but their specific tasks developed over time.[37] Since Hans Böhmcker had not given any specification about the long-term tasks of the JR, there were differing interpretations of its precise function.[38] We have seen that the JR's initial task was to restore order after the fights that had broken out in the Jewish quarter in early February 1941. Additionally, the JR would be held responsible for controlling the identification cards (*Ausweisen*)

---

[35] Griffioen and Zeller, *Jodenvervolging in Nederland, Frankrijk en België,* 216.

[36] Ibid., 222–223; Boterman, *Duitse daders,* 99–104.

[37] After the war, Wilhelm Harster confirmed that the JR had primarily been established to allow mediation with the Jews, adding that the restrictive measures it communicated did not constitute preparations for the deportation of Jews. See Excerpt from the Willy Lages Dossier, statement of Harster, September 1952, Doc. 1 248-0639 Dr. Wilhelm Harster, NIOD; Also see Letter of Reichskommissar Seyss-Inquart concerning the role of the JR, 25 November 1941, Abschrift Landgericht München (8 March 1967), pp. 50–51, Box 2, Dossier W. Harster, CABR, Access No. 2.09.09, Inv. No. 378 I BRvC 292/49, NA.

[38] Letter from Böhmcker to Seyss-Inquart, 17 Feb. 1941, 'Betr. Bildung des Amsterdamer Judenrats, Einrichting des Amsterdamer Ghettos', Inv. No. 149, 014 Reichskommissar für die besetzten niederländischen Gebiete, NIOD. Also see Griffioen and Zeller, *Jodenvervolging in Nederland, Frankrijk en België,* 210.

necessary to enter the ghetto.[39] However, a closed-off ghetto similar to those in Eastern Europe was never established in Amsterdam, despite Böhmcker's wish that it should be. The Waterlooplein area in Amsterdam had only been temporarily cordoned off in February 1941, and JR officials were not held responsible for controlling identification cards in this area.[40] To complicate the matter of the organisation's precise tasks further, there exist various draft statutes (*ontwerpstatuten*), in which its responsibilities are worded differently. In one of these draft statutes, it is indicated that the JR was held responsible for the 'non-religious interests of Dutch Jews'.[41] Another draft statute reads that the JR would act as the 'highest body' of Amsterdam Jewry, without further specifying its tasks.[42]

The imprecise wording of these draft statutes, together with the varying descriptions of the JR's responsibilities, have led to different interpretations on what its exact nature and function was supposed to have been. De Jong, Presser and Herzberg have argued that Böhmcker wanted to establish a Jewish Council headed by the experienced religious authorities of both the Ashkenazi and Sephardi Jewish communities, and that he entrusted Asscher (and Cohen) with its formation.[43] Knoop argued instead that Böhmcker was only aiming for a representative institution of the Jewish quarter – in Amsterdam, and that the idea of the JR as an umbrella organisation was introduced by Abraham Asscher rather than by the Germans.[44] His argument is unconvincing; while the direct pretext for the establishment of the Council were the irregularities that broke out in the Jewish quarter, it was established to do more than just restore order in this particular area. In line with the more broadly defined tasks of similar institutions, the JR was meant to represent Jewry, and to serve as an organisation through which German officials could communicate their regulations. At the same time, the lack of a more clearly defined, specific, (long-term) purpose fostered improvisation and created an atmosphere in which the rivalry between the various German institutions could continue to prosper.

[39] Documents sent by David Cohen to his lawyers during the state investigation of his wartime activities, p. 79, 181j, Inv. No. 11, NIOD; Michman, 'De oprichting van de "Joodsche Raad voor Amsterdam" vanuit een vergelijkend perspectief', 88.
[40] Happe, *Veel valse hoop: de jodenvervolging in Nederland, 1940–1945*, 77–78; Griffioen and Zeller, *Jodenvervolging in Nederland, Frankrijk en België*, 210–211; Presser, *Ondergang*, Vol. 1, 392–398.
[41] The various draft statutes are assembled together in one inventory. See Archief van de Joodse Raad, 182, Inv. No. 1, NIOD.
[42] Ibid.
[43] De Jong, *Het Koninkrijk*, vol. 1, part 2, 884–885; Presser, *Ondergang*, Vol. 1, 81–82; Herzberg, *Kroniek der Jodenvervolging*, 143.
[44] Knoop, *De Joodsche Raad*, 82.

Belgium: Military Administration versus the SiPo-SD

In Belgium, the presence of a Military Administration rather than a Civil Administration (as in the Netherlands) limited the authority of the SiPo-SD, particularly during the first phase of the occupation. Conflicts arose between the SiPo-SD and the Military Administration about the implementation of anti-Jewish regulations and the creation of a representative Belgian Jewish organisation. The nature of the discussion was nevertheless different from that in the Netherlands. The question of *who* should be responsible for the organisation's establishment and functioning was less important in Belgium than *whether* a Jewish representative body should be established at all.

During the first phase of the occupation of Belgium, the different outlooks of the SiPo-SD and the Military Administration were immediately apparent. As a result of the restricted power of the Sipo-SD in relation to the Military Administration and of the limited cooperation of the Belgian authorities, it was initially difficult to institute anti-Jewish legislation in the country. Whereas Heydrich and Himmler wanted a unified, centralised SS policy for Western Europe, the Belgian head of the Military Administration, Eggert Reeder, was not willing to consent to a diminution of his power.[45] In terms of the implementation of anti-Jewish laws, the Military Administration in Belgium preferred to maintain stability, and objected to a rapid implementation of such laws. This position is illustrated by a letter of the Military Commander of Belgium and Northern France, Alexander von Falkenhausen, to the General Commissioner for Administration and Justice, Friedrich Wimmer, on 21 December 1940. In this letter, von Falkenhausen indicated that the Belgian non-Jewish population did not feel that the country had 'a racial problem' (*ein rassisches Problem*). From his perspective, this meant that it would be impossible to implement anti-Jewish regulations in the same way as in Germany or in other countries, where anti-Jewish sentiments had been growing over the years as a result of deliberate German policies.[46]

---

[45] Steinberg, *La Persécution des Juifs en Belgique*, 45–46, 54–58; Griffoen and Zeller, *Jodenvervolging in Nederland, Frankrijk en België*, 197–199.
[46] Letter from the Military Commander of Belgium and Northern France addressed to the Reichskommissar für die besetzten niederländischen Gebiete – Generalkommissar für Verwaltung und Justiz, 21 December 1940, SVG-R.184/Tr 50 077, DOS. Also see Happe, Mayer and Peers, *Die Verfolgung und Ermordung der europäischen Juden*, Vol. 5, DOK. 164, 452–454. It should be noted here that Dan Michman's assumption that the Military Administration did not believe there existed a so-called Jewish question stems from an incorrect translation of the text. See Michman, 'De oprichting van de VJB in internationaal perspectief', 37.

In March 1941, SS-Obersturmführer Kurt Asche tried to increase his control of Jewish affairs. He initiated the institution of a Belgian version of the General Commissariat for Jewish Affairs, the Vichy body that oversaw Jewish affairs in France, so that a local Belgian authority (the Department of Internal Affairs) would be formally involved in the execution of anti-Jewish policies. The reasoning behind this was simple: if Belgians were involved, attention would be deflected from German responsibility. Asche envisioned that this organisation would cooperate closely with his office at the SiPo-SD and also suggested a name for this putative Belgian institution: the Royal Commissariat for Jewish Affairs (Commissariat Royal aux Questions Juives). However, he never succeeded because the Military Administration, fearing that Belgian extremists would take over such an institution, failed to cooperate. They were especially afraid that their position would be threatened by radical Belgian civil servants or by Asche himself.[47]

The institutional rivalry between the Military Administration and the SiPo-SD continued in the following months, and it delayed the establishment of a compulsory Jewish representative body in Belgium. Since the Military Administration in Belgium, in contrast to the Civil Administration in the Netherlands, was strongly preoccupied with the responses of the native non-Jewish population, it opposed the institution of a Belgian alternative to the *Judenräte* from the start. In September 1941, its officials specifically objected that it would be difficult to find a Belgian leadership willing to head the organisation since the upper layer of Belgian Jewry had fled to France at the time of the German invasion in May 1940. This, in turn, raised questions about the financial backing that could be offered by the Jewish communities.[48]

In October 1941, shortly before the AJB was finally established, representatives of the Military Administration, Löffler (Senior War Administration Counsellor), Duntze (Senior War Administration Counsellor) and Höllfritsch (War Administration Counsellor) raised more objections, including the notion that Belgian Jewry was by no means united. They argued that this lack of homogeneity would prevent the emergence of a sense of communal responsibility among the Jews. This in turn would provoke tensions that could endanger German interests. The absence

[47] Steinberg, *L'étoile et le fusil: La question juive 1940–1942*, 122–123; and *La Persécution des Juifs en Belgique*, 118–120; Etienne Verhoeyen, *België bezet 1940–1944: een synthese* (Brussels: BRTN Educatieve Uitgaven, 1993), 440–441; Michman, 'De oprichting van de VJB', 37–40.
[48] Draft of 30 September 1941, p.1, Administration Department, Group 7: Care, SVG-R.184/Tr 50 077, Marburg Documentation, DOS.

of a unified Jewish leadership and the lack of support from the Belgian authorities could also prove problematic. Prominent officials inside the Military Administration argued that these issues could not be ignored.[49]

During the course of the war, the authority of the Military Administration in Belgium was increasingly challenged by the SS. Although Reeder had wanted to take a cautious approach in relation to Belgian Jewry, he was quickly pressured to implement the same anti-Jewish measures that had been implemented in neighbouring countries.[50] The power of the Military Administration was further damaged by the regular meetings of Eichmann's representatives for the Netherlands (Zöpf), Belgium (Asche) and France (Dannecker) in Berlin, during which anti-Jewish legislations in all three countries were discussed.[51] Perhaps to maintain what influence they could over the process, and because they realised that it was necessary to isolate Jews from their non-Jewish neighbours, officials inside the Military Administration took the decision at this point, in autumn 1941, not to hamper the creation of a Belgian Jewish organisation any longer, despite their initial objections.

In light of these developments, the AJB can be considered a compromise between SS-Obersturmführer Kurt Asche's wish for a *Judenrat* modelled on the Eastern European style (not anchored in law and directly subordinate to the local German security apparatus), and the initial reluctance of the Military Administration to institute a representative organ at all.[52] The AJB was eventually set up following the more moderate model of an Association (*Vereinigung*) rather than that of a Judenrat; it was officially subordinate to the Belgian Ministry of the Interior and Health (secretary-general Gerard Romsée), and its existence was anchored in the Belgian legal system. The organisation's subordination to the Ministry of the Interior and Health was of little value in practice, since all fundamental decisions concerning the AJB were taken by the German authorities. Nevertheless, as we will see, the fact that the AJB, unlike the JR (and local *Judenräte* elsewhere), was not directly subordinate to the local German SS, and police apparatus meant that German pressure on this organisation was less severe.

---

[49] Report concerning the establishment of a *Vereinigung der Juden* in Belgium, 15 October 1941, 184/Tr50.077, Marburg Documentation, DOS. Also see Happe, Mayer and Peers, *Die Verfolgung und Ermordung der europaïschen Juden,* Vol. 5, DOK. 176, 478–480.

[50] Steinberg, *L'étoile et le fusil. La question juive 1940–1942,* 23–25; Griffioen and Zeller, *Jodenvervolging in Nederland, Frankrijk en België,* 199–200.

[51] De Jonghe, 'De strijd Himmler-Reeder', 33–35, 41–42.

[52] Michman, 'De oprichting van de VJB in internationaal perspectief', 40–42.

The AJB had a nationwide authority from the outset with a central seat in Brussels and local branches in the most important cities where Jews lived: Brussels, Antwerp, Charleroi and Liège. The leaders of these four cities were also represented in the AJB's central board. As in the cases of the JR, the UGIF-Nord and the UGIF-Sud, there were also representatives of the AJB in other cities where Jews lived, including Gand, Oostende and Arlon, although these were not official local branches.[53] Whereas the SiPo-SD supervised the Eastern European Jewish Councils and eventually the Dutch JR as well, the AJB was directly overseen by the Military Administration.[54] As the SiPo-SD was responsible for the planning and execution of the deportation of Jews to Eastern Europe, it continued to clash with the Military Administration during the course of the war about the question of the supervision of the AJB.

German views about the role of the AJB had already changed a number of times before the organisation was officially established. In line with the antisemitic laws that were already in place, the Military Administration's officials agreed during a meeting in October 1941 that the principal aim of the Association would be the restriction of Jewish economic activities in Belgium and the elimination of Jews from public social life. At the end of this meeting, an important addition was made: the organisation had to support all tasks that in the future might be ascribed to it.[55] In short, while the initial aim of the AJB was to eliminate Jews from social and economic life, all options were kept open. We have seen that the actual establishment order of the AJB on 25 November 1941 indicated that its main task was the 'promot[ion] of emigration of the Jews' and the provision of social welfare and education.[56] This is indeed what was agreed during the first official meeting between the Military Administration and the AJB in April 1942.[57]

[53] Insa Meinen, 'De Duitse bezettingsautoriteiten en de VJB', in van Doorslaer and Schreiber, De curatoren van het getto, 51.
[54] Steinberg, La Persécution des Juifs en Belgique, 182; van Doorslaer and Schreiber, 'Inleiding', in De curatoren van het getto, 8.
[55] Report concerning the establishment of a Vereinigung der Juden in Belgium, 15 October 1941, 184/Tr50.077, Marburg Documentation, Documentatie Oorlogsslachtoffers. Also see Happe, Mayer and Peers, Die Verfolgung und Ermordung der europäischen Juden, Vol. 5, DOK. 176, 478–480.
[56] Michman, 'De oprichting van de VJB in internationaal perspectief', 41–42. For the establishment order, see Verordnungsblatt des Militärbefehlshabers in Belgien und Nordfrankreich, No. 63, 2 December 1941, A012077, JMDV, CNHEJ, Buber Collection, Kazerne Dossin.
[57] Report of the meeting between Maurice Benedictus Salomon van den Berg, Eugen Löffler and Wilhelm von Hahn, 8 April 1942, R497/Tr146.665, DOS.

In addition, the organisation was supposed to function as an executive power for anti-Jewish legislation; all Jews in Belgium had to become members. In doing so, the primary aim of the AJB was to unite Belgian Jewry.[58] The tasks outlined here, on 25 November 1941, differ from those outlined less than a month earlier, and this discrepancy requires consideration.

One might question how carefully the functions and structure of the AJB had been thought through by the Germans. The change in wording in relation to the central tasks of the AJB is indicative of uncertainty about its precise role. The feeling that there must be a representative Jewish organisation simply because these also existed in the Netherlands, Eastern and Central Europe, seems to have been more of a driving force than any carefully considered sense of *how* and *why* such a body would be necessary or helpful in the solution of the so-called 'Jewish problem' in Belgium itself. This conclusion is reinforced by the knowledge that the Military Administration initially did not consider a Jewish representative institution beneficial. As the war progressed, both the SiPo-SD (Asche) and representatives of Reeder (Military Administration) failed to formulate a clear strategy towards the AJB. Their demands were inconsistent and sometimes contradictory, and it was often not clear which department presided over the Jewish body. Partly because of this, it was often not clear to the Jewish leaders which of the two institutions was in charge.[59]

France: Military Administration, SiPo-SD, and Vichy

The situation in France was different from that in other occupied countries in (Western) Europe as direct German control was, until November 1942, limited to the occupied zone. The presence of the collaborationist Vichy regime, which facilitated anti-Jewish policies, had a significant impact on the implementation of anti-Jewish laws, and the establishment of the UGIF specifically. Despite this unique situation in France, similarities can be identified with the Belgian case, as rivalry between the Military Administration and the SS prevailed in France as well.

The Military Administration in France, headed in 1941 by Otto von Stülpnagel, had sole authority at the beginning of the occupation but was increasingly forced to share its powers with other German agencies.

---

[58] Meinen, 'De Duitse bezettingsautoriteiten en de VJB', 46; and *De Shoah in België*, 85.
[59] Meinen, 'De Duitse bezettingsautoriteiten en de VJB', 64–66.

In fact, no fewer than five branches of German government authority were involved in Jewish matters in France.[60] The Security Police, which Reichsführer-SS Heinrich Himmler had, in 1939, merged with the Security Service into the RSHA, was the most important rival to the Military Administration. Differences in approach to the so-called Jewish problem between the two institutions prevailed throughout the occupation. Whereas Military Administration officials recognised that an effective implementation of their policies depended on the French' willingness to cooperate and took a careful approach to safeguard this cooperation, SS-Haupsturmführer Dannecker did not have such reservations.[61] When the Security Police was granted administrative autonomy in May 1942, after which it answered directly to Himmler's office in Berlin, the friction between the two bodies, including on Jewish matters, persisted.

The existence of the Vichy regime made the situation even more complex compared with the two other countries. In recent years, the role of Vichy, and the nature of the relationship between the regime and its Jewish citizens, has been carefully examined. In the early 1980s, Marrus and Paxton published their famous work revising the long-held view that Vichy's policies towards Jews were created as a result of German orders. They provided a detailed overview of the level of collaboration and the initiatives taken by Vichy officials themselves in carrying out anti-Jewish policies. In their view, Vichy's own antisemitism offered the Germans more substantial help than they received anywhere else in Western Europe, and more, even, than they received from allies such as Hungary and Romania.[62] As we shall see, Vichy sometimes resorted to measures even more radical than the Germans proposed, with the aim

---

[60] For an overview of the various German authorities involved, see Marrus and Paxton, *Vichy France and the Jews*, 45–48.

[61] Ibid. In France, the RSHA was headed by SS-Obersturmführer Helmut Knochen, who was appointed as Heydrich's representative in Paris in June 1940. Max Thomas served as Himmler's representative in the RSHA in France. Also see Joly, *Vichy dans la 'solution finale'*, 111–112.

[62] Although their central conclusions have remained unaltered, in the revised and updated version of their first edition, published in 2020, Marrus and Paxton have reformulated their conclusions, and elaborated on their findings from a comparative viewpoint. They emphasise that the actions of the Vichy government and its supporters resulted in a higher death toll of Jews than would have been the case otherwise. The fact that they delivered thousands of foreign Jews from the unoccupied zone into German hands, in their view, is unparalleled in Western Europe (and has only a few equivalents in Eastern Europe). For the comparison with Hungary and Romania, see Marrus and Paxton, *Vichy France and the Jews* (1981 edition), 369. For the conclusions in the 2020 edition regarding the Vichy government's anti-Jewish measures from a comparative viewpoint, see pp. 269–284. Future references to this work concern the 2020 edition.

of maintaining its own authority of the Jews in France. The institution of the UGIF in both the occupied and the unoccupied zones, while the Germans only opted to have such an organisation in the occupied zone, bears witness to this.[63]

Recent studies, however, show that the nature of French society and the Vichy regime was more diversified than has been argued by Marrus and Paxton and by others in the decades that followed. These studies underline its ambiguous nature. Wolfgang Seibel, for example, investigated the negotiations between Vichy officials and the Germans in 1942 and 1943. He demonstrated that Vichy officials provided crucial assistance to the deportations in 1942, but were more hesitant later on. The massive round-ups of foreign Jews in Paris and in the unoccupied zone in summer 1942, which provoked public outrage, resulted in a Vichy–German agreement that the French police would not be responsible for arresting French citizens. Throughout 1943, Vichy cooperation with the solution to the so-called Jewish question decreased, which culminated in Laval's refusal to denaturalise all Jews who were provided French citizenship since 1927.[64] In 1944, deportations intensified again with the aid of the Milice Française, headed by Laval. Vichy thus both facilitated and (temporarily) obstructed the solution to the so-called Jewish problem in France.

More recently, Sémelin emphasised that 75 per cent of the Jews in France managed to survive despite the presence of the collaborationist Vichy regime. Without exonerating Vichy's antisemitism, he argued that historians need to understand the 'French paradox' within a many-layered analytical framework, (controversially) emphasising the assistance ordinary non-Jews in France provided to their Jewish neighbours.[65] As a study by Daniel Lee has convincingly shown, Vichy policies were inconsistent, especially during the first two years. On the one hand, there were senior Vichy officials who considered the marginalisation of Jews an 'absolute priority', as well as those who believed that 'Jewish influence had brought about the defeat'.[66] On the other hand, for a number

---

[63] Laurent Joly, *Xavier Vallat (1891–1972): Du nationalisme chrétien à l'antisémitisme d'État* (Paris: Grasset, 2001), 239; Marrus and Paxton, *Vichy France and the Jews*, 71.

[64] Wolfgang Seibel, *Macht und Moral: Die 'Endlösung der Judenfrage' in Frankreich, 1940–1944* (Munich: Wilhelm Fink Verlag, 2010), 304–317.

[65] Sémelin, *The Survival of the Jews in France*, passim. For the criticisms that were voiced by prominent historians of Vichy France, see, for example, Robert O. Paxton, 'Jews: How Vichy Made it Worse', *The New York Review*, 6 March 2014; Vicki Caron, '*The Survival of the Jews in France, 1940–1944*', book review, *The Journal of Modern History*, Vol. 92, No. 2 (2020), 444–447.

[66] Lee, *Pétain's Jewish Children*, 11.

of Vichy's leading figures 'the antisemitic legislation only served as an inconvenience and a distraction from their principal ministerial responsibilities'.[67] To many, the reconstruction of the country, rather than ideological antisemitism, was the central driving force in this period. Most recently, Laurent Joly has emphasised the ambiguous nature of the Vichy regime, arguing that its policies against Jews can be characterised as a combination of antisemitism, impulses towards sovereignty and the desire for collaboration.[68] We can therefore conclude that Vichy was never a monolithic bloc.

Recent studies have also re-evaluated the relationship between the German Military Administration and the SiPo-SD in occupied Western Europe. Gaël Eismann, for example, has argued, in the case of France, that the differences between these two institutions were not as clear as has been argued in the past. Rather than considering the Military Administration as a restraining factor in the implementation of anti-Jewish legislation in Western Europe, she claimed that it pioneered the radicalisation of antisemitic policy in occupied France, outpacing the SiPo-SD. Eismann showed that the German military and security forces often cooperated closely with each other at the local level.[69] In the case of occupied Belgium, Insa Meinen has similarly highlighted the powerful role of the Military Administration in the deportation of Jews from the country. In doing so, she downplayed the widespread notion that the Military Administration often served as an inhibiting factor in the implementation of anti-Jewish regulations.[70]

These arguments are hard to sustain in the contexts of the AJB and the UGIF, as we have seen that the institutional rivalry between the SiPo-SD and the Military Administration, and the objections of the Military Administration's officials, delayed the establishment of these organisations. At the same time, we shall see that prominent German officials involved with the Jewish organisations did at times disagree while also cooperating, not least because they often had strong ties to both the SS and the Military Administration. Werner Best offers an example of this.

---

[67] Ibid.

[68] Laurent Joly, *L'État contre les juifs: Vichy, les nazis et la persécution antisémite* (Paris: Éditions Grasset, 2018), passim.

[69] Gaël Eismann, *Hôtel Majestic: Ordre et sécurité en France occupée, 1940–1944* (Paris: Éditions Tallandier, 2010), passim. In doing so, she disputed the traditional assumption that a clear line can be drawn between the Military Administration and the SiPo-SD. See, for example, Umbreit, *Der Militärbefehlshaber in Frankreich*; Eberhard Jäckel, *Frankreich in Hitlers Europa. Die deutsche Frankreichpolitik im zweiten Weltkrieg* (Stuttgart: Deutsche Verlags-Anstalt, 1966).

[70] Meinen, *De Shoah in België*, 237–240.

As a senior member of the SS, he also served as head of the administrative section of the civilian branch of the Military Administration in
France.[71]

The inconsistent nature of the Vichy regime, together with the rivalry
between the SiPo-SD and the Military Administration, created a complex situation. The representatives of these institutions all had different
views about the scope of anti-Jewish regulations and the pace at which
they ought to be implemented. Their rivalries and disagreements, in particular between the SS and Vichy officials, affected the course of events
even more in France than they did in Belgium or the Netherlands. In
Belgium, the power of the Military Administration began to fade as the
war continued. In the Netherlands, the position of the Civil Administration in relation to the SS began to weaken. But the presence and influence of Vichy could not be downplayed and it served to influence how
the UGIF was established and how it functioned.

When, after repeated demands from Heydrich and Himmler, army
officials agreed in October 1940 that the development of anti-Jewish
policies in France would be in the hands of the SiPo-SD-led Judenreferat (overseen by Eichmann in Berlin), SS-Haupsturmführer Dannecker became one of the central figures in initiating anti-Jewish
legislation in France.[72] Continuing conflicts of interest over the execution of anti-Jewish legislation seems to have been an important driving
force in allowing Dannecker to establish his authority by forcing a Jewish representative organisation, modelled after Jewish Councils, into
existence.

Shortly after his arrival in France on 5 September 1940, Dannecker
pressured Jewish leaders in Paris to establish an organisation to deal with
all political, social and cultural problems relating to the Jews in France.
It should be noted that although some existing literature asserts that
Dannecker wanted a French *Judenrat* (used to describe the organisations German authorities imposed on the Jewish communities in Eastern

---

[71] Werner Best occupied a multitude of positions across Europe (Germany, Poland,
France and Denmark) during the Second World War. Between August 1940 and mid-
June 1942, as senior member of the SS, he served as the head of the administrative
section of the civilian branch of the Military Administration in France. For an excellent overview of the positions of Werner Best and the complicated relations and over-
laps between the Military Administration, SiPo-SD and German Embassy in France,
see Ulrich Herbert, *Best: biographische Studien über Radikalismus, Weltanschauung und
Vernunft, 1903–1989* (Bonn: Dietz, 1996), 251–322.
[72] Griffioen and Zeller, *Jodenvervolging in Nederland, Frankrijk en België*, 182–183;
Marrus and Paxton, *Vichy France and the Jews*, 47–48; Steur, *Theodor Dannecker*,
47–48.

Europe), he himself did not use this word.[73] This is important because, as we have seen, the Eastern European *Judenräte* were very different in form and function from the Associations in Germany, Belgium and France. Dannecker was affected by his experiences in Eastern Europe and referred to Bohemia and Moravia as proof that an organisation that had been forced into existence could be vital for the progressive removal of Jews from French society. However, rather than using the term *Judenrat*, he instead referred to the French Jewish representative organisation as a *Zwangsvereinigung* (compulsory organisation), modelled on the Reich Association for Jews in Germany.[74] By establishing such an organisation, Dannecker wanted to merge the existing Jewish relief agencies and hoped to gain access to their financial resources.[75]

In order to achieve this, he contacted Chief Rabbi Julien Weill and Rabbi Marcel Sachs, and informed them that he expected the religious leadership, the Israelite Consistorial Association of Paris (Association Consistoriale Israélite de Paris, ACIP) to recognise their representative role for all Jews in Paris and provide for the communities' social and charitable needs. This was the first indication of the German intention to represent Jews officially through a single body. His efforts failed, largely owing to the lack of the support from the Military Administration, which was more concerned with the preparations of the military campaign against England in this period. Furthermore, Dannecker was unable to force the ACIP to act as he wished because the 1905 Law of Church and State Separation ruled that no representatives of religious institutions were permitted to assume responsibilities in secular organisations. Sachs and Weill used this legal principle as the basis for refusing Dannecker's demand.[76]

After this failed attempt, Dannecker changed track, emphasising the philanthropic possibilities for Jews in France once all were united under one umbrella organisation.[77] As the needs of the Jewish people increased,

[73] See, for example, Joly, *Xavier Vallat*, 241; Marrus and Paxton, *Vichy France and the Jews* (1981 edition), 108; Donna Ryan, *The Holocaust and the Jews of Marseille: The Enforcement of Anti-Semitic Policies in Vichy France* (Urbana/Chicago: University of Illinois Press, 1996), 157.

[74] For the use of the term *Zwangsvereinigung*, see, for example, Dannecker's report on the 'Judenfrage in Frankreich und ihre Behandlung', 1 July 1941, XXVI-1, p. 25, CDJC, Mémorial de la Shoah; Report of Dannecker concerning the activities of the SiPo-SD in Paris, 22 February 1942, XXVI-80, CDJC, Mémorial de la Shoah. Also see Happe, Mayer and Peers, *Die Verfolgung und Ermordung der europäischen Juden*, Vol. 5, DOK. 272, 675–690.

[75] Marrus and Paxton, *Vichy France and the Jews*, 71; Adler, *The Jews of Paris*, 58–68.

[76] Adler, *The Jews of Paris*, 57–58; Cohen, *Burden of Conscience*, 27.

[77] In a report written on the 'Jewish question in France and its treatment', published on 1 July 1941, Dannecker referred to an organisation that would provide for the lives of Jews, for their maintenance, and for their 'professional opportunities'. See Report of SS-Obersturmführer Theodor Dannecker of the French SiPo-SD in

both immigrant and French Jewish leaders decided to use this opportunity to improve their relief activity, despite their reservations about
German involvement. As we have seen, this gave rise to the Coordinating Committee, established in January 1941. Dannecker hoped the
organisation would form the essence of a Jewish compulsory organisation comparable to the *Judenräte* in Eastern Europe.[78]

In order to ensure this, on 18 March 1941 he brought two Austrian
Jews, Leo Israelowicz-Ilmar and Wilhelm Biberstein, to Paris. They were
members of the Jewish Community of Vienna (the IKG), which served
as an intermediary between Jews and Germans until December 1942,
when it was transformed into a Council of Elders (*Ältestenrat*). By then,
most Austrian Jews had either migrated or been deported.[79] Irsaelowicz-
Ilmar and Biberstein took control of the Coordinating Committee and
were ordered to transform it into an 'effective' Jewish organisation, using
the experience they had acquired in Vienna.

Dannecker believed the two men to be technical advisors and considered their guidance important. Israelowicz, for example, reported to
Dannecker about the nature and organisation of French Jewry before
the war, and advised him which organisations – he included the Comité
de Bienfaisance de Paris, the OSE and La Colonie Scolaire – could continue their activities through the Coordinating Committee.[80]

Unsurprisingly, the aims of the Jewish community and Dannecker
were different. While participating Jewish organisations were determined
to continue offering aid through the Coordinating Committee without
losing their financial and operational autonomy, Dannecker wanted the
committee to be geared towards the solution of the so-called Jewish
question, which at that moment still meant the emigration of Jews from
the country.[81] In order to achieve this, he felt that the communities had
to be united under the committee's umbrella – an objective that still had
not been achieved at this point (early 1941).

In response to increasing German pressure and the arrest of 3,710
foreign Jews on 14 May 1941, the relief organisation Amelot Committee

---

Paris, titled 'Judenfrage in Frankreich und ihre Behandlung', 1 July 1941, XXV-1,
CDJC, Mémorial de la Shoah. Also see Happe, Mayer and Peers, *Die Verfolgung und
Ermordung der europäischen Juden*, Vol. 5, DOK. 272, 675–690.
[78] Marrus and Paxton, *Vichy France and the Jews*, 71; Adler, *The Jews of Paris*, 53–80;
Moore, *Survivors*, 105.
[79] Klein, 'The Judenrat', 27; Rabinovici, *Instanzen der Ohnmacht*, 311–317.
[80] Laffitte, *Juif dans la France allemande*, 71; Adler, *The Jews of Paris*, 65–72. Also see
Dannecker's report on the 'Jewish question' in France and its treatment, 1 July 1941,
XXV-1, CDJC, Mémorial de la Shoah; Happe, Mayer and Peers, *Die Verfolgung und
Ermordung der europäischen Juden*, Vol. 5, DOK. 272, 683–685.
[81] Adler, *The Jews of Paris*, 175; Cohen, *Burden of Conscience*, 29.

(whose members would later engage in clandestine operations), seceded from the committee four months after its establishment. As we shall see, Amelot then explored the potential for a shift to illegal activity.[82] Since the Coordinating Committee failed to unite Jews in France, Dannecker began to look for alternatives and decided to involve the French government more actively in his plans. He believed that experiences in Germany and the Protectorate of Bohemia and Moravia proved that forcing an organisation into existence would be essential for the progressive removal of Jews from French society.[83]

While exploring the possibilities for a Jewish umbrella organisation, in winter 1940–1941, Dannecker also wished to establish a central Jewish office that would be overseen by the French (Vichy) government. From January 1941, he set up various meetings with the representatives of all German agencies involved in Jewish affairs, including the Military Administration, in order to press ahead with this idea.[84] During one of those meetings, on 21 January, Dannecker proposed the establishment of a central Jewish office – a *Zentrales Judenamt* – to trace Jews, remove them from all professional and social domains, and centralise the administration of their property 'until the date of their deportation'.[85] As we have seen, in Germany, Austria and the Protectorate of Bohemia and Moravia such institutions had been successfully established, and in each locality was referred to as the Central Office for Jewish Emigration (Zentralstelle für Jüdische Auswanderung).

In a detailed report on the supposed function of this central Jewish office in Paris, Dannecker claimed that while the Military Administration had already taken the first steps towards removing Jews from the country, it had become clear that the French authorities until then had wanted to follow the strict letter of the law and showed 'no political understanding of the necessity of a general cleansing [of Jews]'.[86] Indeed, the willingness of Vichy officials to cooperate in this regard was limited at

[82] Adler, *The Jews of Paris*, 175–176; Moore, *Survivors*, 106; Jean Brauman, Georges Loinger and Frida Wattenberg (eds), *Organisation juive de combat: résistance / sauvetage, France 1940–1945* (Paris: Éditions Autrement, 2002), 232.
[83] Report of Dannecker concerning the activities of the SiPo-SD in Paris, 22 February 1942, XXVI-80, CDJC, Mémorial de la Shoah.
[84] Marrus and Paxton, *Vichy France and the Jews*, 47–48; Joly, *Vichy dans la 'solution finale'*, 115.
[85] Dannecker's report on the establishment and function of the central Jewish office in Paris, 21 January 1941, V-59, CDJC, Mémorial de la Shoah. Also see Billig, *Le Commissariat général aux questions juives*, Vol. 1, 46–47.
[86] Dannecker's report on the establishment and function of a central Jewish office in Paris, 21 January 1941, V-59, CDJC, Mémorial de la Shoah.

first, because they were reluctant to carry out a unified anti-Jewish policy dictated by the Germans.[87] Furthermore, they were 'thrown off balance' by the Nazi system of rivalry and conflicting jurisdiction that more than once forced them to deal with several German agencies.[88]

Between December 1940 and February 1941 relations between Vichy and German officials, which had been complicated since the armistice on 22 June 1940, further deteriorated. Marshal Philippe Pétain, head of the Vichy government, had fired his vice-president Pierre Laval whose collaborationist ardour was not always in line with Pétain's perspective on Franco-German cooperation. Laval had formed a close working relationship with the German ambassador Abetz in autumn 1940 and was 'the most visible architect of the policy of collaboration with the German victors'.[89] The German occupying authorities strongly disapproved of Pétain's actions and immediately banned the passage of civil servants and men aged from eighteen to forty-five over the demarcation line, the border that separated the occupied zone from the unoccupied zone. Owing to the position taken by Admiral François Darlan (Minister of the Navy, Minister of Foreign Affairs, Minister of the Interior and, from February 1941, vice-president of the Council of Ministers) Vichy–German relations improved. Darlan was ready to make all necessary concessions to win the favour of Nazi Germany and to restore calm.[90]

In this period of political and diplomatic rapprochement, German agencies recognised that they needed the cooperation of Vichy officials to carry out Dannecker's plan of a central office that would oversee Jewish affairs.[91] In a telegraphic report to Minister of Foreign Affairs Joachim von Ribbentrop on 6 March 1941, Otto Abetz wrote that Vichy's support was necessary because the central Jewish office would then have a legal basis, and the German influence on the office's work in the occupied zone could have such an impact that the unoccupied zone would also be forced to implement the measures taken.[92] Darlan voiced reservations, taking refuge behind objections he attributed to Pétain, who, he said,

---

[87] Joly, *Vichy dans la 'solution finale'*, 113–115.
[88] Marrus and Paxton, *Vichy France and the Jews*, 45.
[89] Ibid., 43. Also see: Joly, *Vichy dans la 'solution finale'*, 116–119.
[90] For a detailed overview of the 'French-German crisis' between December 1940 and February 1941, see Joly, *Vichy dans la 'solution finale'*, 116–120.
[91] Marrus and Paxton, *Vichy France and the Jews*, 48.
[92] Report of Otto Abetz to Joachim von Ribbentrop, 6 March 1941, CCXL-1, CDJC, Mémorial de la Shoah. For more information on Abetz' role in France, see Ahlrich Meyer, *Täter im Verhör: die 'Endlösung der Judenfrage' in Frankreich, 1940–1944* (Darmstadt: Wissenschaftliche Buchgesellschaft, 2005), passim; Barbara Lambauer, *Otto Abetz et les Français: ou l'envers de la collaboration* (Paris: Fayard, 2001); Pascal Ory, *Les Collaborateurs, 1940–1945* (Paris: Éditions du Seuil, 1976), 12–18.

was worried about the impact of the establishment of such an office upon French Jews and about distinguished war veterans.[93] Afraid he would be surpassed by rival institutions and aiming to safeguard a working relationship with the Germans, which, as we have seen, had been seriously dented in the months prior to this, Darlan eventually succumbed, and on 29 March 1941 officially instituted the General Commissariat for Jewish Affairs (CGQJ).[94] The central aim of the organisation was to oversee spoliation and Aryanisation measures. It also supervised and organised the implementation of anti-Jewish policies in France, which until then had been the responsibility of individual ministerial departments. From November 1941, this body would also directly oversee the UGIF.[95]

Although the Germans had provided two lists of candidates they preferred for the position of head of the CGQJ – one signed by Otto Abetz and the other by Kurt Ihlefeld, the Paris correspondent of the NSDAP's newspaper *Völkischer Beobachter* – the Germans gave Darlan the autonomy to make the final decision.[96] He chose Xavier Vallat, a fanatical antisemite and proponent of the extreme nationalist movement *Action Française*. Vallat, a distinguished First World War veteran, was active in conservative and Catholic political circles and a strong supporter of Pétain. In July 1940, he had been appointed secretary for veterans' affairs and he had created the Légion Française des Combattans, 'a single, unified veterans' movement that was supposed to serve as a link between Pétain and his popular base'.[97]

Vallat reflected upon his appointment at the head of the CGQJ when he was brought to court after the war, and claimed that that he felt competent to take up this position because he had been deliberating about the so-called Jewish question for a long time.[98] To Vichy,

---

[93] Serge Klarsfeld, *La Shoah en France: Le calendrier de la persécution des Juifs de France, julliet 1940–août* (Paris: Fayard, 2001), 78; Marrus and Paxton, *Vichy France and the Jews*, 48.

[94] Joly, *Xavier Vallat*, 213; and *Vichy dans la 'solution finale'*, 120; Marrus and Paxton, *Vichy France and the Jews*, 48. According to Paxton, Darlan was arguably the most important figure in the Vichy regime in 1941. He held various offices and was also designated *dauphin*, successor to Pétain in case of incapacity or death. See Robert Paxton, *Vichy France: Old Guard and New Order, 1940–1944* (New York: Columbia University Press, 2001 [revised ed.]; first ed. 1972), 109–135. For an excellent biography of Darlan, see Hervé Coutau-Bégarie and Claude Huan, *Darlan* (Paris: Fayard, 1989).

[95] For a detailed overview of history and function the CGQJ, see Joly, *Vichy dans la 'solution finale'*; Joseph Billig, *Le Commissariat général aux questions juives, 1941–1944*, 3 volumes (Paris: Éditions du Centre, 1955, 1957 and 1960).

[96] Joly, *Xavier Vallat*, 213–214; Marrus and Paxton, *Vichy France and the Jews*, 48.

[97] Marrus and Paxton, *Vichy France and the Jews*, 52. Also see Joly, *Xavier Vallat*, 195–211.

[98] Statement of Xavier Vallat during his post-war trial, 3 December 1947, p.4, LXXIV-8, CDJC, Mémorial de la Shoah.

Vallat was a logical choice given that, as we will see, Vallat had an anti-German outlook and would therefore be able to hamper German influence over Jewish affairs in France. This, in turn, fostered Vichy's autonomy.[99]

During and after the establishment of the CGQJ, Dannecker continued to focus his attention on the establishment of a well-functioning coerced representative Jewish body in France. This remained a problem in the first half of 1941. SS-Sturmbannführer Kurt Lischka, deputy of Helmut Knochen (Chief of the German police forces in France) at the Paris SD department, insisted that the Coordinating Committee would be transformed into such an organisation in early 1941. Dannecker communicated Lischka's demand to Vallat on 3–4 April when they met in the presence of Abetz and Werner Best, who headed the administrative section of civilian branch of the Military Administration in France.[100] Vallat, who ardently hated German interference in Jewish affairs, initially refused to institute a Jewish umbrella organisation.[101] He managed to stall Dannecker's wish for such an organisation until later that year: on 29 November 1941, the law that established the UGIF, in both the occupied zone and the unoccupied zone, was promulgated by the French government. On 2 December 1941, the law was published in the official journal of the French state (*Journal officiel de l'État français*).

In the existing literature, the role of the various German departments involved in the establishment of the UGIF remains unclear. Michel Laffitte has pointed out that the law establishing the organisation, was a state law (*loi d'État*), decreed by Pétain and co-signed by various Vichy officials, including Darlan, but he reflects hardly at all on the role of the Germans in this specific process.[102] Richard Cohen stressed the role of Jonathan Schmid, head of the Verwaltungsstab of the Military Administration, who supposedly pressured Vallat to establish the organisation.[103] Joseph Billig instead emphasised the role of Dannecker who, bypassing the authority of the Military Administration, approached Vallat in September 1941 and threatened to establish a *Judenrat* himself in the event that Vallat refused. According to Billig, it was specifically in response to Dannecker's pressure that Vallat quickly established a Jewish

---

[99] Marrus and Paxton, *Vichy France and the Jews*, 81–83; 87–89; Asher Cohen, *Persécutions et sauvetages: Juifs et Français sous l'occupation et sous Vichy* (Paris: Éditions du Cerf, 1993), 130–133.
[100] Laffitte, *Un engrenage fatal*, 48–49; Joly, *Vichy dans la 'solution finale'*, 150–152.
[101] Joly, *Xavier Vallat*, 239, 246–249; Marrus and Paxton, *Vichy France and the Jews*, 71.
[102] Laffitte, *Un engrenage fatal*, 50–51.
[103] Cohen, *Burden of Conscience*, 50–51.

organisation in both zones, in consultation with the relevant Vichy government officials.[104]

Documentation shows that the Military Administration *was* directly involved in the establishment of the UGIF. A letter of the Military Administration to Vallat as well as a report written by Dannecker in early 1942 indicate that its functionaries had already encouraged Vallat to institute an obligatory Jewish representative organisation in August 1941.[105] From this we can deduce that from the summer of 1941 pressure on Vallat increased, from both the SS and the Military Administration.

In the end, the ongoing institutional rivalry between representatives of the Military Administration, the Vichy regime and the SS were instrumental in the formation of the UGIF. In particular, Dannecker's willingness to overpower those who in his view were not sufficiently radical was crucial to the establishment of the organisation. The pressure he exerted on the Jewish communities' representatives to ensure that a representative organisation was established was probably inspired by his wish to suppress the influence of the Military Administration, which had thwarted his plans and ideas for such an organisation on numerous occasions.[106]

An important motivation for Vichy officials in instituting the UGIF was their belief that they would lose control over the confiscation of Jewish property in the occupied zone if the organisation were to serve under German authority. The choice to have a Jewish representative organisation in both zones was prompted by the fear that foreign Jews would otherwise be expelled to the Vichy-controlled unoccupied zone, which the Germans considered a 'place to dump their unwanted Jews' well into 1941.[107]

Vallat tried to maintain Vichy sovereignty and aimed for complete control over the UGIF. In September 1941, he had written to Dr Storz, the Ministerial Advisor to the Administrative Department of the Military Administration, that three important points had to be settled before a Jewish representative body was established: 1) that the organisation (UGIF) should function across all of France and that the members in the occupied zone should be appointed by *French authorities*; 2) that the

[104] Billig, *Commissariat Général aux Questions Juives*, Vol. 1, 210–212; and *Die 'Endlösung der Judenfrage'*, 100–101. This idea is echoed by Marrus and Paxton in *Vichy France and the Jews*, 71–72.

[105] Letter of Military Administration to Xavier Vallat, 28 August 1941, LXXVI-16, CDJC, Mémorial de la Shoah; Report of Dannecker concerning the activities of the SiPo-SD in Paris, 22 February 1942, XXVI-80, CDJC, Mémorial de la Shoah.

[106] Adler, *The Jews of Paris*, 58; Steur, *Theodor Dannecker*, 52; Griffioen and Zeller, *Jodenvervolging in Nederland, Frankrijk en België*, 182–183.

[107] Paxton, *Vichy France: Old Guard and New Order*, 10, 184; Marrus and Paxton, *Vichy France and the Jews*, 71.

central board of the occupied zone should be under the authority of the CGQJ and 3) that the security of (UGIF) members would be safeguarded.[108] Despite Vallat's attempts to gain the upper hand, the UGIF was formed according to the wishes of the Germans and ultimately controlled by them. The UGIF-Sud's leader Raymond-Raoul Lambert reflected upon this in his diary, and wrote that the promises of Vallat about the protection of First World War veterans, should not be taken for granted 'since he is not free [to act]'.[109]

The third condition in Vallat's letter to Storz is indicative of his particular attitude towards French Jewry, which dated back to his experiences in the First World War. As a French soldier during that war, he had fought alongside Jews at the front. The friendships he formed at that time help to explain the distinction Vallat would continue to make between Jews 'in general' and those Jews whom he believed deserved to remain members of the national community because they had defended the fatherland (la patrie).[110] During a personal meeting with Dannecker on 17 February 1942, Vallat highlighted the ways in which his own antisemitism differed from Dannecker's.[111] He elaborated on this in his memoirs, where he claimed he did not hate Jews and underlined that he had Jewish friends, including three Jewish 'combat friends' made in the period 1914–1918. Instead, he 'mistrusted' and 'feared' strangers or outsiders (l'étranger), a feeling that he considered to be universal.[112]

Vallat was particularly influenced by the Catholic Church and the measures it had passed against Jews through the centuries. His racial laws were therefore 'a continuation of French and Catholic restrictive measures that sought only to reduce Jewish influence in France'.[113] Like Charles Maurras, an intellectual who directed the extremely nationalist and antisemitic Action française, Vallat advocated a form of 'state antisemitism' that attempted to regulate Jewish existence by state agencies in the general interest.[114] Even though his general antisemitic outlook

---

[108] Archives Municipales de Lyon (AML), fonds Vallat, 21ii-42, letter sent to Doctor Storz, September 1941, as cited in Joly, Xavier Vallat, 243.

[109] Lambert, Diary of a Witness, 22 June 1941, 45.

[110] Joly, Xavier Vallat, 90–94.

[111] Report of the meeting between SS-Obersturmführer Dannecker and Xavier Vallat, 17 February 1942, p. 25, XXIV-21 CDJC. Mémorial de la Shoah.

[112] Xavier Vallat, Le Nez de Cléopâtre: souvenirs d'un homme de droite, 1919–1945 (Paris: Éditions 'Les Quatre Fils Aymon', 1957), 221.

[113] Lee, Pétain's Jewish Children, 58–59. Also see: Joly, Xavier Vallat, 107–111.

[114] Marrus and Paxton, Vichy France and the Jews, 53. For further reading on Maurras and the Action française, see: Joly, Vichy dans la 'solution finale', 45–50; Michel Leymarie and Jacques Prévotat (eds.), L'Action française: culture, société, politique (Villeneuve d'Ascq: Presses universitaires du Septentrion, 2008).

did not significantly alter after the First World War, his differentiation between the minority of 'israélites' who were able to forget their origins and the large majority of dangerous, unassimilated Jews, whom he felt constituted a threat to the French race, does suggest a modestly nuanced viewpoint.[115]

Xavier Vallat and German officials such as Theodor Dannecker and Werner Best had different perspectives on the responsibilities of the UGIF and about the role of the Vichy administration (the CGQJ in particular) in the solution of the so-called Jewish question in France. This had become clear during the first meeting between Vallat, Best and Von Stülpnagel (head of the Military Administration) on 3–4 April 1941. Vallat explained that he considered the expulsion and internment of Jews to be a matter for the German administration and its police forces, whereas the Germans had hoped for the cooperation of the French in this regard.[116]

In his memoirs, Vallat reflected upon the disagreements between himself and the Germans, and claimed that he considered Dannecker's attempts to separate Jews from non-Jews in Paris in early 1941 through the formation of a ghetto 'old-fashioned'; he could not grasp how Dannecker imagined a ghetto could exist in a city such as Paris.[117] As to the function of the UGIF, Vallat considered it to be an institution permitting notable Jews to control the untrustworthy and generally lower-class immigrant Jewry. By contrast, the Germans wanted the organisation to be part of a new phase in the process of separation between Jews and non-Jews. Dannecker furthermore intended to finally unite Jewish relief agencies under the UGIF's umbrella.[118]

The physical occupation of the northern half and the western coastal areas of the France until November 1942, and the split of the UGIF into an UGIF-Nord and UGIF-Sud as a consequence thereof, resulted in two distinctive organisations. The framework of UGIF-Sud was entirely different from that of the JR, the AJB and the UGIF-Nord; it was a federative structure in which existing Jewish organisations such as the OSE and FSJF were assembled, retaining their (administrative) autonomy. The UGIF-Sud's main office was situated in Marseille, with regional and local offices in a large number of cities, including Lyon (three offices),

[115] Marrus and Paxton, *Vichy France and the Jews*, 109. Also see: Joly, *Xavier Vallat*, 185–191.
[116] Joly, *Xavier Vallat*, 219–221.
[117] Vallat, *Le Nez de Cléopâtre*, 253.
[118] Joly, *Xavier Vallat*, 241; Marrus and Paxton, *Vichy France and the Jews*, 71.

Nice, Montpellier, Perpignan, Valence, Saint-Etienne, Grenoble, Pau, Limoges, Périgueux and Vichy.[119] The UGIF-Nord had a complex bureaucratic structure that was based on numerous departments and sub-departments. The majority of its services were concentrated at various locations in Paris, with thirty-two localities in different arrondissements. Georges Edinger, member of the UGIF-Nord central board, was responsible for establishing local UGIF branches in the occupied zone, 'wherever there were sizeable communities', and local Consistories were approached to find representative French leaders.[120] Local branches were instituted in Amiens, Besançon, Montbéliard, Le Mans, Lunéville, Montargis, Nancy, Poitiers, Troyes, Versailles, Bayonne, Bordeaux, Epinal and Rouen.[121] Whereas the UGIF-Sud in practice consisted of organisations that were still operating autonomously, the leadership of the UGIF-Nord attempted (in vain) to oversee and control all forty-eight departments of its organisation.[122]

After the German occupation of the southern zone of France in November 1942, there were several attempts to unite the UGIF-Nord and the UGIF-Sud under one umbrella. On different occasions, this wish was voiced by various German and Vichy departments as well as by Jewish functionaries of the UGIF-Nord. These attempts proved futile, however: reorganisation challenged the existence and independence of the UGIF-Sud and could therefore 'not be but rejected by it'.[123]

The Impact of Institutional Rivalry on the Jewish Organisations

The previous examples show that if we want to understand the context in which the Jewish organisations were established, it is important to look beyond the limits of national borders. In all three cases, the Jewish organisations were built using blueprints from elsewhere. The rivalry between the various German institutions in each of the countries found its origin at the very top of the Nazi party in Berlin. This means that the establishment of these organisations should be understood within the broader context of German rule in occupied Europe. Looking at the

---

[119] For an overview of all regional and local UGIF-Sud offices, see Rajsfus, *Des Juifs dans la collaboration*, 148.
[120] Adler, *The Jews of Paris*, 110. Edinger believed that the UGIF should be solely led by French Jews, fearing that foreign Jews were a threat to traditional Jewry.
[121] Rajsfus, *Des Juifs dans la collaboration*, 147.
[122] Adler, *The Jews of Paris*, 115–116.
[123] Cohen, *Burden of Conscience*, x; Also see Adler, *The Jews of Paris*, 133–161.

creation of the Jewish organisations in the three countries, there are a number of important similarities. First, their existence resulted in part from competition between various German (and Vichy) institutions as prominent officials rushed to take the initiative and tried to consolidate their own power over anti-Jewish legislation at the cost of rival institutions and individuals.

The second factor relates to the first, as the examples demonstrate that a clear notion of exactly what the (long-term) tasks of the organisations would be was ambiguous. Therefore, the months and weeks prior to, and even after, the establishment of the organisations were characterised by improvisation more than anything else. This can be explained by the fact that events often followed each other so quickly that German policymaking could not catch up and responses had to be ad hoc. The majority of Nazi bureaucrats did not have any pre-war experience in dealing with the kind of situation they now found themselves in.

It is therefore not surprising that anti-Jewish policies and regulations that had been introduced elsewhere were simply copied, sometimes without any serious account being taken of the particularities of the country in question. The fact that Dannecker planned to establish a ghetto in Paris even though it would have been impossible to do so further supports this view.[124] The foundations on which the organisations were built were therefore far from predetermined and questions about their exact form and long-term function were often moved to the sidelines.

Institutional rivalry surfaced between the various sections of the German occupation regime, and in all three countries the SS encountered obstacles when trying to establish its dominance in the execution of anti-Jewish policies. In practice, the situations varied. In the Netherlands, we have seen that the presence and influence of the SS increased more rapidly during the course of the war than it did in Belgium and France. Rivalry with the Sipo-SD was an important factor in motivating Reichskommissar Seyss-Inquart to make sure that the supervision of the JR would be in the hands of the Civil Administration. In a similar vein, both Asscher and Cohen tried to ensure that the JR would continue to be responsible to Hans Böhmcker rather than to the SS. This made it vulnerable because there was always the threat that the SS would take over if it did not comply with Böhmcker's orders.[125]

---

[124] Adam Rayski, *The Choice of the Jews under Vichy: Between Submission and Resistance*, transl. from the French by William Sayers (Notre Dame, IN: University of Notre Dame Press, 2005; first ed. 1992 [French]), 42–43.

[125] Houwink ten Cate, 'Heydrich's Security Police', 384.

Above all, the increasing influence of the SiPo-SD, together with an overlap of functions, resulted in a rapid succession of anti-Jewish measures in the Netherlands. Unlike its Western European counterparts, the JR was exclusively subordinate to the local German civil and police authorities, Böhmcker and the Zentralstelle, and this was emblematic of the German aim to oust the Dutch government bureaucracy, sitting in The Hague. This is illustrated by the fact that the JR, unlike the AJB and the UGIF, was not anchored in law. The personal order of Hans Böhmcker to institute the JR resembled that of the Eastern European Councils, which were usually established on a personal basis (e.g. by the town commander appointing a prominent Jew).[126]

In Belgium it remained unclear which of the rival institutions supervised the AJB because both the SiPo-SD and the Military Administration continued to be actively involved with it. Furthermore, the Belgian authorities were also in communication with the AJB. Even SS-Obersturmführer Asche was unsure who was responsible for policies vis-à-vis the AJB. This became clear, for example, during a visit of Maurice Benedictus and Saül Pinkous, representative of the AJB Antwerp branch and secretary of the central board respectively, to Asche's office on 17 April 1942. They asked him whom they should approach in order to gain more information about the recently announced legislation concerning the identity card for Jewish workers in Charleroi and Liège (which these workers would need in order to be on the streets after 8pm).[127] Initially, Asche directed them to the Feldkommandatur but a few days later he claimed instead that the Sicherheitspolizei of Charleroi was responsible in this case.[128]

In order to buy time, the AJB could approach different institutions and, in doing so, was able to create organisational confusion to its own benefit. For example, Benedictus used the absence of a formal order to hamper the provisions for forced labour by Jews in the

---

[126] Michman, 'De oprichting van de "Joodsche Raad voor Amsterdam"', 88; and 'Research on the Holocaust in Belgium and in General', 33–35; Michman, Beem and Michman, *Pinkas*, 172; Griffioen and Zeller, *Jodenvervolging in Nederland, Frankrijk en België*, 649.

[127] For the legislation concerning Jewish workers in Charleroi and Liège, see *Verordnungsblatt des Militärbefehlshabers in Belgien und Nordfrankreich*, No. 54, 29 August 1941.

[128] Minutes of the AJB central board meeting, report of the visit of Benedictus and Pinkous to Obersturmführer Asche, 17 April 1942, R497/Tr206891, DOS; Report of the conversation between SS-Obersturmführer Asche with M. Benedictus and N. Nozice, 27 April 1942, R497/Tr206891, DOS as cited in Sophie Vandepontseele, 'De verplichte tewerkstelling van joden in België en Noord-Frankrijk', in van Doorslaer and Schreiber, *De curatoren van het getto*, 153. For an overview of the various German and Belgian authorities involved in the forced labour of Jews, see 149–155.

Organisation Todt (OT) camps in the north of France that had been announced on 11 March 1942.[129] In June 1942, he refused to hand over lists of Jews to the Labour Office (Arbeidsambt) of the Belgian secretaries-general, one of the authorities with which the AJB leaders communicated and which sat in a larger disorganised web of Belgian and German organisations overseeing the forced labour of Jews in the OT camps.[130] He claimed that he could not do so in the absence of a formal order from an 'authorised authority', aiming to use the organisational ambiguity to his own advantage.[131] Even though the Germans in the end did not need the lists because they already had the necessary documentation, this example shows how the AJB leadership used the presence of rival institutions to attempt to frustrate German plans.

In France, the ongoing institutional rivalry between the Military Administration, the SiPo-SD and Vichy officials dominated the politics of the UGIF. As in Belgium, this rivalry delayed the establishment of the UGIF-Nord and the UGIF-Sud in the first place. Furthermore, it affected the implementation of anti-Jewish measures such as that of the yellow star for which the Germans needed the cooperation of the French administration, and, in particular, of the French police. After Louis Darquier de Pellepoix, who succeeded Xavier Vallat, had taken office at the CGQJ, Werner Best and Theodor Dannecker hoped against all odds that the former would see to it that the yellow star was imposed in both zones.[132] However, Vichy officials at this point drew a line between foreign and French Jews, and were unwilling to introduce a measure that would stigmatise all Jews equally. In the unoccupied zone, the star was never introduced, and the UGIF-Sud was the only

[129] Report of a meeting between d'Hoedt of the Labour Office (Arbeidsambt), Benedictus and Feiertag, 27 June 1942, A008453, JMDV, CNHEJ, Buber Collection, Kazerne Dossin. It took the Military Administration almost two months to establish the legal framework for the forced labour of Jews in OT camps. After the general announcement of the regulation on 11 March 1942, the second (final) regulation was circulated on 8 May that year; see *Verordnungsblatt des Militärbefehlshabers in Belgien und Nordfrankreich*, No. 70, 18 March 1942 and *Verordnungsblatt des Militärbefehlshabers in Belgien und Nordfrankreich*, No. 76, 8 May 1942.

[130] For more information on the Belgian *Arbeidsambten* that operated under the *Rijksarbeidsambt*, the successor of the Nationale Dienst voor Arbeid en Werkloosheid, reporting to the Ministry of Labour and Social Security, see Bart Brinckman, 'Een schakel tussen arbeid en leiding: het Rijksarbeidsambt (1940–1944)', *Bijdragen tot de Geschiedenis van de Tweede Wereldoorlog*, Vol. 12 (1989), 85–161; Nico Wouters, *De Führerstaat: overheid en collaboratie in België, 1940–1944* (Tielt: Lannoo, 2006), 141–147.

[131] Report of the meeting between d'Hoedt of the Labour Office (Arbeidsambt), Benedictus and Feiertag, 27 June 1942, A008453, JMDV, CNHEJ, Buber Collection, Kazerne Dossin.

[132] Marrus and Paxton, *Vichy France and the Jews*, 180.

Jewish organisation in Western Europe that was not held responsible for distributing the stars.

In both Belgium and France, institutional rivalry resulted above all in postponements and, from the German perspective, in a looser grip on the organisations. As a result, as we shall see in Chapter 5, there was more room for manoeuvre for the AJB, the UGIF-Nord and the UGIF-Sud, allowing them to foster their engagement in illegal activities.

3 Leadership of the 'Councils'
Continuation or Discontinuation with Pre-war Structures?

Aiming to unite the Jewish communities in the Netherlands, Belgium and France, and to establish a properly functioning representative organisation through which they could communicate their regulations, the Germans appointed at the head of the 'Jewish Councils' Jews whom they believed would achieve these goals. A 1939 report of the SD's Jewish Department shows that its officials analysed the Dutch–Jewish communities prior to the occupation of the Netherlands.[1] In Belgium and France, German authorities also issued reports concerning the structures of the (pre-war) Jewish communities in July 1941.[2] Even though it is impossible to prove that these investigations directly resulted in the appointment of specific individuals at the head of the JR, the AJB, the UGIF-Nord and the UGIF-Sud, it is clear that the power balances in the communities were known to the occupiers.

In all cases, the Germans first approached (Chief) Rabbis. Only in Belgium, however, did the Chief Rabbi, Salomon Ullmann, take up the chairmanship of the Jewish organisation. In the Netherlands and France, Rabbis were not willing to serve in this capacity either because they believed they would not make the most suitable leaders, or because it was decided that religious leaders should not interfere in non-religious matters.[3] Instead, as will be further examined in this chapter, individuals

---

[1] Dan Michman, 'Preparing for Occupation? A Nazi *Sicherheitsdienst* document of spring 1939 on the Jews of Holland', *Studia Rosenthaliana*, Vol. 31, No. 2 (1998), 177.

[2] See Dannecker's report on the 'Judenfrage in Frankreich und ihre Behandlung', 1 July 1941, XXVI-1, CDJC, Mémorial de la Shoah. Also see Happe, Mayer and Peers, *Die Verfolgung und Ermordung der europäischen Juden*, Vol. 5, DOK. 272, 675–690; Steinberg, *L'étoile et le fusil: La question juive*, 75.

[3] We will see that in the Netherlands Rabbis Lodewijk Hartog Sarlouis and David Francès refused to serve as chairs of the JR. In France, Dannecker initially approached Rabbi Marcel Sachs and the Chief Rabbi of Paris Julien Weill, who also refused to serve. For France, see Cohen, *Burden of Conscience*, 27; Adler, *The Jews of Paris*, 57–58. For the Netherlands, see E. Somers (ed.), *Voorzitter van de Joodse Raad: De herinneringen van David Cohen, 1941–1943* (Zutphen: Walburg Pers, 2010), 80. This book contains the post-war memoirs of JR chairman David Cohen. The original transcripts

who had been involved in refugee aid organisations before the war were appointed as chairmen in these countries.

Four aspects are crucial if we want to understand the contexts in which these Jewish leaders in Western Europe took up their positions. First, those who refused to be appointed to the central boards were not punished. By contrast, in many communities in Eastern Europe, the establishment of the Councils was accompanied by intimidation, threats, humiliation, and massacres. The Jews who were appointed, for instance, to the *Judenrat* in Bilgoraj (Lublin district in Poland) were threatened with the death penalty in the event that they refused to accept their appointment. In the case of Kolomyja (Poland, currently Ukraine), Chaim Ringelblum and his family were taken away after refusing to accept his nomination.[4]

Nothing similar occurred in any of the three Western European countries.There were Jews who refused their nomination despite German pressure as well as those who resigned their positions either before or shortly after having been appointed. Yet there were no repercussions in any of these cases. For example, in the Netherlands Rabbis Lodewijk Hartog Sarlouis and David Francès refused to accept their appointment by the Germans.[5] In France, we see that the same applied in the cases of Marc Jarblum, the president of the FSJF (one of the major Jewish immigrant aid organisations), and René Mayer, head of the HICEM, an organisation that was established in 1927 and helped European Jews to emigrate.[6] In Belgium, Joseph Teichmann did not take up his assigned role.

Taking this context into consideration, there is a need to examine the motivation of those who did accept appointments as central board members to lead the 'Jewish Councils'. For some, their appointment was the definitive wider official representation they had been working towards for years. This was particularly the case for Asscher and Cohen in the Netherlands and to some extent for Raymond-Raoul Lambert, leader of the UGIF-Sud in France. For others, including the chairman of the AJB, Salomon Ullmann, this aspect hardly played a role. It is exactly these kinds of differences that this chapter seeks to explain and understand.

The second aspect that needs to be taken into consideration if we want to understand the contexts in which Jewish leaders accepted their

---

of these memoirs can be found at the archives of the NIOD: Prof. D. Cohen, Doc. I 248-0294, Inv. Nos. 10–12.
[4] Trunk, *Judenrat*, 21–26.
[5] Berkley, *Overzicht van het ontstaan*, 12–13; Cohen, *Voorzitter van de Joodse Raad*, 80.
[6] HICEM is an abbreviation of the names of three 'resettlement organisations': HIAS, an American organisation with its headquarters in New York; the Paris-based Jewish Colonisation Association; and Emigdirect, based in Berlin. For further reading, see Valery Bazarov, 'HIAS and HICEM in the System of Jewish Relief Organisations in Europe, 1933–1941', *East European Jewish Affairs*, Vol. 39, No. 1 (2009), 69–78.

nomination is that it was not yet clear in 1941, when the JR, the AJB, the UGIF-Nord and the UGIF-Sud were established, what their precise responsibilities would be over the long term. The basis on which the Jewish leaders accepted their nominations in 1941 were mainly those of uniting the Jewish communities under their organisations' umbrellas, transmitting German orders and providing social welfare. They did not have the benefit of hindsight that is often inherent to analyses of these organisations and the choices of their leaders. These Jews did not know, in short, that persecution would evolve into mass destruction.

Third, it was clear that if appointed leaders were to decline their appointment to the central board, which occurred in all three countries, others would be nominated instead. Thus, even if individuals had refused to take up their designated role, the four Jewish organisations would still have been established. Fourth, a recurring criticism of the Jewish leaders is that they were not representative of their communities since they were 'notables' and could not represent the (highly diversified) nature of these communities.[7] In this context, it is important to acknowledge that the responsible German and Vichy authorities would never have opted for a Jewish representative of the lower echelons of society. Since Nazi officials in all three countries indicated that the organisations ought to unite the Jewish communities, they were specifically looking for Jews who had a prominent pre-war social standing.

The variations in the social backgrounds of the Jews who served as the organisations' chairmen, including their different (pre-war) positions, influenced their self-perception, their acceptance by the Jewish communities and the decisions they made. This, in turn, affected how the Jewish organisations could function. Whether the position of the leaders was either a continuation or discontinuation of pre-war structures played an important role in this regard. We will see that the relatively well-integrated pre-war position of the Dutch Council leadership, Abraham Asscher and David Cohen, in combination with a relatively stable Jewish community, resulted in a more confident self-perception of their role compared with that of their Belgian and French counterparts. In Belgium, a leadership vacuum existed after the pre-war leaders had fled the country in May 1940. In France, the situation was different yet again, since the central board of the UGIF, both in the occupied and the unoccupied zone, consisted of a mixture of people who had belonged to the traditional Consistory and Jews with relatively little leadership experience.

The variations in self-confidence that resulted from these different contexts partly explains why the Dutch leadership remained in place

---

[7] See, for example, Saerens, *Vreemdelingen in een wereldstad*, 502–503; Knoop, *De Joodsche Raad*, 22.

until the JR was dissolved in September 1943, whereas their Belgian and French counterparts were either voluntarily or forcibly removed from their positions during the course of the war. This chapter highlights the impact of these voluntary and forced removals. It argues that the change of leadership in Belgium and France unintentionally created a form of disorder and chaos, and thereby fostered the ideal circumstances to delay the execution of German anti-Jewish measures.

The Joodsche Raad: A Continuation of Pre-war Social Structures

To turn to the Netherlands first, the Germans approached three influential Jews to head the Joodsche Raad on 12 February 1941: the famous diamond merchant Abraham Asscher (illustration 3.1); Lodewijk Hartog Sarlouis, Chief Rabbi of the Amsterdam Dutch–Israelite Hoofdsynagoge (Ashkenazi Community); and David Francès, Chief Rabbi of the Portuguese–Israelite (Sephardi) community. The choice of Asscher, Sarlouis and Francès was well founded, as the three men played a central role in the Jewish communities: Asscher on a social and economic level, and Sarlouis and Francès on a religious level.

Whereas Asscher agreed to his assigned role, Rabbis Sarlouis and Francès refused, because they felt they could not carry out any other task than the provision of religious and spiritual care.[8] They may also have been discouraged by seeing what the Reich Association of Jews in Germany or the Eastern European *Judenräte* had been manipulated into. Even though it is impossible to assess exactly what knowledge people had of Councils elsewhere in occupied Europe at this stage, functionaries of Committee for Jewish Refugees in the Netherlands, including Asscher and Cohen, had been in (close) contact with the Relief Organisation of German Jews (Hilfsverein der Deutschen Juden, renamed Hilfsverein der Juden in Deutschland in 1935) and with the Reich Representation of German Jews (Reichsvertretung der Deutschen Juden) in Germany, which was replaced by the Reich Association of Jews in July 1939.[9] Perhaps information of other Jewish representative organisations filtered through via these connections.

---

[8] Berkley, *Overzicht van het ontstaan*, 13.
[9] In 1939, the Hilfsverein der Juden in Deutschland was officially dissolved, yet it continued to exist as an emigration section of the Reich Association until 1941. For the communication between the Committee for Jewish Refugees in the Netherlands and the Hilfsverein, see Correspondentie met de Hilfsverein der Juden in Deutschland, Berlijn, July 1935–December 1937, Inv. Nos. 135–155, 181b, NIOD. For the history of the (predecessors of the) Reich Association of Jews in Germany, see Meyer, *A Fatal Balancing Act*, passim.

Illustration 3.1 The chairmen of the JR; Abraham Asscher (middle)
and David Cohen (right). On the left: Abraham Krouwer, late 1942.
Photograph by Johan de Haas. Reproduced by kind permission of the
De Haas family and the NIOD.

Once the Dutch Jewish Council was established, Rabbi Sarlouis took
a seat on its central board, though not as chairman. We might also therefore explain his refusal to take on the position of chairman in light of
decreasing religious activity in Dutch Jewish society. Perhaps Sarlouis
did not consider himself to be the most appropriate official representative of the communities. As a result, Asscher turned to David Cohen
(illustration 3.1), with whom he had worked closely together for years
while they had been working to help Jewish refugees in the Netherlands
in the 1930s; the latter agreed to cooperate and both men were appointed
chairmen of the Joodsche Raad.[10]

In the context of pre-war structures, the fact that *two* individuals
chaired the Dutch Jewish Council is not surprising; for years, Asscher

---

[10] Documents sent by David Cohen to his lawyers during the state investigation of his
wartime activities, 10 January 1949, p. 79, 181j, Inv. No. 11, NIOD; Cohen, *Voorzitter
van de Joodse Raad*, 80. In a public speech at the Diamond Exchange (Diamantbeurs)
in Amsterdam, Asscher explained the course of events that led to the establishment of
the 'Representation of the Amsterdam Jews', soon referred to as the Jewish Council,
see Notice of the Permanent Commission of the Dutch-Israelite Hoofdsynagoge, 14
February 1941, D003186, Joods Museum, Amsterdam.

and Cohen had presided over the care to Jewish refugees together. In fact, the Council can be considered a continuation of the pre-war Committee for Jewish Refugees (the CJV). In a wider European context, however, their dual leadership was a unique phenomenon, as other Jewish Councils were all chaired by one individual. The German authorities clearly took the local conditions into consideration and agreed with a leadership structure in which the final responsibility was shared.

Asscher and Cohen were responsible for appointing the other central board members, between fifteen and twenty in total throughout the JR's existence. In his memoirs, Cohen emphasised that they mainly chose Jews who fulfilled official representative functions in the communities – Chief Rabbis, chairmen of the Church councils and leaders of major Jewish organisations.[11] These included Jacob Arons (a doctor), Nochem de Beneditty (a judge), Albert B. Gomperts (a lawyer, and vice-chairman of the Jewish service organisation B'nai B'rith), Isidore de Haan (occupation unknown), Abraham de Hoop (former chairman of the Nederlandse bioscoopbond, the Dutch cinema association), Marinus L. Kan (a lawyer and chairman of the Nederlandse Zionistenbond, the Dutch Zionist Association), Isaac Kisch (a university lecturer), Abraham Krouwer (director of the Handelsmaatschappij Europa-Azië, the Europe-Asia Trading Company), Siegfried J. van Lier (secretary of the Amsterdam municipality), Abraham J. Mendes da Costa (former secretary of the Portuguese–Israelite community), Juda L. Palache (a professor at the University of Amsterdam), Max I. Prins (an expert in constitutional law and director of the labour affairs department at the municipality of Amsterdam), Aaron L. Quiros (a butcher), David M. Sluys (secretary of the Dutch-Israelite Hoofdsynagoge Amsterdam), Abraham Soep (a diamond trader), Herman I. Voet (former chairman of the Algemene Diamant Bewerkers Bond, the General Diamond Workers Union) and Rabbi Lodewijk Sarlouis.[12]

Despite his initial reservations, Isaac Kisch, a member of the Jewish Coordinating Committee (JCC), took a seat on the JR's board in order to have the JCC represented on the newly established body. He did so

---

[11] Cohen, *Voorzitter van de Joodse Raad*, 83.
[12] See *Voorzitter van de Joodse Raad*, 83 n.75; Leden van de Joodse Raad voor Amsterdam, 182, Inv No. 1, NIOD. In 1941, Quiros, Kisch and Voet left the central board. Voet resigned after a few weeks because of ill health. In September 1942, he joined the Council again. See Presser, *Ondergang*, Vol. 1, 82; Meeting report of the Joodsche Raad voor Amsterdam, 18 September 1942, 182, Inv No. 3, NIOD. I.H.J. Vos (liberal politician) and A. van den Bergh (notary) were later included in the board. In February 1942, M. L. Kan resigned, because he disagreed with the notice (published by the Jewish Council) that encouraged individuals to abide by German regulations in order to prevent retaliations. The Jewish Council published this notice on 20 February 1942 in *Het Joodsche Weekblad*, the Jewish weekly published under the auspices of the JR. See Meeting report of the Jewish Council, 25 February 1942, 182, Inv. No. 3, NIOD. From July 1942, some

after consultation with the JCC's head Lodewijk Visser who objected to any form of cooperation with the Germans. His letter of resignation to Cohen shows that Kisch left the board again on 21 September 1941 because he disapproved of the JR's functions. After the second major raid had taken place in June 1941, Kisch believed the Council should have been dismantled, which, as we will see, Asscher had in fact proposed (though the plan was not carried out).[13] Shortly after Kisch sent this letter, the Germans ordered the JCC to cease all its activities.[14] There were two Jews who refused to take positions on the JR board: Professor Herman Frijda, who believed the Council was an instrument in the hands of the Germans, and A. van Dam, for medical reasons.[15]

The central board members were primarily notables: doctors, lawyers, Rabbis, leading functionaries within the Jewish congregation, university professors and affluent and influential traders. As was the case with almost all Jewish Councils throughout Europe, the JR leadership was in the hands of the chairmen rather than those of the entire central board. Neither the other members of the central board, nor the members of the Joodsche Beirat – the sub-department of the Joodsche Raad that consisted of, and represented, German Jews in the Netherlands – and not even the leaders of the local branches established throughout 1941 (when the JR officially became a body with nationwide authority) possessed the power to change the directives of the JR.[16] Nor did they have a voice in any matters of principle. Gertrude van Tijn, who headed the Help for the Departing (Hulp aan Vertrekkenden) section of the JR, highlighted in a 1944 report written in Palestine that local branches were simply informed about the new procedures and about decisions that had already been taken.[17]

of the central board members were deported. This resulted in changes in the central board. For an overview of the central board members on 15 March 1943, see *Gids voor den Joodschen Raad voor Amsterdam*, 15 March 1943, 182, Inv. No. 1, NIOD.

[13] Letter of Kisch to Cohen, 21 September 1941, Doc. I 248-0895A, Prof. Mr. I Kisch, Inv. No. 4, NIOD. Also see Meeting report Joodsche Raad, 29 September 1941, 182, Inv. No. 3, NIOD; Statements of Kisch, 3 November 1947 and 6 December 1947, dossier Abraham Asscher and David Cohen, CABR, Access No. 2.09.09, Inv. No. 107491 III (PF Amsterdam T70982), NA.

[14] Melkman, 'De briefwisseling', 111–114; Meeting report of the Joodsche Raad voor Amsterdam, 16 October 1941, 182, Inv. No. 3, NIOD.

[15] Cohen, *Voorzitter van de Joodse Raad*, 83; Meeting report of the Joodsche Raad voor Amsterdam, 13 February 1941, 182, Inv. No. 3, NIOD.

[16] The Joodsche Beirat initially consisted of ten individuals. Later, this number was increased to twenty. From October 1942, the Beirat leader Prof. Max Brahn was invited to attend meetings of the central Council board. He did not have a right to vote, however. See Gertrude van Tijn, 'Bijdrage tot de Geschiedenis der Joden in Nederland van 10 mei 1940 tot juni 1944', p. 5, Doc. I 248-1720B Gertrude van Tijn, Inv. No. 1, NIOD.

[17] Ibid., p. 8, Doc. I 248-1720B, Inv. No. 1, NIOD. In July 1944, Gertrude van Tijn was part of a group of Jews, also including Mirjam Levie (Bolle), that was released from

While the members of the central board were frequently consulted on matters of principle, which generally revolved around the question whether the Council should continue to cooperate with the Germans, the final decisions were always taken by the two chairmen. A letter written on 26 December 1941 signed by eight central board members, shows they felt resentment about this lack of influence. In this letter, the board members stated they were held responsible for the chairmen's decisions while they neither had any influence on these decisions, nor on the operations of the JR more generally.[18]

We have seen that Abraham Asscher and David Cohen maintained close bonds with Dutch Jewry and were firmly rooted in Dutch social and cultural life.[19] Both men were well integrated into wider Dutch society. In addition, they had fulfilled leading functions in the pre-war refugee aid organisations. Considering the initial social welfare remit of the Western European 'Jewish Councils' the leadership of Asscher and Cohen can be considered a continuation of the pre-war relief activities in which they had both been engaged. The contacts they had established through these organisations ensured they were able to build upon a network of people familiar with social welfare work.

In a society characterised by decades of assimilation and secularisation, in which the influx of immigrants did not drastically affect the existing structures of the Jewish communities as it did in Belgium and France, Asscher and Cohen were in fact more appropriate representatives than has been argued. Of course, they were notables, part of the upper-class bourgeoisie, and they did not mirror the nature of Jewish society at large, which had a large presence of poor Jews and Jewish proletarians who were not represented in the central board at all. At the same time, it would be naive to think that a representative from the lower echelons of the community would have been acceptable to the German occupier. With the absence of an official secular representative of Dutch Jewry, Asscher and Cohen served as spokespersons. As Mirjam Bolle-Levie, former secretary at the Committee for Jewish Refugees, which was incorporated into the Joodsche Raad in 1941, said during an interview:

Bergen-Belsen in exchange for Germans in Palestine. For further reading on this history, see Bernard Wasserstein, *Gertrude van Tijn en het lot van de Nederlandse Joden* (Amsterdam: Nieuw Amsterdam Uitgevers, 2013), 188–210.

[18] Letter signed by J. Arons, A.v.d. Bergh, A. Gomperts, I. de Haan, A. de Hoop, A. Krouwer, Prof. Dr. L. Palache and Mr. Dr. I. Prins, 26 December 1941, 182, Inv. No. 6, NIOD.

[19] For a thorough overview of Cohen's activities in the Jewish community between 1926 and 1941, see Schrijvers, *Rome, Athene, Jeruzalem*, 161–201.

if Asscher and Cohen were not representatives of their community, then who would have been?[20]

Asscher and Cohen also regarded themselves as the most appropriate representatives of the Dutch–Jewish communities. After the war, Cohen stated that he considered that he and Abraham Asscher were the most suitable and capable leaders of the Jews in the Netherlands at that moment. According to Cohen, at different stages during the war, both men had considered resigning. However, he writes, the thought of two other Jews taking over their position was one of the reasons that forced them to take up their position in the first place and to remain until the very end.[21] In a similar vein, Asscher indicated he was convinced he had the confidence of the 'vast majority' of Jews in the Netherlands: 'in view of my various involvements in Jewish affairs [before the war], I considered (and still consider) myself suitable for this [role]'.[22] Their pre-war involvement in the community contributed to the idea that they would be best able to defend the position and rights of the Jews. This idea is supported by, among other things, Asscher's unwillingness to flee the country. Post-war testimonies indicate that the JR leader did not want to abandon the Jewish people: 'he would rather shoot himself through the head than join us in Switzerland [...] he considered that to be treason vis-à-vis the other Jews'.[23] In the 1990s, the son of David Cohen, Herman Cohen, stated it would have surprised him if his father had not taken up the position. He claimed that his father undoubtedly drew on his extensive leadership experience and probably never even hesitated to head the Council, not yet knowing that his task would be very different from his previous leading roles.[24]

There is another motivation that needs to be taken into consideration here. For years, Asscher and Cohen had committed themselves to the

---

[20] Interview with Mirjam Bolle by the author, Jerusalem (June 2016). Also see statement of Gerard Polak in Willy Lindwer (ed.), *Het fatale dilemma: De Joodsche Raad voor Amsterdam 1941–1943* (Den Haag: SDU Uitgeverij Koninginnegracht, 1995), 136.

[21] David Cohen, 'Geschiedenis der Joden in Nederland tijdens de bezetting', 18 August–5 September 1945, p. 13, 181j, Inv. No. 10, NIOD.

[22] Statement of Abraham Asscher, 7 November 1947, dossier Willy Paul Franz Lages, CABR, Access No. 2.09.09, Inv. No. 140-VI (BrC 394/49), NA.

[23] Statement of Abraham van Dam (a bank director who was asked by Asscher and Cohen to join the JR; he had declined their offer), 12 November 1947, dossier Abraham Asscher and David Cohen, CABR, Access No. 2.09.09, Inv. No. 107491 III (PF Amsterdam T70982), NA. Also see the statement of Gerda Jonker in this file who added that Asscher feared he would cause a mood of panic (*paniekstemming*), among Jews in the Netherlands in the event that he left the country.

[24] Herman Cohen in *Het fatale dilemma*, 60.

well-being of the Jews in the Netherlands. Both men had aimed to serve the interests of the Jews in various roles. However, they were not (yet) the undisputed leaders of Dutch Jewry. Taking up the leadership of the JR might have contributed to a feeling that this was a chance to finally and officially establish their leading position in relation to the Dutch authorities. Both Asscher and Cohen had been angling for official government recognition for some years, and their appointment at the head of the JR was an opportunity to achieve that status.

This idea is strengthened when we consider the attitude of the chairmen towards the other major Jewish representative organisation in the Netherlands: the Jewish Coordinating Committee. Between February and autumn 1941, the Jewish Council and the Coordinating Committee had worked together on a variety of matters related to social welfare, including education to Jewish children. This working relationship changed, however, when the Jewish Council extended its control outside the city of Amsterdam and, in doing so, penetrated the Coordinating Committee's sphere of influence. This first occurred in March 1941, when Reichskommissar Seyss-Inquart's representative for the city of Amsterdam, Hans Böhmcker, declared that the Council had to incorporate all non-religious Jewish organisations in the Netherlands under its umbrella.[25]

In early October 1941, Hellmuth Reinhard, chairman of the Central Office for Jewish Emigration (Zentralstelle), ordered Cohen to appoint local representatives in each of the provinces in the Netherlands.[26] The JR leadership then approached local representatives of the Coordinating Committee and asked them to work for the Council. The Committee's leadership did not encourage its employees to consent to this request. On the contrary, chairman Visser and secretary Henri Edersheim hinted at the idea that they should not comply.[27] This angered the JR leadership. During a meeting of the central board on 16 October 1941, Cohen indicated that he wanted the Committee to be dissolved in case it continued to obstruct the world of the JR; it was considered an impediment to the Council's power and control. The entire board supported this viewpoint.[28] Eleven days later, during a meeting with Böhmcker and

---

[25] Letter Hans Böhmcker to the chairmen of the Jewish Council, 18 March 1941, 182, Inv. No. 26, NIOD.

[26] Meeting Cohen and Reinhardt, 3 October 1941, 182, Inv. No. 4, NIOD. More than a week earlier, it had been decided that the Jewish Council would handle the requests of all Jews in the Netherlands that related to an ordinance announced on 15 September (which prohibiting Jews from entering certain public spaces), see Meeting report of the Joodsche Raad voor Amsterdam, 17 September 1941, 182, Inv. No. 3, NIOD.

[27] Circular of the Coordinating Committee, 5 October 1941, 181d, Inv. No. 2, NIOD.

[28] Meeting report of the Joodsche Raad voor Amsterdam, 16 October 1941, 182, Inv. No. 3, NIOD.

SS-Sturmbannführer Lages, Cohen got what he wanted: the Council's sphere of influence was officially extended to the entire Dutch-occupied territory, after which the Coordinating Committee was disbanded.[29]

The UGIF-Sud: A Break with Pre-war Structures?

In France, the social standing of the UGIF-Sud central board in the unoccupied zone was different from that of the UGIF-Nord in the occupied zone. The diverse backgrounds of those on the UGIF central boards has previously been acknowledged without explicitly making this differentiation between the two organisations. Laffitte underlined the heterogeneous nature of those on the UGIF central boards by highlighting that their paternal origins were diverse. They came from Algiers (Alfred Morali and Marcel Stora in the unoccupied zone), from Poland (Joseph Millner) and from Holland (Juliette Stern in the occupied zone). Around half of the central board members were of Alsatian descent. Laffitte also showed that the UGIF consisted of a mixture of lawyers (Lucienne Scheid-Haas, Wladimir Schah and Raphaël Spanien), doctors (Benjamin Weill-Hallé and Alfred Morali), translators or journalists (Marcel Stora and Raymond-Raoul Lambert) and engineers (Marcel Wormser, Joseph Millner and Robert Gamzon) and that some came from the families of Rabbis. Middle-class bankers and merchants were also represented and only a few belonged to the upper middle class: André Baur, a banker from a prominent family that was closely linked to the Rabbinate, and Albert Weil, former member of the Coordinating Committee.[30]

It has also been argued that, with the exception of one individual, Robert Gamzon (whose background and occupations will be discussed later in this chapter), the UGIF central boards (both Nord and Sud) did not consist of true representatives of the Jewish communities.[31] We will see

---

[29] In April 1941, in response to Hans Böhmcker's request that the JR ought to incorporate non–religious Jewish organisations in the Netherlands, the Council's chairmen had already inquired whether the Council's jurisdiction would be extended to the entire country. On 27 October, Böhmcker and Lages ultimately decided that the Coordinating Committee would be disbanded, and that the Coucil's jurisdiction would be extended. On 3 November, Asscher and Cohen communicated to the Coordinating Committee's employees that the Council would take over the Committee's activities, and expressed their hope that they would continue to work under the auspices of the JR. See Meeting Council chairmen with Böhmcker, 15 April 1941, 182, Inv. No. 26, NIOD; Report meeting Asscher, Cohen, Lages and Böhmcker, 27 October 1941, 182, Inv. No. 4, NIOD; Circular of the Jewish Council, 3 November 1941, 182, Inv. No. 2, NIOD.

[30] Laffitte, 'Between Memory and Lapse of Memory', 674–687. It should be noted that Laffitte mistakenly claimed that Robert Gamzon came from Poland when he was in fact born in Lyon (France) in 1905.

[31] See, for example, Rayski, *The Choice of the Jews under Vichy*, 64.

that UGIF central board members in general did indeed not represent the various Jewish communities in France equally, although it would have been difficult to truly represent the many Jewish groups who lived in the country. Yet in order to further examine this matter, we have to differentiate between the two Jewish bodies in France. In doing so, we can identify more common patterns among the UGIF-Nord central board members, and, in turn, among the UGIF-Sud central board members.

Focussing first on the UGIF-Sud, the leaders' appointment at the helm of this organisation on the one hand represented a break with decades of traditional Consistory leadership (a discontinuity), while many had fulfilled prominent leading positions at the same time (a continuity). If we compare the French to the Belgian case, the UGIF-Sud leadership was more fundamentally part of the traditional structures than was the case in Belgium. Rather than being a continuation of pre-war structures as was the case in the Netherlands, however, the core of the UGIF-Sud leadership symbolised an alternative form of representation. While its leaders had been part of traditional structures for years, they represented a deviation from the Consistory rule that had been predominant for decades at the outbreak of the war.

Pre-war instability in French Jewish society (partly owing to the influx of refugees), where the Consistory failed to function as a (religious) representative organisation, had in some respects created a leadership vacuum. After the German order for the establishment of a French Jewish representative organisation, the head of the collaborationist CGQJ, Xavier Vallat, had first approached Jacques Helbronner, president of the General Consistory from 1940. Helbronner was among the most influential Jews in France at the time, and Vallat asked him to cooperate in the institution of an overarching, mandatory organisation (the UGIF). The connection between these two men dated back to the First World War, when Helbronner served in Prime Minister Paul Painlevé's Ministry of War, and the former 'was alleged to have supported Pétain's nomination to lead the French armies in 1917'.[32]

The draft for a Jewish representative organisation that Vallat presented to Helbronner was more comprehensive than the Germans had proposed and grouped all existing Jewish organisations together under one umbrella, undoubtedly in an attempt to show the Germans that 'France was equally capable and determined to deal with the Jewish Question'.[33] Since Helbronner refused to cooperate as he opposed the establishment

[32] Adler, *The Jews of Paris*, 95. Alse see Poznanski, *Jews in France during World War II*, 132; Laffitte, *Juif dans la France allemande*, 46–47.
[33] Adler, *The Jews of Paris*, 89.

Illustration 3.2 Raymond-Raoul Lambert, chairman of the Union Générale des Israélites de France (UGIF)-Sud between 1941 and 1943 in his Strasbourg office in the 1930s. Reproduced by kind permission of the Yad Vashem Photo Archive, Jerusalem.

of such an organisation, there was an opportunity for a new leadership to present itself. As Laffitte demonstrated, the German occupation was a chance for the 'new elite' to establish their power and to break the Consistorial monolithic power for good.[34] The opportunity was used by Raymond-Raoul Lambert, whose disappointment in the Consistory's dealings with the Jewish immigrants made him into someone who aimed to break permanently with centuries of Consistory rule.

Born in 1895 in Montmorency (Seine-et-Oise, currently Val d'Oise), Lambert (see illustrations 3.2 and 3.3) had received several military decorations for his efforts during the First World War. Before the Second World War, he had been involved in several humanitarian (refugee) organisations, among other things, as secretary-general of the Committee for Assistance to Refugees in Marseille. He condemned

---

[34] Laffitte, *Juif dans la France allemande*, 25–26, 45–52.

Illustration 3.3 Raymond-Raoul Lambert, chairman of the UGIF-Sud between 1941 and 1943, walking in a street, France, 1930s. Reproduced by kind permission of Mémorial de la Shoah, Paris.

both the xenophobic responses by French Jewry and those of French society more generally towards the arrival of thousands of refugees and believed that French Jewry had a responsibility to take care of their co-religionists.

Lambert was also a board member of the Zionist Federation in France, where he had tried to improve the integration of Jews in French society while simultaneously preparing them for emigration to Palestine. Former editor of the *Univers Israélite*, the mouthpiece of the Central Consistory, he was a leading figure in French Jewry who, similar to Asscher and Cohen in the Netherlands, held key posts within the non-Jewish community as well.[35] Lambert felt strongly connected to the French state: 'pulling off these roots would be worse than amputation' he wrote in his diary.[36] With

---

[35] Cohen, *Burden of Conscience*, 53; and *Diary of a Witness*, xviii–xxxii; Laffitte, *Un engrenage fatal*, 39–42.

[36] Lambert, *Diary of a Witness*, 15 July 1940, 9.

his background in relief work, one of Lambert's aims was to represent and protect the interests of immigrant Jews through the UGIF, as their voice had often been ignored, particularly by the French ruling class.[37] While he negotiated with Vallat on the establishment of the UGIF, Lambert claimed he was afraid that if *he* did not take up a leading role, there would be a lack of concern for immigrant representation.[38] He thus used the Jewish refugee problem and the need to have a representative Jewish organisation as an opportunity to establish once and for all his leadership position in the community. Although the same has been said about Asscher and Cohen in the Netherlands, the situation was nonetheless quite different. Asscher and Cohen were representative of change in a Jewish community that had gradually developed over the years. Lambert represented an anti-movement and a break with the dominance of the Consistory.

Richard Cohen has indicated that Lambert's meeting with Vallat in preparation for the establishment of the UGIF in the summer of 1941 was the turning point in his career: 'it was to catapult him into one of the most influential positions in Jewish life in unoccupied Europe'.[39] The leading role Lambert took up was not well received by the Rabbinate and the Consistory, and they belittled his actions as the 'unauthorised acts of a layman'.[40] This harsh, publicly voiced, criticism of the religious leadership is unique compared with the Netherlands and Belgium, where the Dutch–Israelite religious community was represented in the JR central board through Rabbi Sarlouis while Chief Rabbi Salomon Ullmann served as head of the AJB in Belgium.

The Consistory's rejection of Lambert's leadership was a constant source of trouble for him, and he often vented his anger and disappointment in his diary. In one entry, Lambert described an encounter with the Consistory's president on 30 July 1942 on the platform of Lyon-Perrache

[37] Michel Laffitte, 'l'UGIF, collaboration ou résistance?', *Revue d'histoire de la Shoah*, Vol. 2, No. 185 (2006), 55.
[38] Raymond-Raoul Lambert's chronicle concerning the establishment of the UGIF, 20 September 1941–9 January 1942 (description and texts of documents addressed to Albert Lévy, president of the Committee for Assistance to Refugees, CAR), Reel 2, MK490, 2.1:2:60 (YIVO), Mémorial de la Shoah.
[39] Cohen, *Burden of Conscience*, 53. For a description of this meeting, which was attended by Pierre Bloch, former socialist deputy of the Aisne department and appointed as assistant commissioner at the Interior Ministry of the Free French government in Algeria on 17 November 1943, see Pierre Bloch, *Jusqu'au dernier jour. Mémoires* (Paris: Albin Michel, 1983), 185.
[40] Zosa Szajkowski, *Analytical Franco-Jewish Gazetteer, 1939–1945* (New York: Shulsinger Brothers, 1966), 49–50. Also see the letter of Rabbi Maurice Liber to Raymond-Raoul Lambert, 11 December 1941, p. 7, CCCLXVI-48, CDJC, Mémorial de la Shoah; Lambert's chronicle concerning the establishment of the UGIF, pp. 3,6, Reel 2, MK490, 2.1:2:60 (YIVO), Mémorial de la Shoah.

station: 'I ask for a meeting the next day, but Mr. Helbronner will not agree to meet before Sunday. [...] The president of the Consistory seems more deaf to me, more pretentious and older than ever. The fate of the foreigners doesn't move him in the least'.[41]

Although the UGIF did not officially represent the Consistory, neither was it disconnected from it. We have seen that Lambert had been closely involved with the Consistory through his work for the *Univers Israélite*. The same applies to Albert Lévy, the first president of the UGIF. Lévy was a member of the Consistory from 1935 until his choice to take up the presidency of the UGIF forced him to resign in February 1942.[42] He had close personal, social and institutional ties to Lambert, not least as leader of the Committee for Assistance to Refugees (the CAR) and also as fellow member of the Paris literary community in the 1930s.[43]

In a report written at the end of February 1942, Lévy indicated that he had been nominated president of the UGIF without having been informed of this beforehand. It was a role he had not been willing to take and he initially signed a collective refusal letter. Eventually, however, after Vallat threatened to choose central board members who had never been involved in welfare activities, Lévy agreed to take on his position in the UGIF, arguing that it was the only way to ensure social care for all Jews living in France. Like Lambert, he felt forced to do so because he believed that the position taken by the Consistory in relation to the refugee problem was wrong. For Lévy, taking up a leading position in the UGIF was a good way to represent and protect immigrant Jewry.[44] After this decision, the Consistory accused him of treason: '[t]he Consistory repudiated me, but it simultaneously tried to hide from responsibilities and it was grateful that I did take on this [responsibility] vis-à-vis the government and French Jewry'.[45] As we shall see, despite the antagonism between the two organisations, the Consistory and the UGIF grew closer again during the course of the occupation, aiming to use their combined efforts to help Jews.

For the central board of the UGIF-Sud, apart from chairman Lambert, Xavier Vallat nominated Jews who had fulfilled prominent positions in the pre-war Jewish society. Gaston Kahn had close ties to the Committee for Assistance to Refugees, where he had served as director. Other

---

[41] Lambert, *Diary of a Witness*, 6 September 1942, 130.
[42] Laffitte, *Juif dans la France allemande*, 35–37.
[43] Ibid., 58.
[44] Memorandum of Albert Lévy to the Central Consistory regarding the UGIF and the attitude of the Consistory to the UGIF, end of February 1942, p. 34, Reel 2, MK490.2 (YIVO), Mémorial de la Shoah.
[45] Ibid., 7.

appointed members were David Olmer and Professor William Oualid, both of whom worked for the ORT, a Jewish professional education and training organisation for rural trades.[46] Oualid, born in 1880 in Algeria, was one of the central leaders of French Jewry before the war. Among other positions, he held the chair of Political Economy at Sorbonne, was chief of the Employment Office at the Ministry of Labour in 1919 and was vice-president of the Universal Israelite Alliance (Alliance Israélite Universelle, AIU), the first transnational organisation (based in Paris) whose members aimed to aid oppressed Jews. As a respected member of the Central Consistory, Oualid was actively engaged in several refugee organisations in the pre-war period and was closely associated with Marc Jarblum, the president of the Jewish immigrant aid organisation FSJF.[47] The other appointed members were René Mayer, Maurice Pléven, representative of the AIU and Dr Joseph Weill, who worked for the OSE. Clearly, the majority had been involved in (immigrant) aid organisations before the war.

Contrary to Lambert, who already had agreed to fulfil a leading position in the UGIF through his negotiations with Vallat, the majority of these Jews had not agreed to work for the Jewish organisation prior to their appointment. Some were uncertain about whether to accept their nomination. The community leaders were split between those who advocated either continuing negotiations in order to improve the UGIF's establishment decree or terminating negotiations, and those 'who recognised the inevitable and resigned themselves to this new form of organisation'.[48] Initially, many refused their nomination. In his diary, Lambert wrote that Mayer and Olmer were the first to do so; 'Oualid and Jarblum then followed them'.[49] Jarblum opposed bringing all Jewish organisations under the control of an antisemitic government (Vichy) that openly collaborated with the Germans. Mayer refused on personal grounds and suggested someone else be appointed in his place. Olmer refused on the grounds of legal principles, and Oualid refused unless Vallat could provide guarantees about the nature of the organisation.[50] Larger underlying factors also played a role here. At this stage, it was not yet clear what kind of organisation the

[46] For further reading on the role of the ORT during the Second World War, see Sarah Kavanaugh, *ORT, the Second World War and the Rehabilitation of Jewish Survivors* (London: Valentine Mitchell, 2008).

[47] Caron, *Uneasy Asylum*, 218, 302. For further reading on Oualid, see Georges Wormser, *Français israélites: Une doctrine – une tradition – une époque* (Paris: Éditions de Minuit, 1963), 143–148; Assan, 'Israël William Oualid', passim.

[48] Cohen, *Burden of Conscience*, 63.

[49] Lambert, *Diary of a Witness*, 28 December 1941, 85.

[50] Adler, *The Jews of Paris*, 102; Poznanski, *Jews in France during WWII*, 133.

UGIF would become. There also existed a general fear that the responsibilities of the organisation would go beyond providing social welfare.

Some members were prepared to accept their nomination. These included Albert Lévy, Raymond-Raoul Lambert, Joseph Millner, secretary general of the OSE, and Robert Gamzon. In 1923, Gamzon had created the first Jewish scout troop (the EIF) in Paris – by then, the scouting movement was highly popular in France with separate Catholic, Protestant and secular scouting associations – and he attempted to create a unified movement among Jewish political youth factions.[51] The EIF members were diverse and Jews from all religious and educational backgrounds were welcome.[52] Before the war, 'the movement's overwhelmingly French leadership had built connections with high-ranking personalities in the national administration and had developed excellent relations with France's other scouting associations'.[53]

Even though these appointed individuals wished to accept their nomination, they decided to support the collective refusal (*réfus collectif*) that was formulated by the other appointed central board members out of solidarity. Lambert reflected upon this episode in this diary: 'Albert Lévy, Millner, Gamzon, and I could not possibly accept under the circumstances. So we decided to go along with the others, and all of us signed the same letter declining the office'.[54]

On 24 December 1941, all appointed members sent a letter to Vallat stating the reasons for declining their nomination: 'the reasons mainly concern the limited competences of the *Union* and its board of directors' and the fact that 'it could not exclusively dedicate its attention to uniting French Jewry and welfare work'.[55] From Lambert's diary, it is clear he was dissatisfied with the course of events: 'I am convinced that this is an imbecilic step to take, but we'll see what happens! Oualid had a failure

[51] Lee, *Pétain's Jewish Children*, 36–40. For further reading on the origins and development of the EIF, see ibid.; Alain Michel, *Les Éclaireurs Israélites de France pendant la Seconde Guerre Mondiale, septembre 1939 – septembre 1944: action et évolution* (Paris: Éditions des Éclaireurs Israélites de France, 1984); *Revue d'Histoire de la Shoah: le Monde Juif: Les éclaireurs israélites de France dans la guerre*, No. 161 (1997). For the memoirs of Gamzon, a diary which was edited and published posthumously, see Robert Gamzon, *Les eaux claires, journal 1940–1944* (Paris: Éclaireurs Israélites de France, 1981).
[52] Lee, *Pétain's Jewish Children*, 76.
[53] Ibid., 70. The history of the EIF and the recognition it (successfully) sought from Vichy in the summer of 1940 lie beyond the scope of this research. It is discussed in ibid., 70–89.
[54] Lambert, *Diary of a Witness*, 28 December 1941, 87. For Lambert's report on the precise course of events that led to the collective resignation, see his chronicle concerning the establishment of the UGIF, pp. 9–14, Reel 2, MK490, 2.1:2:60 (YIVO), Mémorial de la Shoah.
[55] Letter of Gamzon, Mayer, Lambert, Millner, Jarblum, Oualid, Olmer and Lévy to Xavier Vallat, 24 December 1941, XXVIIIa-13, CDJC, Mémorial de la Shoah.

of nerve … I wrote a personal letter to Vallat to notify him of this collective refusal, since I am the only one who has any power to save this
thing any longer – I'm right about that'.[56] Vallat had become increasingly agitated, and, during a meeting on 30 December 1942, threatened
to replace those individuals who had expressed their reservations with
individuals who had no experience in relief work. In his diary, Lambert
reflected upon this episode:

Vallat can't wait any longer. He is leaving for Paris on the 5th [of January].
Besides Mr. Marcel Wormser, whom he chose himself and who had accepted,
he will choose eight Jewish individuals not involved in our social work. He will
have an easy time finding eight 'mercenaries' he says, people living in Vichy
who know nothing about our organizations but will be happy to have a role in
them, if only because this will give them the authorization to stay.[57]

Lambert asked Vallat to reconsider the appointment of alternative 'mercenaries', encouraging him to send personal telegrams to all those who
had initially sent a collective refusal, in which the UGIF's sphere of
activity and the responsibilities of the Jewish functionaries would once
more be outlined.[58] This effort was successful, as most appointees then
(grudgingly) accepted their nomination to the central board. Existing
literature has claimed that Olmer, Oualid and Jarblum refused to work
for the UGIF, and that they saved their honour and that of the Jewish
community in so doing.[59] Nonetheless, the acceptance telegrams sent by
these men on 4 January 1942, sent alongside those of Lévy, Lambert,
Millner and Gamzon, show otherwise. All men emphasised they would
only engage in charity and social work. Olmer and Jarblum added an
attachment to their telegram, outlining three conditions: 1) the tasks of
the entire organisation would be limited to *questions d'assistance*; 2) there
would be no other task than this; and 3) they wanted to personally discuss
the composition of the organisation with Vallat.[60] Lambert's diary shows
that the conditions that were articulated by Oualid, Olmer and Jarblum

[56] Lambert, *Diary of a Witness*, 28 December 1941, 87.
[57] Ibid., 8 January 1942, 91.
[58] Ibid.
[59] See, for example, 'L'organisation de l'UGIF en France pendant l'occupation
(excerpts of an article by Zosa Szajkowsji) in Rajsfus, *Des Juifs dans la collaboration*,
366; Szajkowski, 'The Organization of the "UGIF" in Nazi-Occupied France', 248;
Yahil, 'The Jewish Leadership of France', 323–325.
[60] Telegrams of Lévy, Lambert, Jarblum, Oualid, Gamzon and Millner to Xavier Vallat,
accepting their position in the Conseil d'Administration of the UGIF, January 1942,
CCXIII-31, CDJC, Mémorial de la Shoah. In January 1942, Gamzon sent a letter to
leaders of the EIF, explaining his motives and conditions for joining the UGIF. See
Michel, *Les Éclaireurs Israélites de France*, 105–109.

were not accepted by Vallat. Instead, Lambert proposed three others to serve in the UGIF-Sud board: Raphaël Spanien, Laure Weill and André Lazard.[61]

On 9 January 1942, all positions in the central board of the UGIF-Sud were assigned and approved. Although Albert Lévy was officially the president of the UGIF, Lambert was in fact the one taking the lead.[62] It is therefore not surprising that when Lévy fled to Switzerland in December 1942, Lambert took over his presidency in March 1943.[63] In sum, the UGIF-Sud central board comprised Raymond-Raoul Lambert, Robert Gamzon, Wladimir Schah, Raphaël Spanien, André Lazard, Laure Weill, Marcel Wormser and Joseph Millner, who was replaced on 11 May 1942 by Pierre Seligman. Seligman had been honorary member of the State Council where Helbronner had been his colleague until he was forced to resign as a result of the *Statut des Juifs* that was put in place by Vichy in October 1940 and that, among other things, banned Jews from top government administrative positions. During the war, he also worked for the juridical service of the Consistory. In a letter to Lambert, Seligman showed his reservations about working for the UGIF-Sud: 'Although I could accept being appointed by Mr. X.V. (Xavier Vallat) it did not please me to be named by a note signed by his successor (Louis Darquier de Pellepoix). I am afraid it will be impossible to work with the latter'.[64]

The UGIF-Nord: A Continuation of the Coordinating Committee

In the French occupied zone, the appointment of leaders at the helm of the UGIF-Nord proved less difficult. The central board was a mere continuation of the Coordinating Committee (Comité de Coördination des Oeuvres de Bienfaisance), the umbrella of philanthropic organisations

---

[61] Lambert, *Diary of a Witness*, 8 January 1942, 94.

[62] Cohen, 'Introduction', in *Diary of a Witness*, xlvi; Adler, *The Jews of Paris*, 102–103.

[63] Laffitte, 'l'UGIF, collaboration ou résistance?', 57; Marrus, 'Jewish Leadership and the Holocaust: The Case of France' in Marrus, *The Nazi Holocaust: The Victims of the Holocaust* (part 6), Vol. 2, 786. In the existing literature, Albert Lévy and his actions have at times been misrepresented. Cynthia Haft, for example, confuses Albert Lévy with his namesake who headed the first direction of the UGIF Lyon branch; see Haft, *The Bargain and the Bridle*, 14. Yehuda Bauer mistakenly claimed that Lévy remained president until he resigned because of ill health in February 1943. See Bauer, *American Jewry and the Holocaust*, 237. Mordecai Paldiel incorrectly claimed that Lévy fled to Switzerland only in December 1943: *Saving One's Own: Jewish Rescuers During the Holocaust* (Lincoln: University of Nebraska Press, 2017), 211.

[64] Letter of Pierre Seligman to Raymond-Raoul Lambert, 6 May 1942, CDX-86, CDJC, Mémorial de la Shoah.

established at the end of January 1941. Of the nine central board members of the UGIF-Nord, six had previously worked for this committee.[65] The UGIF-Nord not only inherited Coordinating Committee's staff but also the conflicts that had prevailed within the organisation. These conflicts were primarily consequences of the mass exodus of Jews from Paris in May–June 1940, as a result of which the former centre of Jewish life in the city had been broken apart. Instead, Jews were concentrated in the provinces, which made it difficult for umbrella organisations to carry out their work.[66]

Another point of conflict was the lack of immigrant representation. Whereas in the unoccupied zone immigrant movements had been represented in the negotiations with Xavier Vallat on the establishment of the UGIF, this was not the case in the occupied zone. The Paris negotiations with Vallat only involved leaders close to the Consistory. Therefore, immigrant leaders had little trust in the goodwill of their French counterparts and in their apparent concern for immigrant communities.[67]

André Baur (illustration 3.4), appointed leader of the UGIF-Nord, was a banker from a wealthy family with links to both the Rabbinate and Zionism. He was the grandson of the former Chief Rabbi of France, Emmanuel Weill, and second cousin to the Chief Rabbi of Paris, Julien Weill. Like Lambert, Baur considered Zionism as a lifebuoy, a solution to the crisis in which European Jewry found itself.[68] Other members of the first UGIF-Nord central board were also Zionists, including Juliette Stern, Georges Edinger, Benjamin Weil-Hallé and Fernand Musnik. In that sense, the impact of the large number of refugees who introduced Zionist ideas into French society was visible in the UGIF-Nord leadership.

Baur had played a prominent role in the Coordinating Committee and represented the *haute bourgeoisie* of Paris. He accepted his nomination as UGIF-Nord chairman without hesitation, and to the very end he aimed to preserve the links between the notables of the Consistory and the UGIF-Nord. Baur's close connections to the Consistory decreased the tensions that existed between these two organisations. Cooperation between the UGIF-Nord and the Consistory in fact proved imperative

---

[65] Laffitte, *Juif dans la France allemande*, 75. Of these six, five (with the exception of Lucienne Scheid-Haas) had been part of the directory board of the Coordinating Committee.

[66] Poznanski, *Jews in France during WWII*, 66–67.

[67] Cohen, *Burden of Conscience*, 70–71; Adler, *The Jews of Paris*, 104.

[68] Laffitte, *Juif dans la France allemande*, 35–37.

Illustration 3.4 Chairman of the UGIF-Nord, André Baur, with his wife Odette Baur (neé Kahan) and their four children Pierre, Myriam, Antoine and Francine, early 1943. Reproduced by kind permission of Mémorial de la Shoah, Paris.

as German pressure quickly intensified in the occupied zone, and there was therefore a need to unite Jewish responses.[69]

Many UGIF-Nord central board members belonged to the Jewish elite in France and did have (some) organisational experience, including Juliette Stern (general secretary of the WIZO), Fernand Musnik (a member of the Directory Board of the Federation of the Zionist and Pro-Palestinian Youth of France), Georges Edinger (member of the Relief Committee of the Children of Zion as well as the Union of Jewish Societies and other relief organisations), and Albert Weil (administrator of the Jewish Welfare Committee of Paris).

Some members of the UGIF-Nord's central board were not experienced leaders at all. The experience they had gained through the Coordinating

---

[69] Richard Cohen, 'Le Consistoire et l'UGIF: La situation trouble des Juifs Français face à Vichy' in: *Revue d'histoire de la Shoah: Le Consistoire durant la Seconde Guerre Mondiale*, No. 169 (2000), 29–31; Laffitte, *Juif dans la France allemande*, 55.

Committee was very limited in duration. Marcel Stora, for example had been Baur's secretary at the Coordinating Committee, yet he had lived by doing modest jobs until the 1930s. He had worked as a representative for a funerary marble firm and later obtained a position as translator for the publishing house Gallimard.[70] Lucienne Scheid-Haas, in turn, had had only a minimal prior commitment to and involvement in the Jewish society; she became head of the juridical service of the UGIF-Nord. After the war, Scheid-Haas indicated that she was encouraged to take part in the organisation by her strong feeling that she ought to aid her fellow Jews.[71] Above all, owing to the flight of the traditional leadership to the unoccupied zone, the social foundations of the UGIF leadership in the occupied zone were different from those of the UGIF-Sud and the JR.[72]

The AJB: Improvised Leadership

In Belgium, there was a discontinuity in Jewish leadership after the German occupation of the country. This had two causes. The first of these was the absence of those who had taken up leading positions before the German occupation; the second, the generally disorganised state of the Belgian–Jewish communities and their representative organisations. Although the future Dutch JR leaders had established their positions as key functionaries in the Jewish communities in the 1930s, the large influx of Jewish immigrants in Belgium meant that it was impossible to identify a distinctive Jewish leadership in Belgium before the war. Both the German occupier and the Jews had to look for people who could appropriately fill the leadership vacuum after May 1940. Only Salomon Ullmann (illustration 3.5), Chief Rabbi of Belgium, former head of the Coordinating Committee and military chaplain (who had been made a prisoner of war, but was returned to Belgium on 12 June 1940), as well as Rabbi of Antwerp Markus Rottenberg, both representatives of the former Jewish communities' structures, remained.[73]

---

[70] Laffitte, *Juif dans la France allemande*, 55; Ibid., 'Between Memory and Lapse of Memory', 682.

[71] Interview with Lucienne Scheid-Haas, 24 April 1978, as appendix to Rajsfus, *Des Juifs dans la collaboration*, 345–348. Also see the interview with Scheid-Haas, conducted in July 1963, as appendix III to Laffitte, *Juif dans la France allemande*, 385–391; Cohen, *Burden of Conscience*, 52.

[72] The following individuals took a seat in the first UGIF-Nord's central board: André Baur, Marcel Stora, Georges Edinger, Albert Weil, Alfred Morali, Lucienne Scheid-Haas, Benjamin Weill-Hallé, Fernand Musnik and Juliette Stern; see appendix VI to Laffitte, *Juif fans la France allemande*, 404–409. For further biographical information on the individuals who worked for the UGIF(-Nord), see ibid., 54–66.

[73] Steinberg, *L'étoile et le fusil: Les cent jours de la déportation*, 31; Ibid., 'The Trap of Legality', 799.

Illustration 3.5 Salomon Ullmann, chairman of the Association des Juifs en Belgique (AJB) between 1941 and 1942, in his military uniform in 1933. Reproduced by the kind permission of Musée Juif de Belgique/Joods Museum van België, Brussels.

This leadership vacuum might explain why, despite German disapproval of the way the Comité de Coordination had functioned, the majority of the Jews who had been active in this committee were again appointed to serve in the AJB, including Salomon Ullmann who was appointed as its first head. The choice for Ullmann can very well be explained from the German perspective. In a splintered Belgian–Jewish society where numerous sorts of Jewish life were represented, from non-Zionist to Zionist, from Bundist to communist, and from conservative to Modern Orthodox, the choice of a traditional Rabbinic leadership seems well reasoned.

The position of the AJB central board members in Belgian society was essentially different from that of their Dutch and French counterparts. To some extent, Van Doorslaer and Schreiber were right when they claimed that the leading figures of the AJB in Brussels and Antwerp occupied religious, official or even representative functions prior to the

AJB being established.[74] At the same time, a comparative analysis shows that Salomon Ullmann, as well as the majority of AJB central board members, did not have representative functions before the war in the same way that the JR leadership had had. We will see that many AJB leaders had either not been actively involved in pre-war Jewish communal life or had been involved in activities primarily on a local scale.

We should therefore take a nuanced view of the notion that AJB central board members considered their appointment to be a logical result of their pre-war position.[75] It was only because those Jewish notables who had fulfilled leadership roles in the Belgian pre-war Jewish communities were absent that the appointment of these individuals instead could be considered a logical alternative. From a comparative viewpoint, the AJB central board never obtained the same unequivocal status as their Dutch counterparts. This meant, too, that their position was also not as autocratic.

The first chairman of the AJB, Salomon Ullmann, was not involved in major public activities before the war in the way that Asscher and Cohen in the Netherlands or Lambert in France had been. Ullmann was born in Budapest in 1882, went to school in Antwerp but then returned to Hungary to attend a *yechivah*, a talmudic school. After studying in Frankfurt am Main and Bern, he once more returned to Hungary between 1907 and 1909 to continue his Rabbinic education. Ullmann unsuccessfully applied for the post of Rabbi of the Brussels orthodox community in 1914. After living in the Netherlands for seven years, he eventually became secretary of the Machsike Hadass in Antwerp, a small ultra-orthodox, generally non-Zionist, community. It was a minor movement with a largely immigrant congregation.[76] A few years later, Ullmann became the community's Rabbi. From 1937, he was the main chaplain (*hoofdaalmoezenier*) of the Belgian Army, but his leadership cannot be seen as the product of a long-term development in Belgian Jewish society and Ullmann can hardly be considered typical of Belgian Jewry at this time.[77]

---

[74] Van Doorslaer and Schreiber, 'Besluit', 338. Other historians have made similar observations. See, for example, Laffitte, 'l'Association des Juifs en Belgique (AJB): Des notables postiers de la solution finale', *Revue d'Histoire de la Shoah* (2006), 89–91; Griffioen and Zeller, *Jodenvervolging in Nederland, Frankrijk en België*, 375.

[75] As stated by Van Doorslaer and Schreiber, 'Besluit', 339.

[76] For further reading on the Machsike Hadass community in Belgium see Stamberger, 'Jewish Migration and the Making of a Belgian Jewry', 67–69, 324–326, 333–352.

[77] For an extensive overview of Salomon Ullman's life and (pre-war and wartime) occupations, see Laurien Vastenhout, 'Filling a Leadership Void: Salomon Ullmann's position during Nazi occupation', *Les Cahiers de la Mémoire Contemporaine/Bijdragen tot de Eigentijdse Herinnering*, forthcoming.

After the German occupation of Belgium and the disappearance of Jews who had fulfilled major representative functions before the war, Ullmann had been (unwillingly) put forward as a candidate to become Chief Rabbi of the country. Yitzak Kubowitzki, leader of the Brussels Jewish Zionist community, had been important in the process of reorganisation after the German occupation and was anxiously looking for any Jewish representative left who could take care of the remains of the Jewish community. Via Marcel Blum, the only board member of the Israelite Community of Brussels left in the city, Kubowitzki approached Antwerp Rabbi Halevi Brodt and Rabbi Schapiro to become Chief Rabbi of Belgium. Both of them refused.[78] In a post-war report on the activities of the AJB, Ullmann claimed he was not inclined to accept the job either. However, Rabbis Brodt and Markus Rottenberg declared that a refusal on his part would have a disastrous impact on the Jewish communities of Belgium. Kubowitzki, Brodt and Schapiro therefore encouraged Ullmann to take up the position.[79]

Ullmann claimed that, eventually, his decision to do so was among other things motivated by German Jewish refugees who tried to 'profit' from the lack of representation and leadership within Jewish society by presenting themselves to the Germans as the communities' representatives. He considered this potentially harmful. In addition, the pressure from the German side was severe, he claimed.[80] As a result, he gave in to demands voiced by both the Jewish and German sides and became interim Chief Rabbi of Belgium, in the absence of Joseph Wiener. Quite unexpectedly, Salomon Ullmann therefore suddenly fulfilled a central role in the Jewish communities of Belgium only two years before the AJB was established (and Ullmann was appointed as its chairman). Fela Perelman, wife of Chaim Perelman and who, as we will see in Chapter 5, worked both for the AJB and the Jewish Defence Committee (Comité de Défense des Juifs, CDJ), a leftist organisation uniting various Jewish organisations that were engaged in clandestine activities, claimed after the war that Ullmann was not able to serve as the communities' leader at such an important moment in Jewish history because he lacked the necessary experience:

---

[78] Interview with Yitzak Kubowitzki, 12 November 1964, AA 1196, CEGESOMA; Schreiber, *Dictionnaire Biographique*, 203–204.

[79] Report by Salomon Ullmann 'l'Activité de l'Association des Juifs en Belgique', undated, AA MIC/41, CEGESOMA; Interview with Yitzak Kubowitzki, 12 November 1964, AA 1196, CEGESOMA.

[80] Report by Salomon Ullmann 'l'Activité de l'Association des Juifs en Belgique', undated, AA MIC/41, CEGESOMA. Also see the report of Maurice Benedictus, in which he described how Ullmann was advised by prominent Belgian authorities to accept the nomination, rather than to allow a group of German Jews to take on the chairmanship of the AJB: 'Historique du problème Juif en Belgique depuis le 10 Mai 1940 jusqu'au 21 Décembre 1942', p. 5, 18 Feb. 1943, A006683, Kazerne Dossin.

Illustration 3.6 Maurice Benedictus, secretary of the AJB central board. Reproduced by the kind permission of Archives générales du Royaume/Algemeen Rijksarchief, Brussels.

Seeing as though you've asked me, Chief Rabbi Ullmann was certainly not a traitor in my opinion. He was just ignorant. And he was not able to assume such an important role at such an important moment in Jewish history in general and the Jewish community in Belgium in particular. Chief Rabbi Weiner was gone. Ullmann had never been a Chief Rabbi before. He was a secretary. And suddenly he held this responsibility [.].[81]

The same pattern of having relatively minor pre-war representative positions, if any, can be identified if we look at the other AJB central board members, who were appointed by the German authorities and could only resign if approved by the Military Commander (Militärbefehlshaber, MBF) of Belgium and Northern France, Alexander von Falkenhausen. Ullmann was not involved in this nomination process.[82] Unsurprisingly, the central board members were chosen from among the largest Jewish communities in Belgium, representing Antwerp (Maurice Benedictus, illustration 3.6), Brussels (Salomon van den Berg), Charleroi (Jules Mehlwurm) and Liège (Noé Nozyce).

The appointment of the Antwerp AJB representative, who would also serve as the AJB's vice-chairman, was a complex process. Initially, the secretary of the Antwerp Diamant Club, Louis Judels, was

---

[81] Interview with Fela Perelman-Liwer, conducted by Jean-Philippe Schreiber, 14 April 1988, p. 80, Fondation de la Mémoire Contemporaine.
[82] Interview with Salomon Ullmann concerning Jewish organisations and the resistance, 1970, AA 1196/12, CEGESOMA.

chosen to head the Antwerp branch, but he pretended to be a half-Jew and instead nominated Isaac Benedictus, who belonged to one of the oldest families in Antwerp. As Isaac Benedictus was too old, his son Maurice was put forward in his place. Arguing that he lacked the necessary competence and would not be at all capable as a leader, Maurice refused.

His reluctance was not unreasonable. He had been a cigar-maker before the war and was not at all involved in Jewish public life.[83] Like Ullmann, he had been unwilling to take up a leading position in Jewish society after the German occupation. Despite this, Ullmann informed Benedictus that he was obliged to take on this responsibility owing to intense German pressure.[84] As a result, someone who had only been remotely connected to Jewish public life became leader of the Antwerp AJB branch.[85] The story of Maurice Heiber, head of the social service section of the AJB Brussels branch, is very similar. He reflected on his involvement with pre-war Jewish society: '[until the end of 1940] I did not have any contact with the Jewish community in Belgium, whose problems and members were entirely unfamiliar to me'.[86]

There were also AJB central board members whose pre-war position in the society had been better established. Nico Workum (vice-president of the AJB), had been director of the Belgian Communications Network, and Salomon van den Berg, a wholesale dealer, was vice-president of the Israelite community in Brussels from 1940. After he returned from his flight to southern France in 1940, van den Berg was one of the few members of the pre-war Belgian Israelite establishment who remained in Brussels. His nomination as vice-president of the community occurred in the face of few alternatives. In his diary, van den Berg wrote: 'I allowed myself to be nominated vice-president of the Israelite community, being one of the oldest members present in Brussels in Belgium, which was a rare thing in these times'.[87]

Very much focussed on his own well-being, and with a negative perception vis-à-vis German Jews who continued to play a role in the Aid Organisation for Jews from Germany (Hilfswerk für Juden aus Deutschland) that operated in parallel to the AJB, van den Berg

---

[83] Schreiber, *Dictionnaire Biographique*, 48.
[84] Maurice Benedictus, 'Historique du problème Juif en Belgique depuis le 10 Mai 1940 jusqu'au 21 Décembre 1942', 18 February 1943, p. 5, A006683, Kazerne Dossin.
[85] Ibid. Also see Steinberg, 'The Trap of Legality', 801.
[86] Eyewitness account by Maurice Heiber, 'The Jewish Children in Belgium' (1956), p. 2, 1656/3/9/274, Wiener Library.
[87] Salomon van den Berg, Journal de guerre, p. 36, Buber Collection, A006685, Kazerne Dossin.

seemed to consider the AJB as a mere continuation of and substitute for the Consistory tradition he had been part of before the war.[88] In fact, he did not even try to hide his feeling of repugnance towards foreign Jews. His diary shows that he wished to maintain his privileged position in society, using the AJB to establish his longed-for position of leadership.[89]

When we look at other (central board) members, some of whom joined the AJB at a later stage in the war, we see that some had immigrated to Belgium in the 1920s or the 1930s. Although the existing literature has emphasised the fact that the vast majority of AJB board members possessed Belgian citizenship, the presence of some Jews who did not (yet) have Belgian citizenship constitutes a major difference with the JR, where none of the central board members was an immigrant.[90] The following foreign-born individuals were all involved in the local branches of the AJB, while some simultaneously took a seat on the central board. Noé Nozyce, president of the local AJB Liège board, was born in Cieszyn (Poland), and arrived in Liège in 1928 where he became a fur trader.[91] Grigorijs Garfinkels, secretary of the local Liège board, was born in Liepaja (Latvia) and immigrated to Belgium in 1925.[92] Chaïm Perelman, born in Warsaw, was throughout the 1930s still going through a process of naturalisation to become an official Belgian citizen.[93] Perelman's family had settled in Antwerp in 1925, and while Chaïm quickly pursued a career at the Université Libre de Bruxelles (ULB), he only received Belgian citizenship in 1936.[94] One of the founders of the local Liège AJB branch, Idel Steinberg, born in Rezina (Bessarabia, Romania) was also in the middle of a naturalisation process in the 1930s.[95] The president of the Charleroi branch of the AJB,

[88] Rudi van Doorslaer, 'Salomon van den Berg of de ondraaglijke mislukking van een joodse politiek van het minste kwaad', in van Doorslaer and Schreiber, De curatoren van het getto, 118. Hilfswerk für Juden aus Deutschland was the successor of the Hilfswerk der Arbeitsgemeinschaft von Juden aus Deutschland, the Aid Organisation for Jewish workers from Germany.
[89] Salomon van den Berg, Journal de guerre, p. 36, Buber Collection, A006685, Kazerne Dossin; Van Doorslaer, 'Salomon van den Berg', 111.
[90] See, for example: Steinberg, La Persécution des Juifs en Belgique, 181–182; Saerens, Vreemdelingen in een wereldstad, 502–503.
[91] Report on Noé Nozyce, Inv. No. 19186/45, Conseil de Guerre de Liège, Auditorat Militaire, Algemeen Rijksarchief België (ARA 2).
[92] Report on Grigorijs Garfikels, Inv. No. 4030/44, Conseil de Guerre de Liège, Auditorat Militaire, Algemeen Rijksarchief België (ARA 2).
[93] Report of Foreign Police (Vreemdelingenpolitie), Chaïm Pinchos Perelman, N 682.302/A 143129, Kazerne Dossin.
[94] Schreiber, Dictionnaire Biographique, 271–272.
[95] Report of the Foreign Police (Vreemdelingenpolitie), Idel Steinberg, N 682.302/1313133, Kazerne Dossin; Steinberg, 'The Trap of Legality', 801.

Juda Mehlwurm, who was born in Poland, arrived in Charleroi in 1923 and only received Belgian citizenship after the war, in March 1955.[96]

Mehlwurm's successor, Louis Rosenfeld, nominated at the end of 1942, had not intended to settle in Belgium permanently, yet circumstances forced him to do so in 1939. He was a German trader in women's clothing and visited Belgium occasionally in this capacity. His intention to emigrate to Britain was suddenly thwarted when the British Consul failed to grant him authorisation to enter the country. As a result, he asked for a Belgian visa in April 1939.[97] After the German invasion, he became president of the Aid Organisation for Jews from Germany.[98] Despite this, his prominent position in the AJB, attained only a little over two years after circumstances forced him to remain in Belgium, does seem remarkable. The fact that the board consisted of people whose integration into the pre-war Jewish communities of Belgium was fairly recent suggests that the nomination of the majority of these individuals to prominent positions in the Belgian AJB was done in the face of few alternatives.

Saerens has argued that in the case of the Antwerp AJB branch the board members were not at all representative of the city's Jewish communities, since almost all possessed Belgian citizenship, belonged to the *moyenne bourgeoisie* and lived in non-Jewish neighbourhoods. He has highlighted the fact that these were assimilated Jews and that even Machel Majer (Max) Grätzer, of Polish origin, was representative of the Jewish bourgeoisie because he served as secretary of the Consistory.[99] In a similar vein, Steinberg pointed out that the vast majority of AJB employees were Belgian citizens, which was in accordance with the demands of Wilhelm von Hahn, the liaison officer for the AJB at the Military Administrative Staff (*Militärverwaltungsstab*) of Eggert Reeder. When the mass deportations commenced in summer 1942, Von Hahn indeed indicated to Benedictus and Nozyce that the positions of the AJB ought to be occupied as much as possible by Belgian Jews.[100]

---

[96] Report of the Foreign Police (Vreemdelingenpolitie), Juda (Jules) Mehlwurm, N 682.302/1160919, Kazerne Dossin. Before the German occupation, Mehlwurm was actively engaged in relatively minor revisionist Zionist socialist circles. Their meetings were closely guarded by government officials. The gendarmerie of Charleroi indicated in March 1935 that these kinds of organisations continued to be an object of discreet surveillance on their part. Mehlwurm also fulfilled a representative function as the Charleroi representative of the Israelite Community before the war.

[97] Report of Foreign Police (Vreemdelingenpolitie), Louis Rosenfeld, N 682.302/ A317631, Kazerne Dossin.

[98] Schreiber, *Dictionnaire Biographique*, 295.

[99] Saerens, *Vreemdelingen in een wereldstad*, 502–503.

[100] Report of meeting between Benedictus, Nozyce and Von Hahn, 14 September 1942, A007418, CNHEJ, Buber Collection, Kazerne Dossin; Steinberg, *La Persécution des Juifs en Belgique*, 181–182.

The examples we have seen here suggest that, from a broader perspective, the nature of the AJB leadership was rather different, reflecting a more complex reality. In the organisation's central board, there were in fact a number of Jews who did not possess Belgian citizenship, and, especially compared with their Dutch counterparts, the relative lack of overall experience in leading positions among the board members was significant. They were not representative of the highly diverse Jewish (immigrant) communities of Belgium, but neither were they traditional leaders with years of leadership experience such as Asscher and Cohen.

The social-historical context in which the AJB central board was established meant that its acceptance by the Jewish communities was minimal. In a post-war interview, Ullmann was asked whether those nominated as central board members of the AJB received the confidence of the Jewish communities in Belgium. He answered:

None. They were generally never in touch with Jews. I mean, some of them you have to know, one of them was Benedictus, that was the cigar factory Benedictus in Pienkov, in the Catenstrasse. He was a member. And one of them was Nossatsche (?) [Nozyce], a short man from Liège, A fur trader. Then you had Hellendahl [Hellendall], from Brussels, he had a well-known company in Brussels, he was hardly in touch with Jews.[101]

Whereas Belgian historians Schreiber and Van Doorslaer have argued that there was a general sense of trust among the Jewish population in the AJB at least until summer 1942, the image portrayed here by Ullmann is quite different.[102] It is clear that he believed the weak social status of the organisation's leaders resulted in little trust in the form and function of the AJB.

The fact that the Belgian Jewish leaders' positions were not a continuation of pre-war structures certainly affected their perceptions and the choices they made. The treasurer of the local Brussels AJB board, Alfred Blum, indicated in a post-war interview that Ullmann regretted he had been appointed as director: 'he was very bored'.[103] Without any real previous leadership experience and also a rather unwilling leader, he never seemed to take his role as chairman as seriously as either Asscher or (particularly) Cohen had done in the Netherlands or as Lambert had done in France.

The post-war testimony of Alfred Rosenzweig, who worked for both the AJB and the clandestine CDJ, gives a valuable insight into the way Ullmann was perceived in his role as a communal leader. According to

---

[101] Interview with Salomon Ullmann concerning Jewish organisations and the resistance, 1970, AA 1196/12, CEGESOMA.

[102] Van Doorslaer and Schreiber, 'Besluit', 339.

[103] Interview Alfred Blum, Farde Histoire Oral III, 5 December 1972, p. 4, CNHEJ, Buber Collection, Kazerne Dossin.

Rosenzweig, Ullmann was an honest and good man but was not the most capable person to represent the Belgian Jewish communities, and was even less prepared for his job than other members of the central board. As a consequence, his leadership lacked determination.[104] Ullmann's role in the AJB was therefore secondary. Maurice Benedictus occupied the central position instead, first as secretary and later as head of the administration of the AJB, which presided over the local branches and various of its commissions.[105] Despite Benedictus' initial unwillingness to become a representative, he thus fulfilled his positions with much more confidence and courage than Ullmann.[106]

The unwillingness Ullmann and Benedictus initially felt was shared by others. It has been argued that the AJB leaders did not use the establishment of this body to gain power in Jewish society, but we might take this claim one step further, and conclude that the majority of the central board members were far from willing to take on any representative position whatsoever.[107] They had initially rejected the 'offer' to form the leadership of the Association as they considered it to be a *guet-apens* – a trap.[108] Although only Joseph Teichmann, who was designated to become the local Antwerp representative, refused to work for the Association, the general lack of eagerness to become AJB representatives among the central board members, and in the case of Salomon Ullmann specifically, is an important difference from the examples of the Dutch and French chairmen.[109]

From a comparative viewpoint, two important observations can be made. The AJB's leading functionaries, and specifically its chairman, did not have the same pre-war status as the majority of their counterparts in the Netherlands and France; its leadership was less entrenched in the country's Jewish communities. As a result, the confidence that Asscher and Cohen especially had in their own leadership, and their feeling that they were the right representatives of Jewish society in the Netherlands, was generally absent in the Belgian case. These issues affected the self-perception of the central board membership. In a number of cases, they were either unwilling to (continue to) head the organisation or not

---

[104] Interview Alfred Rosenzweig, 3 February 1972, p. 26, CNHEJ, Buber Collection, Kazerne Dossin. For a short biography of Rosenzweig, see Schreiber, *Dictionnaire Biographique*, 296–297; Steinberg, *La persécution des Juifs en Belgique*, 185.

[105] Steinberg, 'The Trap of Legality', 801. Also see Interview Alfred Rosenzweig, 3 February 1972, 26–27, CNHEJ, Buber Collection, Kazerne Dossin.

[106] Steinberg, *La Persécution des Juifs en Belgique*, 185.

[107] Van Doorslaer and Schreiber, 'Besluit', 338.

[108] Survey of M. Benedictus regarding the experiences of the Jews of Belgium during the war years, until September 1943, Archive Record Group O.29, File No. 17, Document Number 98, Yad Vashem.

[109] For the notice on the refusal of Joseph Teichmann, see AJB central board meeting, 25 November 1941, 497/146 666, DOS.

confident about their leadership. We will see that this eventually resulted in resignations from the organisation's central board.

Opposition to the Jewish Organisations

The nature of the JR, the AJB, the UGIF-Nord and the UGIF-Sud was such that their leaders received criticism. Their function as spokespersons while also cooperating with the Germans led to disagreement, protest and anger among the Jewish communities. In all three countries, people seemed to feel that it was wrong to comply with the German demand of establishing a Jewish representative organisation in the first place. At the same time, many understood the motives of the central board members for taking up their role, especially when the needs of the Jewish populations increased. This ambivalence was inherent in the way the Jewish organisations in all three western European countries were perceived.

Criticism prevailed at all levels of society. The intensity and degree of these criticisms changed during the war and, naturally, the perception of these Jewish organisations varied from person to person. During the course of the occupation, in the case of the Netherlands, the Jewish Council popularly came to be referred to as Jewish treason (*verraad*) or trouble (*onraad*). This was in response to the chairmen's agreement, in early 1942, to hand the Germans over a list of the names of unmarried men between the ages of eighteen to forty for work-camps in the Netherlands in order to 'forestall disruptions as far as possible'.[110] Mirjam Bolle-Levie, secretary of the JR, alluded to a joke that was common among Jews in the Netherlands, highlighting that its leaders were considered too cooperative with German authorities: the Germans summon Asscher and Cohen and inform them that the Jews will be gassed, to which Cohen immediately responds 'do you deliver the gas, or are we responsible for doing so?'.[111]

Disapproval of the Dutch Council was voiced most powerfully by Lodewijk Visser, President of the Dutch Supreme Court, and head of the Jewish Coordinating Committee. Unlike the chairmen of the Jewish Council, Visser refused to cooperate with the German occupier and tried

---

[110] Minutes of Council meeting, 3 March 1942, 182, Inv. No. 3, NIOD as cited in Moore, *Victims and Survivors*, 86–87.

[111] Mirjam Bolle, *'Ik zal je beschrijven hoe een dag er hier uit ziet': Dagboekbrieven uit Amsterdam, Westerbork en Bergen-Belsen* (Amsterdam/Antwerp: Uitgeverij Contact, 2005; first ed. 2003), 123. This 'diary' consists of letters that Mirjam Levie wrote to her fiancé Leo Bolle who resided in Palestine while she was in Amsterdam during the German occupation of the Netherlands. The letters were never sent but were published in 2003, and provide Mirjam Levie's detailed reflections on the activities of the Council and the choices of its leadership. An English translation was published in 2014, see Mirjam Bolle, *Letters Never Sent: Amsterdam, Westerbork, Bergen-Belsen*, transl. Laura Vroomen (Jerusalem: Yad Vashem, 2014).

instead to serve the interests of the Jews by pressuring Dutch authorities into action. Even though the Coordinating Committee and the Jewish Council initially cooperated, Visser thus had a different outlook on Jewish leaders' most appropriate and meaningful attitude during the occupation.

The different approaches of Visser and Council chairman Cohen are underlined in the letters they exchanged after the Coordinating Committee was dissolved in October 1941.[112] Visser strongly disagreed with the decrees that the Jewish Council had complied with, most notably the one that resulted in Jews no longer being allowed to address the Dutch government on their own account.[113] Moreover, as he wrote to Cohen, he believed that the Council chairmen's strategy had proven unsuccessful; they had not been able to negotiate any meaningful concessions through their cooperation.[114] As a result, Visser believed, the Council had lost its dignity. In the following months, Visser protested against the introduction of new anti-Jewish laws and, despite the prohibition to do so, continued to seek contact with Dutch authorities (the Secretaries-General), much to the dismay of Cohen.[115]

Visser was not the only prominent individual who openly disagreed with the Jewish Council. Isaac Kisch and Herman Frijda, for example, had also distanced themselves from the organisation, yet these were all personal efforts and they had little impact. This was underlined by Joop Voet, whose father, Herman Isidore (Ies) Voet, was member of the Council's central board: 'the biggest problem was that there were no individuals of authority who were able, and dared, to withstand Asscher and Cohen and their associates'.[116] Unlike the situation in Belgium and France, during the period of the Dutch Council's establishment as well as in the years that followed, there was never an organised anti-movement that provided an alternative to the strategy of the JR.

[112] For the letters that were exchanged between Visser and Cohen, see 248–1798A, Lodewijk Ernst Visser, Inv. No. 14, NIOD. After the war, Cohen reflected on the differences of opinion between Visser and himself in various documents he sent to his defense lawyers between 18 December 1947 and 25 September 1949, see 181j, Inv. No. 11, NIOD.
[113] Letter Visser to Cohen, 18 November 1941, 248–1798A, Inv. No. 14, NIOD.
[114] Letter Visser to Cohen, 30 December 1941, 248–1798A, Inv. No. 14, NIOD.
[115] Letter Cohen to Visser, 20 December 1941, 248–1798A, Inv. No. 14, NIOD. The following month, Visser again approached Dutch Secretary–General Karel Frederiks, which angered Hans Böhmcker. In response, Böhmcker urged the Jewish Council chairmen to inform Visser he would be sent to a concentration camp if we would again seek contact with Dutch authorities. Cohen followed up on this request, which deeply affected Visser. See Letter of the Jewish Council to Visser, 13 February 1942, 248–1798A, Inv. No. 19, NIOD; Letter Visser to the Jewish Council, 14 February 1942, 248–1798A, Inv. No. 19, NIOD. Visser wrote an extensive report on his personal efforts to minimise the impact of German regulations, see Report of L.E. Visser, 11 December 1941, Doc. 00003185, Joods Museum.
[116] Reflection Joop Voet on the Jewish Council, autumn 1942, Inv. No. 14, 249–0366A, NIOD.

In France, by contrast, there were strong voices of protest against the establishment of the UGIF. Opposition took various (organised) forms and was expressed on different levels. The Jewish communists, who radically opposed the UGIF, remained completely underground and published illegal newspapers in which the organisation's members were referred to as 'little brown Jews', a reference to the Sturmabteilung uniform, and were accused of helping the Germans to organise deportations.[117] Moreover, in the period prior to and after the institution of the UGIF in November 1941, there was strong opposition between the Consistory and the UGIF central board, which lasted for a year.[118]

Helbronner, who became president of the Consistory in 1940, indicated he did not want to be involved in the establishment of the UGIF and openly objected to the course taken by Lambert, fearing that the UGIF would result in the formation of a ghetto.[119] More broadly, leaders of the Consistory objected to the principle of a mandatory organisation because it would place French and foreign Jews in the same group; it would 'implicitly replace the religious definition of a Jew with a racial one, and further widen the gap that each new antisemitic measure was creating between French Jews and their non-Jewish compatriots'.[120] In short, it would separate French Jews from their fellow Frenchmen. The UGIF leadership believed this approach could not be maintained in the context of the antisemitic government decrees of October 1940 and June 1941. As Lambert wrote in his diary on 30 November 1941: 'The Union des Juifs [Union of Jews] will be created with us, without us, or against us'.[121]

The official stance of the Consistory in relation to the UGIF remained deliberately critical. It thereby functioned as a check on the UGIF and provided an alternate source of authority. In his diary entry of 29 March 1942, Lambert compared himself to Léon Blum in 1936, who faced scepticism when he tried to forestall the hatred of the far Right: 'The very wealthy Jews, who are the majority of the Consistory, are afraid the *Union* will make them pay too much for the poor [...] What a sad, confused mentality!'[122] While concerns about the role of the Jewish

---

[117] Annette Wieviorka, *Ils étaient juifs, résistants, communistes* (Paris: Denoël, 1986), 76. For further reading on the protests against the UGIF, see, for example Rayski, *The Choice of the Jews under Vichy*, 58–59, 63–71.

[118] For an overview of the tensions between the two organisations and Helbronner and Lambert specifically in this period, see Cohen, 'Le Consistoire et l'UGIF: La situation trouble des Juifs Français face à Vichy', 28–33; Laffitte, *Juif dans la France allemande*, 46–50.

[119] Szajowski, 'The Organization of the "UGIF" in Nazi-Occupied France', 247; Cohen, *The Burden of Conscience*, 57.

[120] Poznanski, *Jews in France during World War II*, 133.

[121] Lambert, *Diary of a Witness*, 30 November 1941, 76.

[122] Ibid., 29 March 1942, 112.

organisations were raised in all three countries, it was only in France that the level of criticism and discontent was voiced in such an intense and organised manner. Although the power of the Consistory had been fading, the impact of its negative view on the UGIF should not be underestimated, as it had the means and power to frustrate the actions of the organisation. After the German occupation of the south of France in November 1942, the two bodies grew closer to one another and the Consistory acknowledged the value of the UGIF's work to relieve the hardship of the Jews. The deterioration of both of their financial situations furthermore brought the two organisations closer together.[123]

In Belgium, the establishment of the AJB also provoked discussion among Jews. However, the debates between opponents and supporters seemed not so bitter, and did not materialise on such a personal level as they did in the Netherlands and France. While Asscher and Cohen, for example, were often perceived as arrogant, the general unwillingness of the AJB leadership to take up the positions they were assigned probably contributed to less outrage in this regard. The highly decentralised nature of the Belgian Jewish communities undoubtedly played a role here as well. Moreover, whereas in France the Consistory was a strong opponent of the UGIF, the withering of Consistorial power in Belgium combined with Chief Rabbi Ullman's chairmanship of the organisation meant that the AJB never faced the same level of organised protest from a traditional (religious) leadership. Still, anti-AJB attitudes existed. The Belgian Communist Party opposed the AJB and accused the organisation of 'playing cards with the Nazis',[124] while the left-wing Socialist-Zionists appealed to the Jewish people to 'defend its human and national honour', encouraging them not to participate in the mission the AJB represented.[125] We will see that other organisations, including the Jewish Defence Committee, also advised Jews to ignore the regulations of the AJB.[126]

Criticisms of the Jewish leaders were also voiced by the organisations' own members. In France, for example, one month after the liberation of the country, Joseph Lehman, the director of the UGIF-Sud Marseille branch, denounced the actions of Gaston Kahn, interim director of the UGIF-Sud, in the *Notre Voix* newspaper (a French edition of the Yiddish newspaper *Unzer Wort*, which had been published clandestinely since

---

[123] Laffitte, *Juif dans la France allemande*, 212–213; Cohen, 'Le consistoire et l'UGIF: La situation trouble des Juifs Français face à Vichy', 33.
[124] *Temps Nouveaux*, 20 December 1941, p. 7.
[125] *Unzer Wort*, December 1941, No. 1 as cited in Steinberg, 'Three Strategies for Coping with a Tragedy', in *Belgium and the Holocaust*, 362.
[126] Bob Moore, 'Integrating Self-Help into the History of Jewish Survival in Western Europe', Norman J. W. Goda (ed.), *Jewish Histories of the Holocaust: New Transnational Approaches* (New York/Oxford: Berghahn Books, 2014), 196.

June 1940). In Lehman's view, Kahn had failed to prevent the deportation of Jewish children, knowing full well their destination. He claimed that the UGIF never fought against the orders of Vichy or Gestapo officials and instead followed such orders faithfully.[127]

In the Netherlands, Gertrude van Tijn, who headed the Aid to those Departing department of the Jewish Council, highlighted in a report written in 1944 that there were several occasions on which the other central board members showed their discontent with the decisions taken by Asscher and Cohen. For example, on 4 July 1942 there was a meeting of the entire JR central board after the Germans had announced that Jews would be called upon to work in Germany. The task of the JR was to ensure that Jews would report themselves when they received a call to report themselves for 'work in the East'. According to Van Tijn, the meeting became heated: 'many of us thought the Jewish Council should refuse to cooperate in what we rightly assumed to be the beginning of the deportations'.[128] Despite these differences of opinion, however, most central board members in the end formally continued to support the choices of the Councils' chairmen. Above all, the criticisms were not sufficient to make Asscher and Cohen alter their decisions or rethink their position at the helm of the JR. As Mirjam Levie wrote in an unsent letter to her fiancé, Cohen listened to (objections of) the board members but in the end acted the way he wanted.[129] In a post-war interview, she claimed that even though other board members at times voiced their uncertainty about increasing German demands, Asscher and Cohen had often already agreed to cooperate.[130]

Resign or Remain? Jewish Leaders
Faced with a Difficult Choice

The socio-historical foundations of the JR, the AJB, the UGIF-Nord and the UGIF-Sud central boards affected how the organisations' leaders understood their role and the extent of representation they were to offer. Whereas the JR chairmen decided to remain in place until the Council was dissolved in September 1943, despite the challenging context of occupation in which they operated (with a strong presence of the SS) we will see that Salomon Ullmann and Maurice Benedictus in Belgium voluntarily

---

[127] Excerpts of article in *Notre Voix* republished in *La Presse Nouvelle*, 27 September 1944, No. 4, CMXXV-23, Mémorial de la Shoah.

[128] Van Tijn, 'Bijdrage tot de Geschiedenis der Joden in Nederland', Palestine, Nahariah (1944), p. 48, Doc. 1 248-1720 Inv. No. 1, NIOD.

[129] Bolle, *'Ik zal je beschrijven hoe een dag er hier uit ziet'*, 58.

[130] Mirjam Bolle-Levie in an interview with Johannes Houwink ten Cate, 17 September 2003, Doc. I 248-2366, M. Bolle-Levie, Inv. No. 2, NIOD.

withdrew from their positions. The situation was different again in France, where the first chairmen – Lambert of the UGIF-Sud and Baur of the UGIF-Nord – were forcibly removed from their chairmanship by the Germans. In both Belgium and France, the removals necessitated the appointment of new leaders. In addition, substantial parts of the Belgian and French central boards were replaced during the occupation.

The composition of the JR central board also changed over the course of its existence. Whereas some Jews were arrested, others, including Krouwer and Van Lier, were forced to resign because they were not considered so-called full Jews (*Volljuden*), meaning they did not have three or four Jewish grandparents.[131] Both Kisch and Kan raised moral objections and, in September 1941 and February 1942 respectively, refused to work for the JR any longer.[132] Because Asscher and Cohen maintained their solid position in the central board and, despite regular consultations with other board members, exercised their authority when decisions had to be taken, the replacement of these members did not make a real difference to the functioning of the JR. By contrast, during the transitional phase that followed the replacement of board members of the AJB, the UGIF-Nord and the UGIF-Sud, the level of continuity that characterised the JR could not be maintained. As a result, throughout the occupation, the position of the Dutch Council was different from that of its counterparts.

The decision on whether to resign or remain depended on the way Jewish leaders perceived their own positions and strategies. David Cohen never seemed to question his own tactics of cooperation. While he generally aimed to convince prominent members of the Amsterdam Jewish community of the importance and usefulness of the JR, he was open to receive criticism on rare occasions. In early January 1942, for example, he asked for the opinions of those present (including lawyer Marius Levenbach and teacher and historian Jacques Presser) on the impact of the Council's policies. Although Presser indicated after the war that it was a one-sided exposé of the political directions of the JR, the urge Cohen felt to convince others about his policies, as well as his quest for their opinions, does suggest his feelings of vulnerability in regard to the choices that were being made. At the same time, he never truly reconsidered his policies.[133]

---

[131] Somers, *Voorzitter van de Joodse Raad*, 83 n.75.
[132] The JR central board discussed the resignation of both men during their meetings; see Meeting report of the Joodsche Raad, 29 September 1941, 182, Inv. No. 3, NIOD; Meeting report of the Joodsche Raad, 25 February 1942, 182, Inv. No. 3, NIOD.
[133] Statement of Marius Levenbach, 21 January 1948, dossier Asscher and Cohen, CABR, Access No. 2.09.09, Inv. No. 107491 III (PF Amsterdam T70982), NA; Statement of Jacob (Jacques) Presser, 19 January 1948, dossier Asscher and Cohen, CABR, Access No. 2.09.09, Inv. No. 107491 III (PF Amsterdam T70982), NA.

Asscher seemed to harbour more serious doubts about the course of the JR and about his own role in this process. For example, he proposed the dissolution of the JR on 12 June 1941 because there had been a mass arrest of Jews shortly before. The Jewish leaders had demanded they would be informed about upcoming raids ever since the first mass arrest on 22 and 23 February 1941 in Amsterdam, during which around 400 Jewish men were arrested. Out of this group, 389 were deported to Buchenwald concentration camp, and while dozens of them died of maltreatment and inhuman living conditions, others were transported to Mauthausen in May 1941.[134] Reports of the death of these young and healthy men soon reached the Netherlands, causing unrest among the Jews.

Rather than keeping their promise not to undertake another mass arrest without the JR's knowledge, SD officials arranged a meeting with Asscher and Cohen under false pretences on 11 June 1941. While the Jewish leaders were kept in the office of the SD for hours, more than 200 Jews were arrested.[135] The next day, Asscher's proposal to dissolve the Council was rejected during the meeting of the central board, with only one vote in favour of his plan.[136]

Asscher's proposal to dissolve the Council hints at his uncertainty about the role and function of the JR. Similar to his co-chairman David Cohen, he remained in place until the Council was dissolved, yet the two men had a rather different outlook on their responsibilities throughout the occupation. In fact, the personalities of Asscher and Cohen differed to a great extent. Herman Cohen, son of David Cohen, indicated in a post-war interview that the chairmen respected each other greatly, but that they often disagreed when decisions had to be taken. In his view, Asscher, owing to his (pre-war) position in society (as we have seen, he held important positions in both the Jewish and the non-Jewish communities), felt compelled to take on the role of JR chairman.

---

[134] Kirsten Snijders, *Nederlanders in Buchenwald, 1940–1945: een overzicht over de geschiedenis van Nederlandse gevangenen die tijdens de nationaal-socialistische bezetting van 1940–1945 in het concentratiekamp Buchenwald zaten* (Göttingen: Wallstein, 2001); Hans de Vries, 'Sie starben wie Fliegen im Herbst' in Hans de Vries (ed.), *Mauthausen: 1938–1988* (Bredevoort: Achterland, 2000), 7–18. For a detailed study of the fate of these men, see Wally de Lang, *De razzia's van 22 en 23 februari 1941 in Amsterdam: Het lot van 389 Joodse mannen* (Amsterdam: Atlas Contact, 2021).

[135] Cohen, *Voorzitter van de Joodse Raad*, 103–106.

[136] It should be noted that the report of this meeting, cited in, for example, De Jong, *Het Koninkrijk*, Vol. 5, 550 and Somers, 'Kanttekeningen bij de Joodse Raad' in *Voorzitter van de Joodse Raad*, 30 cannot be found in the archives of the JR stored at NIOD. Nevertheless, there are several sources that confirm that this meeting took place, see: Letter of Prof. Mr. I. Kisch (member of the Council's central board) to David Cohen, 21 September 1941, Doc. I 248-0895A, Inv. No. 4, NIOD; 'Nota over mijn pogingen betreffende de Joodsche gijzelaars', p. 4, mr. L.E. Visser, Doc. I 248-1798A, Inv. No. 9, NIOD.

Cohen, by contrast, agreed to chair the JR because he was convinced that the work he was doing was useful and important for the Jewish communities.[137] These differences materialised in the ways both men administered the Council. As Cohen wrote in his memoirs, the day-to-day governance of the organisation was in his (Cohen's) hands; Asscher did not interfere with individual departments and he was hardly involved when important decisions had to be taken.[138] In a post-war report on her work for the JR, former secretary Mirjam Bolle-Levie also emphasised Cohen was in charge when decisions had to be taken – 'he really was a despot' – and that Asscher often played only a secondary role.[139] Above all, however, even though Asscher was less involved in the decision-making processes and occasionally seemed to question the course the JR was taking, he continued to operate alongside Cohen.

On 27 June 1942, another occasion arose on which the JR leadership questioned whether the continued existence of the JR would serve the interests of Jews in the Netherlands. The day before, SS-Hauptsturm-führer aus der Fünten had communicated to Cohen, Abraham de Hoop, head of the Lijnbaansgracht department, and Edwin Sluzker, head of the Expositur, a department of the JR where the registration of so-called *Sperren* (exemptions from deportation) were processed, that all Jewish men and women between the ages of eighteen and forty would be subject to work under police supervision (*Polizeiliche Arbeitseinsatz*). Although this disturbing new regulation caused unrest among the other board members, Cohen decided in the end to continue the activities of the JR, fearing that the Germans would otherwise turn to violent measures to secure the implementation of the measure.[140]

Historian Nanda van der Zee strongly disapproved of the Council leaders' choices to maintain their tactics of cooperation, claiming that they had primarily given in to German demands in order to protect their own livelihoods, and those of their families.[141] However, similar to other historians who approached the Council from a moral perspective, she failed to see the larger context from which it emerged. Sustained by the idea that they were the most suitable representatives of the Jewish communities in the Netherlands, and that they could still provide support

---

[137] Herman Cohen in *Het fatale dilemma*, 39. Also see Erik Somers, 'David Cohen: een biografische schets', in *Voorzitter van de Joodse Raad*, 19.

[138] Cohen, *Voorzitter van de Joodse Raad*, 195.

[139] Report of Mirjam Bolle-Levie concerning her work for the Committee for Jewish Refugees and the Jewish Council, 12 August 1999, p. 8–9, Doc. I 248-A2366, NIOD.

[140] Cohen, *Voorzitter van de Joodse Raad*, 133–136; Berkley, *Overzicht van het ontstaan*, 67–69.

[141] Van der Zee, *Om erger te voorkomen*, 138.

and alleviate the suffering of the Jews, both men decided to stay at the helm of the Council. Until after the war, Cohen remained convinced of the strength and quality of his leadership.

Former Jewish leaders from across the European continent generally either remained silent about their wartime activities, or could no longer comment upon their role because they had been murdered. By contrast, Cohen did not show any reluctance to discuss his choices after the war. On various occasions, he explicitly indicated that he still approved of the choices he had made during the war.[142] At the same time, though, his letter to James G. McDonald, former League of Nations High Commissioner for Refugees, indicates that even though he considered he 'acted in the right way', he also made it clear that if he had ever learned about the fate of those who had been deported (he was adamant that he did not), he would have resigned immediately.[143] The attitude of the JR leadership bears a resemblance to that of Benjamin Murmelstein, who served as head of the Jewish Council in Theresienstadt from November 1944 onwards. Murmelstein was criticised by many after the war for being a collaborator. In a post-war interview with Claude Lanzmann, Murmelstein indicated he had tried to maintain the Theresienstadt ghetto and compared himself to Sancho Panza, 'a pragmatic and calculating realist' who achieved more than Don Quixote, who continued to fight a useless battle.[144]

In Belgium, chairman Ullmann was not the absolute ruler of the AJB. Instead, he was quickly overpowered by the members of the central board. Rather than being personally involved in issues related to the functioning of the AJB, Ullmann seemed to function more as a symbolic figurehead, distanced from the realities of leadership. In the context of scattered Jewish communities that could not be easily united and the general reluctance to head the AJB, Ullmann fulfilled his position very different from that of his Dutch counterparts. On 8 September 1942, supposedly because he felt he could not continue to fulfil his position 'to the satisfaction of superior authorities (the Germans)', Ullmann 'politely requested' von Falkenhausen, the Military Commander of Belgium and Northern France, that he be allowed to resign from his position.[145] A letter from von Falkenhausen

---

[142] See, for example, David Cohen, 'Geschiedenis der Joden in Nederland tijdens de bezetting', 18 August–5 September 1945, pp. 1, 13, 181j, Inv. No. 10, NIOD; Mirjam Bolle-Levie in *Het fatale dilemma*, 99.

[143] Lehmann papers (Columbia Papers, New York), James G McDonald Papers G.70 'C'. Cohen to McDonald, 27 December 1953 as cited in: Moore, *Victims and Survivors*, 248.

[144] Benjamin Murmelstein – Therensienstadt Judenälteste, United States Holocaust Memorial Museum (USHMM) Film, Accession Number: 1996, 166 RG-60.5009.

[145] Letter of resignation Salomon Ullmann, 8 September 1942, AA MIC/41, CEGESOMA.

sent to the AJB on 28 December 1942 shows that only three and a half months later, the Military Commander of Belgium and Northern France officially approved Ullmann's resignation.[146] In the meantime, Ullmann therefore continued to serve as the AJB's official chairman.

In this period, members of the AJB central board were personally targeted for persecution. On 24 September 1942, SS-Obersturmführer Kurt Asche sent Ullmann, van den Berg, Blum, Hellendall and Benedictus to Fort Breendonk, a prison and police detainment camp (*Auffangslager*) where conditions were similar to those of a concentration camp.[147] Here, they were told they would be interned until all Jews had been evacuated from Belgium. They were accused, among other things, of passive resistance, acts of sabotage and seeking contact with the Belgian queen.[148] Eduard Rotkel, a Hungarian Jew, was arrested as well and immediately sent to SS-Sammellager Mechelen (Kazerne Dossin), from where he was deported to Auschwitz.[149]

Salomon van den Berg described these days in the camp as a traumatic experience; after not having eaten for two days, they had to consume 'infected soup with white cabbage'.[150] Thereafter, they were locked with many others in tiny rooms. The conditions during internment were inhumane. The work they were forced to do was physically exhausting 'especially for a Chief Rabbi', and they were beaten if the work was not done fast enough.[151] Ullmann's traditional beard was cut and people were surprised to see this prominent Jew interned.[152] On 3 October, the AJB leadership was released as a result of interventions by the Militärverwaltungschef Eggert Reeder.[153]

In the existing literature, Ullmann's decision to resign as AJB chairman has been understood either in the context of his experiences in Breendonk (which is inaccurate, taken into consideration that Ullmann sent his letter

---

[146] Letter of the head of the Military Administration to the AJB, concerning the demission of Salomon Ullmann, 28 December 1942, A006900, JMDV, CNHEJ, Buber Collection, Kazerne Dossin.

[147] Patrick Nefors, *Breendonk 1940–1945: de geschiedenis* (Antwerp: Standaard Uitgeverij, 2011; first ed. 2004), 24–25.

[148] Report on the arrest of Ullmann, van den Berg, Blum, Hellendall and Benedictus and their stay in police detention camp Breendonk from 24 September 1942 until 3 October 1942, AA MIC/41, CEGESOMA. Also see Van Doorslaer, 'Salomon van den Berg', 127–130.

[149] For a thorough overview of the nature of this camp, and life inside it, see Laurence Schram, *Dossin: l'antichambre d'Auschwitz* (Brussels: Éditions Racine, 2017).

[150] Salomon van den Berg, 'Journal de guerre', p. 65, A006685, JMDV, CNHEJ, Buber Collection, Kazerne Dossin.

[151] Ibid.

[152] For van den Berg's description of the entire course of events during their internment in Fort Breendonk, see ibid., 57–73.

[153] Van Doorslaer, 'Salomon van den Berg', 129.

of resignation before he was interned) or as a response to the mass raids of August 1942.[154] However, the reality was more complex. His resignation should be understood against the background of a combination of factors that include his initial reluctance to become Chief Rabbi and his intrinsic belief that he could not represent the Jews in Belgium. The increasing German pressure on the organisation, the mass arrests and the indignity with which he had been treated also played a role. As we shall see, after the raids in August and September 1942, Belgian and Jewish resistance became more organised and provided alternatives to the AJB. This undermined and weakened the AJB's position, and this may have strengthened Ullmann's notion that his organisation was no longer of use to the Jews.[155]

The role that Ullmann continued to play in the Jewish community as Chief Rabbi from his resignation onwards has been entirely neglected, perhaps because he himself claimed that he had not been in contact with the organisation after he resigned.[156] The exchange of letters between the AJB Antwerp branch and Ullmann nevertheless shows that he remained tied to the organisation. For example, on 6 May 1943, a letter he sent to the administration of the AJB Antwerp branch highlights how he encouraged the AJB to provide care to a woman named De Leeuw, whose husband had died in Breendonk and who had no family to support her.[157] In turn, the AJB depended upon Ullmann's support, for example to ensure the provision of parcels to individuals in the internment camp of Rekem. Ullmann replied to the AJB Antwerp leadership's request that he was taking care of the situation in Rekem, but that the internees themselves had already sent 'hundreds of begging letters', and that there were some who were receiving between five and ten parcels a week.[158]

Ullmann's resignation did not have direct consequences for him personally. He was neither punished nor deported. In fact, he continued to fulfill his position as Chief Rabbi of Belgium. Nevertheless, he indicated

[154] For an overview of existing literature that explains Ullmann's resignation primarily in response to the raids of August 1942 or his internment in Breendonk, see Schreiber, *Dictionnaire Biographique*, 343–344; van Doorslaer and Schreiber, 'Inleiding', in van Doorslaer and Schreiber, *De curatoren van het getto*, 8; Van Doorslaer, 'Salomon van den Berg', 126; Steinberg, *L'étoile et le fusil: Les cent jours de la déportation*, 52–54.

[155] Steinberg, *L'étoile et le fusil: Les cent jours de la déportation*, 223–226; and *La Persécution des Juifs en Belgique*, 180–181; Meinen, 'De Duitse bezettingsautoriteiten en de VJB', 55–56.

[156] Report by Salomon Ullmann 'L'Activité de l'Association des Juifs en Belgique', undated, AA MIC/41, CEGESOMA.

[157] Letter from Ullmann to the AJB Antwerp branch, 6 May 1943, A003931.1, JMDV, Musée National de la Résistance (MNR), Kazerne Dossin.

[158] Letter from the AJB leadership to Salomon Ullmann, 13 May 1943, A003934.1, JMDV, MNR, Kazerne Dossin; Letter from Salomon Ullmann to the Antwerp branch of the AJB, 16 May 1943, A00395.1, JMDV, MNR, Kazerne Dossin.

in a post-war report on the activities of the AJB that the Military Administration had accepted his resignation reluctantly.[159] This reluctance is highlighted by the months it took Alexander von Falkenhausen to accept Ullmann's resignation officially. The lack of potential successors, due to the Jewish leadership vacuum that existed in the country, undoubtedly played a role here.

In addition to Ullmann, Maurice Benedictus, who occupied a central position in the AJB, also became uncertain about his position and the responsibilities that were forced upon him. From the beginning, his role had been complicated and laden with uncertainty. In summer 1942, Benedictus was appointed as the chief individual responsible for the forced labour of Jews in Eastern Europe, and soon became conscience-stricken. In his memoirs, he wrote that some of his colleagues considered him a traitor while others understood his attempt to lighten the burden on the Jewish communities. Benedictus claimed he tried to deal with this difficult task, knowing about the situation in the Netherlands, where the JR had taken up similar responsibilities.[160] Testimonies show that he discussed his difficult position with others, including prominent people in the Belgian resistance.[161]

At the end of 1942, a new threshold was crossed when SS-Obersturmführer Kurt Asche announced that from 1943 onwards, Belgian Jews would be deported alongside immigrant Jews. In doing so, he deliberately thwarted the Military Administration. Wilhelm von Hahn, liaison officer for the AJB at the Military Administration, had promised AJB representatives that he would speak to Asche about arranging a higher level of protection for the AJB leaders and their families. In response, the AJB leaders encouraged those close to them not to go into hiding.[162] However, Asche still decided to deport Belgian Jews. As a result, Benedictus felt he could no longer help the Jewish communities in his role as the AJB's leader. In the second week of December 1942, he embarked on a difficult journey and managed to reach Portugal via France and Spain, where he arrived in January 1943. He returned to Belgium in September 1945.[163]

---

[159] Report by Salomon Ullmann 'L'Activité de l'Association des Juifs en Belgique', undated, AA MIC/41, CEGESOMA.
[160] Maurice Benedictus, 'Historique du problème Juif en Belgique depuis le 10 Mai 1940 jusqu'au 21 Décembre 1942', 18 February 1943, pp. 13–14, A006683, JMDV, CHNEJ, Buber Collection, Kazerne Dossin.
[161] Witness account of Pierre Bolotius, No. 8036 N 1944, Algemeen Rijksarchief Brussel, Krijgsauditoraat.
[162] Report of Rosenfeld concerning his meeting with SS-Obersturmführer Asche on 10 and 14 November 1942, R486/Tr146.666, DOS.
[163] Van Doorslaer, 'Salomon van den Berg', 128; Griffioen and Zeller, *Jodenvervolging in Nederland, Frankrijk en België*, 620; Saerens, *Vreemdelingen in een wereldstad*,

In the meantime, the replacement of Ullmann and Benedictus spawned debate between representatives of the AJB, the Military Administration and the SiPo-SD. Members of the AJB central board proposed Machel Majer Grätzer, originally from Poland and chairman of the representative body of the Israelite communities in Antwerp.[164] Kurt Asche was strongly opposed to the appointment of a Polish Jew and opted for a German candidate instead, most likely because this would have eased communication with the AJB. He proposed Felix Meyer and Louis Rosenfeld, both German Jews. After the interference of Salomon Ullmann and Gerard Romsée, secretary-general of the collaborationist Flemish National Union (Vlaams Nationaal Verbond), the Military Administration voiced its objections to Asche's proposal and argued that a Belgian Jew should take up the position of leader.

In response, the AJB central committee suggested Salomon van den Berg, representative of the AJB Brussels branch, but SS-Hauptsturmführer Fritz Erdmann, Asche's successor as *Judenreferent* for Belgium (serving under the direct responsibility of Eichmann's RSHA in Berlin), rejected this proposal.[165] In December 1942, the SiPo-SD, the Military Administration and the AJB representatives finally agreed that Ullmann would be succeeded by Marcel Blum (illustration 3.7), who served on the board of the Israelite congregation in Brussels and held Belgian citizenship. As a compromise, Meyer and Rosenfeld were appointed as members of the AJB central board and local Charleroi branch respectively.[166]

Four months after Benedictus' flight abroad, Salomon van den Berg replaced him at the head of the administrative section of the AJB (in April

---

505; Schreiber, *Dictionnaire Biographique*, 48. In Portugal, Benedictus wrote several reports on the occupation of Belgium and the catastrophe that had befallen the Jews, including 'Historique du problème juif en Belgique depuis le 10 mai 1940 jusqu'au 31 décembre 1942'. It is not known exactly how Benedictus managed to reach Portugal. His name is neither mentioned in the archives of the Belgian Legation in Lisbon, nor in the archives of the Belgian ambassador, nor in the reports of Belgians who were trying to learn the fate of Belgian refugees in Portugal. He is not listed on the lists of incoming refugees, and he did not refer to his journey in the report he wrote in Lisbon on the Jews in Belgium during the war. Maurice Benedictus, 'Historique du problème Juif en Belgique depuis le 10 Mai 1940 jusqu'au 21 Décembre 1942', 18 February 1943, A006683, JMDV, CNHEJ, Buber Collection, Kazerne Dossin.

[164] Meeting report of the AJB central committee, 29 October 1942, A006745, JMDV, CNHEJ, Buber Collection, Kazerne Dossin. Also see Steinberg, *L'étoile et le fusil: Les cent jours de la déportation*, 52–54.

[165] Meeting report of the AJB central committee, 26 November 1942, A006740, JMDV, CNHEJ, Buber Collection, Kazerne Dossin.

[166] Meeting report of the AJB central committee, 3 December 1942, A007146, JMDV, CNHEJ, Buber Collection, Kazerne Dossin; Steinberg, *L'étoile et le fusil: Les cent jours de la déportation*, 115; Meinen, 'De Duitse bezettingsautoriteiten en de VJB', 54–55.

Illustration 3.7 Marcel Blum, chairman of the AJB from 1942. Reproduced by the kind permission of Musée Juif de Belgique/Joods Museum van België.

1943). In March 1944, Van den Berg became the organisation's vice-chairman. Unlike his colleagues at the AJB central board, Van den Berg did not feel inclined to resign from his position. His diary shows that he was convinced that it was in the interest of the Jewish communities in Belgium to remain in place, and he showed little understanding for the criticisms that were raised regarding the Jewish leaders' cooperation with the Germans.

Throughout the occupation, Van den Berg, similar to Asscher and Cohen in the Netherlands, remained convinced that the legal position taken by the AJB leadership was most effective, and he resented any form of illegal activity that might endanger the existence of this body. Despite some doubts as to whether or not he should go into hiding towards the end of 1943, when an operation was launched against all Jews with Belgian citizenship and many were arrested (Operation Iltis), van den Berg eventually decided to remain in place until the end of the occupation.[167]

Other members of the AJB central board *were* replaced, either because they had been arrested or because they no longer wished to fulfil their representative function. For example, Juda Mehlwurm, the Charleroi

---

[167] For further reading on Van den Berg (and his wartime diary), see Van Doorslaer, 'Salomon van den Berg', 111–145. Van den Berg's diary can be consulted at Kazerne Dossin (A006685).

representative on the AJB, had gone into hiding in September 1942 after the Germans had asked him for an updated list of Jews resident in the city.[168] Eugène Hellendall and his wife were arrested because they had left their home on 23 October 1942 without wearing the yellow star.[169] Neither his Belgian citizenship nor his position in the AJB could help Hellendall. Most likely, the 'passive resistance' for which he was interned in Breendonk played a role in his arrest as well. All these events – the resignations of central board members and the quests for successors – weakened the AJB.

In France, the first general director of the UGIF, Albert Lévy, fled to Switzerland in December 1942 in order to avoid persecution.[170] UGIF-Sud chairman Lambert, in turn, was forcibly withdrawn from the central board because he refused to cooperate with increasing German demands. Throughout 1943, SS-Hauptsturmführer Aloïs Brunner increased the pressure on Jewish society by his brutal actions and by the continuous arrests taking place throughout France. For Lambert, the measures were too much to accept and he spoke out against the direction of events. On 16 May 1943, he wrote in his diary that it had been 'a month of anxiety, or ordeals and actions difficult to carry out'.[171] He objected in particular to the increasing anti-Jewish measures taken by the Gestapo in the weeks preceding his arrest.

In spring 1943, Lambert, as well as Baur and Marcel Stora, negotiated with the SS about the 'redundancy' of foreign employees of the UGIF, whose removal they were not able to prevent. As a result of his attempts to negotiate with the Germans, combined with the objections he was increasingly voicing, Lambert was arrested on 21 August 1943 and interned in Drancy, together with his wife and their four children. Other UGIF central board members who had tried to negotiate with the Germans were arrested as well, including André Lazard and Marcel Stora.[172]

In the UGIF-Nord, in contrast to the JR, the AJB and the UGIF-Sud, none of the central board members voluntarily resigned or fled abroad.

---

[168] André Donnet, 'Het onderzoek door het militaire gerecht: het geheugen buitenspel gezet', in van Doorslaer and Schreiber, De curatoren van het getto, 299; Meinen, De Shoah in België, 89.

[169] Report of conversation between Kurt Asche and Noé Nozyce on the latter's (unsuccessful) intervention on behalf of Eugène Hellendall and his family, 27 October 1942, A007424, JMDV, CNHEJ, Buber Collection, Kazerne Dossin; Letter from Noé Nozyce to Maurice Benedictus, 28 October 1952, A007425, JMDV, CNHEJ, Buber Collection, Kazerne Dossin.

[170] Laffitte, 'l'UGIF, collaboration ou résistance?', 57; Marrus, 'Jewish Leadership and the Holocaust: The Case of France', 786.

[171] Lambert, Diary of a Witness, 16 May 1943, 178.

[172] Laffitte, 'Between Memory and Lapse of Memory', 682.

However, as in the case of Lambert in the unoccupied zone of France, important members of the organisation refused to cooperate with increasing German demands and were forcibly removed from the central board: André Baur, Marcel Stora and Fernand Musnik were deported to Auschwitz in the summer of 1943. Up until this moment the UGIF-Nord had limited itself mainly to social relief activities and had not been called upon to change its course of action. However, when Brunner demanded that the UGIF-Nord become a watchdog over the community, pressuring families to join their arrested family members so they could be deported to 'the East' all at once, rather than individually, the UGIF-Nord leadership refused. In doing so, as the last UGIF chairman, Georges Edinger, declared after the war, Baur saved the soul ('*l'âme*') of the UGIF.[173]

We can identify a pattern in the four case studies under investigation. In those cases where the social foundation of the initially appointed leaders was – relatively speaking – weaker, the fluctuation of central board members was larger. The possible explanations for this vary; the individuals in question were either not sufficiently confident about their leadership, or disagreed with the way their positions were being used by the Germans, and refused to further cooperate as a result. In some cases, this led to the board members' choice to resign. In other cases, German authorities were dissatisfied with their function and arrested the Jewish leaders. The first two factors have much in common. Taking the case of Salomon Ullmann as an example, we can see that he had a low perception of his own leadership qualities. When German pressure on the AJB increased, and he was asked by the Germans to continue and even expand his activities, his limits were quickly reached. The combination of these factors undoubtedly caused him to resign willingly, whereas Asscher and Cohen, who were confident about the quality of their leadership, did not do so.

Naturally, there were other contextual factors that affected these choices as well. The personalities of each of the leaders differed, and they had different motivations for having taken up the leadership in the first place. In the French case, Lambert and Baur, for example, felt that they could no longer cooperate with the Germans in light of the worsening anti-Jewish legislation. They increasingly objected to the regulations and were arrested as a result. This feeling was not shared by their Dutch counterparts, who believed there was a need to maintain their position for the sake of their community. In Chapter 4, we will see that the existence of

---

[173] Georges Edinger, Report on the activities of the UGIF: concerning its 'official work' and 'clandestine work' from 1941 to 1944, p. 17, CCCLXXIX-33, CDJC, Mémorial de la Shoah.

other Jewish representative aid organisations in Belgium and France also played an important role in this context. Whereas the JR quickly became the sole representative body that could effectively aid Jews, the existence of alternatives to the AJB, the UGIF-Nord and the UGIF-Sud might have contributed to the feeling that their work was not indispensable.

Resignation and Arrest: Reorganising the Belgian and French Central Boards

In both French zones, as well as in Belgium, the (voluntary or involuntary) withdrawal of the Jewish organisations' central board members affected the course of events. The continuous changes to the board created a certain disorder that was advantageous to the AJB and to the UGIF leadership as it meant there was room to frustrate German intentions. For example, after Baur and Lambert were arrested in summer 1943, the UGIF was only reorganised towards the end of that year. On 23 November 1943, Georges Edinger was appointed as chairman of the UGIF while Gaston Kahn replaced Lambert as head of the UGIF-Sud. One month later, Kahn was again replaced by Raymond Geissmann, the UGIF regional director for Lyon, Vichy and Clermont-Ferrand and the former head of the French Israelite Mutual Aid Society (Entr'aide Français Israélite), which was devoted to the assistance of French Jews.[174] In Belgium, we have seen that the replacement of Ullmann and Benedictus resulted in tensions between the AJB, the Military Administration and the SiPo-SD and delayed the appointment of new representatives.

The replacement of the organisations' leaders meant that the Germans (and in France the Vichy officials) lost the central contact through which, for a significant period of time, they had communicated with Jewish communities. The period of transition to a new leadership undoubtedly hampered the effectiveness of the Jewish organisations from the German perspective. The change of leadership in Belgium and France unintentionally created a form of disorder that risked delaying the execution of German anti-Jewish measures. In Belgium, for example, the AJB was rendered useless as far as the Germans were concerned. The appointment of Blum months after Ullmann's resignation did not serve German interests either, since the AJB limited itself to social work, while deportation remained in German hands. In September 1942, the AJB leaders had already refused to send out further notices for deportation, and Ullmann's resignation shortly thereafter

---

[174] Michel Laffitte, 'Les rafles de Janvier 1944 à Bordeaux et les raisons de l'aveuglement de l'UGIF', *Revue d'Histoire de la Shoah*, Vol. 203 (2015), 324.

seems to have served as a reminder that the AJB should not become anything but a social welfare organisation.

The successors of the initial organisations' leaders were already much better aware of German aims in relation to the Jewish organisations than those who had taken up leadership at the end of 1941. Their agreements to work for the organisations were therefore based on different premises and principles. By late 1942 and early 1943, in response to the radicalisation of the Nazi policies in the summer of 1942, resistance organisations were fully operative in Belgium and France. There was a gradual trend towards the unification and coordination of the various resistance groups across the countries, even when they had different political, organisational or ideological backgrounds.[175] As a result, being part of the Jewish organisations' central board became an opportunity to, for example, communicate information and financial resources to illegal organisations. This does not necessarily mean that the later heads were more outspokenly anti-German. As Zuccotti claimed in the case of France, especially after the arrests of courageous leaders such as André Baur and Raymond-Raoul Lambert, the UGIF directors and employees were 'weak and terrified of breaking the law'.[176] Nevertheless, as we shall see in Chapter 5, there were central board members, such as Marcel Blum and Juda Mehlwurm in Belgium and Juliette Stern and Robert Gamzon in France, who decided to use their position in the AJB, the UGIF-Nord and the UGIF-Sud to facilitate illegal activities, particularly during the second half of the German occupation.

---

[175] For further reading on (the organisation of the) resistance in Belgium and France, see, for example, Moore, *Survivors*, 99–207; Pieter Lagrou, 'Belgium', in Bob Moore (ed.), *Resistance in Western Europe* (Oxford: Berg, 2000), 27–64; Olivier Wieviorka, 'France', in Moore, *Resistance in Western Europe*, 125–156; José Gotovitch, 'Resistance Movements and the "Jewish Question"', in *Belgium and the Holocaust: Jews, Belgians, Germans*, 273–285.

[176] Susan Zuccotti, *The Holocaust, the French and the Jews* (Lincoln: University of Nebraska Press, 1999; first ed. 1993), 200.

4 Optimism and Frustration
German Perspectives

While all 'Jewish Councils' were established with similar objectives (uniting and representing the Jewish communities in their respective communities and transmitting German orders), their precise functions and responsibilities changed over time, and inherently depended upon local conditions and institutional rivalry between the various German (and Vichy) departments involved. Variations in this regard led to differences in the efficiency and, from the German viewpoint, effectiveness of the JR, the AJB, the UGIF-Nord and the UGIF-Sud. The rivalry between German (and Vichy) departments also meant that the Jewish leaders interpreted their role according to their own understanding and preferences, and these divergent interpretations added to the different organisational structures.

The large majority of the Jewish organisations' operations concerned very basic and practical activities, mostly related to social welfare and assistance. Although historical analyses have been primarily focussed on questions of *whether* and *why* the Jewish leaders collaborated or cooperated with the Germans, these were only questions of minor importance for these leaders during the period of occupation itself. Rather, they were busy providing assistance with housing, education and medical care. In France, for example, one of the major tasks of the UGIF-Nord was to provide aid to Jews suffering from hunger in internment camps in the occupied zone such as those at Pithiviers and Beaune-la-Rolande. The organisation also secured contact between Jews in the camps and their family members outside.[1] A telling example of the minor details with which the JR in the Netherlands busied itself is the notice it sent to Jews in the provinces urging them to make sure they shut down the electricity in their houses before their forced relocation to Amsterdam.[2] A detailed description sent out by the Council's functionaries of how people should pack their bags also bears witness to this.[3]

---

[1] Laffitte, *Un engrenage fatal*, 55.
[2] Letter of JR central board to those Jews outside Amsterdam who would be forcibly relocated to the capital city, 19 March 1942, 182, Inv. No. 2, NIOD.
[3] Ibid. Also see Letter of the Amsterdam central board to the JR Leeuwarden branch, 10 May 1943, M. 19, Inv. No. 2, Yad Vashem.

The provision of social welfare that had previously been carried out by local government organisations characterised all Jewish organisations, but from 1942 the leaders were, to varying degrees, also held responsible for assisting in the preparation of the further isolation of the Jews, and their deportation. For example, with the exception of the UGIF-Sud leadership, they were coerced to distribute the yellow star of David, introduced between May and June of that year across Western Europe.[4] Jews had to wear this sign on their outer clothing in public at all times and, apart from stigmatisation, the badge also facilitated deportation. Furthermore, the organisations' functionaries aided those who were sent eastwards, providing basic necessities they needed for the difficult journey ahead. Above all, they attempted to minimise the impact of anti-Jewish laws on their communities, and tried to arrange exemptions from deportation for individuals (and their families) through negotiations with the overseeing German (and Vichy) authorities.

The ways in which the leaders carried out their activities varied, in part because the JR, the AJB, the UGIF-Nord and the UGIF-Sud were structured differently and operated in different contexts. Whereas the JR quickly gained exclusive power over the Jews in the Netherlands, the existence of still other Jewish (representative) organisations meant that the AJB, the UGIF-Nord and the UGIF-Sud never fulfilled the same function in their respective societies. The autocratic position of the JR in combination with the absolute power of its chairmanship was markedly different from the Belgian case, where local boards were effectively represented in the central board and Jewish welfare organisations continued to operate alongside the AJB. In the French unoccupied zone, the situation was yet again different because the Jewish organisations within the UGIF-Sud generally retained their autonomy.

These differences affected the daily organisational reality and the effectiveness of the organisations, both from the Jewish and the German perspective. Whereas German authorities were reasonably satisfied with the organisational effectiveness of the Dutch Jewish Council, they took issue with how the Belgian and French Associations functioned. Whether or not the Jewish organisations lived up to German expectations is important for our understanding of both the nature of the interaction between these organisations and their German (or Vichy) overseers, and the broader dynamics of occupation in each of the three countries.

---

[4] Vichy was not willing to introduce a measure that would stigmatise all Jews equally. As a result of this bureaucratic resistance, the star was never introduced in the unoccupied zone, even when the German forces occupied these regions in November 1942. Poznanski, *Jews in France During World War II*, 242.

German Perceptions of the Jewish
Organisations' Functionality

The nature of the interactions between the Jewish leaders in Belgium and overseeing German authorities becomes evident when SS-Obersturmführer Kurt Asche indicated in April 1942 that he expected the AJB to scrupulously carry out the tasks laid down by the Germans. Maurice Benedictus – Antwerp representative on the AJB central board – candidly replied that, from his perspective, the AJB only existed in order to serve the interests of the Jewish communities in Belgium. Asche declared that he did not want the AJB to become a continuation of the passive resistance previously offered by other Jewish organisations. Benedictus replied in his defence that the AJB had busied itself exclusively with the obligations imposed on it since the organisation's establishment. Asche's fear was therefore, he said, unfounded.[5] This lack of trust so soon after the AJB's establishment encapsulates the nature of the communications between German authorities and the AJB leadership throughout the war.

These communications intensified in the summer of 1942. On 15 July, the SiPo-SD announced the first deportations of Jews from Belgium as part of the so-called *Polizeilicher Arbeitseinsatz* (work under police supervision, which was a euphemistic term that concealed the Nazis' true intentions – the mass destruction of Jews), and demanded that the AJB make the necessary preparations for this. These preparations included the creation of a new registry of Jews in the country by AJB personnel, and the distribution of the summonses for labour deployment (*Arbeitseinsatzbefehle*). The AJB leadership consented, aiming to negotiate exemptions from deportation for as many Jews as possible.[6]

On 25 July, the AJB distributed the first summonses, yet only half of the Jews who were called for reported themselves to Kazerne Dossin in Mechelen. As a result, in August, the SiPo-SD pressured the AJB to encourage Jews to comply with the calls for deportations in order to avoid retaliation measures. During a meeting of the AJB with twelve representatives of other central Jewish representative organisations, not including the communist Immigrant Workers Organisation (Main d'Oeuvre Immigrée, MOI) and the Zionist-socialist Labourers of Zion, Left Faction (Linke Poale-Zion), chairman Ullmann was pressured by the other community representatives to sign a 'call for obedience' that encouraged the Jews to obey the German orders.[7]

---

[5] Report of the visit of M. Benedictus and S. Pinkous to SS-Obersturmführer Asche, 17 April 1942, A007399, JMDV, CNHEJ, Buber Collection, Kazerne Dossin.

[6] Schram, 'De oproepen voor "tewerkstelling" in het Oosten', 251–252.

[7] Steinberg, *L'étoile et le fusil: les cent jours de la déportation*, 184–188; Ibid., *La persécution des Juifs en Belgique*, 233–251. Also see the personal accounts of Salomon Ullmann

Despite this commitment, the Germans did not consider the AJB to be useful in helping with the deportation of Jews in the period that followed.[8] The SiPo-SD did not manage to gain a direct and definitive grip on the Jewish leadership, and SS and Belgian police officials began to seize Jews from their homes during raids, hoping to ensure that the quotas of deportees (which were decided in Berlin) were met.

German discontent with the AJB's function led officials of both the Military Administration and the SiPo-SD to maintain contact with employees of the former Aid Organisation for Jews from Germany (Hilfswerk für Juden aus Deutschland), which had been officially incorporated in the AJB in March 1942. In doing so, both German institutions undermined the power of the AJB. The German motivation for turning to representatives of this alternative organisation has been described as laziness.[9] However, in the context of German dissatisfaction with how the AJB was functioning, the choice to turn to Hilfswerk as an alternative representative body can be differently explained. Officials from both the SiPo-SD and the Military Administration were anxiously looking for Jewish representatives who would promote two of their major aims: 1) a steady transmission of German orders to the Jewish communities; 2) an increase in their own authority at the expense of their rival German institution. Securing the cooperation of Hilfswerk might have helped achieve both aims.

In this period, representatives of the two Jewish organisations (the AJB and Hilfswerk) ended up in rivalry themselves, and this increased still further when one of the Hilfswerk committee members falsely presented himself to the Oberfeldkommandantur in Brussels (the local representative of the Military Administration) as an AJB representative in June 1942. Without informing the AJB leadership or asking for its consent, he agreed that the AJB would be responsible for the distribution of the yellow star.[10] In the end, German attempts to create a more functional line of communication with Jewish community representatives by approaching Hilfswerk functionaries did not contribute to a more effective implementation of anti-Jewish regulations. On the contrary, the existence and position of the Hilfswerk complicated an already difficult situation in which the AJB aimed to serve as an umbrella relief organisation for all Jews in Belgium.[11] Therefore, the plan was a failure.

---

and Alfred Rosenzweig on this episode: Report of Salomon Ullmann, L'Activité de l'Association des Juifs en Belgique, p. 3, undated, AA MIC/41, CEGESOMA; Interview with Alfred Rosenzweig, p. 26, 3 February 1972, JMDV, CNHEJ, Kazerne Dossin.

[8] Steinberg, *L'étoile et le fusil: les cent jours de la déportation*, 223–227; Ibid., *La traque des Juifs*, Vol. 1, 65–81.

[9] Meinen, 'De Duitse bezettingsautoriteiten en de VJB', 55.

[10] Ibid.; Meeting report of Maurice Benedictus and Salomon Ullmann with dr. Gentze, 6 June 1942, R497/Tr146.666, DOS.

[11] Meinen, 'De Duitse bezettingsautoriteiten en de VJB', 55.

The AJB dealt with the various departments of the Military Administration and the SiPo-SD through a complicated network of communication. The fact that it was unclear to which German authority the AJB
leaders ought to address themselves prevented effective communication.
For example, when the central board members approached the Military Administration and asked who was directly responsible for the daily
functioning of the AJB, Johannes Duntze, responsible for social affairs,
directed them to three different functionaries.[12] At the SiPo-SD, the Jewish leaders were forced to address four subsequent *Judenreferenten* (who
supervised the deportation of Jews and directly served under Eichmann's
Referat IV B4): first SS-Obersturmführer Kurt Asche (until the end of
November 1942); then SS-Hauptsturmführer Fritz Erdmann; from mid-
October 1943 SS-Hauptscharführer Felix Weidmann; and from March
1944 SS-Obersturmführer Werner Borchardt. Moreover, the AJB also
had to communicate with the Antwerp Jewish department of the SiPo-
SD, headed by Erich Holm, and with the administrators of Mechelen
camp: SS-Hauptsturmführer Steckmann, SS-Sturmbannführer Philipp
Schmitt and SS-Sturmscharführer Johannes Frank.[13]

This complex network of communication led to tensions among those in
responsibility in the German authorities. In September 1942, Kurt Asche,
who felt he was losing his grip on the AJB, summoned twenty of the organisation's leading members to his office, blaming them for disloyalty and
sabotage. He then interned five members of the central board and the local
Brussels board, including chairman Ullmann and vice-chairman Benedictus, in the police detention camp Breendonk.[14] They were told they would
not be released until all Jews were deported from the country.[15] Although
these AJB leaders were released nine days later, after both the Belgian
authorities and the Military Administration put pressure on Asche, the
SiPo-SD's ongoing dissatisfaction with how the AJB functioned is clear.

We have seen that after Salomon Ullmann and Maurice Benedictus resigned in late 1942, SS-Obersturmführer Asche put forward Felix
Meyer and Louis Rosenfeld as possible successors. Asche's plan failed,
and instead both men took a seat on the AJB central board and the board
of the Charleroi branch respectively. During their negotiations with Asche,
both men voiced a number of demands that they wished to have met in

---

[12] Letter of Duntze to the AJB, 25 March 1942, A007397, JMDV, CNHEJ, Buber
Collection, Kazerne Dossin; Minutes of the AJB central board meeting, 19 March
1942, A006709, JMDV, CNHEJ, Buber Collection, Kazerne Dossin.
[13] Meinen, 'De Duitse bezettingsautoriteiten en de VJB', 47–48.
[14] Ibid., 55–56.
[15] Report of Salomon Ullmann, L'Activité de l'Association des Juifs en Belgique,
undated, AA MIC/41, CEGESOMA; Salomon van den Berg, Journal de guerre, p.
57–58, A006685, JMDV, CNHEJ, Buber Collection, Kazerne Dossin.

order to relieve the situation of the Jews in Belgium, including an immediate amnesty for those Jews who had been arrested after they had failed to wear the yellow star, a halt to deportations until the spring of 1943 and the possibility of establishing an intermediary service for those who had already been deported. Asche replied that he might be able to give in to these demands, and he simultaneously again criticised the AJB's lack of effectiveness up to that point. Perhaps hoping the leadership would become more amenable to his own aims, Asche proposed to organise a new inscription of Jews in Belgium onto a 'special register'. The Jews inscribed in this register would not have to fear deportation until spring.[16] There are no indications, however, that this plan was implemented.

Above all, the AJB leadership generally adhered to social welfare aims, hoping to use the negotiations as a way of protecting their community (although often without much success), and this did not correspond to Asche's perceptions of what the Jewish organisation should be. Furthermore, German functionaries were convinced that the AJB was engaged in illegal activities and were concerned that the organisation was offering help to Jews who were in hiding. As late as spring 1944, there was an official prohibition for the AJB on offering financial aid to these illegal Jews, proving the level of German suspicion about the organisation's activities.[17]

In France, the situation was different from both Belgium and the Netherlands, as the Vichy-led CQGJ, which directly oversaw the UGIF, functioned in practice as an intermediary between the UGIF and the Germans.[18] The relation between the German departments responsible for Jewish Affairs in France (most notably representatives of Referat IV B4) and the Vichy CGQJ, headed by Xavier Vallat until May 1942, was complicated. SS-Hauptsturmführer Theodor Dannecker did not feel supported by Vallat in his ferocious attempt to remove the Jews from France as soon as possible, and he harboured a strong sense of mistrust towards him. Vallat, in turn, believed his role did not stretch beyond isolating Jews socially, and categorically refused to collaborate with the Germans in the arrest, internment and deportation of Jews. He only wished to implement French laws.[19]

<hr>

[16] Report of Louis Rosenfeld on the conversations at the Sicherheitsdienst with SS-Obersturmführer Asche, 10 and 14 November 1942, A007428, JMDV, CNHEJ, Buber Collection, Kazerne Dossin.

[17] Report of the general meeting of the central board and the local Brussels board, 30 March 1944, R497/Tr146.665, DOS. This report can also be found in the archives of Kazerne Dossin. See A006822, JMDV, CNHEJ, Buber Collection.

[18] Towards the end of this analysis, a distinction will be made between the observations on the UGIF-Nord and the UGIF-Sud. The communications between the CGQJ and the Germans mostly concerned the functioning of the UGIF in general. In spite of the fact that the bodies operated differently in both zones, the UGIF was still perceived as one organisation by the various German departments.

[19] Steur, *Theodor Dannecker*, 69; Joly, *Xavier Vallat*, 248.

As Joly has highlighted, the relation between these two men was calamitous, and Vallat considered Dannecker, who was twenty-two years his junior, to have a 'juvenile impulsiveness' and 'a deceitful intransigence'.[20] The difference in understanding between the two men in how to approach the so-called Jewish problem is indicative of the difference between the Germans and the Vichy regime more broadly. As Paxton has argued, without German pressure Vichy would probably have been content with professional discrimination and measures to hasten the departure of foreign Jews.[21] Whereas Vichy was mostly concerned with expropriating Jewish wealth and removing foreign Jews (while taking the reactions of French citizens carefully into consideration), Dannecker was striving for a swift and total removal of all Jews from France.[22] Vallat was reluctant to execute German orders and, as we have seen, believed that French and immigrant Jews should not be treated identically. This is why he had opposed the establishment of a Jewish compulsory organisation (the UGIF) in the first place.

To be sure, Vallat was an ardent antisemite and, like Dannecker, he aimed to remove Jews from French society. However, his feeling of revulsion towards the Germans, and Dannecker in particular, was as strong as, and perhaps even stronger than, his antisemitic outlook.[23] Dannecker became angry with Vallat's attitude, and believed that the UGIF was still not functioning properly as a Jewish representative organisation in France by February 1942. He wondered why Vallat had not financially supported the UGIF to help them establish an effective organisation. In line with a wider policy of the Vichy government to maintain at least some form of autonomy, Vallat replied that Dannecker was not supposed to interfere as this was his responsibility alone.[24] Their conflicting views continued to hamper their relationship and, in the end, resulted in the discharge of Vallat in mid-May 1942. Dannecker's outspoken dissatisfaction with Vallat's obstinate attitude and with his refusal to become a tool in German hands played a major role in this decision.[25]

---

[20] Joly, *Xavier Vallat*, 247.
[21] Paxton, *Vichy France: Old Guard and New Order*, 174.
[22] Griffioen and Zeller, *Jodenvervolging in Nederland, Frankrijk en België*, 182–183.
[23] Joly, *Xavier Vallat*, 246–249.
[24] Report of the meeting between SS-Obersturmführer Dannecker and the French General Commissioner for Jewish Affairs Xavier Vallat on 17 February 1942, XXIV-21, CDJC, Mémorial de la Shoah.
[25] For the process of the marginalisation of Xavier Vallat and the disputes that led to his discharge, see: Joly, *Vichy dans la 'solution finale'*, 277–313; and *Xavier Vallat*, 287; Gerard Reitlinger, *The Final Solution* (New York: Beechurst Press, 1953), 312–313.

It is not surprising that Dannecker loathed the way Vallat dealt with anti-Jewish policies and that the UGIF's ineffectiveness angered him. In neither zone did the UGIF become an organisation uniting Jews in France, though this was one of the central aims the Germans had voiced prior to its establishment. The UGIF-Sud in particular was still largely dysfunctional in early 1942; the first meeting of its central board was held as late as 4 May 1942, almost six months after its official establishment order.[26] By then, the Louis Dutch JR had already been fully operative for more than a year.[27]

Hoping to make the UGIF more instrumental in achieving German aims, the SiPo-SD was closely involved in the appointment of Vallat's successor, Louis Darquier de Pellepoix. As former director of the Anti-Jewish League (Rassemblément Antijuif), a federation of antisemitic organisations officially instituted in 1938, Darquier was in several ways different from his predecessor. Whereas Vallat was 'a personage of rank and distinction' at Vichy, Darquier – an 'unsuccessful businessman and a marginal journalist'– always remained an outsider. He also did not carry out his work at the CGQJ with the same care and diligence as Vallat. Moreover, he did not share any of Vallat's principled anti-Germanism, and can be considered an even more radical antisemite than his predecessor.[28]

Even after the appointment of Darquier de Pellepoix, the German perspective on the effectiveness of the UGIF did not significantly alter. In May 1942, Darquier de Pellepoix presented his vision for the role of the CGQJ in dealing with Jewish affairs. He underlined that he wanted to take a different approach from his predecessor by ensuring that the *Statut des Juifs*, the anti-Jewish legislation passed by the Vichy regime, was implemented and applied to all Jews.[29] A letter Darquier sent to Albert Lévy, written on 18 July 1942, shows that he was keen to tell the UGIF's president about the changes he was planning to make. He noted that, in terms of its expenses, the UGIF had gone through a phase of trial and error that he considered 'inevitable' for a newly instituted organisation and he claimed that new responsibilities would soon be given to the UGIF.[30] The letter demonstrates that the UGIF's sphere of

[26] Lambert, *Diary of a Witness*, 5 May 1942, 118. In Belgium, the first meeting of the central board took place on 15 January 1942; see Meeting report of the central board, 15 January 1942, A006700, JMDV, CNHEJ, Buber Collection, Kazerne Dossin.

[27] The first meeting of the JR's central board took place on 13 February 1941, the same day it was established. For the report of this first meeting, see 182, Inv. No. 3, NIOD.

[28] Joly, *Vichy dans la 'solution finale'*, 294–299, 313–315; Marrus and Paxton, *Vichy France and the Jews*, 213–261. For an excellent biography of Darquier de Pellepoix, see Laurent Joly, *Darquier de Pellepoix et l'antisémitisme français* (Paris: Berg, 2002).

[29] Joly, *Vichy dans la 'solution finale'*, 314.

[30] Letter from the General Commissioner of Jewish Affairs Darquier to Albert Lévy, 18 July 1942, XXVIIIa-109, Mémorial de la Shoah.

activity was still not strictly defined in July 1942. Despite his ambitions, Darquier was unable to make the UGIF more effective in implementing anti-Jewish legislation and the Germans continued to be dissatisfied with how it worked.

When the mass deportations began in summer 1942, the UGIF was not yet ready to play the role Dannecker assigned to it. Its formal basis had just been established in this period and it was now drawn into the 'concentration camp vortex'.[31] The UGIF was not helpful in achieving the number of deportees Dannecker wanted; in July, he was enraged when only 5,000 Jews (out of 20,000 he had anticipated) were interned in the unoccupied zone.[32] Whereas in Eastern Europe, Jewish Councils were directly held responsible for delivering the required number of Jews for each transport, the UGIF, like its Western European counterparts, was never made to do so.[33] This was because, despite attempts by the Gestapo, no ghetto system similar to that in Eastern Europe was introduced in any of these countries. The fact that the Jewish populations lived dispersed in the Netherlands, Belgium and France made internment a necessary transitional stage.[34] In the end, the organisation's leaders persisted in their refusal to be responsible for the internment of Jews, and primarily focused their energy on providing social welfare to those who were deported.

[31] Adler, *The Jews of Paris*, 118.

[32] Report of Dannecker on his visit to the internment camps in the unoccupied zone, 10 July 1942, XXVI-43, CDJC, Mémorial de la Shoah; Steur, *Theodor Dannecker*, 84; Laffitte, *Un engrenage fatal*, 70–78.

[33] For the history and function of the *Judenräte* in Poland (from a comparative viewpoint), see: Trunk, *Judenrat*, passim. Since Trunk's publication in 1972, many studies on ghettos in Poland, and Jewish representation in these ghettos, have been conducted. See, for example, Israel Gutman, *The Jews of Warsaw, 1939–1943: Ghetto, Underground, Revolt* (Bloomington: Indiana University Press, 1982; originally published in Hebrew in 1977); Yehuda Bauer, *The Death of the Shtetl* (New Haven/London: Yale University Press, 2009); Freia Anders, Katrin Stoll, and Karsten Wilke (eds.), *Der Judenrat von Białystok: Dokumente aus dem Archiv des Białystoker Ghettos 1941–1943* (Paderborn: Ferdinand Schöningh, 2010); David Silberklang, *Gates of Tears: The Holocaust in the Lublin District* (Jerusalem: Yad Vashem, 2013); Katharina Friedla, *Juden in Breslau/Wrocław 1933–1949: Überlebensstrategieen, Selbstbehauptung und Verfolgungserfahrungen* (Cologne/Weimar/Vienna: Böhlau, 2015).

[34] For further reading on the role of the JR, the AJB and the UGIF in the process leading up to the deportation of Jews from Western Europe to 'the East', see Laurien Vastenhout, 'The Jewish Council of Amsterdam: A (More) Useful Tool in the Deportation Process?' in Peter Black, Michaela Raggam-Blesch and Marianne Windsperger (eds.), *Deportations of the Jewish Population in Territories under Nazi Control. Comparative Perspectives on the Organization of the Path to Annihilation*, Beiträge zur Holocaustforschung des Wiener Wiesenthal Instituts für Holocaust-Studien (VWI), Vol. 9 (Vienna: New Academic Press, forthcoming).

Throughout 1942, Dannecker's radical approach to the Jews and towards Vichy officials had become a source of irritation for Helmut Knochen, head of the Security Police in France. Both men had successfully increased the authority of the SiPo-SD over that of the Military Administration in the previous months. After they succeeded in doing so, Knochen, having reached his goal, seemed to lose interest in the Jews. He wanted to cooperate with the Vichy regime for the sake of order and to safeguard his authority.[35] Knochen's unwillingness to jeopardise collaboration with the Vichy regime, or to further alienate French public opinion, was highlighted when he vetoed SS-Obersturmführer Heinz Röthke's plan for a major round-up of French Jews by the German police in Paris in September 1942.[36] By contrast, Dannecker, like Röthke and SS-Hauptsturmführer Aloïs Brunner, wanted to deport all Jews from France as quickly as possible. Dannecker's 'undiplomatic' attitude towards Vichy undermined Knochen's work and his authority. In July 1942, Dannecker, who became Eichmann's representative in Bulgaria (and later in Italy and Hungary), was replaced by Heinz Röthke.[37]

In summer 1943, in order to make the UGIF in the northern zone more amenable to their aims, the German authorities altered their approach to the organisation. While the Vichy-led CGQJ was given a free hand in overseeing its affairs in the first years of its existence, the presence of Aloïs Brunner, who directed Drancy transit camp from 2 July 1943, drastically changed things. Between 1938 and 1942 Brunner had worked for, and later headed, the Central Office for Jewish Emigration in Vienna. In February 1943, he was posted as expert of Jewish affairs (*Judenreferent*) to Greece, where he brutally and efficiently organised the deportation of at least 43,000 Jews. Sent by Eichmann, Brunner arrived in Paris in early June 1943, seeking to speed up the process of deporting Jews from France.

In order to strengthen the position of Röthke's department for Jewish Affairs, Brunner brought his own task force with him, consisting of around twenty-five Austrian SS men. While Röthke remained *Judenreferent* for France, Brunner was authorised to act independently of the German police chain of command and was accountable only to Berlin. Both men competed to gain the upper hand in the so-called Final Solution to the Jewish Question in France. Brunner soon managed to secure the leading role.[38]

---

[35] Steur, *Dannecker*, 86.
[36] Zuccotti, *The Holocaust, the French and the Jews*, 159–160.
[37] Ibid., 176; Marrus and Paxton, *Vichy France and the Jews*, 160; Seibel, *Macht und Moral*, 60–61.
[38] Meyer, *Täter im Verhör*, 192–193; Adler, *The Jews of Paris*, 148–149; Marrus and Paxton, *Vichy France and the Jews*, 182.

Aiming to outmanoeuvre the French police, Brunner 'launched a violent press campaign against René Bousquet, head of the French police, and Pierre Laval and accused them of "protecting" the Jews'.[39] After Brunner's takeover of the direction of Drancy camp, Vichy lost control over the administrative network of deportation, and no longer had any influence on the composition of convoys to Eastern Europe.[40] In June 1943, in response to Germany's need for manpower and the Compulsory Labour Service (Service du Travail Obligatoire, STO) that Laval had introduced in February 1943, Brunner and Röthke ordered the UGIF-Nord to open its own factories.[41] One month later, in his attempt to remove the Jews from France as quickly as possible, Brunner aimed to directly oversee the UGIF, thereby sidestepping Röthke as well as the CGQJ.[42]

On 30 June, Brunner identified one of the main 'problems' of the UGIF during a discussion with UGIF-Nord leader Baur: 'the discipline and solidarity among the Jewish population in Paris is not sufficiently developed ... [therefore] the UGIF does not have any authority among this population'.[43] He indicated to Baur that he wanted the UGIF-Nord to take on two key tasks in order to speed up the process of deportation. First, the organisation would oversee the administrative management of the camp at Drancy, which Brunner now wanted to transform into a concentration camp under the direct control of the SS. Second, the UGIF-Nord should encourage families of interned Jews to report themselves so that the whole family could be deported together. The UGIF-Nord leadership refused to turn their organisation into an arm of the Gestapo and was unwilling to carry out or participate in any police measures.[44] André Baur, afraid that the UGIF would become a 'docile

---

[39] Marrus and Paxton, *Vichy France and the Jews*, 253. Also see Jacques Delarue, *Histoire de la Gestapo* (Paris: Fayard, 1987), 389; André Brissaud, *La dernière année de Vichy* (Paris: Perrin, 1965), 42–43.

[40] Marrus and Paxton, *Vichy France and the Jews*, 253. Also see Meyer, *Täter im Verhör*, 193.

[41] Minutes of the Administrative Council of the UGIF in the Northern Zone, 8 June 1943, Reel 3, MK490.4.3:3:1 (YIVO), Mémorial de la Shoah. For further reading on the STO and Germany's need for manpower, see: Paxton, *Vichy France: Old Guard and New Order*, 367–370. Across Europe, being productive offered a possibility for (temporary) survival for Jews and Jewish leaders adopted this strategy in order to safeguard the survival of (part of) their communities, see: Yisrael Gutman, 'The Concept of Labor in Judenrat Policy', in Gutman and Haft, *Patterns of Jewish Leadership*, 151–180.

[42] Cohen, *Burden of Conscience*, 89–90; Laffitte, *Un engrenage fatal*, 154–156.

[43] CDJC YIVO 3-116 as cited in Laffitte, *Un engrenage fatal*, 155.

[44] Minutes of the Administrative Council UGIF-Nord, 6 July 1943, Reel 3, MK490.4.3:3:1 (YIVO), Mémorial de la Shoah; Report of the meeting between Baur and Brunner, 30 June 1943, Reel 3, MK490.4.3:3:1 (YIVO), Mémorial de la Shoah; Edinger, Report on the activities of the UGIF, p. 16, CCCLXXIX-33, CDJC, Mémorial de la Shoah; Laffitte, *Un engrenage fatal*, 159–164; Adler, *The Jews of Paris*, 150; Cohen, *Burden of Conscience*, 89.

instrument' of a new, more radical German policy, agreed only to function as an intermediary between Brunner and the French administration in the reorganisation of the camp, and made it clear the UGIF-Nord would only engage in relief activities that would ease the situation of the Jews as they departed.[45]

Baur's refusal to do more was not taken lightly, and tensions between the UGIF-Nord leadership and Brunner increased still further when two men, including Baur's cousin Adolphe Ducas, escaped from Drancy and the UGIF-Nord, despite its best efforts, failed to find them. Shortly thereafter, Baur was arrested together with his wife and their four children. On 4 September, Stora and Musnik, the other main protagonists of the UGIF-Nord who had temporarily assumed the leadership of the organisation, were arrested as well because they failed to meet Brunner's previously voiced demands. All three men were deported on 17 December 1943 and none of them survived the war.[46]

Brunner's pressure on the UGIF's leaders and his dissatisfaction with the organisation's effectiveness in the deportation of Jews from France did not change the UGIF-Nord's policies after Baur's arrest. Its newly appointed leadership, headed by Georges Edinger and Juliette Stern, viewed the organisation as the only relief agency still available to the Jews and continued to focus on its relief work.[47]

The UGIF-Sud was even less successful in living up to German expectations. The heterogeneous federative structure of the organisation meant that there was anything but a unified UGIF policy in the unoccupied zone. The UGIF-Sud central board had neither any real authority over their departments, nor any influence over the Jewish communities.[48] In summer 1943, the German authorities were still not satisfied with the numbers of Jews being deported from France; those arrested had already been taken from the camps and it became harder to find Jews.[49] As we shall see in Chapter 5, rather than acting to achieve the German aim of swiftly arresting and deporting Jews from France, functionaries of the UGIF-Sud in this period increasingly used the organisation as a cloak for clandestine activities, both with and without the direct participation and knowledge of its leaders. The arrest of Raymond-Raoul Lambert,

---

[45] Laffitte, *Un engrenage fatal*, 161–162.

[46] Adler, *The Jews of Paris*, 151–152; Serge Klarsfeld, *Le mémorial de la déportations des juifs de France* (Paris: Klarsfeld, 1978), liste alphabétique du convoi No. 63.

[47] Adler, *The Jews of Paris*, 152–153; Cohen, *Burden of Conscience*, 105–106.

[48] For an overview of all organisations that were incorporated into the UGIF-Sud, and their sphere of activity, see Cohen, *Burden of Conscience*, 138–153. Also see Laffitte, *Juif dans la France allemande*, 408–409.

[49] Marrus and Paxton, *Vichy France and the Jews*, 246.

who refused to cooperate with the Germans any longer in summer 1943 is indicative of the level of German dissatisfaction with the UGIF-Sud's function and the position taken by its leadership.

The Vichy-led CGQJ was also not content with the organisation's effectiveness. Auguste Duquesnel, director of the CGQJ's Control Department (Service du Contrôle) of the UGIF, believed that the problem stemmed from organisational deficiencies and claimed that the UGIF was not cooperating sufficiently. In order to improve the efficiency of the organisation, it was proposed to reorganise the entire UGIF, centralising its organisation in Paris. This idea had been discussed by both the Germans and CGQJ officials, in liaison with the UGIF-Nord leadership, from the summer of 1942 onwards. The plan became even more relevant when the financial situation of the UGIF-Nord reached a critical state in April and May 1943 and it was considered that the resources of UGIF-Sud could be applied to resolve the problem.[50] However, the UGIF-Sud's leadership rejected any proposals for unification and resolutely maintained the organisation's independent structure.

In September 1943, the CGQJ leadership changed its perspective and opposed the unification of the UGIF under one umbrella, possibly fearing that it would lose its authority over the organisation. This fear was voiced as early as March 1943 by Duquesnel, who had claimed in a report that centralisation would result in the elimination of the UGIF-Sud's leadership and a loss of control by Vichy.[51] That the CGQJ was uncertain about the role and future of the UGIF-Sud becomes clear from a statement in the same period, which said there was no alternative for the UGIF's deplorable situation but to dismiss the UGIF-Sud leadership and 'proceed with the centralisation in Paris'.[52] The ongoing discussions about the reorganisation of the UGIF show that both German and Vichy officials were dissatisfied with the way it worked.

The nature of the occupation and of the Jewish communities in France meant that the function and structure of the UGIF was not significantly altered during the course of the war, despite the occupier's pronounced dissatisfaction with the organisation. The German authorities took a number of measures to improve the effectiveness of the UGIF. First, we have seen that CGQJ-head Xavier Vallat, who was considered too moderate by Dannecker, was replaced by Louis Darquier de Pellepoix who,

---

[50] Adler, *The Jews of Paris*, 146.
[51] See the report of Robert Duquesnel sent to the General Commissioner of Jewish Affairs Darquier, 4 March 1943, XXVIII-136, CDJC, Mémorial de la Shoah. For an overview of the discussion on the centralisation of the UGIF, see Adler, *The Jews of Paris*, 133–161; Cohen, *Burden of Conscience*, 154–166.
[52] UGIF-Nord board meeting, 3 September 1943, as cited in Adler, *The Jews of Paris*, 152.

in turn was replaced by Charles du Paty de Clam in February 1944. In June 1944, Du Paty de Clam was himself replaced by Joseph Antignac.[53] Second, Dannecker was replaced in July 1942 in order to improve the communication of the department of the SiPo-SD responsible for Jewish Affairs with both Vichy officials and the Military Administration.[54]

Third, as we have seen, those UGIF leaders who refused to cooperate and who displayed troubling signs of independence were interned and deported. Ultimately, though, even apparently compliant leaders such as Edinger and Geissmann were no more obedient to German rule than their predecessors had been.[55] The UGIF failed to unite Jews in France or to become a tool in the hands of the German occupier. Instead, it continued its social welfare activities within the limits provided by the Germans and, as Chapter 5 will show, at times also outside these limits (resistance).

At the same time, like their Western European counterparts, the Jewish leaders in France were forced to make decisions that harmed their communities and that even led to arrests and deportations. An infamous example of this is the arrest of Jewish children who were taken care of by UGIF personnel in their facilities because their parents were no longer able to do so (they were either interned or deported). Despite warnings of some leading Jewish functionaries, including Lambert who was by then interned in Drancy, the UGIF leadership refused to disband the organisation (which would have enabled a mass escape of these children).[56] As a consequence, in summer 1944, many children and staff were seized by the Gestapo and sent eastwards.

---

[53] Du Paty de Clam was a career colonial official who had been serving in Damascus in the interwar years. His appointment at the head of the CGQJ was primarily because of his name, as descendant of the famous staff officer Du Paty du Clam who arrested Captain Alfred Dreyfus in 1894. Antignac was a former cavalry officer who had become the director of the Police for Jewish Affairs in Limoges in 1940. Marrus and Paxton, *Vichy France and the Jews*, 159–161, 215–229, 256–261; Joly, *Vichy dans la 'solution finale'*, 237–238, 742–745. Also see Dossier Joseph Antignac, AJ38 6278, Archives Nationales, Paris; Dossier Charles du Paty de Clam, AJ38 6302, Archives Nationales, Paris.

[54] Marrus and Paxton, *Vichy France and the Jews*, 160.

[55] Laffitte, *Un engrenage fatal*, 176; for the role of Edinger in the UGIF after the arrest of its first leadership, see 175ff.

[56] Lambert unsuccessfully attempted to persuade the remaining leaders to dissolve the entire UGIF, which had been weakened since his removal. See Lambert's letter to Maurice Brener sent from camp Drancy, 26 October 1943 as published in *Diary of a Witness*, 205–206. It should be noted that in February 1943, following the raids in Marseille, Wladimir Schah had attempted to convince Lambert that the physical UGIF offices ought to be closed (while the UGIF continued its activities). By that point, Lambert was not yet convinced of the benefit of doing so. See Laffitte, *Un engrenage fatal*, 319.

The failure of the UGIF leadership to overcome these mass arrests was one of the three points for which the UGIF leadership was criticised during the commission of inquiry imposed on the organisation after liberation by the Representative Council of the Israelites of France (Conseil Representatif des Israélites de France, CRIF).[57] The CRIF had been established in January 1944, officially representing both immigrant and French Jews, and created a jury of honour to investigate Jewish leaders' wartime conduct.[58] The UGIF-Sud leadership's decision not to dissolve the organisation was inspired by the feeling that it still had an important role to play as a relief organisation, and its continued existence was considered imperative for the maintenance of the remaining Jews in France.[59]

As in Belgium and France, Dutch JR leaders clashed with their German overseers. These conflicts were mainly caused by the fact that the JR believed the Germans were not living up to the promises they had made. The frustration thus originated from the Jewish leadership, rather than, as we have seen in Belgium and France, from the German authorities. For example, the leadership protested against the raid of 11 June 1941, during which many so-called Palestine Pioneers (Palestina Pioniers), formerly residents of the training centre in the Wieringermeer (province of North Holland) which prepared them for emigration to Palestine, were arrested and sent to Mauthausen concentration camp in Austria. In March, the village of the Palestine Pioneers had been evacuated. When the Germans had ostensibly agreed in June to allow the Palestine Pioneers to go back to the working village in order to continue their preparations for emigration to Palestine, the JR had provided the names and addresses of the Jews concerned.[60] Thereafter, the Jews were arrested and deported. The Germans had thus asked the JR's

---

[57] Jacques Fredj, 'Le Consistoire Central et la création du CRIF', *Revue d'histoire de la Shoah: Le Consistoire* durant *la Seconde Guerre Mondiale*, Vol. 169 (2000), 177.
[58] The name of the Conseil Representatif des Israélites de France was subsequently altered to Conseil Representatif des Juifs de France because the term *Israélites*, commonly used to refer to French Jews specifically, was considered too narrow. For an overview of the establishment of the CRIF, see Fredj, 'Le Consistoire Central et la création du CRIF'; and *La Création du C.R.I.F. 1943–1967*, mémoire de maîtrise sous la direction de Jean-Marie Mayeur (Université de Paris, 1988), which can be consulted at the CDJC, Mémorial de la Shoah, Paris; Adler, *The Jews of Paris*, 157, 219; Shannon Fogg, *Stealing Home: Looting, Restitution, and Reconstructing Jewish Lives in France, 1942–1947* (Oxford: Oxford University Press, 2017), 155. For an overview of all organisations associated with the CRIF, see 'Sous l'égide du CRIF', undated report, CRIF MDI-192, CDJC, Mémorial de la Shoah.
[59] Adler, *The Jews of Paris*, 158–159.
[60] Somers, 'Kanttekeningen bij de Joodse Raad', 30.

functionaries to provide this information under false pretences, and the Jewish leaders then expressed their discontent with the situation.[61]

There were also other occasions on which the JR's leadership objected to the course of events, for example when the head of the Central Office for Jewish Emigration (Zentralstelle), Ferdinand aus der Fünten, indicated during a meeting on 21 May 1943 that 7,000 JR employees ought to report themselves for forced labour in Germany only four days later. Until then, these employees had been exempted from deportation because they worked for the JR. Abraham Asscher, David Cohen and Edwin Sluzker, head of the Expositur, protested, and claimed that it would be impossible to continue the work of the JR without these individuals. The meeting report indicates that Lages then threatened to arbitrarily deport individuals in the event that they would not comply.[62] Asscher and Cohen therefore agreed to compile a list of 7,000 employees who would no longer receive protection through the JR, and consequently were put at risk of being deported.

When the chairmen communicated this measure to the other central board members, some considered resigning from their position, including Gertrude van Tijn and Asscher himself, who apparently reconsidered his decision to comply.[63] This objection was short-lived, however, and both Van Tijn and Asscher continued to work for the Council until it was dissolved in September 1943.

Despite these occasional clashes with German functionaries, the JR leadership tried to make communication with the Germans as efficient as possible, aiming to win time by giving in to certain demands while at the same time asking for concessions, in order to prevent worse (*om erger te voorkomen*). This phrase was repeatedly used to explain and excuse the tactics of the Jewish leaders in that they had attempted to 'prevent worse', including deportation to Mauthausen, by complying with German regulations. Mauthausen gained an unsettling reputation in the Netherlands

---

[61] Gertrude van Tijn, who headed the Emigration department of the JR and later its department named Help for the Departing (Hulp aan Vertrekkenden), had been responsible for providing the lists. In her memoirs, Van Tijn wrote that she then decided she would never again provide any list of Jewish names to the Gestapo, 'no matter what they promised or threatened to do'. Gertrude van Tijn, 'The World was Mine', undated (1950s), p. 32, Doc1 248-1720B, NIOD.

[62] Report of meeting between aus der Fünten, Lages, Blumenthal, Asscher and Cohen, 21 May 1943, 182, Inv. No. 4, NIOD. It should be noted that Cohen mistakenly claimed after the war that they were forced to hand over a list of 7,500 names. The previously mentioned meeting reports of that period show that the number amounted to 7,000. See Cohen, *Voorzitter van de Joodse Raad*, 166.

[63] Minutes of the JR, 21 May 1943, 182, Inv. No. 3, NIOD; Wasserstein, *Gertrude van Tijn en het lot van de Nederlandse Joden*, 176–177.

in spring 1941 when a group of Jewish hostages was sent there and reports of their death soon reached their families. After that, the Germans used Mauthausen as a threat to make the JR carry out its instructions.[64] Apart from the situation in this particular camp, Cohen claimed after the war that he had not known the fate of the Jews who were deported to camps in 'the East'; a claim that was widely criticised by historians such as Hans Knoop and Nanda Van der Zee.[65]

Cohen also said after the war that in order to make their tactics work, he and Asscher at times divided the meetings with particular German officials between themselves, because, for example, Cohen got along better with Ferdinand aus der Fünten and Asscher with Willy Lages.[66] He elaborated on their strategy and indicated that the central aim had been to receive exemptions from deportation, to gain time and, in doing so, to serve the interests of the Dutch Jewish community at large.[67] Whether or not this was a successful strategy has been, as we have seen, a subject of debate in the historiography of the persecution of the Jews in the Netherlands for decades.

The case of the Jewish Council of Tunis, which only existed for six months, shows that the strategy of cooperation with the Germans, while simultaneously trying to delay the implementation of measures, could be successful in the short term.[68] In the Netherlands, this tactic failed, because the occupation lasted years rather than months. Moreover, the local conditions, including the nature of the German occupation, the nature of the Jewish community and the quality of the infrastructure of deportation, were very different.

---

[64] Henny Dominicus, *Mauthausen: een gedenkboek* (Amsterdam: Stichting Vriendenkring Mauthausen, 1999; first ed. 1995), 13; Knoop, *De Joodsche Raad*, 102; De Jong, *Het Koninkrijk*, part V, 567.

[65] See, for example, Cohen, *Voorzitter van de Joodse Raad*, 136. For the criticism on Cohen's statements see van der Zee, *Om erger te voorkomen*, 97–140; Knoop, *De Joodsche Raad*, passim. In 2012, after the publication of Dutch historian Bart van der Boom's *'Wij weten niets van hun lot': gewone Nederlanders en de Holocaust* (Amsterdam: Boom, 2012), a fierce debate emerged on the knowledge of Dutch citizens of the fate of the deported Jews. See, for example, Remco Ensel and Evelien Gans, 'Nivellering in de geschiedenis: wij weten iets van hun lot', *De Groene Amsterdammer*, No. 50, 12 December 2012; and 'Over "Wij weten iets van hun lot', *De Groene Amsterdammer*, 6 February 2013.

[66] Statement of David Cohen, 19 July 1949, dossier Willy Paul Franz Lages, CABR, Access No. 2.09.09, Inv. No. 140-VIII (BrC 394/49), NA.

[67] Ibid. This strategy was emphasised by Cohen on numerous occasions, including during the pre-trial investigations of the Dutch State into the wartime activities of the JR, and the role of the two chairmen. See, for example, his statement on 1 December 1947, dossier Abraham Asscher and David Cohen, CABR, Access No. 2.09.09, Inv. No. 107491 VII (PF Amsterdam T70982), NA.

[68] Friedl, 'Negotiating and Compromising', 231–235.

In contrast to the situation in Belgium and France, despite the inevitable conflicts between the JR leaders and the German authorities, the apparently friendly 'cooperation' was emphasised by both sides after the war. Reichskommissar Arthur Seyss-Inquart as well as commander of Westerbork transit camp Albert Conrad Gemmeker, SS-Sturmbannführer Willy Lages, Commander of the SiPo-SD in the Netherlands Wilhelm Harster and SS Hauptsturmführer aus der Fünten all claimed that the Germans would never have been able to deport so many Jews without the aid of the JR. Lages even referred to the Jewish body as a 'German department' because Asscher and Cohen were so cooperative that it was not necessary to appoint a German official at the head of the Council.[69]

Lages also indicated that his German colleagues in Belgium and France were surprised about the results that had been accomplished: 'they indicated they were incapable of achieving the same in Belgium and France'.[70] While these statements need to be treated with caution, given that the Nazis were trying, in court, to downplay their own involvement in the deportation of the Jews and to shift blame onto the JR, we must acknowledge that the level of cooperation in which Asscher and Cohen were prepared to engage went beyond what their Belgian and French counterparts were forced to do or were willing to do.

The fact that the JR's leadership in May 1943 agreed to compile a list of 7,000 of its own employees who would be called to 'work under police supervision' (*Polizeilicher Arbeitseinsatz*) is an example of this. After the war, David Cohen wrote in his memoirs that he had agreed to provide these lists because it would enable the JR leadership to save from deportation those employees who were indispensable for the day-to-day functioning of the organisation.[71] He also made the controversial admission that he had done this in order to save from deportation prominent Jews who would be able to rebuild the Jewish community after the war.[72]

[69] Statement of Lages, 23 September 1947, dossier Abraham Asscher and David Cohen, CABR, Access No. 2.09.09, Inv. No. 107491 I (PF Amsterdam T70982), NA. Also see: Statement of Ferdinand aus der Fünten, 6 October 1947, dossier Abraham Asscher and David Cohen, CABR, Access No. 2.09.09, Inv. No. 107491 I (PF Amsterdam T70982), NA; Statement of Gemmeker, 15 September 1947, dossier Abraham Asscher and David Cohen, CABR, Access No. 2.09.09, Inv. No. 107491 I (PF Amsterdam T70982), NA; Statement of Harster, 15 October 1947, dossier Abraham Asscher and David Cohen, CABR, Access No. 2.09.09, Inv. No. 107491 I (PF Amsterdam T70982), NA.

[70] Statement of Lages, 23 September 1947, Dossier Abraham Asscher and David Cohen, CABR, Access No. 2.09.09, Inv. No. 107491 I (PF Amsterdam T70982).

[71] Cohen, *Voorzitter van de Joodse Raad*, 166.

[72] David Cohen, 'Geschiedenis der Joden in Nederland tijdens de bezetting', p. 21, 181j, Inv. No. 10.

While the cooperation of JR functionaries was considered more effective than that of their counterparts in Belgium (as well as France), we
can identify similarities between the responsibilities that the Germans
imposed on, and that were carried out by, the JR and the AJB. Apart
from the provision of social assistance to the Jewish communities, both
organisations were pressured early on to compile registries that recorded
the names and addresses of Jewish citizens. In the Netherlands, such
a registry (the so-called *bevolkingsregister*) existed prior to the German
occupation, but in October 1941, aus der Fünten pressured the JR leadership to produce another inventory that also listed what the Nazis defined
as 'quarter-Jews', 'half-Jews' and 'mixed-marriages'.[73] In Belgium, AJB
officials were held responsible for the registration of Jews in early 1942.[74]
Both the JR and the AJB were also engaged in the creation and distribution of the summonses for labour deployment (*Arbeitseinsatzbefehle*),
and, in various ways, encouraged their Jewish communities, albeit reluctantly, to report themselves once they had received a summons.[75]

By contrast, apart from the provision of social welfare, the UGIF-
Nord and the UGIF-Sud were never involved in these activities, in part
because the system of summonses for labour deployment was never used
in France. Instead, German and French police forces arrested Jews during raids – a tactic the Germans turned to in the Netherlands and Belgium when the *Arbeitseinsatzbefehle* system proved inadequate because
many Jews refused to reported themselves.[76]

Above all, despite the fact that we can identify similarities in the
responsibilities that were carried out by the AJB and the JR, the Dutch
Council seemed to have met the constantly changing German expectations much better than its Belgian or French counterparts. The disagreements between the JR and the Germans never reached a point of outright
conflict. This partially explains why Asscher and Cohen, in contrast to

[73] A reference to the registration of Jews by the Jewish Council is made during a meeting
with the organisation's central board at the end of October; see Meeting report of the
JR, 30 October 1941, 182, Inv. No. 3, NIOD. Also see Cohen, *Voorzitter van de Joodse
Raad*, 102–103.
[74] Frank Seberechts, 'De Duitse instanties en de anti-Joodse politiek', in Rudi van
Doorslaer, Emmanuel Debruyne, Frank Seberechts et al., *Gewillig België: overheid en jodenvervolging tijdens de Tweede Wereldoorlog* (Amsterdam: Meulenhoff/
Antwerp: Manteau, 2007), 277–278; Seberechts., 'De Belgische overheden en de
Jodenvervolging, 1940–1942', in *Gewillig België*, 304–313; Laurence Schram, 'De
oproepen voor "tewerkstelling" in het Oosten', in van Doorslaer and Schreiber, *De
curatoren van het getto*, 247–249.
[75] See *Het Joodsche Weekblad: uitgave van den Joodschen Raad voor Amsterdam*, 14 July
1942; Steinberg, *La persécution des Juifs en Belgique*, 233–251.
[76] For further reading on the responsibilities that were imposed on the JR, the AJB and
the UGIF in the context of mass deportation, see Vastenhout, 'The Jewish Council of
Amsterdam', passim.

Jewish leaders in other localities, including Belgium, France and Poland, were able to remain leaders of the JR from the moment it was established until the Council was dissolved in September 1943.[77]

Explaining the Dutch Jewish Leaders' Level of Cooperation

The difference in functionality and effectiveness of the Joodsche Raad in the Netherlands can be, and has been, explained by the specific personalities of its leaders. Asscher and Cohen's will to gain power and control over the Jews in the Netherlands was significant. We have seen that the country's Jewish communities had been moving in a particular direction, of which both Asscher and Cohen were representative: they were secular, well-integrated Jews.

The initial outlook of the JR's chairmen, in February 1941, was different from that of their counterparts in Belgium and France, who were appointed nine months later. Although anti-Jewish regulations had already been implemented by the time Asscher and Cohen took up their positions (for example, Jews had to register themselves, Jewish civil servants were fired and Jews were not allowed to visit cinemas), mass arrests and deportations had not yet taken place in Western Europe. Whereas the UGIF and the AJB came into existence as German policies were slowly evolving from antisemitic regulations into the attempt to remove all Jews from these countries, this was by no means the case in the Netherlands. The Dutch Council leadership accepted their nomination on different grounds, and, as the months went by, were gradually drawn into the radicalisation of the persecution process. In fact, the situation faced by the two chairmen was more comparable with that of Jewish leaders in Poland in 1939–1940.

Asscher and Cohen's strong belief in their own ability to make the right decisions and their trust in the legal path they had chosen, perhaps combined with a feeling they could not truly obstruct German policies even if they wanted to, resulted in a degree of blindness with respect to German intentions. The wish to maintain order was central to the leadership's policies, and this is highlighted in Asscher's speech of 14 February 1941, made in response to the unrest that had broken out in the Jewish quarter. At this event, his first public appearance as chairman

---

[77] In Poland, some Jewish leaders voluntarily resigned from their positions (because they were unwilling to acquiesce to German policies), and many were liquidated or voluntarily removed. See Aharon Weiss, 'Jewish Leadership in Occupied Poland: Postures and Attitudes', *Yad Vashem Studies*, Vol. 12 (1977), 363. Trunk, *Judenrat*, 317–331.

of the Council, Asscher encouraged Jews to hand over their weapons so that order could be reinstated.[78]

There were further occasions when the JR's leaders voiced this aim. During a meeting between Willy Lages, Ferdinand aus der Fünten and the two Council chairmen on 4 August 1942, for example, Asscher and Cohen discouraged the Germans to spread information that would cause distress in the community. They were referring to Generalkommissar Schmidt's public statements on the tough fate that awaited Jews once they were deported to Eastern Europe. Although Asscher and Cohen were interested in the accuracy of this information, they emphasised above all that these type of statements caused disquiet in the community that would hamper their own work.[79]

The feeling that they, Asscher and Cohen, were the most capable leaders of the Jewish communities in the Netherlands, and the concessions they were prepared to make in order to safeguard their position and the continued existence of the JR, contrasts with the outlook of the first leaders of the Belgian AJB and the French UGIF-Nord and UGIF-Sud. We have seen that on a number of occasions the JR leaders exhibited doubts about the role of the JR, but they were more afraid that if the Council were to be dissolved, the Germans would be free to impose arbitrary measures.[80]

By contrast, in Belgium and France, important board members (they included Ullmann, Baur and Lambert) stepped down from their positions, or were forced to do so, when they disagreed with German regulations and when pressure on their organisations increased. Save for some exceptions, the boards here were more reluctant to carry out policies that went beyond the realm of welfare activities. For example, the chairman of the UGIF-Sud, Lambert, refused to cooperate when pressure on the Jewish communities, and on him personally, was increased. On 1 May

---

[78] Notice of the Permanent Commission of the Dutch-Israelite Hoofdsynagoge, 14 February 1941, Doc. 00003186, Joods Museum. For other documents that testify to the leadership of the JR's overarching wish to maintain order, see, for example, Cohen, *Voorzitter van de Joodse Raad*, 81–82; Letter of the JR to the Sicherheitspolizei in Amsterdam, 7 May 1941, 182, Inv. No. 22, NIOD; Statement of Laura Mazirel, 7 November 1947, dossier Abraham Asscher and David Cohen, CABR, Access No. 2.09.09, Inv. No. 107491 III (PF Amsterdam T70982), NA. In the court case against Asscher and Cohen, the Dutch State Prosecutor, mr. L.W.M.M. Drabbe wanted to use Mazirel as a crown witness. See Houwink ten Cate, 'De justitie en de Joodsche Raad', in Ed Jonker and Maarten van Rossem, *Geschiedenis en cultuur: achttien opstellen* ('s Gravenhage: SDU, 1990), 158.

[79] Report of the meeting between Lages, aus der Fünten, Asscher and Cohen, 4 August 1942, 182, Inv. No. 4, NIOD; Cohen, *Voorzitter van de Joodse Raad*, 141.

[80] Somers, 'Kanttekeningen bij de Joodse Raad', 28.

1943, a bombing in Marseille left two SS men seriously wounded. In response, the Germans asked the UGIF-Sud for a list of persons to be arrested in retaliation. On 5 May Lambert's diary records:

At 6 p.m. I am called to the German police who demand, under the threat of arresting me and 10 per cent of my staff, a list of two hundred prominent Jews of Marseilles. I refuse, as I must. Their answer is that I will find out in the morning the decision of the German authorities as a result of my refusal, and that I will be informed of this decision by telephone during the morning.[81]

His growing refusal to cooperate with the Germans in this period resulted in his arrest in May 1943. Similarly, when on 30 June 1943 Brunner presented André Baur in the northern zone with an outline of his proposed changes and an account of the role he expected the UGIF-Nord to play in carrying out his demands, the UGIF-Nord board refused to carry out, or participate in, any police measures.[82]

Their successors were also not willing to cooperate. As Adler has noted, the 'arrest of most of the leaders of the UGIF in Paris did not [...] mean a change of policy on its part'.[83] This is not to say that the UGIF leaders never gave in to German demands, or that they were immune to threats. For example, on 4 March 1943, André Baur wrote to Lambert that the threat of measures against the rest of their personnel and against the French Jews had compelled him to reconsider his resistant, anti-German attitude. After weeks of negotiation the UGIF-Nord central board agreed to the German concession that they might retain up to 15 per cent of their foreign workers, surrendering the rest of them (they had until then been exempt from deportation) to the Nazis.[84]

The nature of the German occupation played an important role in the level of cooperation of the Dutch Council's leaders. In the Netherlands, the presence and control of the SS was soon felt, despite several attempts by Reichskommissar Seyss-Inquart to outmanoeuvre them.[85] Compared to the AJB, the UGIF-Nord and the UGIF-Sud, the JR had fairly limited room for manoeuvre. The strong presence of the SS and the German

[81] Lambert, *Diary of a Witness*, 18 May 1843 [reflection upon the events of 5 May], 181. Also see: Cohen, *Burden of Conscience*, 127–128; Laffitte, 'Between Memory and Lapse of Memory', 682.
[82] Minutes of the Administrative Council UGIF-Nord, 6 July 1943, Reel 3, MK490.4.3:3:1 (YIVO), Mémorial de la Shoah; Edinger, Report on the activities of the UGIF, p. 16; Laffitte, *Un engrenage fatal*, 154–164; Adler, *The Jews of Paris*, 150.
[83] Adler, *The Jews of Paris*, 152.
[84] Ibid., 137; Laffitte, *Juif dans la France allemande*, 179–189.
[85] For Seyss-Inquart's attempts to outmanoeuvre the SiPo-SD, with varying degrees of success, see: Griffioen and Zeller, *Jodenvervolging in Nederland, Frankrijk en België*, 207–226.

police meant that the JR gradually became completely subordinate to the orders of the German police in Amsterdam.[86] The fact that the Dutch Jewish Council, in contrast to its Western European counterparts, and similar to Jewish Councils in Poland, was not anchored in local law, enabled this.

In Belgium and France, by contrast, the Jewish bodies had a legal backing and, as a result, their complete subordination to radicalising German policies was more difficult to achieve. Moreover, the AJB, the UGIF-Nord and the UGIF-Sud had a broader scope for negotiation with rival German institutions. In both countries, as we have seen, the Military Administration (and in the case of France the Vichy regime as well) in some instances delayed or even restricted the implementation of anti-Jewish measures during the first phase of the occupation.

Despite the increasing authority of the SS in France and Belgium through the course of the war, the situation remained markedly different from that in the Netherlands. For example, although Dannecker aimed to increase pressure on the Jewish communities, he was not able to meet the expectations he set for himself in terms of the solution to the so-called Jewish question. The nature of the occupation in France, including the presence of the Vichy regime and the fact that, initially, only the north-western part of the country was occupied, obstructed the SiPo-SD-led Judenreferat (responsible for Jewish affairs) in this country from effectively carrying out the deportation of Jews from the country.[87] In Belgium did the SiPo-SD only enlarge its influence shortly before the start of the mass deportations and even then its authority was still restricted by the Military Administration.[88]

The institutional rivalry between the various departments involved in anti-Jewish politics worked out favourably for the Jewish Associations in Belgium and France. Because there was no unified policy, and as rival departments obstructed one another with competing interests, there was a delay in the implementation of anti-Jewish measures compared with the Netherlands.[89] This lessened the pressure on the AJB and the UGIF relative to that exerted on the JR. We can say how this played in, for example, the display of the yellow star, which was implemented

---

[86] Michman, 'The Uniqueness of the Joodse Raad', 377.
[87] Griffioen and Zeller, *Jodenvervolging in Nederland, Frankrijk en België*, 401–418. For the shifting power balances between the Military Administration and the SS in France (and Belgium) throughout the war, see, for example, Marrus and Paxton, *Vichy France and the Jews*, 45–48; Griffioen and Zeller, *Jodenvervolging in Nederland, Frankrijk en België*, 179–206.
[88] Griffioen and Zeller, *Jodenvervolging in Nederland, Frankrijk en België*, 235–236.
[89] For an overview of anti-Jewish regulations and the preparation for deportations between 1940 and 1942 as well as the differences in terms of the scale, pace and implementation of anti-Jewish regulations in the Netherlands, Belgium and France,

in the Netherlands six weeks earlier than in Belgium and France. The delay was largely due to practical constraints, together with the Military Administration's concern about the response of the non-Jewish population in these two countries.[90] The measure was not even introduced in the French unoccupied zone because of the objections of Xavier Vallat. The leaders of the AJB, the UGIF-Nord and the UGIF-Sud could use disagreements between rival institutions to their own advantage.

In the case of Belgium, we know that the central board of the AJB used the rivalry between the SiPo-SD and the Military Administration to create room for manoeuvre in their negotiations with both of these departments.[91] In the Netherlands, by contrast, the struggle for dominance did not result in a delay in the implementation of anti-Jewish legislation because the various German institutions overall agreed on the nature of the policies. The JR was directly subordinated to the Zentralstelle and the Judenreferat (IV B4), headed by SS-Haupsturmführer (in November 1942, he was promoted to Sturmbannführer) Zöpf and overseen by Commander of the Security Police and Security Service (SiPo-SD) Harster; rivalry resulted in an overlap of responsibilities, and these were carried out faithfully by the departments involved. As a result, anti-Jewish measures followed one another with increasing rapidity, and the JR functionaries felt this pressure on a day-to-day basis.[92]

Centralised versus Decentralised Power

Apart from the motivations of individual leaders and the nature of occupation, there are other factors that played a decisive role in shaping the organisations' effectiveness in carrying out German demands. It has become clear that German dissatisfaction in Belgium and France often followed from the Jewish bodies' failure to serve as true umbrella organisations, uniting all Jews in these countries. Therefore, the organisational structures and level of representation of the Jewish bodies are aspects that need to be considered.

---

see Griffioen and Zeller, *Jodenvervolging in Nederland, Frankrijk en België*, 231; for an overview of the impact of the institutional rivalry in the three countries, see, 642–651 and the schematic overview on 652.

[90] Marrus and Paxton, *Vichy France and the Jews*, 179; Schram, 'De distributie van de davister', 204–205.

[91] Meinen, 'De Duitse bezettingsautoriteiten en de VJB', 63–64; Griffioen and Zeller, 'Jodenvervolging in Nederland en België tijdens de Tweede Wereldoorlog: Een Vergelijkende Analyse', *Oorlogsdocumentatie '40–'45*, Vol. 8 (1997), 45.

[92] Boterman, *Duitse daders*, 99–101; Griffioen and Zeller, *Jodenvervolging in Nederland, Frankrijk en België*, 236.

Unlike the AJB, the UGIF-Nord and the UGIF-Sud, the JR quickly gained exclusive control over the Jewish communities in the Netherlands. This is especially remarkable taken into consideration that the JR was initially established as an organisation with only local authority. When the Amsterdam Jewish Council officially became a body with nationwide authority in October 1941, eight months after its establishment, it had to incorporate all remaining Jewish associations and foundations.[93] While these organisations were allowed to maintain their name and outward independence, their activities and financial resources were directly overseen by the JR. Representatives of local JR branches were appointed in each of the provinces, eleven in total, and each was obliged to report directly back to Asscher and Cohen.[94] Whereas Jozeph Michman has argued that there was relative autonomy for the local brancheswe will see that, compared with Belgium and France, local branch representatives in the Netherlands generally had little or no impact on the central board's policies and decisions; they were dependent on the decision that were taken by the Council's chairmen.[95]

The functionaries of some local branches, however, used whatever freedom they had to formulate a strategy on their own. The Enschede chairman, Sig Menko, was convinced that the directions of the central board in Amsterdam ought not to be followed). As various testimonies indicate, the Enschede leaders encouraged Jews to go into hiding while being seemingly loyal to the Germans.[96] This was in contrast to what Asscher and Cohen were doing in Amsterdam. In the end, around half of the Jews in Enschede managed to survive, a higher rate than the countrywide average (25 per cent), and this can partly be ascribed to the position taken by Menko.[97] It should also be noted that Enschede

---

[93] The first move in this direction had been made as early as 18 March 1941, when Böhmcker ordered all other Jewish associations and foundations to be incorporated into the JR, see Letter Hans Böhmcker to the chairmen of the Jewish Council, 18 March 1941, 182, Inv. No. 26, NIOD.

[94] Communications of the Joodsche Raad, 18 November 1941, pp. 1–2, M.19, No. 4, Yad Vashem. In this letter, the JR leaders aimed to create an overview of the organisation and functions of the JR local branches 'because there seem[ed] to be misunderstandings' in this regard. In total, there were twelve provincial representatives as the province of Zuid-Holland was divided up in a northern and southern zone, with The Hague responsible for the northern half of the province and Rotterdam for the southern half.

[95] Jozeph Michman, 'The Controversy Surrounding the Jewish Council of Amsterdam. From its Inception to Present Day', in Michael Marrus (ed.), *The Nazi Holocaust: Victims of the Holocaust* (Westport, CT/London: Greenwood, 1989), 826.

[96] 'Resisting Forces – the Jewish Council in Enschede 1941–1943', item ID 8413288, Film Center, Yad Vashem; Cecile Kanteman in *Het fatale dilemma*, 115–121.

[97] Schenkel, *De Twentse Paradox*, 94–95; Marnix Croes and Peter Tammes, *'Gif laten wij niet voortbestaan': Een onderzoek naar de overlevingskansen van joden in de Nederlandse gemeenten, 1940-1945* (Amsterdam: Aksant, 2006), 40.

is situated near the border with Germany, through which many German Jewish refugees had passed in the 1930s, so it is likely that the Jews there may have been more aware of the consequences of German persecution and were therefore more willing to go into hiding. The presence of an active organised resistance group in the area, the Overduin group, which arranged hiding places for Jews, together with the considerate attitude of Enschede's non-Jewish population, should also be emphasised in this context.[98] Other contributory factors include the presence of an anti-German police commissioner until the end of December 1942 and a mayor who protested against the German measures on a number of occasions.[99]

The dependence of the other local branches was in part the result of their (financial) reliance on the Amsterdam main office. The JR central board was unwilling to give the local branches freedom to act. Wartime exchanges between the central board and the local Leeuwarden branch show that the central board encouraged local branches to execute the instructions of the central board in Amsterdam as quickly and precisely as possible.[100] In the blueprint of May 1941 about the transformation of the Amsterdam Jewish Council to the Jewish Councils for the Netherlands (Joodse Raad voor Nederland), the specific role of the local branches as perceived by the JR leadership was outlined. The text highlights the intended centralised power of the Amsterdam main office: 'The provincial Jewish Councils are subject to the Joodse Raad voor Nederland and execute its orders and decrees in their respective areas. They communicate externally only with consent of the Joodse Raad voor Nederland'.[101]

There was extensive communication on an almost daily basis between the central JR board and its local branches. Indeed, on one occasion, the representative of the province of Friesland (Leeuwarden), Maurits

---

[98] Presser, *Ondergang*, Vol. 1, 407. The Overduin group was centred around Leendert Overduin, a Reformed pastor in the city of Enschede in the Eastern part of the Netherlands. From summer 1942, the group took care of Jews in hiding. In cooperation with other (small) resistance groups in the area, the Overduin group managed to save at least 800 Jews (30 per cent of the Jews in the larger Twente area) from deportation. For further reading on Overduin, see Arnold Bekkenkamp, *Leendert Overduin: het levensverhaal van een pastor Pimpernel, 1900–1976* (Enschede: Van de Berg, 2000).

[99] Schenkel, *De Twentse Paradox*, 131–132.

[100] Letter of the JR central board to Mr Troostwijk (representative of the Leeuwarden branch), 28 May 1943, p. 29, M. 19, Inv. No. 2, Yad Vashem. Also see the statement of Franz Fischer, who worked for the Judenreferat in The Hague, 22 December 1947, dossier Abraham Asscher and David Cohen, CABR, Access No. 2.09.09, Inv. No. 107491 I (PF Amsterdam T70982), NA. Fischer indicated that the Hague branch of the JR never took any decision on its own and that the central office in Amsterdam always had to be consulted first.

[101] 'Ontwerp statuut Joodsche Raad voor Nederland, Memorandum – samenstelling van de Joodsche Raad', 1941, p. 1 182, Inv. No. 1, NIOD.

Troostwijk, expressed dissatisfaction that there had not been communication for several days, showing just how often the central board was
usually in touch with local branches.[102] Local branches were not only
subject to the Amsterdam central board. They also worked under the
direct supervision of the SiPo-SD – the German authorities thus had the
power to intervene without informing the Amsterdam leaders.[103]

In addition to the local branches that were responsible for the Jews in
certain towns and regions, the JR had numerous sub-departments that
were responsible for particular social sectors, including the department
of immigration, the office for Help for the Departing (Hulp aan Vertrekkenden), the education department and the socio-pedagogic department. Whereas the local branches were simply taken over from the Jewish
Coordinating Committee that was dismantled in November 1941, these
social departments were newly established. Administrative documents
show that they all frequently reported back to the JR's central board.[104]

There was also the so-called Joodsche Beirat, which was formed by,
and represented, German Jews in the Netherlands. In a post-war report,
Cohen indicated that the task of the Beirat was to advise the JR and that,
as such, it had a major impact on the decisions of the organisation.[105]
However, in practice, the Beirat was never officially part of the JR. It had
neither substantial autonomy nor a real say in the Council's decisions or
regulations, in part because its members did not have the right to vote.[106]

By contrast, the Expositur department of the JR, headed by Austrian Jew Edwin Sluzker, was more important in its function. Initially, it
exclusively aided Jews in completing their emigration forms. However,
its responsibilities increased as the war progressed, in particular after the
evacuation of Jews in the Netherlands to Amsterdam and the first deportations to Eastern Europe commenced in summer 1942. It was responsible for providing social welfare to Jews in the Hollandsche Schouwburg
(a Dutch theatre, during the war renamed Joodsche Schouwburg, Jewish

[102] Letter of Troostwijk to the Amsterdam central Council board, Joodse Raad voor
Leeuwarden, 27 May 1943, p. 31, M.19, Inv. No. 2, Yad Vashem. Troostwijk indicated that the last internal information (interne informatie) had been received on 20
May 1943 and that they wished to receive an update about the course of events.
[103] Michman, 'De oprichting van de "Joodsche Raad voor Amsterdam"', 91.
[104] See: Joodse Raad voor Amsterdam, 182, NIOD.
[105] Cohen, Voorzitter van de Joodse Raad, 200.
[106] Report of Gertrude van Tijn, 'Bijdrage tot de Geschiedenis der Joden in Nederland',
p. 5, 248-1720B, Inv. No. 1, NIOD. For the interactions between the Beirat and the
central board in Amsterdam, see: Beirat 'voor niet-Nederlandse joden', 182, Inv. No.
36, NIOD. For Cohen's reflections on the establishment of the Beirat and its role, see
Statement of David Cohen, dossier Abraham Asscher and David Cohen, 24 March
1947, CABR, Access No. 2.09.09, Inv. No. 107491 V (PF Amsterdam T70982), NA.

theatre), an assembly place of Jews before they were sent to Westerbork in the north of the country. The Expositur also arranged exemptions at the office of the Zentralstelle, headed by aus der Fünten.[107]

As in the case of its Dutch counterpart, the Belgian AJB was instructed to incorporate into itself Jewish charitable institutions, as stated in its establishment order of 25 November 1941. The Military Administration could either insist upon incorporation or alternatively give the order to dissolve social welfare organisations other than the AJB, transferring their possessions and financial resources to the newly established Jewish organisation.[108] Yet this centralisation never succeeded, which obstructed the AJB's organisational effectiveness.

In order to achieve the centralisation of welfare activities under the organisation's umbrella, the AJB planned several meetings with existing organisations in early 1942, including with the most important ones in Brussels: The Rusthuis voor Bejaarden, a home for the elderly, the Central Israelite Relief Work (Oeuvre Centrale Israélite de Secours, OCIS), the central Jewish relief society established in 1920, and the Israelite Orphanage (Israëlitisch Weeshuis).[109] At this point, the AJB central board still granted these organisations financial autonomy, allowing them to receive membership dues and gifts.[110] During the following months, individual local AJB branches developed different policies in relation to the social welfare organisations that still operated largely outside the structures of the AJB. For example, while the Brussels branch in February 1942 ruled that none of these organisations would be allowed to receive memberships dues any longer, the Antwerp branch still allowed Beth Lechem, a Jewish organisation dedicated to poor relief, to do so.[111]

---

[107] Presser, Ondergang, Vol. 1, 465; Cohen, Voorzitter van de Joodse Raad, 90–94.
[108] Report concerning the establishment of a *Vereinigung der Juden* in Belgium, 15 October 1941, 184/Tr50.077, Marburg Documentation, DOS; *Verordnungsblatt des Militärbefehlshabers in Belgien und Nordfrankreich*, no. 63, 2 December 1941, JMDV, CNHEJ, Buber Collection, Kazerne Dossin; Report of meeting of M. Benedictus, E. Hellendall and S. Pinkous with the Comité de la Rue Ruysbroeck, 27 March 1942, A008428, JMDV, CNHEJ, Buber Collection, Kazerne Dossin; Schreiber, 'Tussen traditionele en verplichte gemeenschap', 73.
[109] Catharine Massenge, 'De sociale politiek' in van Doorslaer and Schreiber, *De curatoren van het getto*, 216–218.
[110] Minutes of the meeting of the local Brussels board, 28 January 1942, A006941, JMDV, CNHEJ, Buber Collection, Kazerne Dossin; Massenge, 'De sociale politiek', 218.
[111] Minutes of the AJB central board, 5 February 1942, A006703, JMDV, CNHEJ, Buber Collection, Kazerne Dossin; Massenge, 'De sociale politiek', 218. For the discussions of the incorporation of Jewish welfare organisations under the AJB's umbrella, see, for example, Minutes of the meeting of the local Brussels board, 28 January 1942, A006939, CNHEJ, Buber Collection, Kazerne Dossin; Minutes of the meeting of the local Brussels board, 11 February 1942, A006941; Minutes of the meeting of the local Brussels board, 4 March 1942, A006944.

In May 1942, despite the formal incorporation of organisations such as the Aid Organisation for Jews from Germany, the centralisation of Jewish social welfare remained ineffective and the AJB leadership accepted at this point that it would merely oversee the organisations rather than incorporate them.[112] In the report 'La Centralisation de la Bienfaisance' (The Centralisation of Charity), written in spring 1942, Oscar Teitelbaum, a member of the AJB Antwerp branch, indicated that centralisation was no longer the main aim. He claimed it would be detrimental to poor relief and that members of the individual organisations were reluctant to serve in a subservient role under the leadership of the AJB.[113] Whereas social welfare was centrally organised by the Dutch JR in late 1941, the AJB in spring 1942 thus still depended upon autonomously operating welfare organisations that worked in conjunction with its local branches.

During a meeting in this period (spring 1942) between the Jewish leaders and Wilhelm von Hahn, liaison officer for the AJB at the *Militärwaltungsstab* of Eggert Reeder, the decentralised nature of Jewish social welfare was highlighted. Individual Jewish aid organisations continued to receive support from a variety of Belgian institutions in response to the financial difficulties they faced in the wake of the liquidation of Jewish enterprises. Von Hahn voiced his dissatisfaction with the Jewish communities' dependence on the financial aid of non-Jewish organisations, emphasising that the Reich Association of Jews, the Jewish body that was established to unite the Jewish communities in Germany under its umbrella, successfully took care of all the costs of social work.[114] This comparison with the Reich Association underlines that this organisation continued to be seen as the AJB's reference point.

Some social welfare organisations continued to function outside the AJB throughout the course of the occupation in Belgium, including the OCIS, the central Jewish relief society established in 1920. The situation was similar in the southern zone of France, where Jewish welfare organisations also maintained their autonomy. However, in France, organisations were still officially grouped under the umbrella of the UGIF-Sud, whereas the OCIS in Belgium was not officially part of the AJB. The diverse nature of the Jewish communities in both Belgium and France and the influx of large numbers of Jews in the decades before 1940

---

[112] Steinberg, *L'étoile et le fusil. La traque des Juifs 1942–1944*, 94.
[113] Oscar Teitelbaum, 'La Centralisation de la Bienfaisance', spring 1942, A005269, JMDV, MNR, Kazerne Dossin.
[114] Report of meeting between Dr Löffler, Von Hahn, S. van den Berg and M. Benedictus, 8 April 1942, A007599, JMDV, CNHEJ, Buber Collection, Kazerne Dossin.

necessitated the existence of a large variety of Jewish aid organisations.[115] As there were no retaliation measures for the failure to bring all organisations under the umbrella of the AJB, these social welfare groups did not feel pressured to surrender their autonomy. According to Schreiber, the fact that the Belgian administration legally recognised organisations such as the OCIS, which was part of the Israelite congregation, made it impossible for the Germans to disband this organisation.[116]

The unwillingness of the OCIS to be incorporated in the AJB Brussels branch led to increasing tension between the two organisations in February 1943, because the former wanted to remain functionally autonomous while the AJB was trying to strengthen its hold on the Jewish communities in Brussels. By then, the OCIS was no longer financially autonomous since it received substantial financial support from the AJB.[117] Leo Feiertag, secretary of the Brussels AJB branch, complained about the function of the OCIS, arguing that it was not working properly because it failed to help people who were ill and depended on social support.[118] When the OCIS finally agreed that it would be incorporated in the AJB's social service division on the condition that its executive committee remained in existence, the AJB disagreed, and its leadership's wish for close cooperation between the two organisations was therefore not realised.[119]

On 28 June 1943, the Military Commander of Belgium and Northern France, Alexander von Falkenhausen, aware that the unification of Belgian Jewry under the AJB's umbrella had not been successful, in an ultimate attempt commanded that all Jewish welfare organisations had to be incorporated into local AJB branches as soon as possible. Among these were local aid organisations such as the Israelite Association for Effective Relief (Société Israélite des Secours Efficaces), the Association of Israelite Mothers and Orphans (Société des Mères et Orphelines Israélites) and the Israelite Orphanage in Brussels (Orphelinat Israélite de Bruxelles), as well as the OCIS.[120]

---

[115] Massenge, 'De sociale politiek', 238.
[116] Schreiber, 'Tussen traditionele en verplichte gemeenschap', 85–86. For an overview of the Belgian judicial structure during the German occupation, see David Fraser, *The Fragility of Law: Constitutional Patriotism and the Jews of Belgium, 1940–1945* (Abingdon: Routledge-Cavendish, 2009), passim.
[117] Minutes of the 49th meeting of the local Brussels board, 3 March 1943, A006996, JMDV, CNHEJ, Buber Collection, Kazerne Dossin.
[118] Minutes of the 48th meeting of the local Brussels board, 24 February 1943, A006994.04, JMDV, CNHEJ, Buber Collection, Kazerne Dossin.
[119] Minutes of the 51st meeting of the local Brussels board, 17 March 1943, A006998, JMDV, CNHEJ, Buber Collection, Kazerne Dossin.
[120] Minutes of the 68th meeting of the local Brussels board, 30 June 1943, A007021.03, JMDV, CNHEJ, Buber Collection, Kazerne Dossin.

One month later, Chaïm Perelman was appointed to function as an intermediary between the AJB Brussels board and the executive committee of the OCIS in order to see if von Falkenhausen's demand could be met.[121] Whether or when these organisations were officially incorporated into the AJB remains unclear. In April 1944, the OCIS still operated in parallel to the social service department of the AJB and the two bodies cooperated in providing care to 753 families in Brussels.[122] The difference with the Netherlands, where the JR served as the sole representative body of the Jews, even more so after the Coordinating Committee was dissolved in November 1941, is striking.

The position of the AJB's local branches was also different from that of its counterparts in the Netherlands. Whereas the chairmen of the JR's local branches only had an advisory role to the central board, the local AJB leaders of the largest communities in Belgium were also part of the central board themselves. Juda Mehlwurm, for example, headed the local AJB Charleroi board and was also a member of the central board.[123] This gave these local leaders a much larger role in determining AJB policies. Meeting reports of the central board show that at least one representative of each of the local boards was required to be present in order to make the meetings, and the decisions made in them, legitimate.[124]

That local communities were represented differently in the central boards of the JR and the AJB might be explained by the fact that, as we have seen, the vast majority of the Jews in Belgium lived in one of the country's four major cities (45 per cent in Brussels, 45 per cent in Antwerp and 9 per cent in both Liège or Charleroi). In the Netherlands, by contrast, 60 per cent of the Jews lived in Amsterdam while others lived dispersed in numerous localities across the country. As a result, the JR had more than three times as many local branches than the AJB had. From early 1942, more Jews settled in the Dutch capital city, as a result of an active policy of forced relocation of Jews that was implemented by the Germans.[125] Jewish life was thus centred in Amsterdam, yet the

---

[121] For a biographical overview of Perelman, see Alan Gross and Ray Dearin, *Chaïm Perelman* (New York: State University of New York Press, 2003); Schreiber, *Dictionnaire Biographique*, 271–274.
[122] Massenge, 'De sociale politiek', 238.
[123] Nico Workum, Juda Mehlwurm, Noé Nozyce (Nozice) headed the Antwerp, Charleroi and Liège local AJB board respectively and, consequently, were also part of the AJB's central board.
[124] Document explaining the organisation of the AJB, December 1941, A003710, MNR, Kazerne Dossin.
[125] Presser, *Ondergang*, Vol 2, 203–211.

dispersion of those who lived elsewhere continued to make it difficult to represent local communities in the JR's central board. Another explanation for the lack of local representation might be the fact that the JR chairmen maintained an autocratic position in the central board, and they were not inclined to have local community representatives interfere in their policies.

In spite of their representation in the central board, local AJB branches also faced restrictions, and they remained subordinate to the central administration throughout their existence. That is, members of the local boards implemented the decisions made by the central board and had to provide a monthly report of their daily activities. Moreover, the central board supervised the expenses of the local branches and, as a document on the organisation of the AJB dating from December 1941 indicates, their financial resources were considered the exclusive property of the AJB central board.[126] Above all, local branches were only allowed to communicate with the Germans through the central board.[127]

On 3–4 September 1943, Operation Iltis was launched against all Jews of Belgian nationality, with the purpose of placing them to work in 'the East'. As a response, all local AJB branches, except for the Brussels local office that merged with the central office, ceased to exist. Between April and October 1943, all the Jewish communities of Antwerp, Charleroi, Ghent, Mons, Arlon and Liège were liquidated. Those members of the local branches who were not immediately arrested and deported were relocated to the central board in Brussels.[128]

Whereas the AJB central board had a different kind of relationship to its local branches than the JR, the organisation and structure of the social welfare provision was almost identical. Departments such as Social Assistance (Maatschappelijke Hulp), Education (Centrale Onderwijscommissie), Special Aid (Speciale Hulp), Housing Management (Centrale Huisbeheer) and Immediate Assistance (Onmiddelijke Bijstand) all had their own specific function and fell under a more broadly defined division of labour (including local committees, the secretary, finances, welfare, education, emigration, and culture and the arts).[129]

---

126 Document explaining the organisation of the AJB, December 1941, A003710, MNR, Kazerne Dossin.
127 Ibid.; Meeting report of the 58th meeting of the local Antwerp board, A007213, JMDV, CNHEJ, Buber Collection, Kazerne Dossin.
128 The Iltis Plan for the Detainment and Expulsion of Jews who are Belgian Subjects, 1 September 1943, AA556, CEGESOMA; Schreiber, 'Tussen traditionele en verplichte gemeenschap', 104–105.
129 Letter of the Antwerp AJB board to the Labour Office (Arbeidsambt) concerning the statute and the role of the AJB, 29 June 1942, A005945.01, MNR, Kazerne

These departments were responsible for large numbers of Jews and this, together with rapidly changing circumstances and the lack of pre-war organisational working experience for most of the function-airies involved, meant that communication and cooperation between the various departments was strained. Those who worked in the education department had almost no experience, for example, in how to set up, structure and operate an education system. The only exception was Chaïm Perelman, who had been a professor at the ULB before the war.[130] The lack of coordination in some sections resulted at times in the development of complex and confusing organisational structures at the highest level of the AJB. The Jews in Belgium therefore depended far more than their counterparts in the Netherlands upon local organisational branches and their initiatives.

In France, the UGIF in neither zone became an umbrella organisation similar to the JR in the Netherlands. This was particularly the case in the southern zone where the UGIF-Sud's federative structure resulted in a situation where a substantial number of Jewish (welfare) bodies were officially administered by the organisation while in practice they remained autonomous. Its different sections (*directions*) in fact represented organisations that already existed before the war. In designing the UGIF-Sud, Lambert had been well aware of the differences between the groups of Jews who resided in France. When he instituted the seven departments with subsections, he therefore allowed a wide range of welfare activities that represented the prevailing currents in the different communities.[131]

For example, the first department ('family') of the organisation consisted of two sections, incorporating the CCOJA, the French Israelite Mutual Aid Society of Marseille (Entr'aide française Israélite de Société de Bienfaisance Israélite de Marseille), the Israelite Refuge House (Maison Israélite de Refuge) in Lyon and the Union of Israelite Charity Societies (Union des Sociétés de Bienfaisance Israélite) in Toulouse. The second department incorporated the Organisation for the Social Aid to Displaced Populations of Alsace Lorraine (Oeuvre d'Aide Sociale Auprès des Populations Repliées d'Alsace Lorraine) in Périgueux. Other departments incorporated Jewish welfare organisations such as the ORT, OSE, EIF and HICEM.[132]

Dossin; Dickschen, 'De VJB en het onderwijs' in van Doorslaer and Schreiber, *De curatoren van het getto*, 183.

[130] Dickschen, 'De VJB en het onderwijs', 191.
[131] Cohen, *Burden of Conscience*, 137.
[132] For a full overview of the administrative apparatus of the UGIF-Sud, including its departments and subsections, see: Laffitte, *Juif dans la France allemande*, 408–409.

In contrast to the situation in the Netherlands and Belgium, the individual departments of the UGIF-Sud were also financially autonomous. The OSE and the Jewish scouts were, for example, only loosely associated with the UGIF-Sud and 'could follow their own policies with little intervention'.[133] These organisations legally aided the Jewish communities in the unoccupied zone by providing social welfare such as clothing and food. As we shall see in Chapter 5, they simultaneously engaged in clandestine activities, including the provision of hiding places for children.

The UGIF-Sud was similar to the JR, the AJB and the UGIF-Nord, in that local branches were put in place in cities with a (large) Jewish presence (Marseille and Toulouse, for example). Compared with the JR and the AJB, the number of local branches of both the UGIF-Nord and UGIF-Sud was considerable and, in the case of the UGIF-Sud, these remained operative well into 1944. Correspondence between the various UGIF directors show that some of the UGIF-Sud branches were centralised in April/May 1944.[134]

Initially, the UGIF-Sud leadership expected a gradual dissolution of welfare organisations and their transference into the UGIF structures. However, this did not happen. In contrast to its Western European counterparts, owing to the decentralised nature of Jews in France, the UGIF-Sud remained a federation of many different departments and subsections, in which its leadership lacked any real authority and influence over departments or the Jewish communities.

As a result of its federative structure, the organisation was never exploited by the Germans to carry out arrests, deportations or selections. Moreover, the leadership never attempted to direct the communities into a particular course of action. Since the UGIF-Sud did not have independent financial resources and only had a few autonomous areas of activity, which included its relations with German and Vichy authorities and their engagement in relief work, it had limited influence. The organisation was functioning as a polyarchy 'unable to serve the German designs even if it so desired'.[135]

---

[133] Cohen, *Burden of* Conscience, 121.
[134] Correspondence of Raymond Geissmann (the last chairman of the UGIF) with other UGIF leaders and with Rabbi Deutsch on the liquidation of regional offices, 7 April 1944–30 May 1944, CDX-59, CDJC, Mémorial de la Shoah. In early April 1944, the local branches of le Brive, Périgueux and Vichy were closed, after the Chambéry-Grenoble branch had been dismantled two months earlier and the personnel arrested. As a consequence, the UGIF's last director Geissmann sent a letter to Kurt Schendel, who as *chef de liaison* served as an intermediary between the UGIF and the Germans, and indicated that the local branches of Chateauroux, Guéret and St. Amand had transferred their activities to the regional office of Limoges, while the Pau branch had been transferred to Toulouse.
[135] Cohen, *The Burden of Conscience*, 153.

Turning to the UGIF-Nord, we see that its bureaucratic structure was highly complex. As in the cases of the JR, the AJB and the UGIF-Sud, the Jewish body was divided into individual departments, each with particular social welfare responsibilities. The majority of the UGIF-Nord central board members were assigned to administer individual departments. For example, Georges Edinger, Fernand Musnik and Juliette Stern were responsible for administration and finances (section 2), youth and redeployment (section 4) and social services (section 3) respectively. Section 2 had direct control over certain UGIF provincial offices such as Seine-et-Oise, Lunéville, Nancy, Bordeaux and Rouen.

Section 1, including all general services and headed by Marcel Stora, was the most important department. Besides the general secretariat, it included the population card index, the legal department, dispatch of food supplies to camp inmates, the official journal of the UGIF (*Bulletin de l'UGIF*), liaison with the Germans and the Préfecture de Police, the control commission, the administrative committee and the administration of the UGIF's provincial committees. In the second half of 1942, the UGIF-Nord consisted of as many as forty-eight different departments. The leadership's wish to maintain firm control over all these departments resulted in an impractical situation in which '[n]o independence of operation within departments was tolerated'.[136]

In a similar way to its predecessor the Coordinating Committee, the UGIF-Nord suffered from a lack of cooperation from immigrant community leaders. This has been explained by the fact that the UGIF-Nord leaders followed a legalistic model of behaviour, 'rooted in a trust in France and fostered by generations of emancipation'.[137] However, this analysis is too narrow since we know that clandestine activities were undertaken under the cloak of the UGIF-Nord and by its own members. The strong divisions among French Jewry and its non-unified nature, combined with Central and Eastern European Jewish immigrants' distrust of Nazi policies, better explain the lack of immigrant support for the UGIF. They had, after all, already voiced their opposition during the establishment of the UGIF, when communists and Bundists stated that no collaboration with Vichy was acceptable.[138] As a result of these factors, the power of the UGIF-Nord leadership over the Jewish communities was restricted. Above all, despite the negative public perception of both the UGIF-Nord and the UGIF-Sud, which increased during the war, we have to conclude that their actual scope of

[136] Adler, *The Jews in Paris*, 115–116.
[137] Cohen, *Burden of Conscience*, x.
[138] Adler, *The Jews of Paris*, 87.

action was limited. This explains, in part, why the Germans were dissatisfied with their function.

Powerful Alternative Representations in Belgium and France

The presence or absence of alternative kinds of representation that operated (largely) independently of the JR, the AJB, the UGIF-Nord and the UGIF-Sud could affect the extent of the control that the organisations were able to exercise over the communities. Therefore, from the German perspective, this was another important factor in the Jewish organisations' potential effectiveness.

As discussed, large numbers of immigrants in both Belgium and France had brought with them whole new sets of ideas and convictions before the war. In these two countries, the highly diversified and scattered nature of the Jewish communities made it impossible to represent the Jews through umbrella organisations such as the AJB, the UGIF-Nord and the UGIF-Sud. The wide range of social welfare organisations that were established to take care of these different groups of Jews, such as the Foreign Working Force (Main d'Oeuvre Étrangère, MOE), a communist foreign workers' organisation, and the Jewish Solidarity (Solidarité Juive), which was created in 1939 specifically to aid political refugees from Poland, continued to exist after the German invasion of Belgium and France in May 1940.[139]

The existence of other Jewish representative organisations in both Belgium and France, compared with an absence of alternative powerful Jewish representative bodies in the Netherlands, is an aspect that has been overlooked in the existing historiography because there has until now been no solidly comparative approach. Whereas Adler, for example, has indicated that the UGIF, as the sole official source of support and assistance, occupied a central place in the Jews' struggle for survival, we will see that there were strong alternative representative groups in the French Jewish communities that continued to operate in parallel to this organisation.[140] These included both the Consistory and secular aid institutions. In Belgium, alternative forms of representation came primarily in the form of secular aid institutions. These alternatives served to hamper the potential organisational effectiveness and absolute power of the AJB, the UGIF-Nord and the UGIF-Sud.

---

[139] Steinberg, *L'étoile et le fusil: Les cent jours de la déportation*, 60–61; Van Doorslaer, 'Jewish Immigration and Communism in Belgium', 68–81; Moore, *Survivors*, 175.
[140] Adler, *The Jews of Paris*, 133.

The German (and Vichy) officials who oversaw the establishment of the 'Jewish Councils' considered it a necessity that these would coordinate both social and religious life. In order to achieve this, the inclusion of all Jews, and Jewish organisations, under the umbrella of the JR, the AJB, the UGIF-Nord and the UGIF-Sud was considered a necessity. We have seen, for example, that Dannecker, inspired by the examples of Jewish Councils and similar organisations elsewhere in occupied Europe, attempted in the first instance to convince Rabbis Sachs and Weill to transform the Paris Consistory into an organisation representative of the Jews in Paris, responsible for all social, religious and charitable needs of the Jewish people.[141]

Nevertheless, the nature of the Jewish communities in France was such that the Consistory continued to represent religious Jewry independently. The law even required that religious institutions should be able to execute their practices autonomously.[142] Above all, the vast number of Jewish immigrants, whose religious orientation varied widely, could not be represented by a singular umbrella organisation that failed to respect the specificity of their spiritual beliefs. Although the Consistory did not represent the large variety of religious beliefs either, it was at least focussed on religious life exclusively, whereas the UGIF-Nord and the UGIF-Sud were not.

In the Netherlands, the religious NIK remained in existence during the war and, as Michman has shown, the Jewish Coordinating Committee, headed by Visser, encouraged cooperation between the leaders of the NIK and liberal Jewry in order to face difficult times together during the first phase of the German occupation.[143] However, the dissolution of the Coordinating Committee meant that pressure to unify the two community federations faded from November 1941. This can be explained by the fact that the JR received national authority in this period and Asscher and Cohen were attached to the traditional community federations of the NIK, whose Chief Rabbis remained reluctant to cooperate with the liberal Jews.[144]

---

[141] For SS-Obersturmführer Dannecker's attempt to transform the ACIP into a *Zwangsvereinigung*, see his report titled 'Judenfrage in Frankreich und ihre Behandlung', 1 July 1941, XXVI-1, CDJC, Mémorial de la Shoah. Also see Happe, Mayer and Peers, *Die Verfolgung und Ermordung der europäischen Juden*, Vol. 5, DOK. 272, 675–690.

[142] Lucien Lazare, *Rescue as Resistance: How Jewish Organizations Fought the Holocaust in France*, transl. Jeffrey Green (New York: Columbia University Press, 1996), 82.

[143] Michman, *Het Liberale Jodendom in Nederland*, 134–137.

[144] Ibid., 137.

Above all, even though the Portuguese–Israelite (Sephardi) and Dutch–Israelite (Ashkenazi) community federations continued to cooperate in parallel to the JR, increasing secularisation, shown in the decline in regular synagogue attendance, diminished their power and influence before the war.[145] The waning influence of the religious federations was further reinforced by internal disputes among and between the various Jewish factions, most notably the Liberals, zionists and the Dutch-Israelite representatives.[146] Therefore, unlike in France, there was no powerful religious authority in the Netherlands that could function as an alternative to the JR.

The existence of alternative representative organisations affected the position of the Jewish organisations in Belgium and France. In France, the Consistory at times (vehemently) opposed the UGIF's existence and policies. Disagreements between the UGIF leadership and the Consistory were omnipresent, especially in the period prior to, and immediately after, the organisation's establishment.[147] The Consistory believed that the institution of the UGIF would be a major mistake. Although tensions decreased during the course of the occupation, and the two bodies even cooperated, some discord was always present.[148]

That UGIF central board members were closely watched by highly esteemed members of the French Jewish community, who still exerted a significant influence, at times led the UGIF officials to re-evaluate their decisions or encouraged its leaders to dissolve the organisation.[149] The fact that the first meeting of the UGIF-Sud's central board was held as late as 4 May 1942, can be explained in this context. While this delay was partly caused by the problems that surfaced during the formation of the board, which took two months, the further delay in the UGIF's organisation resulted from the Jewish communities' internal

---

[145] Moore, *Victims and Survivors*, 25; Michman, Beem and Michman, *Pinkas*, 130–131.
[146] Michman, *Het Liberale Jodendom in Nederland*, 107–122.
[147] Cohen, 'Le Consistoire et l'UGIF: La situation trouble des Juifs Français face à Vichy', 28–33; Ibid., *The Burden of Conscience*, 57–63; Szajowski, 'The Organization of the "UGIF" in Nazi-Occupied France', 247.
[148] See, for example, the memorandum of Albert Lévy to the Central Consistory regarding the UGIF and the attitude of the Consistory to the UGIF, end of February 1942, Reel 2, MK490.2 (YIVO), Mémorial de la Shoah; Meeting reports of the Commission Central des Organisations Juives d'Assistance (CCOJA) on the establishment of the UGIF: 16 and 22 October 1941, CCXIII-72; 26 October 1941, CCXIII-74; 12 November 1941, CCXIII-76, CDJC, Mémorial de la Shoah. Several organisations were represented during these meetings, including CAR, EIF, FSJF, OSE and Rabbinical authorities.
[149] For an overview of the opposition between the Consistory and the UGIF, see Cohen, 'Le Consistoire et l'UGIF: La situation trouble des Juifs Français face à Vichy', 28–37.

disputes and from the disapproval shown by leading Consistory members towards the UGIF. Lambert reflected upon the continuing anxiety in this period: 'There continues to be agitation and back-fence talk among the Jews, led by people who have nothing to do and are jealous of our useful action, jealous especially of the trust the authorities have shown in me...the least.'[150]

In Belgium, the situation was different because Rabbi Ullmann presided over the Consistory while he simultaneously headed the AJB. In contrast to France, where the opposition to the UGIF took a solid, organised form, the protests against the AJB were therefore not centrally orchestrated by the Consistory. The fact that pre-war Consistorial leaders had fled abroad at the outbreak of war removed the main potential mouthpiece for criticism of Ullmann's policies. Only in France did the criticisms voiced by the Consistory therefore actually serve as a constraint on the policies of the UGIF-Nord and the UGIF-Sud.

Secular aid institutions that obstructed the authority of the AJB, the UGIF-Nord and UGIF-Sud were manifold in Belgium and France. In Belgium, zionist youth movements engaged in welfare activities and increasingly cooperated with one another during the war. As Moore has indicated, 'the cooperation between different welfare and resistance organizations in Belgium during the occupation, coupled with the willingness of Jewish and non-Jewish groups across the political spectrum to work together, provided the basis for an organization unique in Western Europe'.[151]

This attempt at unity materialised through the CDJ, a leftist charitable organisation that united various Jewish organisations and originated among members of the Independent Front (Front d'Indépendance, FI).[152] The FI was a resistance movement founded on 15 March 1941 by journalist Fernand Demany, who brought together leaders from various political strands. The initiative for the CDJ emerged from far-left Jewish circles almost simultaneously in five major cities in response to the first threats of deportation in July 1942.[153]

---

[150] Lambert, *Diary of a Witness*, 11 February 1942, 97.
[151] Moore, *Survivors*, 175; for an overview of the history of the organisations that helped Jews to avoid persecution and deportation in Belgium, see 166–207.
[152] The Front d'Indépendance was referred to as the Onafhankelijkheidsfront (OF) in Dutch.
[153] Steinberg, *Le comité de défense des Juifs en Belgique*, 39; René de Lathouwer, *Historique du Comité de Défense des Juifs* (Témoignages et documents recueillis entre 1947 et 1951 par Renee de Lathouwer), introduction, AB2167, CEGESOMA; Lieven Saerens, 'Die Hilfe für Juden in Belgien', in Wolfgang Benz and Juliane Wetzel (eds.), *Solidarität und Hilfe für Juden während der NS-Zeit*, Vol. 2 (Berlin: Metropol, 1998), 250. Also see Jeanine Levana Frenk, 'Le Linké Poalé Zion et la Résistance en

The CDJ functioned in close connection with the FI and was eventually taken under its wing.[154] Hertz Jospa, a communist of Romanian/ Bessarabian origin and member of the Conseil National of the FI, proposed the establishment of the CDJ as a way to assist the Jewish population.[155] He was supported by his wife, Yvonne Jospa. Another important individual was Emile Hambresin, former editor of the periodical *Avant Garde* and president of the Belgian Committee Against Racism (Comité Belge Contre le Racisme), who knew Jospa from their shared membership in the Association to Combat Antisemitism (Ligue pour Combattre l'Antisémitisme) in the 1930s.[156] Jospa and Hambresin were joined by six others, including Abusz (Abous) Werber of the left-wing Poale-Zion, and Israël (Maurice) Mandelbaum of Solidarité Juive.[157] In order to create a broad base of representation in the CDJ, the right-wing-oriented Chaïm Perelman, who was associated with the AJB, was also included.[158] Other CDJ representatives were Benjamin (Benno) Nykerk, industrialist, Edouard Rothkel, secretary of the Brussels Jewish community, and Eugène Hellendall, a wealthy industrialist who also served for the Brussels branch of the AJB.[159] They all set aside their fears about becoming involved with left-wing organisations, including the communists, in order to create an organisation that would help the Jewish communities in Belgium.[160] The only major Jewish organisation that was not represented in the CDJ was the Bund, a secular Jewish socialist party that was originally established in the Russian Empire at the end of the nineteenth century, and sought to unite all Jewish workers under one umbrella.[161]

From September 1942, the CDJ was a powerful alternative to the AJB for the Jews in Belgium, helping an estimated 15,000 people into

Belgique durant la Seconde Guerre mondiale', *Cahiers de la Mémoire Contemporaine/ Bijdragen tot de Eigentijdse geschiedenis*, Vol. 12 (2016), 63–98.

[154] Gotovitch, 'Resistance Movements and the "Jewish Question"', 280–228; Steinberg, *Le comité de défense des juifs en Belgique*, 36. It should be noted that many of the CDJ's records remained in private hands or were lost in the post-war period.

[155] Steinberg, *Le comité de défense des Juifs en Belgique*, 38. Herz Jospa is also referred to as Ghert or Joseph.

[156] Steinberg, *L'étoile et le fusil. La traque des Juifs*, Vol. 1, 66.

[157] Moore, *Survivors*, 175; Frenk, 'Le Linke Poalé Zion', 90–91.

[158] Saerens, *Vreemdelingen in een wereldstad*, 695; Also see the interview in the USC Shoah collection with Noémi Mattis (Perelman), daughter of Chaïm Perelman and Fajga Perelman, where she describes the life, including the wartime activities, of her father: Interview Noémi Mattis (Perelman), 24 November 1995, Interview No. 9178, USC Shoah Foundation. Accessed at the American University of Paris, Paris.

[159] De Lathouwer, *Comité de défense des Juifs*, 22–23.

[160] Steinberg, *Le comité de défense des Juifs en Belgique*, 68; Moore, *Survivors*, 176.

[161] Lucien Steinberg, 'Jewish Rescue Activities in Belgium and France', in Yisrael Gutman and Efraim Zuroff (eds.), *Rescue Attempts during the Holocaust: Proceedings*

hiding.[162] In total, the organisation 'may have helped up to 30,000 individuals with false papers, encompassing not only the Jews in Belgium but also those passing through the country, and several thousand labour draft evaders'.[163] The group also attempted on a number of occasions to sabotage the German war machine by derailing trains and setting fire to factories. In fact, the CDJ became one of FI's most effective groups.[164] While focussing on propaganda, and the provision of false papers and material aid, the rescue of children was its central occupation.[165] We will see in Chapter 5 that its members actively aimed to hamper the actions of what they considered the collaborationist AJB, for example by encouraging Jews not to cooperate with its directives, even though the opposition of CDJ members to the AJB was not as uniform as has been suggested in the literature.[166]

In addition to the CDJ, there were other social welfare organisations still functioning in parallel to the AJB, including Mutual Aid (Secours Mutuel), Popular Aid (Secours Populaire), Zionist Aid (Secours Sioniste), Jewish Solidarity (Solidarité Juive), National Children's Aid (Oeuvre Nationale de l'Enfance, ONE) and, as noted, OCIS. The existence of these organisations meant that the organisation and unification of Jewry by means of the AJB (which was what the Germans wanted), had not been achieved by the middle of 1943, despite SS-Obersturmführer Asche's demand (reiterated in the summer of 1942) to ban any autonomous activity of organisations other than the AJB.[167] These organisations continued to provide alternatives to the assistance offered by the AJB. Indeed, after the first wave of deportations in summer 1942, the AJB's importance lessened for the majority of non-Belgian Jews. In contrast to its counterpart in the Netherlands, the organisation also became less important to the occupier towards the end of 1942 because it was not managing to effectively represent the Jews in Belgium.[168]

of the Second Yad Vashem International Historical Conference (Jerusalem: Yad Vashem, 1977), 603–604; Steinberg, *L'étoile et le fusil. La traque des Juifs*, Vol. 1, 67–69; Betty Garfinkels, *Les Belges face à la persécution raciale, 1940–1944* (Brussels: ULB, 1965), 88–89.

[162] Moore, *Survivors*, 176.
[163] Ibid., 179; Also see De Lathouwer, *Comité de défense des Juifs*, 8.
[164] De Lathouwer, *Comité de défense des Juifs*, 2.
[165] Steinberg, *Le comité de défense des Juifs en Belgique*, 74–75; De Lathouwer, *Comité de défense des Juifs*, 2–18; Moore, *Survivors*, 176.
[166] See, for example, Moore, *Survivors*, 179.
[167] Report on the order given by SS-Obersturmbannführer to Robert Holzinger on the incorporation of Jewish organisations under the AJB's umbrella, 21 August 1942, A007415, JMDV, CNHEJ, Buber Collection, Kazerne Dossin.
[168] Steinberg, *L'étoile et le fusil: les cent jours de la déportation*, 223–227; and *La traque des Juifs*, Vol. 1, 65–81.

In France, there were various secular organisations that offered aid to Jews (illegally) with the aim of ensuring that they could escape from Vichy and from German persecution. George Weller has divided Jewish resistance in France into three categories: 1) those devoted to self-help through escape or hiding, including the Amelot Committee and the OSE; 2) those who were part of both the Jewish resistance and the armed French resistance, including Organisation Juive de Combat, Franc-Tireurs et Partisans – Main d'Oeuvre Immigrée (FTP-MOI)[169] and the EIF; and 3) the communist armed resistance organisations that included Jews but had no direct contact with the Jewish community.[170] Alternatives to the UGIF primarily belonged to the first group.

The Amelot Committee was made up of three political groups (the Bund and the left and right wings of the Poale-Zion), and two other organisations, the FSJF and the Colonie Scolaire. Its leaders had been politically active long before they arrived in France. Léo Glaser, Amelot's first treasurer, had been sought by the Tsarist police after the 1905 uprising in Russia, and the first secretary-general of the organisation, Yéhuda Jacoubovitch, was a Bundist from Poland who had been imprisoned for his opposition to Tsarism.[171] David Rapoport had been involved in the Russian revolutions of 1905 and 1917 before he arrived in France in 1920. As Moore has shown, the leftist background of these men did not result in the cooperation of the Amelot Committee with the communists, in part because cooperation of this sort would have increased the chance of surveillance by the Gestapo. Instead, the communists were organised under the umbrella of the Solidarité, which was founded in September 1940.[172]

---

[169] After the German invasion of the Soviet Union in June 1941, the French Communist Party developed its own armed wing: the Operation Spéciale, which later became the FTP. In the summer of 1942, after the Paris police's arrest of hundreds of clandestine immigrant MOI members, the FTP seconded 10 per cent of its members to form armed detachments, which became known as the FTP-MOI. David Drake, *Paris at War, 1939–1944* (Cambridge, MA: The Belknap Press of Harvard University Press), 320; Robert Gildea, *Fighters in the Shadows: A New History of the French Resistance* (London: Faber & Faber, 2015), 220–226. For a general overview of the role of the immigrants of the MOI in the resistance, see Stéphane Courtois, Denis Peschanski and Adam Rayski, *Le Sang de l'étranger: Les immigrés de la MOI dans la résistance* (Paris: Fayard, 1989), passim.

[170] As cited in Lazare, *Rescue as Resistance*, 26; for an overview of the different reflections on the Jewish identity of Jewish communist organisations, see 26–27. There are many memoirs and histories by the FTP-MOI workers and their leaders. See, for example, Adam Rayski, *Nos illusions perdues* (Paris: Balland, 1985); Louis Gronowski-Brunot, *Le Dernier grans soir: Un Juif de Pologne* (Paris: Éditions du Seuil, 1980); Boris Holban, *Testament* (Paris: Calmann-Lévy, 1989).

[171] See: Le Douarion, 'Le Comité "Rue Amelot"'; Moore, *Survivors*, 104–105; Lazare, *Rescue as Resistance*, 39–47.

[172] Moore, *Survivors*, 105.

We have seen that the Amelot Committee was represented on the Coordinating Committee instituted on 30 January 1941 to oversee the distribution of relief in the French occupied zone. After Amelot seceded from the Coordinating Committee twice, finally in summer 1941, it continued its ameliorative aid alongside the communist Solidarité, primarily helping immigrant Jews in the larger cities and those held in internment camps.[173] Another prominent organisation that provided aid to the increasingly deprived Jews in France was the Jewish scout movement EIF.

After the institution of the UGIF in November 1941, all these organisations – whether legal, illegal or quasi-legal – remained operative and assisted those in need. The EIF, for example, was incorporated into the UGIF as the Social Youth Service (Service Sociale des Jeunes, SSJ), but it also engaged in clandestine operations from July 1942. Its members primarily focused on the provision of aid to young people, but they also developed a section to help adults in securing hiding places and false identity papers. Some of its members also became involved in armed resistance activities, although this kind of activity had never been envisaged by the group's founders.[174]

From summer 1942, after the indiscriminate mass arrests and deportations of foreign Jews (including men, women, children and the old and sick), these (aid) organisations faced serious problems. The communist Solidarité had lost a high portion of its members as many immigrant Jews had either been arrested or were in hiding. The Amelot Committee was paralysed and had not yet decided whether it would make use of the protection offered by the UGIF's identity cards, which provided temporary exemption from deportation.[175] In the end, both organisations managed to resume their operations: Solidarité increased its armed resistance activities and Amelot, encouraged by Solidarité, sought to direct its welfare activities towards close liaison with non-Jewish organisations.[176]

We will see in Chapter 5 that some of the organisations that remained in existence after summer 1942, most notably Amelot, operated in parallel to

---

173 Ibid., 105–107.
174 See the report on the activities of the EIF from 1939 until shortly after the liberation, CCXVII-8, CDJC, Mémorial de la Shoah; Moore, *Survivors*, 112.
175 Adler, *The Jews of Paris*, 196–197. We will see that in the summer of 1942 the Amelot Committee decided to use these cards after all, despite moral objections to the use of protective cards issued by the Germans.
176 Ibid., 198–201. The conflict that existed between the various immigrant organisations, including the communists and the Amelot Committee, about the nature of their organisations' activities lies beyond the scope of this research. For further reading, see Adler, *The Jews of Paris*, 206–209.

the UGIF-Nord while at the same time providing a counterweight to the collaborationist agenda forced upon it. These organisations were important alternatives to the UGIF-Nord, especially for immigrants, because they provided advice and, even more important, they provided contacts with trustworthy people who could help. Although immigrant organisations in Paris suffered as a result of arrests, deportation and continuous supervision by the Gestapo, they were nonetheless firmly established by mid-1943, not least because a constant stream of refugees continued to need their help.[177]

In the unoccupied zone of France, the fact that the UGIF-Sud served as an umbrella for welfare organisations that in practice continued to function autonomously created a unique situation: such organisations were officially part of the UGIF while also serving as an alternative to it. Before the establishment of the UGIF-Sud, both national and international Jewish organisations were part of a committee (the Nîmes Committee) that coordinated assistance for those in internment camps, as decreed by the Vichy Ministry of the Interior on 20 November 1940. They included the OSE, EIF, HICEM and Joint Distribution Committee.[178] Among these organisations, the EIF, whose headquarters were moved to unoccupied France in June 1940, was the largest and most important Jewish youth movement during the occupation; its predominantly French leadership had access to a substantial network of high-ranking officials in the Vichy administration. The organisation was restructured in summer 1940 and worked, among other things, in the Vichy internment camps to improve conditions for internees, and specifically for children (at the behest of the Ministry of Youth).[179]

The incorporation of the EIF into the UGIF-Sud in 1941 had very little effect on the daily activities of the organisation, even though it officially lost its independent juridical status.[180] Through his contacts with General Lafont, Robert Gamzon, the head of the Scoutisme Français whose friendship with Vallat was known to many, was able to secure a special status for the EIF: while the organisation was part of the UGIF, it was under direct control of the Ministry of Youth and Scoutisme

[177] Ibid., 214.
[178] Other French and international organisations were also part of this commission, including the French Red Cross, Secours Nationale, CIMADE, the American Friends Service Committee (Quakers) and YMCA. See Moore, *Survivors,* 123–138; Lazare, *Rescue as Resistance,* 90–91.
[179] Lee, *Pétain's Jewish Children,* 70–75.
[180] Poznanski, *Jews in France,* 134. As Daniel Lee has shown, this was mainly thanks to General Lafont, head of the Scoutisme Français, who wanted the EIF to continue to practise scouting. Lee, *Pétain's Jewish Children,* 81–82.

Français.[181] Gamzon furthermore managed to obtain a position on the UGIF's central board.

Lambert's diary entry for 28 December 1941 notes that Gamzon was already involved in the organisation from early on. According to him, Gamzon had encouraged André Weil, William Oualid and Joseph Millner to agree to work for the UGIF at the end of 1941.[182] Robert Gamzon's wife Denise indicated in her memoirs that there had been doubts among the EIF's leadership about whether the organisation should become part of the UGIF.[183] Refusing to join the UGIF would mean that all rural and local scout groups and the EIF children's homes would be dissolved. She indicated that, as most French citizens were indifferent or even hostile towards the Jews, it would therefore have become much harder to secure hiding places for Jewish children and youth. In the end, therefore, the decision was taken to join the UGIF.[184] After summer 1942, the EIF launched its programme to hide foreign Jewish children and, in so doing, it relied strongly on the network it had established among the Scoutisme Français.[185] As we shall see in Chapter 5, the interconnections between the illegal work of the organisation and the legal UGIF were many, and this was in part because of Gamzon's dual role.

Another long-standing welfare organisation from which Jewish children in France particularly benefited was the OSE. Established in 1912 in St Petersburg, the OSE provided aid for children and Jewish victims of Tsarist persecution. When it moved its headquarters to Berlin in 1923, the organisation became an international organisation, also gaining an office in Paris established by Professor Eugène Minkowski.[186] From 1938, the OSE primarily dedicated its efforts towards refugee aid, mainly helping children from Austria, Czechoslovakia and Germany.[187]

---

[181] Lee, *Pétain's Jewish Children*, 81.
[182] Lambert, *Diary of a Witness*, 28 December 1941, 85. Lambert's statement is verified by Alain Michel in *Les Éclaireurs Israélites de France pendant la Seconde Guerre Mondiale* (Paris: EIF, 1984), 101–108. Also see Gamzon's acceptance telegram to Vallat, 4 January 1942, CCXIII-31, CDJC, Mémorial de la Shoah.
[183] Denise Gamzon, *Mémoires* (Jerusalem: published by author, 1997), 80.
[184] Ibid. There exist different views on the attitude of 'ordinary' French citizens towards the Jews in France during the Second World War. Whereas Sémelin has argued that there existed a generally sympathetic public opinion towards Jews, Paxton, Caron and others have disagreed, arguing, among other things, that Sémelin has overlooked the pervasiveness of antisemitism in France. See Paxton, 'Jews: How Vichy Made it Worse'; Caron, 'The Survival of the Jews in France, 1940–1944'.
[185] Lee, *Pétain's Jewish Children*, 84.
[186] Sabine Zeitoun, 'L'OSE au secours des enfants Juifs' in: *Le Sauvetage des Enfants Juifs de France. Actes du Colloque de Guéret – 29 et 30 May 1996* (Guéret: Associations pour la recherche et la sauvegarde de la vérité historique sur la Résistance en Creuse, undated), 95.
[187] Laurence Rosengart, 'Les maisons de l'OSE: parcours d'une enfance fragmentée', in Martine Lemalet (ed.), *Au secours des enfants du siècle* (Paris: Nil, 1993), 83.

After May 1940, the organisation continued its pre-war activities, centred on the coordination of children's homes.

In 1941, the OSE started transferring children out of the camps in France, where they were interned with their parents. By November 1941, it controlled nine homes housing 1,200 children and in 1942 the number of children's homes under its direct control had grown to fourteen.[188] By the end of 1941, although it remained operative in the northern zone, the OSE's main office had been moved to Montpellier in the unoccupied zone. From there, it concentrated on the improvement of conditions and medical care in the internment camps where Jewish children were being held. It also organised help for children across the country.

Joseph Millner, born in Poland, headed the OSE in the southern zone. As Laffitte has indicated, Millner's life course reflects that of many Jewish immigrants who were forced to adapt to the new conditions in their host countries. Born in Chelm in Poland in 1882 (some documents indicate 1888), then part of the Russian Empire, Millner fled to France in 1921, where he was unable to practise his profession as a chemical engineer until his naturalisation in 1938.[189] During the negotiations with Vallat about the establishment of the UGIF, Millner had been Lambert's confidant, but in January 1942, he was deprived of his French citizenship and forced to resign from the organisation's central board. Millner continued to play a central role in the OSE and used the organisation to arrange the clandestine passage of Jewish children to Switzerland until the end of 1943, at which time he advised the UGIF to disperse those children who were still resident in the homes overseen by the organisation.[190]

On 8 March 1942, the OSE was forced to function under the umbrella of the UGIF, but it continued to work largely autonomously in cooperation with the ORT and EIF even as pressure on its facilities increased with the liberation of children from the camps and the disbandment of many smaller charitable organisations.[191] Though the OSE initially only operated

---

[188] Ibid., 87; Renée Poznanski, 'De l'Action philanthropique à la résistance humanitaire', in *Au secours des enfants du siècle*, 59; Cohen, *Persécutions et sauvetages*, 103; Sabine Zeitoun, *L'Oeuvre de secours aux enfants (O.S.E.) sous l'occupation en France* (Paris: Éditions L'Harmattan, 1990), 124. For further reading on the OSE and its efforts to help Jewish children, see: Katy Hazan and Georges Weill, 'l'OSE et le sauvetage des enfants juifs. De l'avant-guerre à l'après-guerre' in Jacques Sémelin, Claire Andrieu and Sarah Gensburger (eds.), *La résistance aux génocides. De la pluralité des actes de sauvetage* (Paris: Presses de Science Po, 2008), 259–276.
[189] Michel Laffitte, 'L'OSE de 1942 à 1944: Une survie périlleuse sous couvert de l'UGIF', *Revue de la Shoah*, Vol. 2, No. 185 (2006), 66–67.
[190] Ibid., 67; Cohen, *Diary of a Witness*, 81 n.4.
[191] Moore, *Survivors*, 271; Hillel J. Kieval, 'From Social Work to Resistance: Relief and Rescue of Jewish Children in Vichy France', BA Harvard University (1973), 3; Laffitte, 'L'OSE de 1942 à 1944', 67–70.

legally, from summer 1942 it engaged in clandestine operations in both the occupied and unoccupied zones. The operational autonomy of organisations such as the OSE and the EIF ensured that there was a wider range of welfare organisations available to Jews in the unoccupied (later: southern) zone of France than anywhere else in occupied Western Europe.

The existence of alternative (welfare) organisations as late as summer 1943 and even thereafter undermined the exclusive authority of the AJB and the UGIF. In both Belgium and France, Jews could turn for advice and social welfare to representative organisations that were not directly supervised by the Germans, when they were willing to take the risks that were frequently involved in this. Doing so offered more opportunities for Jews not to follow the legal approach and to investigate non-legal ways to escape German persecution, for example by going into hiding.

The large number of independent organisations and the range of beliefs they represented fostered strong internal divisions that lasted until after the war. This became apparent in the case of the Committee for the Unity and Defence of the Jews of France (Comité d'Unité et de Défense des Juifs de France, CUDJF), established in 1944 in Paris by organisations including the OSE and the Amelot Committee.[192] In August 1944, after the liberation of Paris, the CUDJF arrested Edinger, the last head of the UGIF, and instituted a purge commission. The CUDJF transferred its documents to the CRIF, the commission of inquiry established after liberation headed by members of organisations that had provided alternatives to the UGIF, including Marc Jarblum (president of the FSJF) and André Weil (from the Central Consistory).

The CRIF held the UGIF leadership accountable for its failure to remove children from the homes that were overseen by the Germans.[193] These children had become easy targets for arrest and deportation, but when the Allies drew closer in July 1944 and Brunner aimed to seize as many Jews as possible, the UGIF workers in Paris had not taken special measures to protect these children.[194] Between 21 and 25 July, Gestapo agents raided eight of the eleven UGIF children's homes and all but around ten of the children were deported to Auschwitz on the large last convoy on 31 July 1944.[195]

---

[192] Fredj, 'Le Consistoire Central et la création du CRIF', 176n. For an overview of the welfare activities of the CUDJF that were intended to ameliorate the situation of the Jews in Paris after the liberation, including financial assistance and lodging, see 'Mesures à envisager pour l'amélioration immediate de la situation des Juifs de Paris' (c. 1944), Fonds CRIF, MDI-192, CDJC, Mémorial de la Shoah.

[193] Fredj, 'Le Consistoire Central et la création du CRIF', 176–177.

[194] Zuccotti, The Holocaust, the French and the Jews, 200–201.

[195] Ibid. For the list of those who were taken to Auschwitz on the last convoy (No. 77), see Klarsfeld, Le mémorial de la deportation des Juifs de France.

In the Netherlands, organised Jewish self-help groups were rare. In contrast to Belgium and France, the secular community organisations that existed before May 1940 had no political or representative role; they 'continued to eschew any involvement with political refugees and kept a distance from any communist or social democratic organizations'.[196] Furthermore, the ban on political activity by foreigners prevented refugees from organising their own representation.[197]

In addition, as early as May 1941, many Jewish organisations in the Netherlands were dismantled and their activities taken over by the JR.[198] There were some organisations that continued to operate illegally outside the JR, but their area of influence was limited. One of these was the Palestine Pioneers, which, in response to the first deportation in August 1942, planned an escape line for its group to Switzerland. Although the plan failed and the initial group of ten was arrested, one of the group's members, Joop Westerweel (a non-Jew), continued the organisation's work and managed to help between 150 and 200 Jews. Among them were seventy Palestine Pioneers, and while most were given shelter in France, around eighty crossed into Spain. Westerweel also helped to find hiding places for Pioneers who could not leave the country.[199]

Other illegal organisations, including the Nanno and Oosteinde resistance groups, were engaged in similar activities in the Netherlands. The Oosteinde group, which consisted of German Jewish refugees, was assisted by the JR member Jacques van de Kar.[200] The Oosteinde group had come into existence in the years before the German occupation. Its activities included taking care of illegal immigrants by trying to ameliorate their living conditions in the refugee camps. When it became clear that refugees from Germany would first be targeted for deportation, the group's area of activity increased. From the first deportation in July 1942 until spring 1944, the Oosteinde group distributed illegal papers,

---

[196] Moore, *Survivors*, 211. Also see: ibid., *Victims and Survivors*, 34–35.

[197] Ibid., *Refugees from Nazi Germany*, 158–159.

[198] For an overview of the Jewish organisations that existed in this period, and the meetings that preceded their official dismantlement, see 'Opheffing verenigingen', May–June 1941, Archief van de Joodse Raad 182, Inv. No. 189, NIOD.

[199] Moore, *Victims and Survivors*, 168. For further reading on Joop Westerweel and (the origins of the) the so-called Westerweel group (a resistance group that was led by Joop Westerweel), see Hans Schippers, *Westerweel Group: Non-Conformist Resistance against Nazi Germany, A Joint Rescue Effort of Dutch Idealists and Dutch-German Zionists* (Berlin/Boston: De Gruyter Oldenbourg, 2019). Westerweel was recognised as a Righteous Among the Nations; see Mordecai Paldiel, *The Righteous Among the Nations: Rescuers of Jews during the Holocaust* (Jerusalem: Yad Vashem/New York: HarperCollins, 2007), 549–556.

[200] Moore, *Victims and Survivors*, 169.

including *Het Parool*, *Vrij Nederland* and *De Waarheid*, and falsified documents for itself and other resistance groups. It also took care of people in hiding.[201] Nevertheless, the scope of these Jewish organisations, considered in terms of the number of Jews they helped, was not on the same scale as those Jewish aid organisations operating in Belgium in France alongside the AJB, the UGIF-Nord and the UGIF-Sud. They therefore never had the capacity to serve as an alternative to the JR.

The Jews in the Netherlands continued to depend on the JR, because it was the only organisation that provided social welfare for them. Their dependence increased even further when, from 1 January 1943, the JR began to supervise the 26,000 bank accounts held by Jews at Lippmann, Rosenthal & Co. (LiRo), a Jewish bank that was taken over by the Germans with the aim of registering and then plundering the money and possessions of these Jews.

The year before, on 21 May 1942, the office of Reichskommissar Seyss-Inquart had introduced Verordnung 58/1942, which was a continuation of previous regulations regarding private property and financial resources of Jews. Verordnung 58/1942 ruled, among other things, that any financial claims involving Jews, from then (May 1942) on had to be reported at the LiRo. With only a few exceptions (such as wedding rings and pocket watches), all personal belongings furthermore had to be registered at the bank. In return, individuals received a (monthly) 'stipend'.[202]

From January 1943, Jews could no longer directly withdraw their monthly stipends and instead became dependent upon the JR for financial support.[203] On 18 December 1942, the *Joodsche Weekblad*, the Jewish weekly published under the auspices of the JR, announced:

Since the firm of Lippmann, Rosenthal & Co., Sarphatistraat, will cease to make payments to Jews from 1 January and since, from that date, such benefits will be paid by the Jewish Council, it is essential that everybody who has been drawing, or has applied for, benefits in accordance with Verordnung 58/1942 in November and December 1942 from the above mentioned firm, resubmits these applications to the Jewish Council.[204]

---

[201] For further reading on the Oosteinde group, and the ways in which its activities transformed throughout the occupation, see Ben Braber, *Passage naar vrijheid: Joods verzet in Nederland 1940–1945* (Amsterdam: Uitgeverij Balans, 1987), passim.

[202] Berkley, *Overzicht van het ontstaan*, 55–56.

[203] Philip Staal, *Roestvrijstaal: speurtocht naar de erfenis van Joodse oorlogswezen* (Delft: Eburon, 2008), 186.

[204] *Het Joodsche Weekblad: uitgave van den Joodschen Raad voor Amsterdam*, 18 December 1942, Vol. 2, printed by Omniboek (The Hague) in 1979. In France, the UGIF also published a weekly newspaper, the *Bulletin d'Information de l'UGIF*. In Belgium, all local AJB representatives refused to publish a journal under the auspices of the organization, see Schreiber, 'Tussen traditionele en verplichte gemeenschap', 107.

The fact that the authority of the JR, unlike that of the Belgian and French Associations, was hardly constrained by the existence of alternative groups, meant that it gained a more solid representative power. This allows us to better understand why these organisations functioned differently. It also serves to explain different German perspectives about the effectiveness of the organisations because it was precisely the lack of representative power held by the AJB, the UGIF-Nord and the UGIF-Sud that led the Germans to become dissatisfied with them.

In order to understand the positive perspective on the JR's functionality and effectiveness, other factors also played their part. The effectivity with which the organisation carried out the responsibilities that German officials forced upon it is important in this regard. Many of the JR's responsibilities were not unique in the wider Western European context. In fact, in the context of preparations for (mass) deportations, similarities can be identified between the duties of the AJB and those of the JR. We have seen that both organisations engaged in activities related to the creation and distribution of summonses to report for deportation, and encouraged individuals to respond to these summonses. Yet a few aspects were unique to the JR, including a leadership that remained in office until the Council was dissolved, which, in turn, led to a clear line of communication between German officials and the Jewish leadership. Moreover, the level of cooperation that the Dutch leadership was prepared to engage in on some occasions went beyond that of the Belgian and French Jewish leadership (for example the agreement to provide a list of JR officials who would no longer be exempted from deportation in May 1943). However, whether, or to what extent, the JR was indeed more instrumental to the deportation process than their Western European counterparts, as senior Nazis hinted after the war, is difficult to precisely determine.

We do know that, partly as a result of the nature of the occupational regime, the lines of communication between the Germans and the Jewish leaders were more functional and effective in the Netherlands. Moreover, as will be explored in Chapter 5, the JR leadership remained devoted to their 'legal approach', whereas some of the (central board) members of the AJB, the UGIF-Nord and the UGIF-Sud, throughout the course of German occupation, used their position to enable clandestine activities. All these factors influenced the nature of the activities in which these organisations were engaged, and affected German perceptions of their effectivity.

5   Between Legality and Illegality
Cloaking and Resistance

In August 1942, Irène Zmigrod entered the social welfare department of the AJB in Belgium and was in direct contact with those Jews who needed help. Her main task was to take care of children whose parents had been arrested. In order to achieve this, Belgium, like France, had specifically designated children's homes that were, directly or indirectly, associated with the AJB.[1] Zmigrod used her legal position in the organisation to give clandestine aid to Jewish children whose parents had not (yet) been deported. During an interview in 1953, she outlined how the AJB operated alongside the illegal Jewish Defence Committee (the CDJ):

Many parents came to the AJB and asked us to put their children in the homes. We refused this placement, since the Gestapo forbade us to keep children whose parents were not deported. However, we took note of the name and addresses of these people, which we forwarded to the CDJ. [The CDJ] then sent a social worker to the address and made every effort to hide the child.[2]

Even though Jewish Councils, and similar Jewish representative organisations, have traditionally been seen as channels of collaboration, this example shows that the wartime reality was more complex.

The 'Jewish Councils' in Western Europe were either wittingly or unwittingly used as cloaks for various forms of illegal activities that

---

[1] Massenge, 'De sociale politiek', 220. In an attempt to safeguard the protection of children and the elderly, the number of institutions in which they were housed by the AJB increased during the course of the war. For further reading on the AJB children's homes, see Sylvain Brachfeld, *Ils n'ont pas eu les gosses: l'histoire de plus de 500 enfants juifs dans parents 'fichés à la Gestapo' et placés pendant l'occupation allemande dans les homes de l'Association des Juifs en Belgique,* AJB (Herzliya: Institute for Research on Belgium Judaism, 1989).

[2] An eyewitness account by Irène Zmigrod is entitled 'A Social Worker's Report on her Experiences in Belgium during the Time of the Nazi-Occupation', 1956, p. 8, 1656/3/9/262. Testimony Collection, Wiener Library. Also see the interview with Maurice Heiber in which he corroborates Zmigrod's statement, R.715/Tr248.00, Archives Marcel Blum, DOS.

aimed to prevent Jews from being deported throughout the course of the war. Although the provision of social welfare was at the centre of the organisations' activities, increasing German pressure on the Jewish communities made some leaders reconsider the law-abiding position they had adopted. For UGIF-Sud chairman Raymond-Raoul Lambert and AJB chairman Salomon Ullmann, for example, their original motivation for leading the organisations, namely that by cooperating with the Germans they could serve the interests of the Jewish communities through law-abiding means, began to change over the course of time. They either passively allowed the organisations to be used as cloaks for clandestine operations or they became actively involved in facilitating such activities.

The purpose of this chapter is twofold. First, it highlights the diverse ways in which the Jewish organisations were wittingly and unwittingly used as cloaks for clandestine activities by individuals and groups. Second, it examines the active engagement of the organisations' leadership and membership in these activities. The central aim is to explore the concepts of opposition and resistance in relation to the legal character of these 'Jewish Councils'. Existing scholarship has focussed primarily on individuals who crossed the line between legality and illegality, outwardly conforming while also working outside the legal organisations.[3] This research takes these analyses one step further and investigates whether and how the organisations were used for clandestine activities in ways that extended beyond this individual level. By examining the interconnections between the legal existence of the JR, the AJB, the UGIF-Nord and the UGIF-Sud, and illegal organisations more broadly, we shall see that the very existence of the Jewish organisations led to a wide range of activities that were not necessarily consistent with their official policies, but would nevertheless have been impossible without their existence.

---

[3] See, for example, Laffitte, *Juif dans la France allemande,* 261–262; Massenge, 'De sociale politiek', 229–230; Van Doorslaer and Schreiber very briefly reflected upon the nature of the interrelations between the AJB and illegality in their conclusion to *De curatoren van het getto* (pp. 349–350), questioning whether the presence of some resistance members in the AJB (Perelman, Heiber and Ferdman) was the personal choice of those involved or part of a wider strategy of the resistance. However, they do not provide a satisfactory answer to this question. In Dutch historiography on the Jewish Council, only a few attempts have been made to investigate the interrelations between clandestine activity and the JR, most likely because, as we shall see, there were comparatively few direct interconnections in this regard. See, for example, Mark Schellekens, *Walter Süskind: Hoe een zakenman honderden Joodse kinderen uit handen van de nazi's redde* (Amsterdam: Athenaeum, 2011).

'Jewish Resistance': The Evolution of a Term

The historiography on the subject of 'Jewish resistance' is large and the concept itself remains contested by many scholars.[4] In the period following 1945, there was little appreciation of Jewish resistance because 'so few Jewish resisters survived' and because their efforts had been carried out in secret.[5] The overwhelming focus on Nazi documents in this period contributed to a distorted view of Jewish behaviour in which those who either did not offer armed resistance or fled Nazi persecution were considered to have gone to their death 'like lambs to the slaughter'.[6] In the early 1960s, Raul Hilberg and Hannah Arendt invoked this famous phrase and stressed the passivity of the victims of the Holocaust in their respective works *The Destruction of the European Jews* (1961) and *Eichmann in Jerusalem* (1963).[7] Hilberg emphasised that the Jewish victims had exhibited little, if any, outward defiance. Their behaviour was characterised by 'an attempt to avert action and, failing that, automatic compliance with orders' that was consistent with a 2,000-year-old experience of 'placating and appeasing', rather than resisting, their enemies.[8] Arendt focussed on how the Jewish Councils had served as instruments in the hands of the German occupiers.[9]

Assertions of Jewish passivity in the late 1950s and early 1960s stimulated research into their resistance. In this period, the term resistance was exclusively used to indicate the armed struggle against the enemy, and research on Jewish resistance predominantly focused on ghetto

[4] For a thorough (theoretical) overview of the concept of 'Jewish Resistance' in historiography, see Dan Michman, *Holocaust Historiography, A Jewish Perspective: Conceptualizations, Terminology, Approaches and Fundamental Issues* (London/Portland, OR: Valentine Mitchell, 2003), 217–248.
[5] Michael Marrus, 'Jewish Resistance to the Holocaust', *Journal of Contemporary History*, Vol. 30, No. 1 (1995), 96; Yehuda Bauer, *They Chose Life: Jewish Resistance in the Holocaust* (New York: American Jewish Committee, Institute of Human Relations, c. 1973), 25, as cited by Richard Middleton-Kaplan, 'The Myth of Jewish Passivity', in Patrick Henry (ed.), *Jewish Resistance against the Nazis* (Washington, DC: The Catholic University of America Press, 2014), 15.
[6] Middleton-Kaplan, 'The Myth of Jewish Passivity', 15; Robert Rozett, 'Jewish Resistance', in Dan Stone (ed.), *The Historiography of the Holocaust* (Houndmills: Palgrave Macmillan, 2004), 341–342.
[7] Arendt, *Eichmann in Jerusalem*, 104–111; Hilberg, *The Destruction of the European Jews*, passim. The phrase itself was taken from contemporary testimonies. See, for example, Emmanuel Ringelblum, *Notes from the Warsaw Ghetto: The Journal of Emmanuel Ringelblum*, ed. Jacob Sloan (New York: McGraw Hill, 1958), 316; Abraham Lewin, *A Cup of Tears: A Diary of the Warsaw Ghetto*, ed. Anthony Polonsky (Oxford: Blackwell, 1988), 151, as cited in Moore, *Survivors*, 369n.
[8] Hilberg, *The Destruction of the European Jews*, 666.
[9] Arendt, *Eichmann in Jerusalem*, 104–111.

uprisings and armed struggles in Eastern Europe.[10] In 1972, Isaiah
Trunk's comparative work on the Jewish Councils in Poland and the
Baltic states led to a broader understanding of the term that went beyond
armed confrontation. Trunk highlighted that the Jewish leadership had
been very active in supporting cultural and spiritual resistance against
Nazi efforts to dehumanise the Jews.[11] This notion of retaining spiritual
integrity and dignity in the context of persecution and dehumanisation
altered the perspective about Jewish responses, including Jewish resistance, to German rule.

In the decades that followed, concerted attempts were made to define
the complex nature of Jewish resistance. This resulted in a more nuanced
understanding of the term. The concept of *amidah*, a Hebrew term that
can be literally translated as 'making a stand', was central in refram-
ing the discussion on Jewish resistance during the Holocaust. Mark
Dworzecki argued that the term included 'all expressions of Jewish
"non-conformism" and [...] all the forms of resistance and all acts by
Jews aimed at thwarting the evil designs of the Nazis'.[12] In addition to
their physical destruction, this also included the German aim to deprive
Jews of their humanity 'and to reduce them to dregs before snuffing out
their lives'.[13] Rather than perceiving resistance exclusively as an armed
form of revolt, historians in the field began to formulate more inclusive
definitions. Among those doing so were Yehuda Bauer, Isaiah Trunk,
Dan Michman, Michael Marrus and Lucien Lazare.[14] They all stressed

[10] See, for example, Philip Friedman (ed.), *Martyrs and Fighters: The Epic of the Warsaw Ghetto* (New York: Praeger, 1954); Keshev Shabbetai, *As Sheep to the Slaughter? The Myth of Cowardice* (Bet Dagan: Keshev Oress, 1962); Meyer Barkai (ed.), *The Fighting Ghettos* (Philadephia: Lippinicott, 1962); Yuri Suhl, *They Fought Back: The Story of the Jewish Resistance in Nazi Europe* (New York: Crown Publishers, 1967); Lucien Steinberg, *La Révolte des justes: les juifs contre Hitler, 1933–1945* (Paris: Fayard, 1970).
[11] Trunk, *Judenrat*, 388ff.
[12] Mark Dworzecki, 'The Day to Day Stand of the Jews', in Israel Gutman and Livia Rotkirchen (eds.), *The Catastrophe of European Jewry: Antecedents, History, Reflection* (Jerusalem: Yad Vashem, 1976), 367.
[13] Ibid. Also see Rozett, 'Jewish Resistance', 346; Michman, *Holocaust Historiography: A Jewish Perspective*, 217–219. For the criticisms some scholars (such as Raul Hilberg and Lucy Dawidowicz) voiced on this conceptual development of the term 'resistance', see ibid., 219–221.
[14] Bauer, *They Chose Life*, passim; Yehuda Bauer, *The Jewish Emergence from Powerlessness* (London: Macmillan, 1980); Isaiah Trunk, *Jewish Responses to Nazi Persecution: Collective and Individual Behavior in Extremis* (New York: Stein and Day, 1979); Lazare, *Rescue as Resistance*, passim. For an overview of the studies in the 1970s and 1980s that assessed Jewish behaviour from the perspective of resistance, see Rozett, 'Jewish Resistance', 352. Amos Goldberg analysed the historiographical importance of Yehuda Bauer's conceptualisation of 'Amidah' in 'The History of the Jews in the Ghettos. A Cultural Perspective', in Dan Stone (ed.), *The Holocaust and Historical Methodology* (New York /Oxford: Berghahn, 2012), 79–100.

in their own manner that Jewish resistance took many forms, including those of everyday sabotage and survival.

Bauer argued that 'any Jewish action, whether by a group or by an individual, that ran counter to real or perceived Nazi-German policies, has to be regarded as active nonacceptance of such policies, that is, resistance'.[15] In direct opposition to the claim that Jews passively complied with their destruction, he contended that 'in Poland, after the war had begun, German rules were so brutal that, had the Jews passively acquiesced – even though every infringement of Nazi law was punishable by death – they would have died out in no time at all'.[16] While scholars had (slightly) different interpretations of the term, for Bauer, *amidah* included:

> smuggling food into ghettos; mutual self-sacrifice within the family to avoid starvation or worse; cultural, educational, religious, and political activities taken to strengthen morale; the work of doctors, nurses, and educators to consciously maintain health and moral fiber to enable individual and group survival; and, of course, armed rebellion or the use of force (with bare hands or with 'cold' weapons) against the Germans and their collaborations.[17]

Marrus contributed to the debate by arguing that Jewish resistance encompassed symbolic, polemic, defensive, offensive and enchained resistance. Symbolic resistance in his understanding included gestures and (religious) expressions that showed that Jews remained committed to their religion or culture.[18]

Amidah has broadened the definition of Jewish resistance to such an extent that some scholars have questioned whether this development is fruitful. In their view, the fact that 'resistance' then includes all Jewish responses to Nazism – from collaboration to armed resistance – has led to a neutralisation of the term that prevents us from differentiating and understanding the wide range of responses that can be identified in this period.[19]

---

[15] Yehuda Bauer, 'Jewish Resistance in the Ukraine and Belarus during the Holocaust', in Henry, *Jewish Resistance against the Nazis*, 483.

[16] Bauer, *They Chose Life*, 23–24.

[17] Bauer, *Rethinking the Holocaust*, 120; and 'Jewish Resistance in the Ukraine and Belarus during the Holocaust', 483.

[18] Michael Marrus, 'Varieties of Jewish Resistance: Some Categories and Comparisons in Historiographical Perspective', in Yisrael Gutman (ed.), *Major Changes within the Jewish People in the Wake of the Holocaust* (Jerusalem: Yad Vashem, 1996), 269–300; and 'Jewish Resistance to the Holocaust', 92–103.

[19] Tom Lawson, *Debates on the Holocaust* (Manchester/New York: Manchester University Press, 2010), 252-255.

These discussions concerning the definition of Jewish resistance are particularly interesting in the context of the legal nature of the JR, the AJB, the UGIF-Nord and the UGIF-Sud, as their leaders and members tried to act against the interests of the Germans while they continued to serve as spokesmen of a legal representative body. Their actions were prompted by a wide range of motivations that were aimed at appeasing the occupier while simultaneously serving the interests of the Jewish communities. This makes it difficult to categorise their behaviour and responses. Yet depending on the context and the definition used, the provision of social assistance by these organisations can be seen as a form of resistance, as it was primarily aimed at securing the well-being and, in some cases, survival of the Jewish communities.

As French historian Michel Laffitte asserted, assistance to impoverished Jews in France was vital up until the very last weeks before the liberation.[20] Richard Cohen, in turn, highlighted that the UGIF was criticised by the Germans for distributing financial resources for welfare purposes beyond what was deemed necessary, but noted that 'the council ignored the criticism and continued to allocate close to 4 million francs monthly for welfare purposes to more than 7,000 Jewish families'.[21] The last president of the UGIF, Georges Edinger, reflected on this idea and argued that the official work of the UGIF was resistance to the extent that it served to alleviate the suffering of the Jews and reduce the impact of racial persecution.[22]

In a similar vein, Klarsfeld showed that UGIF aid was of the utmost importance, since it allowed the majority of the Jews in France to survive. In his view, even though the organisation was not established for the purpose of resistance, the UGIF was primarily an instrument of survival. According to Klarsfeld, the UGIF-leaders Baur and Lambert, deported with their families to Auschwitz in 1943, had risked their lives to aid the Jewish communities and had died as courageous men.[23] Overall, the Jewish leaders were not in a position to stop German anti-Jewish legislation from being implemented, but they could certainly aim to alleviate the suffering of the Jews. We have

---

[20] Michel Laffitte, 'Was the UGIF an Obstacle to the Rescue of Jews?', in Jacques Sémelin, Claire Andrieu et al. (eds.), *Resisting Genocide: The Multiple Forms of Rescue* (New York: Columbia University Press, 2011), 407.

[21] Cohen, *The Burden of Conscience*, 103.

[22] Edinger, Report on the activities of the UGIF, p. 1, CCCLXXIX-33, CDJC, Mémorial de la Shoah.

[23] Klarsfeld, *Vichy-Auschwitz: la 'solution finale' de la question juive en France*, 291.

seen that the central board members in all three cases were clearly determined to provide social welfare even though they were operating under severe pressure.

This determination played a part in Jewish leaders' motivations to maintain their position throughout the occupation. Whereas some members of the central boards – including Raymond-Raoul Lambert, André Baur, Salomon Ullmann and Maurice Benedictus – decided that it was no longer in the interests of the Jews for them to keep their posts when the implementation of anti-Jewish legislation increased, others decided to remain in place. Kurt Schendel, liaison officer between the UGIF and the Germans, explained his motivation for maintaining his position during the post-war honour trial initiated by the commission of inquiry (CRIF). To Schendel, it would have been fairly easy to abandon his position at the UGIF, to get himself fake papers (*faux papiers*) and to go into hiding along with his wife. However, he decided not to:

Time and again, people whom I had saved proposed this to me (going into hiding). I did not do it and stayed in my position until the liberation, despite all the risks that my work entailed. I considered it my duty to fulfil my task until the last moment: to save as many Jews as possible and to relieve the fate of the internees.[24]

His willingness to provide aid to the Jews in France outweighed the dangers inherent in that choice.

Similar explanations have been voiced by those in the Dutch leadership who decided to remain in office until the end of the Jewish Council's existence, despite receiving encouragement from others to go into hiding.[25] Even though the Council's leaders, like their counterparts in Belgium and France, had the financial means and social connections to go into hiding, they continued to serve at the helm of the organisation. They believed that they could still aid the Jewish communities by continuing to act legally. Whether or not this was a viable thought, and whether their continued cooperation with German functionaries was indeed beneficial to the Jews, is open for discussion.

While the provision of social welfare as a potential form of resistance to German intentions and actions is important in the context of the 'Jewish Councils', we will shortly be focussing primarily on those (organised)

---

[24] Statement of Kurt Schendel, 2 December 1946, CRIF MDI-310.7, Mémorial de la Shoah; For Schendel's report on his career and his activity within the liaison office, see 'Rapport sur le service de liaison et mon activité dans ce service', 2 September 1944, CCXXI-26, CDJC, Mémorial de la Shoah.

[25] See, for example, the notes of David Cohen: 'Aantekeningen II', 181j, Inv. No. 11, NIOD.

clandestine activities that aimed to prevent Jews from being deported and help them survive. This will allow us to examine the level of interplay between legality and illegality.

Organised Resistance in the Netherlands, Belgium and France

In order to help Jews escape German persecution, and, especially, avoid deportation, Jewish organisations operated in parallel to non-Jewish bodies, and vice-versa. The types of interconnections between Jewish and non-Jewish organisations were different in Belgium, France and the Netherlands. Considerable differences can be identified between the Netherlands on the one hand and Belgium and France on the other. In the Netherlands, there was comparatively little engagement in (organised) clandestine activities during the first phase of the German occupation.[26] A number of factors have been used to explain this: geographical position and topography; the fact that the main response to occupation after 1940 remained one of reaching an accommodation with the occupier; and the absence of a First World War experience.[27] It was fairly easy for the Germans to track down and dissolve the earliest organised illegal activities, as those arranging them had little relevant knowledge or experience.[28]

In both Belgium and France, large numbers of immigrant Jews who had experienced persecution in Eastern Europe were generally less inclined to follow official regulations and were often the first to become involved in clandestine movements.[29] In both countries, the echo of the First World War moreover fed patriotic feelings and stirred very early expressions of resistance after the defeat in 1940.[30] However, this did not immediately yield organised forms of resistance because resistance

---

[26] Bob de Graaff, 'Collaboratie en Verzet: Een Vergelijkend Perspectief', in Joost Jonker and Albert Kersten (eds.), *Vijftig jaar na de inval: geschiedschrijving en de Tweede Wereldoorlog, bijdragen aan het congres gehouden aan de Vrije Universiteit te Amsterdam op 11 en 11 mei 1990* ('s Gravenhage: SDU Uitgeverij, 1990), 96; Dick van Galen Last, 'The Netherlands', in Moore, *Resistance in Western Europe*, 190.

[27] Van Galen Last, 'The Netherlands', 189–190; Hilberg, *The Destruction of the European Jews*, 365–382; Moore, *Survivors*, 234.

[28] Van Galen Last, 'The Netherlands', 194–195.

[29] Renée Poznanski, 'A methodological approach to the Study of Jewish Resistance in France', *Yad Vashem Studies*, Vol. 18 (1987), 3; Griffioen and Zeller, *Jodenvervolging in Nederland, Frankrijk en België*, 658.

[30] Gildea, *Fighters in the Shadows*, 37–38; Lagrou, 'Belgium', 33. Lagrou has argued that we can identify three decisive moments in the entry of different categories of individuals into active resistance in Belgium; for an overview thereof, see 33–48.

groups, in the case of Belgium, were barely organised and individual groups functioned inefficiently and suffered from internal crises.[31]

At the start of the mass deportation of Jews to Eastern Europe in summer 1942, the FI in Belgium was the first major umbrella organisation to unite different social and political forces. It was instituted on the initiative of the communists in March 1941. The FI connected various groups and included the communist Solidarité, which focused on helping the persecuted, including those in hiding.[32] Among the wide spectrum of social and political forces united in the organisation were representatives of the Catholics, socialists and liberals as well as the communists.[33]

At first, the FI did not have a department dedicated to helping persecuted Jews. The organisation's foremost ambition was to mobilise support in all social circles and to fight against the labour draft. Jews were considered a marginal group in society, and the small number of assimilated Jews who joined general resistance groups did not establish Jewish resistance organisations because they were reluctant to be associated with immigrants who, as we have seen, had failed to integrate into Belgian society.[34]

After the major raids in summer 1942, representatives of leftist Jewish circles decided to institute a committee that would centre its activities exclusively around the creation of aid networks for Jews who were threatened with deportation. Organised Jewish resistance was most visible among the communists. The MOI, which worked in affiliation with the FI, was a communist foreign workers' organisation that predated the German occupation under the name Foreign Working Force (Main d'Oeuvre Étrangère, MOE). It was the Communist Party's liaison unit, intended to recruit immigrant workers into the party and to unite communist immigrants.[35] The MOI strongly opposed the law-abiding course

---

[31] Griffioen and Zeller, *Jodenvervolging in Nederland, Frankrijk en België*, 537.

[32] For an overview of all organisations that were included in the FI, see Jul Puttemans, *De bezetter buiten: beknopte historiek van het onafhankelijkheidsfront, nationale verzetsbeweging, 1941–1945* (Lier/Almere: NIOBA, 1987), 19–24.

[33] Lagrou, 'Belgium', 49–50.

[34] Gotovitch, 'Resistance Movements and the "Jewish Question"', 279–280; and *Du Rouge au tricolore: les communistes belges de 1939 à 1944: un aspect de l'histoire de la résistance en Belgique* (Brussels: Éditions Labor, 1992), 204–220; Puttemans, *De bezetter buiten*, 27–54; Lagrou, 'Belgium', 50–51; For an overview of FI member Jean Terfve's post-war attempts to ensure that all meritorious Belgians, not just those who had engaged in armed resistance, were recognised, see Pieter Lagrou, *The Legacy of Nazi Occupation: Patriotic Memory and National Recovery in Western Europe, 1945–1965* (Cambridge: Cambridge University Press, 2000), 52–58.

[35] Van Doorslaer, 'Jewish Immigration and Communism in Belgium, 1925–1939', 68–81; Gotovitch, 'Resistance Movements and the "Jewish Question"', 280; Steinberg, *L'étoile et le fusil. Les cent jours de la déportation*, 60–61.

taken by the AJB leadership and, sponsored by the FI, its members organised concerted acts of resistance.

Among the earliest operations of the MOI were the murder of Robert Holzinger in summer 1942, a German Jew who worked for the AJB, and the destruction of copies of AJB files that contained the personal information of Jews who were to be called for 'labour' in 'the East'.[36] Even though the destruction of the AJB files was ineffective because the original files were saved, both actions underline the resentment felt by organised Jewish resistance groups against the AJB.

On the initiative of MOI-member Hertz Jospa, the CDJ was established in September 1942; it functioned in close connection with the FI, focussing primarily on social welfare work, the production of false identity papers and securing hiding places for Jews.[37] It went on to become the most important clandestine Jewish aid organisation. As Moore has argued, the activities and success of the CDJ rested largely on the assistance of non-Jewish individuals and organisations, including the Catholic Church.[38] While the story of the rescue of Jews was primarily a story of Jews saving Jews, the Catholic Church was indeed an important institution that assisted Jews, and Jewish children in particular, who were in search for help.[39] Help was initially given in the form of providing (false) baptismal certificates, and later 'also encompassed requests for shelter, ration cards, or help to escape the country altogether'.[40] In order to secure these lines of assistance, many priests acted in cooperation with the CDJ and vice-versa, mainly in Brussels but also outside the capital.[41]

In France, the presence of the Vichy regime initially hampered the emergence of resistance activities. A large majority of the population trusted the Vichy government, feeling that it had ended a useless war. The resulting 'wait-and-see' policy meant that, apart from small groups of communists and supporters of General Charles de Gaulle (a previously

[36] Maxime Steinberg and José Gotovitch, *Otages de la terreur Nazi: Le Bulgare Angheloff et son groupe de Partisans juifs Bruxelles, 1940–1943* (Brussels: Uitgeverij VUBPRESS, 2007), 85.
[37] Gotovitch, 'Resistance Movements and the "Jewish Question"', 280–281. Many of the records of the activities of the CDJ remained in private hands or were lost in the post-war period. De Lathouwer, *Comité de défense des Juifs*, introduction; Steinberg, *Le comité de défense des Juifs en Belgique*, 36.
[38] Moore, *Survivors*, 188.
[39] Suzanne Vromen, *Hidden Children of the Holocaust: Belgian Nuns and Their Daring Rescue of Young Jews from the Nazis* (Oxford: Oxford University Press, 2008), passim.
[40] Moore, *Survivors*, 192.
[41] Ibid., 194; Vromen, *Hidden Children of the Holocaust*, 11–12. The discrepancy between non-Jewish rescuers in the French-speaking Walloon region and the Flemish-speaking areas is an interesting phenomenon that extends beyond the limits of this research. For further reading, see: Moore, *Survivors*, 205–207.

202 Between Legality and Illegality

little known army officer who had gone to London and denied the legitimacy of the armistice and the Vichy regime), there was no organised resistance in the country in 1940 or during the first half of 1941.[42]

In terms of Jewish engagement in clandestine activities, the presence of the Vichy regime resulted in a profound split between French Jews on the one hand and immigrant Jews on the other. Especially during the first years of occupation, responses to the persecution and willingness to engage in illegal activities varied widely. Many Jews, in particular those with French nationality, believed at first that the French state was submitting to pressure from the German occupier and hardly recognised the fact that it was carrying out its own policy. These Jews believed, falsely, that they would be protected against German anti-Jewish legislation.[43]

A striking example of this attitude can be seen in a proclamation by Jacques Helbronner, president of the Central Consistory: 'The only hope resides in the presence as the head of the State of Monsieur le Maréchal Pétain, with whom I have been in contact regularly who gives me hope of future reparations for the injustice imposed.'[44] In a similar vein, Lambert referred in his diary to Xavier Vallat, head of the Vichy-led CGQJ, as his friend; a friend who was always 'very open and frank' with him.[45] Lambert trusted Vallat, 'and believed that owing to his animosity towards the Germans and his respect for veteran French Jews, he was willing to ease somewhat the suffering of French Jewry'.[46] As Poznanski has shown, these feelings were fed by the apparently warm and friendly attitude of leading Vichy officials towards the French Jewish leaders.[47] As a result, many French Jews complied with the regulations of the Vichy regime and adapted themselves to the new reality. The need for (organised) resistance was not (yet) recognised.

This attitude of compliance, combined with the belief that Vichy officials would protect Jews, was also visible in the UGIF's policies. Throughout 1942, UGIF leaders Albert Lévy and Raymond-Raoul

[42] Olivier Wieviorka, 'France', in Moore, *Resistance in Western Europe*, 127. The fact that the legal authority of Vichy was contested by some created ambivalence and confusion. The different perceptions of events in the occupied and unoccupied zones during the earliest phases of the war, and their impact on the development of resistance activities is a subject that extends beyond the limits of this research. For an overview thereof, see Nathan Bracher, 'Up in Arms: Jewish Resistance against Nazi Germany in France' in Henry, *Jewish Resistance against the Nazis*, 74–75.

[43] Poznanski, *Jews in France during WWII*, 68–74, 272; Adler, *The Jews of Paris*, 88; Rayski, *The Choice of the Jews under Vichy*, 27, 30–32.

[44] Meeting of March 16–17 1941, AIU, CC-1-b as cited in Poznanski, *Jews in France during World War II*, 2.

[45] Lambert, *Diary of a Witness*, 8 January 1942, 90.

[46] Cohen, 'Introduction' in: *Diary of a Witness*, xlvii.

[47] Poznanski, *The Jews in France during WWII*, 78–79.

Lambert continued to send telegrams to Pétain and other prominent Vichy officials asking for their intervention in various affairs, including the deportation of foreign Jewish children and women – 'whose only crime is that they are non-Aryans' – to the occupied zone.[48]

In some ways, the situation can be compared to that in the Netherlands, where the relative integration of Dutch Jews into non-Jewish society is often considered to have created a false sense of security against German persecution. Because of this integration, and because many considered themselves to be primarily Dutch rather than Jewish, Jews were less susceptible to the fear of being singled out as Jews.[49]

Despite this similarity, the presence of large numbers of immigrants in France makes the situation different from that in the Netherlands. Jews who had recently immigrated to France did not share the feeling of 'trust' in the French state. Immigrant Jews, many of whom had already suffered the burden of persecution, were at this stage already more inclined not to follow the path of legality. Even though resistance groups were drawn from all parts of the political spectrum, especially communists and Zionists engaged in clandestine operations.[50] Throughout 1941 and the beginning of 1942, various immigrant Jewish resistance groups operated in the French occupied and unoccupied zones individually, without strong, central coordination.

The help offered by non-Jewish organisations to the Jews, who were increasingly suffering under the yoke of the occupation, was marginal in this period. Racist and xenophobic prejudice, partly inherited from the nineteenth century and further encouraged by the economic and political crises of the 1930s, fed the notion that the Jews were not, and could never become, truly French.[51] Members of the French resistance were ideologically susceptible to these ideas and also showed caution for strategic reasons, suspecting that much of the population would have been influenced by antisemitic propaganda, and therefore not wanting to

[48] See telegrams of Albert Lévy and Raymond-Raoul Lambert to Marechal Pétain and Jacques Guérard, 4 September 1942, LVII-54, CDJC, Mémorial de la Shoah. Also see, for example, the telegram of Lambert to the secretary-general of the police on the UGIF members interned at Rivesaltes camp, 13 September 1942, CDXVI-139, Mémorial de la Shoah.
[49] Hans Blom, 'De vervolging van de joden in Nederland in internationaal vergelijkend perspectief', Gids, Vol 6–7 No. 150 (1987), 501–505.
[50] Olivier Wieviorka, The French Resistance, transl. from the French by Jane Marie Todd (Cambridge, MA/London: The Belknap Press of Harvard University Press, 2016; first ed. 2013 [French]), 401; Lazare, Rescue as Resistance, 104–105; Gildea, Fighters in the Shadows, 43, 58–82.
[51] Renée Poznanski, Propagandes et persécutions: La Résistance et le 'problème juif', 1940–1944 (Paris: Fayard, 2008), 43.

alienate French citizens. They believed that if they supported the Jews, they would validate Nazi propaganda that condemned the war as Jewish.

Fear of alienating the Arabic–Islamic world, and the failure to perceive the gravity of the threat to the Jews, contributed to the decision not to make a distinction among victims. As a result, 'with very rare exceptions […], the organised resistance did not engage in the battle against antisemitism' during the first phase of the occupation.[52] Exceptions were the communists, who condemned the measures of exclusion, and those Christians who raised their voices to repudiate antisemitic persecution.[53] However, the communists, including the FTP-MOI units, were still primarily concerned with a national, anti-fascist resurrection rather than the provision of aid to Jews.[54]

As more anti-Jewish legislation was enacted in 1942 – most importantly, the introduction of the yellow star in May in the occupied zone and the mass round-ups that began during the summer – the responses of the French population to the persecution of the Jews changed. The distressing scenes that unfolded in the occupied zone and later in the southern zone, including the round-ups of women and children, resulted in open opposition. When the categories of the persecution multiplied, including not only Jews but also communists and Freemasons, as well as French workers who were forced to work in Germany after February 1943 (with the introduction of the Compulsory Labour Service), more Frenchmen actively supported, or were engaged with, resistance activities.[55]

This included acts of sabotage, attacks and the provision of false identity papers and hiding places as well as gathering intelligence and distributing it to the Allied powers.[56] However, according to some historians, there was still very little help for persecuted Jews. The infringement of the sovereignty and honour of France in their view remained the central focus of non-Jewish underground groups and newspapers. As Olivier Wieviorka concluded, 'the fight against antisemitic persecution had mobilised Jewish and Christian organisations, but the internal resistance movements and the Free France organisations [led by

---

[52] Wieviorka, *The French Resistance*, 210–211.
[53] Ibid., 211–213.
[54] Gildea, *Fighters in the Shadows*, 18; Bracher, 'Jewish Resistance in France', 84. The organisational structure of the FTP-MOI units, their relation to the Communist Party and to the FTP are highlighted in Courtois, Peschanski and Rayski, *Le sang de l'étranger*, 143–155.
[55] Poznanski, *Propagandes et Persécutions*, 286. Also see Marus and Paxton, *Vichy France and the Jews*, 205–211; Sémelin, *The Survival of the Jews in France*, 203–206.
[56] Cohen, *Persécutions et sauvetages*, 359–362; Wieviorka, 'France', 134–136.

Charles de Gaulle] remained largely apart from that process'.[57] In his view, antisemitism had by no means completely disappeared and, with the exception of a few isolated examples, French resistance groups remained silent.[58]

Lucien Lazare saw this history differently, claiming that 'the Resistance, many members of the clergy, part of the administration, and elements of the population all took risks in actively and effectively participating in the rescue of Jews', particularly after the Compulsory Labour Service and the deportation of Jews from summer 1942 onwards.[59] In his view, the public disapproval by some bishops of the persecution was decisive in bringing many French people to assist in rescuing Jews.[60] Recently, Jacques Sémelin has claimed in a similar vein that individual acts of resistance or acts of support were more prominent than has previously been thought. He argued that while only a portion of the Jews escaped France or were saved by organised rescue networks, the vast majority of Jews were aided by small gestures from the French population, including the provision of food and help in finding hiding places and ways to escape.[61] Sémelin has been criticised for his views by leading historians in the field, including Robert Paxton, for failing, among other things, to recognise the power of the antisemitism that was inherent in French society and for reinforcing the redeeming myth of the 'good French'.[62] While these criticisms are well founded, Sémelin has nonetheless convincingly shown that Jews could survive in France in many ways, with or without the aid of French people.

Above all, from summer 1942, Jewish resisters of different nationalities began to work together with non-Jews of foreign nationalities under the umbrella of the MOI, which relied on the leadership of Jewish immigrants and other foreigners who had gained military experience. Robert Gildea finds that there were important connections between the French communist resistance and immigrant Jews in France.[63] His work underlines that Jews, especially foreign Jews, cooperated with a wide spectrum of other foreigners and that their role in the resistance, contrary to what other research has suggested, was substantial.

---

[57] Wieviorka, *The French Resistance*, 219.
[58] Ibid., 220.
[59] Lazare, *Rescue as Resistance*, 30.
[60] Ibid.
[61] Sémelin, *The Survival of the Jews in France*, passim.
[62] Paxton, 'Jews: How Vichy Made it Worse'. Also see Caron, '*The Survival of the Jews in France*'; Gildea, *Fighters in the Shadows*, 474.
[63] Gildea, *Fighters in the Shadows*, 46–57, 222–223. Also see Rayski, *The Choice of the Jews under Vichy*, 239–240.

Jews were indeed both recipients of Gentile help and contributors to the wider strategy of resistance. We have seen in Chapter 4 that there were a number of Jewish organisations that (illegally) aided Jews and *specifically* aimed to shield them from persecution. The help of these organisations, including the Amelot Committee and the OSE, materialised predominantly on the initiative of Jews who had immigrated to France before the war. Their ideological and cultural differences meant that these organisations were initially suspicious of each other, but we will see in this chapter that the interrelations that existed in France between Jewish and non-Jewish groups as well as between French and immigrant Jews began after a time to foster mutual clandestine operations under the cloaks of the UGIF-Nord and the UGIF-Sud.

In the Netherlands, contrary to Belgium and France, 'the inexperience in matters of war, occupation and illegal activity soon became apparent' when the German troops crossed the border on 10 May 1940.[64] Initially, acts of resistance were individual in nature. In early 1941, a sequence of anti-Jewish legislation, including raids in the Jewish quarter of Amsterdam, when over 400 Jewish men were arrested, resulted in the famous and unique February strike (*Februaristaking*) on 25 and 26 February. Encouraged by the illegal Dutch Communist Party, this was a coordinated strike during which tram drivers and dock workers refused to work and factories, stores and restaurants in Amsterdam were closed; at its peak, around 300,000 people took part. Surrounding towns such as Zaandam, Utrecht, Hilversum and Haarlem followed Amsterdam's example.[65]

In the end, this strike turned out to be an isolated incident: accommodation with the occupier remained the primary response in the following period. As in France, only with the introduction of compulsory labour service, more than one and a half years later in September 1942, did citizens on a wider scale disobey German regulations or support clandestine activities. At the end of 1942, the nature of resistance in the Netherlands was changed by the institution of the National Organisation for Aid People in Hiding (Landelijke Organisatie voor Hulp aan Onderduikers, LO), whose leaders and early members were all from Christian backgrounds, and which helped workers go underground. However, with some exceptions, the provision of aid to Jews was only a minor part of the LO's work, and was sometimes entirely absent. Overall, because organised

---

[64] Van Galen Last, 'The Netherlands', 191.
[65] For an overview of the history and nature of this strike, see Sijes, *De Februari-staking: 25–26 Februari 1941*, passim; Happe, *Veel valse hoop*, 74–88.

resistance took longer to develop than in Belgium and France, it came too late to help the majority of Jews in the Netherlands.[66]

The absence of large numbers of Jewish (political) immigrants in the Netherlands explains why (organised) resistance activities by Jewish individuals and organisations developed much later in that country than in Belgium and France. We have seen that the large number of immigrant Jews in Belgium and France had experienced persecution in Eastern Europe and were well aware of the dangers of German occupation. As soon as the Germans occupied Western Europe, these Jews were the first to begin organising clandestine activities, operating as organised groups in parallel with the legal organisations via groups such as the Amelot Committee and the FI.

The nature of migration, as well as the sheer number of immigrants, had been different in the Netherlands. As Moore has shown, the Netherlands, despite its proximity to Germany, was never considered a place of refuge for political refugees from the Third Reich in the 1930s, not even for the many Jews who had fled from Poland to Germany earlier on.[67] The country was unattractive for a large group of (left-wing) immigrants, especially for those who wished to continue their political activities. This can be explained by the fact that the Dutch government did not allow political activity by aliens who were considered subversive and undesirable elements. In contrast, France absorbed most of the organised left-wing immigrants during and after 1933, and these individuals became important in establishing clandestine networks.[68]

In addition to the absence of large numbers of (political) immigrants in the Netherlands, the fact that Jews were relatively integrated into non-Jewish society, which allowed them to develop a false sense of security, also explains the relative lack of engagement in (organised) resistance activities early on. Like the majority of the Dutch population, Jews in the Netherlands complied with the German occupation, responding with a traditional deference to authority and the Dutch sense of 'civic duty'.[69]

---

[66] Moore, *Survivors*, 234–237. Also see: Johan Snoek, *De Nederlandse kerken en de joden, 1940–1945: de protesten bij Seyss-Inquart, hulp aan joodse onderduikers, de motieven voor hulpverlening* (Kampen: Kok, 1990).

[67] Moore, *Refugees from Nazi Germany*, 12.

[68] Ibid., 110–112, 158. Moore outlined various reasons why political refugees still decided to come to the Netherlands, of which the geographical location, being the nearest foreign border to the heavily populated industrial areas of Germany, is considered most important. Also see Braber, *Passage naar vrijheid*, 12–13.

[69] Moore, *Survivors*, 208; Griffioen and Zeller, 'Jodenvervolging in Nederland en België tijdens de Tweede Wereldoorlog', 41; Blom, 'The Persecution of the Jews in the Netherlands', 344; Ben Braber, *This Cannot Happen Here: Integration and Jewish Resistance in the Netherlands, 1940–1945* (Amsterdam: Amsterdam University Press, 2013), 158.

In contrast to the situation in Belgium and France, therefore, no Jewish armed resistance groups were formed. Jews in the Netherlands had not experienced anti-Jewish violence on a large scale and therefore they 'were unused to forming defence groups and few had professional military experience'.[70]

The works of Braber have shown that there was Jewish participation in early non-Jewish resistance groups, but only in small numbers.[71] There were Jews who set up specific Jewish welfare and resistance groups, most notably the Nanno and Oosteinde group and the Palestine Pioneers whose activities we examined in Chapter 4, but again, their impact and representation was limited. The delay in the development of resistance activities in the Netherlands, together with the fact that the Dutch Jewish Council was disbanded relatively early (in September 1943), in comparison with its counterparts in Western Europe (which were disbanded close to the liberation in summer 1944), partly explains why few resistance groups operated alongside the JR, and why these groups hardly used the Council as a cloak for their clandestine operations.

Cloaking: Covert Actions Under the Councils' Legal Cover

During the course of the war, the JR, the AJB, the UGIF-Nord and the UGIF-Sud attracted, or had connections with, clandestine operators because their leaders and members had information and resources valuable to the resistance. In France, the president of the Central Consistory, Léon Meiss, who was a known critic of the UGIF, opposed the immediate dissolution of the UGIF in summer 1944 precisely for this reason.[72] In various ways, clandestine organisations used the legal Jewish bodies to facilitate, or cloak, their illegal activities. The term 'cloaking' can be used to describe this phenomenon of covert actions taking place under the legal cover of the Jewish bodies. It is a term best understood as the concealment or camouflage of illegal activities using the legality of the Jewish organisations, either with or without knowledge of its functionaries. Cloaking was a complex phenomenon that was often more central to the history of the 'Jewish Councils' in Western Europe than has previously been argued.

---

[70] Braber, *This Cannot Happen Here*, 161.
[71] Ibid., 92–98; Ben Braber, *Zelfs als wij zullen verliezen: Joden in verzet en illegaliteit, 1940–1945* (Amsterdam: Balans, 1990), 49–56.
[72] Laffitte, *Juif dans la France allemande*, 324.

The level of cloaking activities undertaken under cover of the Jewish organisations differed. The same is true for the central board members' awareness of, and participation in, these activities. Although it is impossible to generalise given the complicated nature of the occupation and changes in the compositions of the boards throughout the war, it is possible to broadly identify three different levels of cloaking. First, in the French southern zone, the federative structure of the UGIF-Sud, in which Jewish social welfare organisations were operating independently, made it relatively easy to engage in clandestine activities that obstructed Nazi policies, using the legality of the organisation as a protective shield. On various levels, and in relatively large numbers, members of the UGIF-Sud central board played an active role in accommodating clandestine activities.

Second, in Belgium, there were some individuals who took on a crucial dual position within the legal AJB and the illegal CDJ. The top level of leadership seems to have had knowledge of this, but intentionally turned a blind eye so as not to hamper these actions. In the northern zone of France, the situation was rather similar, although here the leadership's involvement in cloaking activities was more active. Third, in the case of the JR in the Netherlands, there were some initiatives to use the Council in this way but, compared with the other two countries, these were few and far between. There was relatively little knowledge among the Jewish leadership of illegal activities that were taking place in parallel with the activities of the Council.

The UGIF-Sud and its Multiple Interactions with Clandestine Organisations

The last president of the UGIF, Georges Edinger, claimed in a post-war report on the organisation's activities that the UGIF was the most important 'semi-clandestine, semi-official' organisation. In an attempt to overcome the criticism that prevailed after the liberation regarding the UGIF and, especially, Edinger himself, he asserted that its legal work primarily served to camouflage clandestine activities.[73] While the reality was far more complex than Edinger suggested, the interconnections between the resistance and the UGIF were substantial. When we compare the UGIF-Sud with the JR, the AJB and the UGIF-Nord, we find that the boundaries between legality and illegality were highly permeable in the southern zone of France. The welfare organisations that operated under the UGIF-Sud's umbrella were largely autonomous and not bound by UGIF policy. As a result, it was easy for the leadership of some welfare

---

[73] Edinger, Report on the activities of the UGIF, p. 1, CCCLXXIX-33, CDJC, Mémorial de la Shoah.

organisations to provide social assistance, both legally and illegally, under the guise of the UGIF-Sud and without fear of its intervention.[74] Through the official channels provided by the UGIF-Sud, organisations such as the EIF and the OSE gained access to internment camps and developed important relations with non-Jewish relief societies. As a result, these organisations could engage in the rescue of Jewish children from round-ups and deportation. This was initially achieved legally, but from summer 1942, after the massive round-ups of foreign Jews throughout the southern zone, these practices became increasingly illegal.[75]

From summer 1942, some of the organisations that had been trans-formed into departments or sections of the UGIF-Sud set up illegal parallel bodies, including the third (health) department (administered by the OSE), the fourth (youth) department (administered by the EIF) and the various sections of the fifth (assistance to refugees and those interned) department (administered by the CAR and the FSJ). Crucially, the very top of the UGIF-Sud leadership was aware of, and even encour-aged, illegal activities. Existing pre-war relations played a major role in fostering such activities. For example, the OSE's leader Joseph Millner was close to Lambert because they had worked together for the *Univers Israélite* during the 1930s, and he benefitted from Lambert's leading role in the UGIF-Sud while establishing clandestine activities.[76] The Jewish leadership could also capitalise on its connections with non-Jews that had been established in the decades before the war.[77]

During the first stages of the war, French Jews were similar to their non-Jewish compatriots in holding the belief that the French state would protect citizens against persecution. From the end of 1942, prominent members of the UGIF-Sud – Lambert, Schah, Spanien and Gamzon – came to 'a more realistic appraisal of Vichy' and realised they would not be protected.[78] After the German invasion of the south of France in November 1942, which put an end to legal emigration possibilities for Jews, these four men began to support or condone clandestine activities, including the illegal migration or hiding of Jewish children.[79] Although there had traditionally existed a division between French and immigrant

[74] Cohen, 'Introduction', in *Diary of a Witness*, lii.
[75] Lazare, *Rescue as Resistance*, 172–215; Nancy Lefenfeld, 'Unarmed Combat: Humanitarian Resistance in France' in Patrick Henry (ed.), *Jewish Resistance against the Nazis* (Washington: The Catholic University of America Press, 2014), 111; Cohen, *Burden of Conscience*, 120–121.
[76] Laffitte, 'L'OSE de 1942 à 1944', 67.
[77] Laffitte, 'Was the UGIF an Obstacle to the Rescue of Jews?', 408.
[78] Cohen, 'Introduction', in *Diary of a Witness*, liii.
[79] Ibid; Cohen, *Burden of Conscience*, 123. Also see Rayski, *The Choice of the Jews under Vichy*, 259–261.

Jews, these differences were partly overcome in the context of the UGIF-Sud. The organisation has often been considered elitist, but Lambert's background in Jewish relief work and his willingness to serve the interests of the immigrant Jewish communities, combined with the connections between the UGIF-Sud and clandestine groups that mainly consisted of immigrant Jews, shows that the reality was more complex.

One group that set up a clandestine parallel organisation under the legal umbrella of the UGIF-Sud was the EIF (the Jewish Scouts). We have seen that the EIF in the southern zone had to be dissolved after the UGIF-Sud's establishment, and was incorporated as the Social Youth Service (the SSJ) into the sixth section of the UGIF-Sud's youth department.[80] From summer 1942, the clandestine division of this sixth section (*la sixième*) was active on three levels: in the occupied zone, the unoccupied zone and in the armed resistance known as 'the maquis'.[81] In January 1943, Vichy officials dissolved the entire youth department. A letter from Darquier de Pellepoix, chairman of the Vichy-led CGQJ, to the UGIF-Sud, sent on 5 January 1943, shows that he was dissatisfied with the way the EIF had been reorganised under the umbrella of the UGIF. Darquier accused the Jewish leaders of having appeared to integrate the EIF into the UGIF's services while in fact allowing the organisation to remain intact. He indicated that the dissolution of the EIF's services was supposed to have been total, and should have included the full transfer of its resources to the UGIF.[82]

In the end, while the EIF was officially dissolved in January 1943, some of its functions continued under the official cover of the UGIF. In his diary, Lambert reflected upon the discussions he had had on this issue with Joseph Antignac, chief of staff *(chef de cabinet)* of the CGQJ, during a trip to Vichy on 12 and 13 January 1943. He noted that, in the end, he had managed to save two of the four EIF sections through his negotiations with Antignac.[83] While some of the organisation's functions were moved to the second (work) department, the SSJ was moved to the third department (health), which also incorporated the OSE. Ironically, this Vichy measure to dissolve the EIF thus facilitated cooperation between OSE and the SSJ's *sixième*, both of which were becoming increasingly clandestine by this point.[84] The illegal activities of the *sixième*, such as

---

[80] See the report on the activities of the EIF from 1939 until shortly after the liberation, CCXVII-8, CDJC, Mémorial de la Shoah.
[81] Brauman et al., *Organisation Juive de combat*, 245.
[82] Letter of Darquier de Pellepoix to the UGIF, 5 January 1943, XXVIII-116a, CDJC, Mémorial de la Shoah.
[83] Lambert, *Diary of a Witness*, 13 February 1943, 173.
[84] Zuccotti, *The Holocaust, the French and the Jews*, 348 n.35; Michel, *Les Éclaireurs*, 123–128.

the manufacture and use of false identity papers and ration tickets and the clandestine placement of children, were always conducted under the official cover of the SSJ (and thus that of the UGIF-Sud).[85]

Robert Gamzon, founder of the EIF and also member of the UGIF-Sud's central board, explained in his memoirs that in each city's UGIF office, the *sixième* was represented. When someone turned to the youth service of the UGIF and it was clear that he needed more than 'official aid', they arranged a meeting outside the organisation's office and offered clandestine help.[86] This was done particularly in the cases of foreign Jewish children and adolescents, or those French Jews whose parents had been arrested or were being sought by the Gestapo or the French police. Gamzon's memoirs also show that clandestine organisations such as the EIF, the OSE and the Zionist Youth Movement (Mouvement de Jeunesse Sioniste, MJS) cooperated closely with members of the UGIF's Marseille branch.[87]

Gamzon used his legal position in the UGIF-Sud to prevent Jews from being arrested and deported while he actively looked for people who could help with clandestine operations. In a post-war interview, Liliane Klein-Lieber described how Gamzon recruited her for clandestine work in Moissac in the Tarn-et-Garonne department. She had been a youth member of the EIF in Grenoble and helped with hiding children and the production of false identity papers. She claimed this was relatively easy because the local police were complicit in these activities. As a result, hardly any of her illegal group members were caught. This was very different from the situation in Nice, where almost all Jews responsible for the *sixième* were arrested.[88]

While he combined his role as member of the legal UGIF-Sud central board with participating in the clandestine rescue of Jews, Gamzon also used his position to inform illegal workers about forthcoming German actions and regulations. Member of the clandestine *sixième* Roger Fichtenberg, for example, claimed that Gamzon warned him when the Germans planned to raid Jewish houses.[89] Despite his successful dual role, by the end of 1943, Gamzon felt that it was morally impossible to

---

[85] Lazare, *Rescue as Resistance*, 197.
[86] Gamzon, *Les eaux claires*, 78–79.
[87] Ibid., 86–87.
[88] Interview with Liliane Klein-Lieber, 21 June 1996, Interview No. 16095, USC Shoah Foundation. Accessed at the American University of Paris, Paris. Klein-Lieber was also interviewed for a project of the Association pour l'Histoire du Scoutisme Laïque; see Alain Vincenot, *La France résistante. Histoire de héros ordinaires* (Paris: Les Syrtes, 2004).
[89] Testimony of Roger Fichtenberg, undated, CMXX-33, CDJC, Mémorial de la Shoah.

continue working for the UGIF. During a meeting between the UGIF and the Consistory on 6 October 1943, he recommended the dissolution of the UGIF.[90] After this failed to happen, Gamzon left the organisation. In the months that followed, he continued his resistance activities and, among other things, created a Jewish partisan unit within the Maquis de Vabres, a resistance organisation that operated in the east of the Tarn department (south of France) in 1943.[91]

The chairman of the UGIF-Sud, Raymond-Raoul Lambert, was actively engaged in facilitating the actions of illegal workers. For example, in the wake of the mass arrests of French and foreign Jews in Marseille in January 1943, Lambert appointed Dika Jefroykin and his cousin Maurice Brener as 'social inspectors' of the UGIF-Sud. By then, these men were important members of the armed Jewish resistance movement (Armée Juive, AJ) and acted as financial intermediaries between resistance groups and the Joint Distribution Committee.[92] In this capacity, they were able to finance illegal operations. Gamzon's diary shows that his clandestine activities were financially supported by the Joint with the help of Brener and Jefroykin.[93] A post-war statement by Albert Akerberg, who coordinated both the EIF and the MJS in the northern zone, also testifies to the financial support Brener provided to clandestine operations, in this case in order to save Jewish children.[94]

The protection Brener and Jefroykin received (through the UGIF identity card) after Lambert appointed them as 'social inspectors' allowed them to move freely in the southern zone and gave them 'protected access' to the north.[95] Their ten-day 'special mission' to the north in May 1943, ostensibly to discuss the reorganisation of the UGIF, enabled the two men to establish further contact with resistance groups that were active in both zones.[96] There is little doubt that Lambert deliberately appointed Brener and Jefroykin without a well-defined task so that they could continue their clandestine activities.

---

[90] Rayski, *The Choice of the Jews under Vichy*, 259.
[91] For reflections of Robert's wife Denise on this episode, see Oral history interview with Denise Gamzon, 2006 Accession number: 2012.296.1, RG number: RG-50.710.0001, USHMM; Denise Gamzon, *Mémoires*, 90ff.
[92] Bauer, *American Jewry and the Holocaust*, 241–242.
[93] Gamzon, *Les eaux claires*, 88.
[94] Interview with Albert Akerberg, conducted by Anny Latour after the war (exact date unknown), p. 7, DLXI-3, CDJC, Mémorial de la Shoah.
[95] Lazare, *Rescue as Resistance*, 220.
[96] Cohen, 'Introduction', in *Diary of a Witness*, lvii–lviii; and *The Burden of Conscience*, 160; Adler, *The Jews of Paris*, 142.

After the war, Jefroykin testified to the close contact the UGIF-Sud maintained with the Jewish armed resistance (the AJ) specifically and resistance groups more broadly. He indicated that meetings between representatives of the UGIF-Sud, the Consistory and resistance organisations took place fairly regularly.[97] As a result, even though the organisations were established with different purposes, and their leading functionaries had different perspectives on how to respond to the German occupation, the relation between the UGIF-Sud and the AJ was generally one of trust and approval. Jefroykin specifically noted that, even though the UGIF leadership continued to cooperate with the Germans and Vichy officials, he did not consider the UGIF leaders traitors: 'we simply thought they had made a dangerous error'.[98]

Apart from facilitating clandestine operations, the UGIF-Sud chairman Lambert was also personally engaged in such activities. Throughout 1943, he was in contact with Angelo Donati, an Italian Jew who planned a mass evacuation of Jews from the Italian-occupied French zone.[99] In November 1942, more than 15,000 Italian soldiers had invaded France following the Allied invasion of North Africa, occupying nine departments in south-eastern France, a zone that was delimited by the Rhône on its western border and the Savoy to the north.[100] The Italians refused to give in to German pressure and opposed anti-Jewish legislation, allowing Jews to flee from persecution to the Italian zone.[101] Even though Jews benefitted from this situation, the myth of the *brava gente* (good fellow), fostered by this relatively low-key Italian occupation of the French regions, in contrast with

---

[97] Interview with Dika Jefroykin, undated, CMXX-43, CDJC, Mémorial de la Shoah. For more information on the role of Dika Jefroykin as director of the AJ, see: Brauman et al., *Organisation Juive de combat*, 73–74.

[98] Interview with Dika Jefroykin, undated, CMXX-43, CDJC, Mémorial de la Shoah.

[99] Léon Poliakov, *La condition des Juifs en France sous l'occupation italienne* (Paris: CDJC, 1946), 39; Marrus, 'Jewish Leadership and the Holocaust: The Case of France', 327; Cohen, *Burden of Conscience*, 129–130. For the full story of Donati, who managed to prevent thousands of Jews from falling into the hands of the Nazis during the ten months of the Italian occupation of southern France, see Luca Fenoglio, *Angelo Donati e la 'questione ebraica' nella Francia occupata dall'esercito italiano* (Turin: Silvio Zamorani, 2013). Also see two articles by Fenoglio that reflect on Donati's role: 'On the Use of the Nazi Sources for the Study of Fascist Jewish Policy in the Italian-Occupied Territories: The Case of South-Eastern France, November 1942–July 1943', *Journal of Modern Italian Studies*, Vol. 24, No. 1 (2019), 63–78; and 'Between Protection and Complicity: Guido Lospinoso, Fascist Italy, and the Holocaust in Occupied Southeastern France', *Holocaust and Genocide Studies*, Vol. 33, No. 1 (2019), 90–111.

[100] Emanuele Sica, *Mussolini's Army in the French Riviera: Italy's Occupation of France* (Urbana/Chicago/Springfield: University of Illinois Press, 2016), 77.

[101] Paxton, *Vichy France: Old Guard and New Order*, 182–183.

comparatively brutal Italian occupation of the Balkans, has recently been reconsidered by some scholars.[102]

To the UGIF-Sud leadership, the Italian invasion provided opportunities to foster clandestine operations in this region. Even though he does not reflect upon this directly in his diary, it is clear that Lambert met Donati several times during his visits to Nice in the spring and summer of 1943.[103] Donati had strong connections with France as he had been a liaison officer during the First World War and was a respected banker in Paris in the interwar period. Furthermore, he had helped Jewish refugees who fled to Paris in order to escape persecution in Germany in the 1930s and he continued his work in the unoccupied zone after 1940. During the war, Donati was associated with Father Pierre-Marie Benoît, who acted as an intermediary between the inmates of Les Milles internment camp and its authorities and had access to a large network of Catholics and Protestants in and around Marseille.

Father Benoît used his position to obtain false identity papers and hiding places and he helped individuals to escape the camps. He also became involved with armed resistance groups that organised escape routes via Spain to North Africa.[104] The connections between Donati and Father Benoît and, in turn, between Donati and Lambert suggest that clandestine operations in this region may have been planned, or even carried out, with the knowledge of the UGIF-Sud's leadership. However, as Cohen has pointed out, the collapse of Mussolini's regime in July 1943 prevented an actual long-term collaboration between Lambert and Donati.[105]

After his arrest, Lambert showed other clear signs of his (intimate) connections with illegality. From Drancy, he sent several coded messages to Maurice Brener that referred to illegal activities carried out under the guise of the UGIF-Sud. For example, when the children of the La Verdière home had been seized and arrived in Drancy, Lambert

---

[102] These scholars have highlighted the complex triangular relationship between the French, the Italians and the Germans. See, for example, Davide Rodogno, 'La politique des occupants italiens à l'égard des Juifs en France métropolitaine, Humanisme ou pragmatisme?', *Vingtième Siècle, Revue d'histoire*, Vol. 93, No. 1 (2007), 63–77; Fenoglio, 'Between Protection and Complicity', passim; and 'On the Use of Nazi Sources', passim. Sica has provided a thorough and multi-dimensional perspective on the question of why the Italians displayed such a surprising and lenient attitude towards south-eastern France in *Mussolini's Army in the French Riviera*, passim.

[103] See Lambert, *Diary of a Witness*, 22 June 1943, 189 n.1; Cohen, *Burden of Conscience*, 130; Poliakov, *La condition des Juifs en France sous l'occupation italienne*, 121.

[104] Moore, *Survivors*, 153–154; Yisrael Gutman and Sara Bender (eds.), *The Encyclopaedia of the Righteous Among the Nations: Rescuers of Jews during the Holocaust: France* (Jerusalem: Yad Vashem, 2003), 69–70.

[105] Cohen, *Burden of Conscience*, 130.

indicated that this could have been avoided if they had been sent to Lorraine and then over the border to Switzerland.[106] We have seen that Brener, in addition to his role as 'social inspector' of the UGIF-Sud, was active in the Armée Juive and was charged with establishing connections with non-Jewish resistance movements that specialised in creating false papers.[107] In the post-war trial investigations against former head of the Vichy-led CGQJ Joseph Antignac, Brener claimed that he busied himself mostly with illegal activities, with the support of Lambert and 'other leaders of the UGIF'; Lambert was an important (silent) source and supporter of their illegal actions.[108]

The previous paragraphs have shown that the negative and morally weighted image of the UGIF provided by those such as Maurice Rajsfus should be refuted.[109] At the same time, it would be wrong to argue that the UGIF-Sud was in fact an extension of illegal groups, or indeed the other way around. The UGIF was never actually led into outright resistance and its structures remained legal. However, Cohen's assertion that Lambert 'wavered and opted for a middle road' between legality and illegality does not fully recognise his significant role in supporting clandestine activities.[110]

Lambert deliberately chose to facilitate activities that obstructed German policies and that he allowed the UGIF-Sud to be used as a cloak for clandestine activities on various levels. There was an intrinsic relationship between the two spheres. In contrast to Belgium and the Netherlands, the leadership was strongly involved in this process. Taking into consideration the fact that the UGIF's policies were largely defined by Lambert, this is important. As the course of the war changed and both the UGIF-Sud members and the illegal workers who had been engaged in these activities were arrested, the nature of these relations changed as well. Nevertheless, as Cohen made clear, since none of them advocated the organisation's dissolution, the 'twilight activity' of legality and illegality continued to exist.[111]

After summer 1943, when Lambert had been deported, the UGIF rapidly began to lose credibility and hostility towards the organisation grew. Whereas communists and immigrant Jews had been fighting against the UGIF from very early on, others too now realised that

---

[106] Letter from Lambert to Brener, 26 October 1943, in Lambert, *Diary of a Witness*, 205–207.
[107] Brauman et al., *Organisation juive de combat*, 52.
[108] Testimony of Maurice Brener, 26 June 1946, XCVI-8, CDJC, Mémorial de la Shoah.
[109] Rajsfus, *Des Juifs dans la collaboration*, passim.
[110] Cohen, *Burden of Conscience*, 129.
[111] Cohen, 'Introduction', in *Diary of a Witness*, liii.

its position was no longer politically viable. Beginning in spring 1943, the French resistance had set out to unite all its movements, pressuring the UGIF to abolish itself. In the meantime, Raymond Geissmann, the last chairman of the UGIF-Sud, continued to underline that all of its work had been designed to respond to the needs of the Jewish community. On 13 August 1944, Léon Meiss, president of the Consistory, supported the position taken by Geissmann.[112] Meiss argued that the UGIF provided social support and security to many of the Jews living in France and that it succeeded in preserving the independence of traditionally important Jewish services. He furthermore underlined that some of the UGIF members had paid for these activities with their lives.[113] However, as president of the CRIF, which officially represented both immigrant and French Jews, Meiss proposed in the end to liquidate the UGIF.[114] On 23 August 1944, during the battle for the liberation of Paris, Geissmann ordered the dissolution of the UGIF.[115] Two days later, the French capital city was liberated.

The UGIF-Nord, the Amelot Committee and Other Illegal Groups

Similar to their counterparts in the unoccupied (later southern) zone of France, many organisations in the occupied (later northern) zone moved from legal to clandestine activity with increasing demands from Vichy and German authorities. The Amelot Committee was initially mainly preoccupied with rebuilding Jewish welfare, aiming to unite several pre-existing legal immigrant Jewish organisations.[116] Its representatives encouraged French Jews to engage in relief work as well. In September 1940 it organised a special meeting to this effect, at which the Paris Consistory was also represented.[117] The Amelot Committee's central focus shifted after the mass arrest on 14 May 1941, when 6,500 Polish, Czech and

[112] For further reading on Léon Meiss, see André Blumel, *Un grand Juif: Léon Meiss* (Paris: Éditions Guy-Victor, 1967), passim.
[113] 'Polémique sur le role de l'UGIF sur l'occupation', 13 August 1944, CMXX-17, CDJC, Mémorial de la Shoah.
[114] Ibid.; Minutes of the CRIF (Meiss Grinberg, Adamitz, Geissmann), from July 1944 to 13 August 1944, CDXXX-38, CDJC, Mémorial de la Shoah.
[115] Poznanski, *Jews in France during World War II*, 459–461.
[116] These organisations included the OSE, ORT and the Hachomer Hatzaïr. Hillel J. Kieval, 'Legality and Resistance in Jewish France: The Rescue of Jewish Children', *Proceedings of the American Philosophical Society*, Vol. 124, No. 5 (1980), 342–343; Lazare, *Rescue as Resistance*, 39–47; Adler, *The Jews of Paris*, 62, 166–167.
[117] Adler, *The Jews of Paris*, 62.

Austrian Jews who were encouraged to report themselves to the prefectures, ostensibly in order to discuss their status, were placed in the camps at Pithiviers and Beaune-la-Rolande.

On 20 August, Jews of other nationalities were arrested as well, including some French Jews, and taken to Drancy camp. By then, the Amelot Committee had become a semi-clandestine organisation growing closer to the communist MOI and its Solidarité organisation, although their alliance backfired after the German attack on the Soviet Union, 'when the communists attempted to dominate the other groups whose objectives were more narrowly based than the outright ideological and armed struggle against fascism'.[118] As Moore indicated, the path of the Amelot Committee towards illegality 'was a gradual one, and its relationship with the Jewish communist movement MOI and its Solidarité remained fraught, but all were directly involved in ameliorative relief for a Jewish population that was economically and socially marginalized from mainstream society'.[119]

After the establishment of the UGIF-Nord in November 1941, the legal activities of the Amelot Committee were formally dissolved and transferred into its administration. However, the Committee continued to operate separately from the UGIF-Nord leadership, and the latter was aware that it needed the support and trust of immigrant Jews to establish a solid basis of support among the Jews in France. In order to neutralise immigrant opposition and to gain a position of authority within the Jewish communities, the UGIF-Nord organised a meeting with the Amelot Committee on 28 January 1942.

This meeting shows that there were crucial interrelations between central individuals of the UGIF-Nord central board – Baur, Musnik, Stern, Stora, and Weil-Hallé – and the Amelot Committee. Knowing that the UGIF-Nord leaders could have forced Amelot to be integrated into the organisation, and refusing to dissolve itself, the Amelot Committee was prepared to set aside its moral objections to the UGIF as an organisation that cooperated with the German occupier, and it promised to refrain from attacking the organisation and focus instead on its relief activities.[120]

At the same time, the Amelot Committee continued to disavow all responsibility for the UGIF-Nord's activities. The UGIF-Nord,

[118] Moore, *Survivors*, 106.
[119] Ibid., 110.
[120] Meeting UGIF and Amelot Committee, 28 January 1942, Archive of Marc Jarblum P.7–8, Identifier 4019673, Yad Vashem.

in turn, promised not to impose control on the Amelot Committee or interfere with its activities.[121] Amelot was able to use the financial resources of the UGIF-Nord, while it in turn provided the UGIF-Nord with access to its social infrastructure and to the immigrant population. The interrelation between the two organisations was thus based on pragmatism: they exchanged information, 'referred clients to each other's programs, collaborated in the sending of packages to Drancy, and so on'.[122]

With financial assistance from the UGIF-Nord, the Amelot Committee was able to provide by running soup kitchens, two dispensaries and a cloakroom for Jews who were in need of clothing and shoes. Until June 1943, the canteens functioned autonomously under the surveillance of the UGIF-Nord and were at the centre of the provisions of food for Jews. They also served as gathering places where Jews discussed the latest anti-Jewish regulations and possible ways to escape or impede them.[123]

While availing themselves of the legal structures of the UGIF-Nord when necessary and maintaining their organisational autonomy, the Amelot Committee also engaged in various kinds of extra-legal activity. Amelot helped Jews who wanted to go into hiding, and 'systematically scattered out as many children as they could'.[124] They also secured hiding places for those Jews who had escaped the raids and found ways to bring them to the southern zone. In addition, they helped those who came to their offices to obtain false papers.[125]

The Amelot Committee remained separate from the UGIF-Nord leadership as an organisation engaged in illegal activities, while it used the organisation's funds to provide legal social aid. Although UGIF-Nord functionaries André Baur and Marcel Stora had initially unsuccessfully tried to engage members of the Amelot Committee inside the legal sphere of the UGIF-Nord, the Jewish leadership nonetheless accepted its role as a façade for Amelot's independent activities.[126] In the second half of 1942, Amelot definitively shifted its main emphasis from relief work to humanitarian resistance. While the group had considered permanently shutting their legal canteens, the leadership eventually came to believe

---

[121] Author unknown (probably David Rapoport), 'Notre relations avec l'UGIF', 30 January 1942, CCXIII-48, CDJC, Mémorial de la Shoah.

[122] Poznanski, *Jews in France during World War II*, 232.

[123] Laffitte, *Juif dans la France allemande*, 217.

[124] Poznanski, *Jews in France during World War II*, 343.

[125] Lazare, *Rescue as Resistance*, 39–47; Brauman et al., *Organisation juive de combat*, 231–233; Poznanski, *Jews in France during World War II*, 343.

[126] Adler, *The Jews of Paris*, 203–204.

that deprivation posed a greater threat than police raids and decided not to dissolve its activities.[127]

The ways in which the UGIF-Nord functioned as a façade for the Amelot Committee and its closely associated illegal groups, varied. One of the most obvious and basic forms of cloaking was the use of the UGIF's identity cards, which allowed illegal workers to operate more freely while carrying out its clandestine activities. The Amelot leaders had previously objected to the use of UGIF identity cards on moral grounds, but reconsidered their decision in summer 1942 and this ensured that they were better able to continue their activities.[128] The importance of access to these cards should not be underestimated. It provided a major benefit to the quasi-legal Amelot Committee compared with other illegal groups that had been forced to go underground.

Cloaking activities occurred at other levels as well. A wartime report of the Amelot Committee gives us an insight into the tactics that were used. In October 1942, a member of the Committee wrote: 'We provide the first assistance because the machinery of the UGIF is slower [...] If the UGIF rejects a request, we keep the case in our charge [...] Relations, both within this committee and in general between the UGIF and ourselves are cordial.'[129] The Amelot Committee took up tasks the UGIF-Nord either did not want to, or could not, carry out. For example, around 900 families in Paris were in such a precarious situation that they did not dare contact the UGIF-Nord. Instead, they were aided by the Amelot Committee.[130]

In addition, the use of the UGIF-Nord's legal façade enabled the organisation to maintain its secret office on the second floor of the rue Amelot, where the committee resided. A report of 22 April 1943 shows that the Vichy-led CGQJ was aware that the dispensary 'La Mère et l'Enfant' had a 'secret bureau' and that it clandestinely dispersed children among non-Jewish families.[131] On 1 June 1943, when David Rapoport, leader of the Committee, was arrested, all of the projects of the Amelot Committee were incorporated into sections of the UGIF-Nord.[132]

---

[127] Lefenfeld, 'Unarmed Combat', 106.
[128] Lazare, Rescue as Resistance, 150–151; Brauman et al., Organisation juive de combat, 233.
[129] Wartime report of the Amelot Committee, coll. 343, file 4 and 116, YIVO, as cited in Lazare, Rescue as Resistance, 151.
[130] Poznanski, Jews in France during WWII, 336–337.
[131] Report of the CGQJ to SS-Obersturmführer Röthke on the clandestine activities of the UGIF, 22 April 1943, XXVIII-159, CDJC, Mémorial de la Shoah. For an overview of the organisation and resistance activities of the 'La Mère et l'Enfant' centre on rue Amelot, see Jacqueline Baldran and Claude Bochurberg, David Rapoport, La mère et l'enfant, 36 rue Amelot (Paris: CDJC, 1994).
[132] Lazare, Rescue as Resistance, 82. For an overview of the organisation and resistance activities of the 'La Mère et l'Enfant' centre on rue Amelot, see Jacqueline Baldran and Claude Bochurberg, David Rapoport, La mère et l'enfant, 36 rue Amelot (Paris: CDJC, 1994).

There were also other groups that used the legality of the UGIF-Nord to engage in undercover activities. In a post-war interview, Denise Schorr Khaitman noted that while she worked in the children's homes of the organisation, there was a whole network of clandestine organisations that attempted to move these children from the occupied to the unoccupied zone, or even to Switzerland. Khaitman stated that this happened under the legal cover of the UGIF-Nord and in cooperation with its members, including Fernand Musnik and Juliette Stern, head of the social services division of the UGIF-Nord from January 1942, whose main responsibility was the social governance of Jewish children.[133]

Organisations such as the EIF did indeed use the legal cloak of the UGIF-Nord to undertake illegal activities. Before the war, the EIF had already established a unique organisational foundation throughout the entire country that included both immigrant and French Jews.[134] Similar to the situation in the southern zone, the organisation was integrated into the fourth direction of the UGIF-Nord as the SSJ, where it became the sixth section, which also had a clandestine division (*la sixième*).[135]

The administration of the illegal *sixième* in Paris, established in May 1943, was in the hands of Fernand Musnik, who officially worked for the Youth and Professional Regrouping (Jeunesse et Reclassement Professionel) department of the UGIF-Nord and Emmanuel Lefschetz, director of the UGIF-Nord home in rue Claude Bernard, Paris.[136] Before the war, Musnik had been actively involved in Parisian youth movements, including as a member of the directory board of the Federation of the Zionist and Pro-Palestinian Youth of France (Fédération de la

---

[133] Interview with Denise Schorr Khaitman, 5 December 1996, Interview No. 23092, USC Shoah Foundation. Accessed at the American University of Paris, Paris. It should be noted that Khaitman erroneously claimed that attempts were also made to smuggle children to 'Israel' – which did not exist as such at the time. Even though Jews from Central and Eastern Europe indeed managed to reach Palestine throughout the war, it is questionable whether Jewish children from France were smuggled into this country between 1942 and 1944. It *is* known that the EIF smuggled children from France to Switzerland and Spain.

[134] Lee, *Pétain's Jewish Children*, 36–40, 76; Lazare, *Rescue as Resistance*, 55.

[135] In the southern zone, the EIF had been officially dissolved by Vichy in January 1943. While, after Lambert's negotiations with Antignac, some of its functions were maintained and transferred to sub-departments of the UGIF-Sud, a few EIF members were sent to Paris to encourage and participate in illegal activities there. Adler, *The Jews of Paris*, 156; Michel, *Les Éclaireurs*, 123–128.

[136] Laffitte, *Juif dans la France allemande*, 86, 151. Emmanuel Lefschetz was a French citizen of Russian origin who had arrived in France at the very beginning of the twentieth century and had fought for the French army during the First World War. His memoirs can be found in the Weill family archive and are cited in Camille Ménager, *Le Sauvetage des Juifs à Paris: Histoire et Mémoire* (Paris: Presses de Sciences Po, 2005), 156–157, 159, 202.

Jeunesse Sioniste et Pro-Palestinienne de France). From 1939, he also played an active role in the EIF. Between 1940 and 1944, he was in charge of the EIF and, among other things, participated in the creation of false papers in the northern zone.[137]

After the so-called Vél d'Hiv round-up in the night of 16–17 July, during which over 13,000 Jews in Paris were arrested and two-thirds were temporarily confined in the Vélodrome d'Hiver (an indoor sporting arena in Paris's fifteenth *arrondissement*), Lefschetz established a Jewish youth network that served under the auspices of the EIF.[138] This group, in which his daughter Denise Lefschetz was involved, traced Jewish children in the Paris area whose parents had been deported and provided false identity papers and hiding places for them.[139] The notion that clandestine groups were created in parallel to existing welfare institutions in direct response to the Vél d'Hiv round-up is reinforced by a post-war testimony from Denise Gamzon, whose husband Robert Gamzon was the founder of the EIF.[140]

Another organisation that used the legal cloak of the UGIF-Nord was the Zionist Youth Movement (MJS). We have seen in Chapter 1 that during the 1920s and 1930s, Zionist activity increased in France and numerous Zionist youth organisations were established, with each reflecting a particular political ideological orientation. At the initiative of Simon Lévitte, a national leader of the Jewish scouts, representatives of various Zionist youth organisations came together in Montpellier in May 1942 for a Zionist Unification Congress. An ardent Zionist, Lévitte was born in Ukraine and had published a book on modern Zionism in 1936, after which he and his wife emigrated to Palestine where he worked on a kibbutz. On the eve of the war, they returned to France.[141] During the Unification Congress, Lévitte convinced the individual organisations' leaders to disband their organisations and to form a unified Zionist youth organisation to provide young Jews with a 'Zionist education, physical training and vocational skills they would need to create successful communities in Palestine'.[142]

---

[137] Adler, *The Jews of Paris*, 203.
[138] See the testimony of Emmanuel Lefschetz, undated, CMXXI-53, CDJC, Mémorial de la Shoah.
[139] In 2009, Jacques Sémelin conducted an interview with Denise Weill (born Lefschetz), the daughter of Emmanuel Lefschetz. This interview has been used as a source in *The Survival of the Jews in France, 1940–1944*. Also see the interview with her in the USC Shoah Foundation Collection, 10 May 1996, Interview No. 144775.
[140] Oral history interview with Denise Gamzon, 2006, Accession number: 2012.296.1, RG number: RG-50.710.0001, USHMM.
[141] Simon Lévitte, *Le Sionisme: quelques pages de son histoire* (Paris: Éditions des Cahiers Juifs, 1936); Lefenfeld, 'Unarmed Combat', 115.
[142] Lefenfeld, 'Unarmed Combat', 115. Also see Nicault, 'L'Utopie sioniste du "nouveau Juif" et la jeunesse juive dans la France de l'après guerre: Contribution à l'histoire de l'Alyah française', *Les Cahiers de la Shoah*, Vol. 5, No. 1 (2001), 123.

The MJS was established in May 1942 with Lévitte as general secretary and Jules 'Dika' Jefroykin, founder of the Jewish Resistance (Résistance Juive) and later the AJ, as president. Soon after the organisation's establishment, foreign Jews in France were arrested and deported and the organisation's activities shifted to relief work and humanitarian resistance.[143] Refusing to be integrated in the legal UGIF, the MJS became a clandestine Zionist youth organisation, whose members consisted primarily of foreign-born Jews.[144] As well as rescuing Jews and promoting Zionist education, the organisation's leaders wanted to participate in the armed resistance for the liberation of France and they sent volunteers to the Allied armies. In the end, many MJS members participated in the rescue of Jewish children and in arranging the illegal passage of Jews to Switzerland, in close cooperation with the OSE, the EIF and the AJ. In addition, the majority of MJS members were directly connected to the armed AJ.[145]

While the existing literature has primarily underlined the MJS's operations in the southern zone, the organisation was also active in the Paris area.[146] In a post-war interview, Albert Akerberg, who was responsible for the coordination of the MJS and the *sixième* in Paris from 1943, emphasised the permeable nature of the boundaries between illegality

---

[143] Tsilla Hershco, 'Le Mouvement de la jeunesse sioniste (MJS)', in Catherine Richet (ed.), *Organisations juive de combat. Résistance/sauvetage, France 1940–1945* (Paris: 2006), 127; Lefenfeld, 'Unarmed Combat', 115.

[144] Hershco, 'Le Mouvement de la jeunesse sioniste (MJS)', 127; Lazare, *Rescue as Resistance*, 67–70. There exists no comprehensive account of the history and activities of the MJS. Its activities are considered in various articles, including that of Tsilla Hershco, and in numerous published and unpublished accounts of individuals who worked with the MJS. For further reading, see Hélène Gorgiel-Sercarz, *Memoirs of a Jewish Daughter* (Tel Aviv: H. Gorgiel-Sercarz, 1990); René S. Kapel, *Un rabbin dans la tourmente, 1940–1944* (Paris: CDJC, 1986); Anny Latour, *La résistance juive en France* (Paris: Stock, 1970); Georges Schnek, 'Être jeune en France, 1939–1945', address presented at the Colloque International de Grenoble, January 1996 and reproduced in Jean-William Dereymez, *Être jeune en Isère, 1939–1945* (Paris: l'Harmattan, 2001), 59–64; David Knout, *Contribution à l'histoire de la résistance juive en France, 1940–1944* (Paris: Éditions du Centre, 1947), 126–131 and unpublished testimonies of Tony Gryn, DLXI-35, CDJC, Mémorial de la Shoah and Toto Giniewski (Guinat), DLXI-31, CDJC, Mémorial de la Shoah. As cited in Lefenfeld, 'Unarmed Combat', 115 n.50.

[145] Hershco, 'Le Mouvement de la jeunesse sioniste', 128–130; Lefenfeld, 'Unarmed Combat', 116.

[146] For example, Hershco mentioned the activities of the different MJS groups in places such as Grenoble, Annecy, Cambéry, Nice, Toulouse, Montpellier, Montauban and Périgueux: Hershco, 'Le Mouvement de la jeunesse sioniste', passim. Lefenfeld also focused on the organisation's function in cities in the southern zone. Lefenfeld, 'Unarmed Combat', passim.

and legality in the UGIF-Nord. He explained that he had weekly meetings with Juliette Stern and Benjamin Weill-Hallé to discuss the illegal activities that took place under its cloak. He furthermore cooperated with Toni Stern, who also worked for the Paris UGIF office.[147] These examples highlight not only the strong analogies between the clandestine groups, but also show that the boundaries between legality and illegality were porous.

The connections between the legal UGIF-Nord and illegal organisations went beyond the passing of information or the use of the organisation as a (passive) cloak to cover clandestine activities. In fact, members of the UGIF-Nord actively used illegal organisations to support Jews. This can be seen in the cases of Lucienne Scheid-Haas and Hélène Berr, who combined their legal work for the UGIF-Nord with secret operations. For example, while voluntarily employed as a social worker for the UGIF, Berr was also Denise Milhaud's secretary at the Mutual Assistance (Entraide Temporaire), a clandestine organisation that was instituted in 1941 under the cloak of the Social Service of Assistance to Emigrants (Service Social d'Aide aux Émigrants, SSAE).[148] Even though Berr did not reflect upon this dual role in her diary, she underlined the ambiguous feeling she had towards working for the UGIF:

[A]ll we were doing was trying to relieve other people's misfortunes. We knew what was happening; every extra regulation, every deportation squeezed greater pain out of us. People called us collaborators, because those who came to see us had just had a relative arrested, and it was natural that they should react that way when they saw us sitting behind desks. Department for the exploitation of other people's misfortunes. Yes, I can see why other people thought that's what we were [...]. Why did I accept the job? To be able to do something, to come as close as I could to misfortune. We did all we could to assist the internees. People who knew us well understood and judged us fairly.[149]

The cases of Eugène Minkowski and Juliette Stern, who were both closely associated with illegality, also show that UGIF-Nord functionaries were actively engaged in clandestine organisations. Minkowski worked for the 'socio-medical' department of the UGIF-Nord while also heading the illegal OSE. When four OSE children's homes (two in Montmorency,

[147] Interview with Albert Akerberg, conducted by Anny Latour after the war (exact date unknown), p. 5, DLXI-3, Mémorial de la Shoah. Also see Adler, The Jews of Paris, 156.
[148] Laffitte, 'Was the UGIF an Obstacle to the Rescue of Jews?', 401–403; and 'L'UGIF, collaboration ou résistance?', 62.
[149] Hélène Berr, Journal: The Diary of a Young Jewish Woman in Occupied Paris, transl. from the French by David Bellos (London: Maclehose Press, 2008), 13 November 1943, 210–211.

and the others in Soisy and Eaubonne) were closed in 1940 and the Paris office only retained eight employees, Minkowski, in cooperation with the EIF, intensified the OSE's work to hide Jews in the summer of 1942. As a result, the organisation managed to save 600 Jewish children in the Paris region from deportation.[150]

As head of the social services of the UGIF-Nord, Juliette Stern was mainly responsible for children, including those whose parents had been arrested and interned in Drancy, and who were in need of care after they had been (temporarily) released from the camp. These children were 'blocked' and were not allowed to be transferred to another location because they would eventually be interned in Drancy again. While some of them went to UGIF homes, others were placed in foster homes through the so-called Service 42. After the raids of Vél d'Hiv in the summer of 1942, Stern decided, against German orders, to transfer the children to non-Jewish families and institutions. In order to facilitate this, Stern created a secret parallel institution to the legal and social Service 42, called Service 42B, through which she was able to disperse around a thousand children. A network of organisations involved in the illegal dispersion of Jewish children among non-Jewish families, including the Amelot Committee and Minowski's OSE, allowed her to do this.[151]

A report of the Vichy CGQJ's head of office Antignac to SS-Obersturmführer Röthke on 22 April 1943 concerning the 'clandestine activities of the UGIF' shows that Vichy and German officials were aware of the existence of the illegal Service 42B and the placement of Jewish children in Aryan families.[152] While Antignac encouraged Röthke to start an investigation into these activities, the Gestapo instead arrested the members of the department that was responsible for the children's homes (*groupe 5*); all were deported and murdered.[153] At the time of the arrest, Stern was not present in the UGIF facilities and she managed to escape arrest.

In the period that followed, Stern cooperated with illegal groups to make sure the children were removed from the homes as soon as possible. In order to do so, she made an agreement with the communist underground

---

[150] Brauman et al., *Organisation juive de combat*, 208–209; Laffitte, 'L'OSE de 1942 à 1944', 66. It should be noted that Lazare has erroneously claimed that the OSE, as well as the EIF, was not active in the occupied zone. See Lazare, *Rescue as Resistance*, 137.

[151] Lefenfeld, 'Unarmed Combat', 106–107; Poznanski, *Jews in France during World War II*, 343–344.

[152] Report of the CGQJ to SS-Obersturmführer Röthke on the clandestine activities of the UGIF, 22 April 1943, XXVIII-159, CDJC, Mémorial de la Shoah.

[153] Lazare, *Rescue as Resistance*, 205–206.

organisation National Movement against Racism (Mouvement National Contre le Racisme) which 'kidnapped' the children from the UGIF-Nord homes with her complicity and that of members of the organisation's local branches.[154] Stern not only tried to protect these children from deportation, but she also wanted their Jewish identity to be preserved, which is of crucial importance taking into consideration that the Nazis aimed to deport and murder the entirety of the Jewish population in Europe. This was an extraordinary act of identity politics.

Involvement in illegal or quasi-legal activities were mutually beneficial and were taking place at more than the purely individual level. We have seen that at an early stage of the occupation, the UGIF-Nord leadership had already agreed to function as a cloak for the quasi-legal activities of the Amelot Committee. The leadership allowed the Committee to operate independently, and did not exercise any control over its activities or accounts.[155] There was therefore a degree of trust between the two organisations and the interplay between legality and illegality worked for both 'sides'. While the Amelot Committee worked in tandem with the UGIF-Nord to hide their clandestine activities, without disclosing information about the identity of its clients, UGIF employees such as Juliette Stern, in turn, used undercover organisations to transfer Jewish children to safer locations.

The UGIF-Nord also provided access to financial resources to the Amelot Committee, which was indispensable for any underground activity. In addition to this financial support, Amelot also relied on the FSJF for the financing of its illegal activities and, in turn, supported the illegal Solidarité with its finances when this organisation ran short of funds.[156] The FSJF, which operated in the southern zone, received funds from the Joint Distribution Committee, and from July 1943 until the liberation in August 1944, the organisation sent 600,000 francs per month to the Amelot Committee in the northern zone.[157] Rapoport, the head of the Amelot Committee, also collected funds by borrowing from Jews who wished to shelter their savings. On the basis of an agreement with the Joint Distribution Committee, it was agreed that those who had provided loans would be reimbursed no longer than three months after the official end of the war.[158]

---

[154] Jean Laloum, 'L'UGIF et ses maisons d'enfants: l'enlèvement d'une enfant', *Monde Juif*, Vol. 124 (1990), 172–176.
[155] Laffitte, *Juif dans la France allemande*, 492–493.
[156] Adler, *The Jews of Paris*, 208.
[157] Ibid., 214.
[158] Poznanski, *Jews in France during WWII*, 344.

It remains unclear until when the UGIF-Nord was used to camouflage resistance. Georges Edinger, who succeeded Lambert as the president of the UGIF and headed the UGIF-Nord after André Baur was interned, claimed that the UGIF-Nord continued to be used as a cloak for clandestine activities from summer 1943 onwards.[159] However, cloaking clandestine activities became increasingly difficult during this period. Moreover, the veracity of Edinger's statements and his motivations have been questioned by some. After the war, a former UGIF employee who had worked for the social welfare department, Berthe Libers, referred to Edinger when she attacked 'certain dubious elements' for having tried to save their own skins and having collaborated with people such as Xavier Vallat, who had overseen the day-to-day function of the UGIF as head of the Vichy General Commissariat for Jewish Affairs.[160]

As the last serving president of the UGIF, Edinger responded to these claims in an unpublished work titled *La vérité sur l'UGIF. Enfin!*, in which he emphasised the multiple links between the UGIF and resistance networks. French historian Michel Laffitte refers to Edinger's defence as 'densely written and sometimes contradictory in details' and underlined that Edinger failed to mention 'the immense element of uncertainty, the moments of distress, terror and improvisation, and the leaders' lack of action plan with regard to an extermination policy which they had the greatest difficulty understanding and anticipating'.[161] Since Edinger refused to hand over personal documents to the CDJC, part of his records therefore remaining inaccessible to researchers, Laffitte seems to doubt the truthfulness of Edinger's statements. Whether or not Edinger's statement should be taken at face value is questionable. Yet we have seen that while it is sometimes not clear whether UGIF officials were aware of, or actively facilitating, the cloaking of clandestine activities, there were definitely multiple links between the UGIF-Nord and resistance networks in France at least until summer 1943.

Belgium: The Comité de Défense des Juifs and the AJB

In Belgium, the CDJ was without doubt the most important clandestine organisation that used the legal cover of the AJB to carry out its operations. The perspectives of members of the CDJ on the relation between

---

[159] Edinger, Report on the activities of the UGIF, p. 16, CCCLXXIX-33, CDJC, Mémorial de la Shoah.
[160] Laffitte, 'Between Memory and Lapse of Memory', 677.
[161] Ibid., 677–678. For Edinger's papers, see Fonds Georges Edinger, unlisted documents, Archives du Consistoire Central, Paris.

this illegal organisation and the AJB vary. It is generally understood that the CDJ's propaganda activities were mainly directed against the AJB, 'advising Jews to ignore its directives and to resist German measures'.[162] This notion is confirmed in various post-war statements. For example, according to Alfred Rosenzweig, who worked for both the AJB and the CDJ, there was a hostile and disapproving outlook towards the AJB's decisions and its activities among CDJ members.[163] Some post-war documents, including a report on the CDJ's wartime activities, indeed indicate that the organisation's central aim was to combat and sabotage the actions of the AJB.[164] According to people who worked at the top of the FI (a coalition of resistance organisations of which the CDJ was part), such as Rudolf Roels and Roger Katz, president of the Former Combatants and Armed Jewish Resistants (Anciens Combattants et Résistants Armés Juifs), they never authorised contact with the AJB.[165] According to historian Lucien Steinberg, the CDJ also actively discouraged people from approaching the AJB for help.[166]

Yet other testimonies and documents indicate that there were important connections between the two organisations. This is illustrated by a letter that prominent FI member Jean Terfve sent after the liberation on 17 October 1944, in which he claimed that the presence of the AJB was instrumental to the FI's activities in defence of the Jews.[167] Moreover, in 1964, former AJB head Marcel Blum sent a letter to the president of the Central Jewish Social Work (La Centrale d'Oeuvres Sociales Juives), founded in 1952 by Rabbi Robert Dreyfus and Max Gottschalk, in which he underlined that the AJB had worked in close collaboration with the services of the CDJ.[168] While we should be careful of taking this statement at face value, we will see that connections indeed existed between the two organisations.

Maurice Heiber personified the fluidity between the official AJB and the clandestine CDJ. In his capacity as head of the children's

---

[162] See, for example, Moore, 'Integrating Self-Help into the History of Jewish Survival in Western Europe', 196.

[163] Interview Alfred Rosenzweig, 3 February 1972, JMDV, CNHEJ, Buber Collection, Kazerne Dossin.

[164] De Lathouwer, Comité de défense des Juifs; 'Historique et les activités de le CDJ', CDLXI-19, CDJC, Mémorial de la Shoah. Also see the interview with Yvonne Jospa on the children's rescue work initiated by the CDJ, 1956, PIII.g.253, Testimony Collection, Wiener Library; Archives of Esta and Maurice Heiber, AA1915/13, CEGESOMA.

[165] Letter of Rudolf Roels to Roger Katz, 18 May 1966, AA753, CEGESOMA; Letter of Katz to an unknown person, 19 May 1967, AA753, CEGESOMA.

[166] Steinberg, Le comité de défense des Juifs en Belgique, 86.

[167] De Lathouwer, Comité de défense des juifs, appendix, letter of the 'Direction Nationale du Front de l'Indépendance'.

[168] Letter of Marcel Blum to the president of the Centrale d'oeuvres sociales juives, 18 May 1964, CDLXI-20, CDJC, Mémorial de la Shoah.

service section of the Brussels branch of the AJB, Heiber established an orphanage in Wezembeek-Ophem. During the course of the war, more children's homes were placed under the AJB's umbrella (seven in total). In these homes, AJB functionaries took care of children whose parents were unable to take their children with them into hiding or whose parents could no longer provide (financially) for them. Moreover, there were children whose parents had been arrested (and deported) and who were taken to the AJB homes by German officials. The homes were directly overseen by the Gestapo.[169]

After the first major round-ups in summer 1942, Emile Hambresin, a left-wing Catholic working for the FI approached Heiber and asked him to join the CDJ, which operated under the FI's umbrella. After the war, Heiber claimed to have realised at this point that the AJB was in reality 'an organism that collaborated with the occupier and ultimately facilitated its control over the Jewish population'.[170] When he was introduced to Hertz Jospa, Abusz Werber and Chaïm Perelman, all prominent individuals in the CDJ, Heiber agreed to work for the illegal organisation.

Shadowing his legal role within the AJB, Heiber became primarily responsible for the children's section of the CDJ.[171] He worked together with Yvonne Jospa, the wife of Hertz Jospa, and Yvonne Nèvejean, head of the National Children's Aid (Oeuvre Nationale de l'Enfance, ONE), an official governmental agency that was created to promote children's health and remained associated with the FI. A letter written on 7 November 1968 by Jean Terfve, who had played an active role in the FI, indicates that Heiber wanted to leave the AJB on several occasions. However, time and again, the FI leadership collectively decided it was in the interest of the resistance that he should continue to work for the AJB.[172]

The use of the AJB's legal cover by the CDJ was complex. As soon as a parent applied to the legal AJB to request aid, the child would be sent from one office to another. All details about the child's family

---

[169] For further reading on the AJB children's homes, see Sylvain Brachfeld, 'Jewish Orphanages in Belgium under the German Occupation', in Michman, *Belgium and the Holocaust*, 419–432.

[170] Maurice Heiber's story, 'recit de Maurice Heiber', undated, AA1915/22, CEGESOMA. Also see Eyewitness account of Maurice Heiber, 'The Jewish Children in Belgium' (1956), 1656/3/9/274, p. 4, Wiener Library.

[171] Steinberg, *Un pays occupé et ses juifs*, 98.

[172] De Lathouwer, *Comité de défense des Juifs*, appendix, letter of Jean Terfve to M. Heiber, 7 November 1968; Maurice Heiber's story, 'recit de Maurice Heiber', undated, AA1915/22, CEGESOMA.

background would then be deleted before the child was sent to the CDJ. The clandestine workers therefore made it impossible for the authorities or the parents to know the whereabouts of these children. After that, the 'childhood' section of the CDJ would be alerted and its members would facilitate contact with the parents. They persuaded parents to give up their children to the organisation and the child would then receive a false, non-Jewish identity.[173] Yvonne Nèvejean, who joined the CDJ as a member of the children's section and sat on its finance committee, quickly organised an elaborate illegal network and was able to place between 3,000 and 4,000 Jewish children, including those from the Wezembeek orphanage, at various locations.[174] The CDJ benefitted from the existence of the legal AJB children's homes because of the resources available there and because many children were transferred through the organisation's homes.

Heiber actively facilitated the illegal dispersion of these children to non-Jewish families, and there was a wider awareness among AJB officials of the dual position that he held. David Ferdman, for example, who had fled from Poland to Belgium at the end of the 1930s and who himself worked for both the AJB and the CDJ, knew of Heiber's illegal activities and covered for him whenever necessary. In March 1942, Ferdman had been appointed as inspector-general of charitable institutions at the AJB Brussels branch. He occupied a position in the AJB's central board and, as an active member of the CDJ, had a direct connection to Chaïm Perelman, the CDJ's co-founder.[175]

Perelman was another individual who worked for both the AJB and the CDJ. In January 1942, AJB chairman Ullmann had asked him to join the organisation's Brussels branch, but Perelman was cautious and, as a technical advisor, he initially wanted to deal solely with matters related to teaching. He only became a fully committed AJB member in November 1942, encouraged by the resistance, which saw his infiltration into the AJB as another opportunity to use its existence for their own benefit. Hoping to benefit from the AJB's existence, Heiber and Perelman aimed to get access to the deportation lists and other official documents that

[173] De Lathouwer, *Comité de Défense des Juifs*, 11; Eyewitness account of Maurice Heiber, 'The Jewish Children in Belgium' (1956), 1656/3/9/274, pp. 5–7, Wiener Library.

[174] Steinberg, *Un pays occupé et ses juifs*, 132–136; Sylvain Brachfeld, *Ils ont survécu. Le sauvetage des juifs en belgique occupée* (Brussels: Éditions Racine, 2001), 93.

[175] Maurice Heiber's story, 'recit de Maurice Heiber', undated, AA1915/22, CEGESOMA; Meeting report of the local Brussels department, 11 March 1942, A006946, CNHEJ, Buber Collection, Kazerne Dossin; Meeting report of the central board, 12 March 1942, A006708, JMDV, CNHEJ, Buber Collection, Kazerne Dossin.

provided insight into anti-Jewish policies, and to exert influence on the AJB's decisions and policies.[176]

During the course of the occupation, Perelman gained a prominent position in the AJB, especially after the organisation was centralised in response to the Iltis operation in September 1943, an extensive operation launched against all Jews of Belgian nationality, and this enabled him to take full advantage of his dual role in the legal AJB and illegal CDJ.[177] Importantly, the necessary funds for the operations of the FI and CDJ were obtained in part through fraudulent subtractions from the AJB via David Ferdman and Perelman.[178] In this way, the AJB also served to finance clandestine activities. According to Marcel Blum, a member of the central board and chairman of the AJB from the end of 1942, many millions of Belgian francs, received from the Ministry of Finance, were clandestinely distributed through the AJB via the ONE and the Winter Aid (Secours d'Hiver/Winterhulp, a charitable organisation established by the Belgian Secretaries General in October 1940 in order to meet the needs of the population), with the AJB serving as an official cloak for clandestine activity (*rideau officiel pour la clandestinité*).[179]

In addition to Maurice Heiber, David Ferdman and Chaïm Perelman, there were others, including Eugène Hellendall, Max Katz and Irène Zmigrod, who were involved in both the CDJ and the AJB.[180] In the introduction to this chapter, we saw that Zmigrod testified about the interconnections between the organisations and how they operated alongside one another to safeguard Jewish children. Throughout the occupation, the social services of the AJB increasingly became an intermediate station where the boundaries between legality and illegality were unclear and permeable. At times, the AJB offices served as a meeting place for Jews who wanted to go into hiding and for the 'distributors' of the CDJ who facilitated this.[181] At the same time, CDJ members aimed to influence the AJB's workers by encouraging them not to follow the

---

[176] Schreiber, *Dictionnaire Biographique*, 272; De Lathouwer, *Comité de Défense des Juifs*, 19.

[177] Veerle Vanden Daelen and Nico Wouters, 'The Absence of a Jewish Honor Court in Postwar Belgium', in Laura Jokusch and Gabriel N. Finder, *Jewish Honor Courts: Revenge, Retribution and Reconciliation after the Holocaust* (Detroit, MI: Wayne State University Press, 2015), 202–203.

[178] De Lathouwer, *Comité de défense des Juifs*, 19.

[179] Statement of Marcel Blum, AA753, CEGESOMA.

[180] Steinberg, *Le comité de défense des Juifs en Belgique*, 62.

[181] Eyewitness account by Irène Zmigrod entitled 'A Social Worker's Report on her Experiences in Belgium during the Time of the Nazi-Occupation', 1956, p. 8, 1656/3/9/262, Testimony Collection, Wiener Library; Massenge, 'De sociale politiek', 229.

German directions. Thus, the AJB served both as a useful cloak and an organisation with whose policies the CDJ continued to disagree.

The first chairman of the AJB, Salomon Ullmann, passively supported these illegal activities. Yitzak Kubowitzki, one of the leaders of the Brussels Zionist movement who disagreed with the actions of the AJB and engaged in clandestine activities instead, testified to this. He claimed there were clear signs that Ullmann was aware of the undercover activities undertaken by individuals who worked for the AJB. During a conversation between the two men, Ullmann warned Kubowitzki to prepare Jewish refugees for imminent arrests, and encouraged him to approach Perelman in the event that anything went wrong.[182] Clearly, Ullmann was aware of the function that the AJB fulfilled for the CDJ. At the same time, Roger van Praag, who had worked for the CDJ and filed a complaint against the AJB leaders immediately after the war, indicated that his contact with Ullmann was less constructive. According to Van Praag, Ullmann had not wanted to help him with his clandestine aid for Jews and even indicated that he, Van Praag, was putting all Jews in danger by encouraging them to go in hiding.[183] Ullmann probably considered it too risky to actively cooperate himself with the organisation.

After the war, Ullmann was asked whether the CDJ was founded with the support of the AJB. Ullmann answered that the AJB officially had nothing to do with the CDJ because the Germans had appointed the AJB as the exclusive Jewish authority. At the same time, he claimed that they did meet on a personal level on a daily basis.[184] As Ullmann officially resigned in December 1942 and the CDJ was officially established in September 1942, it could have been only in the first three months of the CDJ's existence that Ullmann, as head of the AJB, and members of this clandestine organisation were in touch. However, we have seen that links between the illegal CDJ and the AJB were indeed established and maintained during the war.

During the course of the occupation, there seems to have been a wider awareness among the AJB leadership about the nature of illegal activities that were carried out (under the cloak of the AJB), and how these activities were being financed. In late January 1943, Salomon van den Berg, who chaired the organisation's Brussels branch (and who would become vice-chairman of the AJB in March 1944), wrote in his diary that he knew that money was unofficially being distributed to clandestine organisations in order to secure aid for Jews and children in hiding.

[182] Interview with Yitzak Kubowitzki, 12 November 1964, AA1196, CEGESOMA.
[183] Report by Roger van Praag entitled 'Organisation and Administration of the Belgian Resistance', 1956, p. 16, 1656/3/7/1112, Testimony Collection, Wiener Library.
[184] Interview with Salomon Ullmann, 1970, AA 1196, CEGESOMA.

He claimed he was not aware of the sums involved in this process, but it is clear that he possessed detailed knowledge of what kind of illegal activities were taking place and how these were financed. Despite the fact that he resented illegal activities, and strongly believed in the legal position he took as member of the AJB central board, the chairman of the AJB Brussels branch was clearly well informed, which again highlights that the boundaries between legality and illegality were porous.[185]

Above all, from the evidence presented here, we can say that there was a large grey area inside the AJB in which connections between legality and illegality were established. Although the AJB cannot be considered a resistance organisation, the actions of clandestine organisations under the cover of the AJB, most importantly the CDJ, at times with the passive consent of the leadership, were of great importance, allowing these organisations to thwart German goals and actions.

The JR: Cloaking and Illegal Activity on an Individual Level

In the Netherlands, illegal activities under the cloak of the JR were limited compared with Belgium and France. We have seen that there was comparatively little engagement in (organised) clandestine activity during the first phase of the German occupation in this country. Whereas the presence of large numbers of immigrants was a major catalyst for the emergence of clandestine activities in parallel to the AJB, UGIF-Nord and UGIF-Sud, the nature and scope of immigration prevented this from happening in the Netherlands. This was furthermore hampered by the attitude of the JR leadership, who strongly believed in the legal course of the JR and did little to encourage illegal activities. Despite these limitations, there was still a tendency for some JR members, who were not part of the central board, to use the Council as a cloak for clandestine activities. This idea is reinforced by several witness statements that were taken during the pre-trial investigations, instigated by the Dutch state, into the wartime activities of Asscher and Cohen.[186]

The case of JR member Walter Süskind, born in Germany in 1906, is illustrative of illegal activities that were carried out under the Council's

[185] Salomon van den Berg, Journal de guerre, pp. 137–138, JMDV, CNHEJ, Buber Collection, A006685, Kazerne Dossin.
[186] See, for example, the statement of Levi Gobits during the pre-trial investigations of Abraham Asscher and David Cohen, 16 January 1948, dossier Abraham Asscher and David Cohen, CABR, Access No. 2.09.09, Inv. No. 107491 II (PF Amsterdam T70982), NA.

cloak. After the JR's leadership appointed Süskind head of the Holland-sche Schouwburg, where Jews were assembled before being transported to Westerbork transit camp, he used his position, his knowledge of German and his close relationship with some German officials to smuggle Jews out of the Schouwburg. Süskind's work was initially dedicated to liberating Jewish adults from captivity, but he also organised the escape of children from January 1943 onwards.[187] While parents were forced to stay in the Schouwburg during the day, their babies and small children were taken across the road to a crèche, the 'Kweekschool', headed by Henriëtte Pimentel.[188]

Süskind and the Jewish women who worked in the crèche managed to save many Jewish children from deportation by smuggling them out of the day-care facility because the crèche was not as closely guarded as the Schouwburg. The children's registration documents were removed from the Schouwburg files and the children were then handed over to resistance groups, for example during the daily walks the nurses organised for the children in the Schouwburg area. Although the German guards on the opposite side of the road carefully scrutinised activities in the surroundings of the Schouwburg, the crèche's employees were able to use the trams that passed outside as a cover to hand the children over to the rescuers, who would in turn use the trams as a way to get away quickly from the scene.[189]

Initially, only those children whose parents had given approval were smuggled out of the crèche. Children who were caught in hiding and subsequently placed in the crèche were an exception because it was generally not known where the parents were. As a result of the hazardous position in which these children found themselves – being caught in hiding meant you would be put on transport as a 'punishment case' (*strafgeval*) – these children received priority to be moved to a safer place.[190]

Süskind and the crèche employees cooperated with at least four organised non-Jewish resistance groups in order to provide a safer place for

[187] Schellekens, *Walter Süskind*, 70–196; Braber, *This Cannot Happen Here*, 124; Moore, *Survivors*, 305.

[188] For further reading on the life and work of Henriëtte Pimentel, see Esther Shaya and Frank Hemminga, *Wacht maar: het veelbewogen leven van Henriëtte Pimentel* (Amsterdam: Amphora Books, 2020).

[189] For a thorough overview of the ways in which Jewish children were smuggled out of the crèche, see Bert Jan Flim, *Omdat hun hart sprak: Geschiedenis van de georganiseerde hulp aan Joodse kinderen in Nederland, 1942–1945* (Kampen: Uitgeverij Kok, 1996), 121–159.

[190] Ibid., 136–137.

the children: the Utrecht Children's Committee (Het Utrechts Kinder-comité), the Amsterdam Student Group (Amsterdamse Studentengroep, ASG), the Anonymous Association (Naamloze Vennootschap) and the Trouw Group (Trouwgroep).[191] The children were distributed to non-Jewish families and hiding places throughout the country. The daughter of JR chairman David Cohen, Virrie Cohen, became the crèche's leader after Pimentel was arrested, and she was also involved in these clandestine activities. Estimates of the number of children who were smuggled out of the crèche and saved from persecution vary, but amount to at least several hundred.[192]

Although some JR members who worked in the Schouwburg distanced themselves from Süskind's illegal activities, there was a core group that actively participated.[193] Some, including Edwin Sluzker, Jacques van de Kar and Sam de Hond, worked for the Expositur, the JR department that served as the liaison between the Council and the Central Office for Jewish Emigration. Van de Kar initially operated in the southern part of Amsterdam (Adama van Scheltemaplein), where German authorities first used a former school building as a collection centre for Jews. As a JR employee, van de Kar had free access to the building, and smuggled Jews out simply by telling the guard that they had been exempted from deportation. Since he had access to a large network of non-Jews, he was sometimes able to provide these individuals with hiding places.[194]

With the aid of Süskind, van de Kar received a position in the Schouwburg, which became the central assembly place for Jews from August 1942 onwards, and where he continued to help people escape by using a set of duplicated keys. In this way, van de Kar and his group managed to free hundreds of Jews from the Schouwburg. Many of them were initially taken to van de Kar's house nearby, where they were then helped

---

[191] Schellekens, *Walter Süskind*, 139. Other organisations involved in this process were members of the Boogaard family from Nieuw-Vennep, members of the Westerweel group and numerous other individuals. Flim, *Omdat hun hart sprak*, 121–123, 464 n.4. For further reading on the efforts that were undertaken by various clandestine groups to aid Jewish children in the Netherlands, see Bert Jan Flim, *Saving the Children: History of the Organized Effort to Rescue Jewish Children in the Netherlands, 1942–1945* (Bethesda, MD: CDL Press, 2005).

[192] Presser has indicated that, according to an eyewitness testimony, around a thousand Jewish children were smuggled out of the crèche. Somers provided an estimate between 600 and 1,100, although it is unclear on what sources he based his information. Flim has argued that this estimate is too high, claiming that the number must have been somewhere in between 500 and 700. Presser, *Ondergang*, Vol. 2, 11; Somers, *Voorzitter van de Joodse Raad*, 149 n.239; Flim, *Omdat hun hart sprak*, 122.

[193] Schellekens, *Walter Süskind*, 101–102.

[194] Jacques van de Kar, *Joods Verzet: terugblik op de periode rond de Tweede Wereldoorlog* (Amsterdam: Stadsdrukkerij van Amsterdam, 1984; first ed. 1981), 50–53.

to find hiding places.[195] Although it is clear that van de Kar and his group helped many Jews to escape the Schouwburg, there are differing accounts of the precise ways in which he managed to do so, some saying that he acted with the help of the Germans who guarded the location, some that he acted without. Van de Kar is himself in part responsible for these discrepancies because he highlighted different methods that he used across a number of interviews between 1961 and 1991.[196]

It is clear that some members of the JR carried out activities that were not in line with the policy of legality that its leadership officially propagated, even if these activities were on a more limited scale than those of the JR's Belgian and French counterparts. The same is true in the case of the Jews who were involved in the JR department that operated in Westerbork transit camp, the so-called Contact Department (Contact Afdeling, CA). This department had been established after the first deportation began in July 1942. As with most of the camp's bureaucracy, the CA was headed by German Jews. The arrangement dated back to before the war when Westerbork transit camp had been built as a central refugee camp to house German Jews who had fled to the Netherlands, especially after The Night of the Broken Glass (*Kristallnacht*), a wave of violent anti-Jewish attacks on 9–10 November 1938 throughout Germany, annexed Austria and the Sudetenland (Czechoslovakia). In the period when Westerbork still served as a refugee camp, these German Jewish immigrants instituted an organisational structure for the camp. They continued to be largely responsible for it when the Germans took over and, from 1 July 1942 onwards, changed the function of the camp to that of a *Polizeiliches Judendurchgangslager*, a transit camp where the Jews stayed temporarily before being deported to concentration camps and death camps further east.[197]

There was a lot of animosity between the German Jewish members of the camp organisation and the Dutch Jews who were later interned in the camp, not least because the Dutch Jews blamed the German Jews for acting primarily to protect their own interests. Philip Mechanicus, for example, described in his diary how the German Jews were constantly giving orders to Dutch Jews and how they misused their power.[198] Similar objections

---

[195] Van de Kar, *Joods Verzet*, 67–71; Ralph Polak in *Het fatale dilemma*, 96.
[196] For an overview of these statements, see Mark Schellekens and Elma Verhey, 'De zaak Alfons Zündler', 1994, pp. 56–60, Doc. I 248-A2390, Inv. No. 2, NIOD.
[197] For further reading on the history of the refugees in Westerbork and on the German camp bureaucracy, see Eva Moraal, *Als ik morgen niet op transport ga...kamp Westerbork in beleving en herinnering* (Amsterdam: De Bezige Bij, 2014), 222–240; Gino Huiskes and Reinhilde van der Koef, *Vluchtelingenkamp Westerbork* (Hooghalen: Herinneringscentrum Kamp Westerbork, 1999).
[198] Philip Mechanicus, *In dépôt* (Amsterdam: Van Gennep 1989; first ed. 1964), 29.

have been raised regarding the CA, headed by Walter Heynemann, Frits Grünberg, Hans Eckmann and Hans Heinz Hanauer, all German Jews.

In its function as a JR department in Westerbork, the CA maintained relations between the camp and various Council departments in Amsterdam, initially in order to register Jewish capital for the Lippmann, Rosenthal & Co., the Jewish bank the Germans used to plunder Jews, but eventually its activities expanded. Among other things, it arranged last-minute exemptions for Jews who were interned in Westerbork. In doing so, it operated in parallel to the Petition Office (*Antragstelle*) of the camp administration, a section that also arranged exemptions from deportations for Jews with a distinctive status (for example, Jews who were in a 'mixed marriage').[199]

Apart from its legal occupations, the CA seems to have been engaged in a variety of illegal activities as well. The fact that this department consisted of *German* Jews who did not have the same deference to authority and were not integrated into non-Jewish society in the way that the Dutch Jews were might have made them more inclined not to follow German orders; that they spoke the same language as their German overseers undoubtedly helped them in their efforts. They tried to bribe the Germans to arrange deportation exemptions for Jews and they continuously negotiated about the number of Jews sent on transport. In the same way that Süskind tampered with German filing systems, Heynemann claimed he attempted to remove the letter 's', standing for *strafgeval* (punishment case) from individual files, so that these Jews could be removed from the punishment barrack (*strafbarak*). These punishment cases had to carry out the dirtiest jobs inside the camp and were generally the first to be put on a transport to Eastern Europe.[200]

[199] Hans Ottenstein, 'Lager Westerbork, een persoonlijk verslag', Inv. No. 510 – Verslagen van kampingezetenen en andere getuigen over de omstandigheden in Kamp Westerbork, 250i, NIOD; Walter Heynemann, Frits Grünberg, Hans Eckmann, and Hans Heinz Hanauer, 'Het werk van de Contact-Afdeeling te Westerbork', February 1945, pp. 10–11, Inv. No. 716, Archief 250i, NIOD; Witness statements, Inv. No. 1007 – Proces-verbaal van het Bureau Opsporing Oorlogsmisdrijven, 250i, NIOD; Presser, Ondergang, Vol. 2, 310–311. For an overview of all groups that were eligible to receive an exemption from deportation, see Inv. No. 550, Archief Westerbork, Judendurchgangslager (250i), NIOD.

[200] Heynemann, Grünberg, Eckmann and Hanauer, 'Het werk van de Contact-Afdeeling te Westerbork', Inv. No. 716, Archief 250i, NIOD; Interview Liesel Reichstaler-Heynemann (daughter of Walter Heynemann), 2012, Herinneringscentrum Kamp Westerbork. Also see the statements of Heynemann and Hanauer during the pre-trial investigations by the Dutch state into the wartime activities of Abraham Asscher and David Cohen on 5 March 1948 and 12 April 1948 respectively, dossier Abraham Asscher and David Cohen, CABR, Access No. 2.09.09, Inv. No. 107491 I (PF Amsterdam T70982), NA; Statement of Walter Heynemann, 22 July 1949, dossier Willy Paul Franz Lages, CABR, Access No. 2.09.09, Inv. No. 140-VI (BrC 394/49), NA.

According to a post-war report written by the CA directors, official documents such as 'Palestine certificates', passports, and parentage certificates (*afstammingspapieren*) were forged and the organisation sought connection with illegal workers in Amsterdam. Personal documentation including photographs and films was also smuggled out of Westerbork. Heynemann furthermore claimed that the CA administered a hidden budget (*zwarte kas*), which was money provided by the JR to finance their clandestine activities. After the JR was dismantled in September 1943 and its leadership interned in Westerbork, individual donations continued to finance the activities of the CA.[201] Although the members of the CA were criticised during the war because of the better conditions they lived in, and were accused of corruption after the war, their involvement in these illegal activities and the fact that they had put their own lives at risk ensured that they were eventually exonerated.[202]

These activities show that the existence of the JR, like that of its Belgian and French counterparts, allowed a range of activities that would have been impossible without the protection it provided to the members involved. However, the boundaries between legality and illegality were not as permeable as they were in Belgium and France. It is likely that the strong focus of the JR's leaders on legal activities discouraged clandestine groups from operating alongside the Council and from infiltrating the organisation, which, as we have seen, *did* occur in Belgium and France.

It was only through people such as Jakob Hermann van Bier, who worked for the Beirat department of the JR and also forged illegal documents, as well as van de Kar, Süskind and the CA members, all of whom operated more on the periphery of the JR, that illegal activities were initiated or, as in the case of Pimentel, Virrie Cohen and the other crèche employees, that the organisation was used to cloak the hiding of children. There are indications that the local JR branch leaders were more directly involved in clandestine activities. For example, Hans van Dam, who worked for the Rotterdam branch of the JR, indicated in a letter to Jacques Presser in 1965 that this JR branch had cooperated substantially with illegal workers, including those who provided hiding places and

---

[201] Heynemann, Grünberg, Eckmann and Hanauer, 'Het werk van de Contact-Afdeeling te Westerbork', Inv. No. 716, Archief 250i, NIOD.

[202] For accusations, see, for example, the statement of Siegfried van den Berg, 19 March 1948, dossier Abraham Asscher and David Cohen, CABR, Access No. 2.09.09, Inv. No. 107491 I (PF Amsterdam T70982), NA; M. de Jong, 'Beantwoording van het exposé betreffende het werk van de Contact-Afdeling te Westerbork', July 1945, Inv. No. 716, 250i, NIOD; Presser, *Ondergang*, Vol. 2, 311–312. Also see Schellekens, *Walter Süskind*, 224–226.

false identity cards.[203] Whether or not this cooperation indeed existed, considering the concentration of Jews in Amsterdam (and the centralisation of the JR's policies in the capital city), the scale of these activities was nevertheless much smaller than in Belgium and France.

When, in 1946, an honour trial was instituted by leading members of the Jewish community in the Netherlands in order to evaluate 'every Jew whose attitude or behaviour during the occupation [...] had been incompatible with the most basic form of Jewish solidarity', JR chairmen Asscher and Cohen, most notably, were investigated.[204] During this trial, Cohen indicated that on a number of occasions he knew about cloaking activities and particularly the clandestine removal of Jews from the Schouwburg and the crèche (through his daughter Virrie).[205] He also gave a very detailed overview of the illegal actions that took place in and around the Schouwburg, claiming that JR cars were used to smuggle Jews out.[206] Asscher further stated that he and Cohen held secret meetings with Süskind and that they permitted the illegal activities that were undertaken under the official guise of the JR.[207]

Views about the role played by the JR leadership are contradictory, however. Former head of the resistance group ASG, Piet Meerburg, said that Cohen actually obstructed his activities and even started an investigation into the whereabouts of children who had disappeared with the help of his group, while he – Cohen – knew full well that these children had been 'safely' taken care of by the resistance.[208] In his defence, Cohen stated that the wrong child had been taken and that he had had to cope with the angry responses of parents who did not want their children to be taken into hiding.[209] Later in his statement, Meerburg was more neutral, claiming that he was not sure whether the JR leaders were aware of the illegal activities, but he continued to insist that they had definitely not been actively involved.[210]

---

[203] Letter of Hans J. van Dam to Jacques Presser, 15 October 1965, p. 1, fiches of L. de Jong in preparation for *Het Koninkrijk*, Vol. 7, chapter 2, NIOD.

[204] Nanno K.C. In 't Veld, *De Joodse Ereraad* (The Hague: SDU Uitgeverij), 43–44.

[205] Statement of David Cohen, 6 November 1947, dossier Abraham Asscher and David Cohen, CABR, Access No. 2.09.09, Inv. No. 107491 VII (PF Amsterdam T70982), NA.

[206] Statement of David Cohen, 17 March 1947, dossier Abraham Asscher and David Cohen, CABR, Access No. 2.09.09, Inv. No. 107491 V (PF Amsterdam T70982), NA.

[207] Statement of Abraham Asscher, 7 November 1947, dossier Willy Paul Franz Lages, CABR, Access No. 2.09.09, Inv. No. 140 VI (BrC 394/49), NA.

[208] Statement of Piet Meerburg, 2 February 1948, dossier Abraham Asscher and David Cohen, CABR, Access No. 2.09.09, Inv. No. 107491 III (PF Amsterdam T70982), NA.

[209] Documents sent by David Cohen to his lawyers during the state investigation of his wartime activities, 181j, Inv. No. 11, NIOD.

[210] Statement of Piet Meerburg, 2 February 1948, dossier Abraham Asscher and David Cohen, CABR, Access No. 2.09.09, Inv. No. 107491 III (PF Amsterdam T70982), NA.

The paucity of wartime sources and the existence of different views on the matter make it difficult to offer a clear assessment of the extent to which the JR leadership was passively aware, or more actively sympathetic to, the use of the structures of the JR as a cloak for clandestine activities. The best way to sum it up is perhaps in the terms of Cohen's own claim that organised resistance groups never attempted to approach him because the position he had taken vis-à-vis the German occupation was simply different.[211] The JR's leadership may indeed have been aware of the activities surrounding the Schouwburg, but it seems unlikely that the role of its leadership in facilitating clandestine operations went beyond (intentionally) turning a blind eye in order not to hamper these actions. As Rafaël (Felix) Halverstadt, who aided Süskind in forging lists, stated, 'Asscher and Cohen neither positively nor negatively influenced the course of events in this respect.'[212]

In sum, even though the connections between legality and illegality are often poorly documented precisely because of their illegal nature, we can conclude that the JR, the AJB, the UGIF-Nord and the UGIF-Sud were all linked in various ways to clandestine activities. To varying degrees, Jewish officials who worked for these organisations used their cooperation with the Germans to simultaneously resist their policies, aiming to protect Jews against persecution and to prevent them from being deported through illegal means. Overall, the existence and legality of the Jewish organisations enabled clandestine activities that would otherwise have been impossible. Particularly in Belgium and France, the interconnections between clandestine groups on the one hand and the AJB, the UGIF-Nord and the UGIF-Sud on the other were manifold. It was even true in the case of the Netherlands, where organised resistance activities were undertaken relatively late and where Jewish Council leaders insisted on maintaining the legal principles on which the JR had been established, that illegal activities were carried out under the Council's cloak.

The nature of these activities was complex, and the role of the Jewish leaders herein varied from passive acceptance to active support of the illegal activities of these groups. In Belgium and France, some of the Associations' leaders and members were actively involved in illegal undertakings

---

[211] Statement of David Cohen, 9 November 1947, dossier Abraham Asscher and David Cohen, CABR, Access No. 2.09.09, Inv. No. 107491 V (PF Amsterdam T70982), NA.

[212] Statement of Felix Halverstadt, 4 February 1948, dossier Abraham Asscher and David Cohen, CABR, Access No. 2.09.09, Inv. No. 107491 II (PF Amsterdam T70982), NA.

themselves. The extent to which this was the case varied and fluctuated. Above all, the Jewish Council functionairies' attempts to provide social welfare to the Jewish communities, during a period when conditions worsened, could itself be seen as a series of courageous acts intended to maintain these communities as they came under increasing threat.

The interrelations we have seen between legality and illegality force us to have a nuanced understanding of the behaviour of the Jewish organisations' leaders and memberships. Their responses were those of ordinary people under the threat of an occupying power. Terms such as 'collaboration', 'cooperation' or 'resistance' are often too narrow to describe the choices of the Jewish leaders during the Holocaust. Over-all, none of these terms suffices to describe their conduct. On an indi-vidual level, we have seen varying choices at different times. Lambert, for example, maintained his policy of legality on the one hand while also allowing clandestine activities to take place under the cloak of the UGIF-Sud on the other, and even participated in some of these activi-ties himself. In circumstances that continuously changed, the central board members often took on shifting roles, oscillating between coop-eration and resistance, and the many shades of behaviour that exist in between.

These shifting roles are not unique to the Jewish leaders of Western Europe. The chairman of the Judenrat in Bialystok (situated in the north-east of Poland), Efraim Barasz (Barash), for example, cooper-ated with the Germans while he simultaneously helped the resistance.[213] Other examples demonstrate that Jewish functionaries across the Nazi occupied territories indeed used their legal position in the Jewish Coun-cils, and similar organisations, to support, or engage in, various forms of clandestine activity.[214] These findings strengthen the notion that,

---

[213] Zvi Gitelman and Leonore J. Weitzman, 'Jewish Resistance in Ghettos in the Former Soviet Union During the Holocaust', in Wendy Z. Goldman and Joe William Trotter, *The Ghetto in Global History* (London: Routledge, 2017), 148–168; Finkel, *Ordinary Jews*, 88–93; Sarah Bender, *The Jews of Bialystok during World War II and the Holocaust*, transl. Yaffa Murciano (Waltham, MA: Brandeis University Press, 2008), 160–161.

[214] See, for example, Freiga Anders, Katrin Stroll and Karsten Wilke (eds.), *Der Judenrat von Bialystok. Dokumente aus dem Archiv des Bialystoker Ghettos, 1941–1943* (Paderborn/Munich/Vienna: Schöningh, 2010). Other Judenrat leaders, or func-tionaries, who maintained their legal position while they simultaneously engaged in clandestine activities, or otherwise shifted in their roles, included Elchanan Elkes, chairman of the Ältestenrat in Kovno (Lithuania), Il'ia Mushkin, the first chairman of the Minsk Judenrat, and members of Jewish Councils in Lachva and Tuchnin. See Finkel, *Ordinary Jews*, 75–77.

even though scholars often continue to use categories that are by definition static to describe the behaviour of the Jewish leaderships, there is a need to recognise the dynamic and hybrid nature of their conduct. Individuals could adopt different types of behaviour over the course of time, as Finkel has stated, and different behaviours could even exist simultaneously.[215]

---

[215] Finkel, *Ordinary Jews*, 72–73.

Epilogue
Looking Back on the 'Jewish Councils'

'I got the impression that [...] not a day and not even an hour passed by in which he (David Cohen) did not think about the persecution of the Jews and his own role in it. He (Cohen) said things like: "[...] every day I wonder how I could have done the things I did".'[1]

David Cohen reflected upon his role in the Dutch Jewish Council (the JR) on 25 September 1964 during a conversation with historian Loe de Jong, who had encouraged Cohen several times to tell his wartime story. Cohen always seemed very confident about his decisions as the Council's leader and often emphasised he could not have done otherwise; this statement therefore is a rare indication that he also had his doubts.[2] After he returned from Theresienstadt, where he was deported on 4 September 1944, Cohen retained his job as professor at the University of Amsterdam. The other Dutch Council chairman, Abraham Asscher, was deported to Bergen-Belsen on 13 September 1944, where he lived in dire circumstances from which he barely recovered after the war.

After their return to the Netherlands, Asscher and Cohen no longer played prominent roles in their communities because they were denounced for their wartime activities. In 1946, both chairmen were brought before a so-called court of honour (*ereraad*), which was instituted by Jewish community members to 'purge the ranks of the Jewish survivors in order to start with a clean slate for the reconstruction of the Jewish community'.[3] While the court dealt with twenty-six cases, those

---

[1] Reflections of Loe de Jong after his meeting with David Cohen on 25 September 1964, fiches of L. de Jong in preparation for *Het Koninkrijk*, Vol. 7, chapter 2, NIOD.

[2] For Cohen's postwar justifications of his wartime actions and decisions, see, for example David Cohen, 'Pro Domo' in Schrijvers, *Rome, Athene, Jeruzalem*, 237–264; Various reports on the Jewish Council and his (Cohen's) role in the organisation, Inv. Nos. 10–11, 181j, NIOD; Trial documents, CABR, Access No. 2.09.09, Inv. No. 107491, NA; Personal records prof. dr. David Cohen, 248-0294, NIOD.

[3] De Haan, 'An Unresolved Controversy: The Jewish Honor Court in the Netherlands, 1946–1950', in Laura Jokusch and Gabriel Finder, *Jewish Honor Courts Revenge, Retribution and Reconciliation in Europe and Israel after the Holocaust* (Detroit, MI:

of Asscher, Cohen and five other members of the JR were considered the most important and attracted the most attention.[4]

At the time the honour court was operative, the two men were arrested on 6 November 1947 on order of the Special Court of Justice (Bijzonder Gerechtshof), instigated by the Dutch state in December 1943. This court tried those accused of high treason, treason and war crimes, including SS-Hauptsturmführer Ferdinand aus der Fünten and SS-Sturmbannführer Willy Lages. Even the its strongest opponents of the JR were outraged by the arrest of the its former chairmen, which was motivated by the fear that they might flee abroad, and Asscher and Cohen were released again on 5 December after questions were raised in the Dutch parliament.[5]

Shortly thereafter, on 26 December 1947, the verdict of the honour court was publicised in the Jewish weekly *Nieuw Israëlietisch Weekblad* (NIW), even though Cohen had not had a chance to make his final plea: Asscher and Cohen were no longer allowed to fulfil any honourable or representative function in the Jewish community.[6] The honour court ruled that the former JR chairmen's decision to comply with the German demand to establish the Council was reprehensible; their agreement in May 1943 to draw up lists of names of Jews who would no longer benefit from the temporary protection of the JR and, consequently, were put on transport was considered 'very reprehensible'.[7] Cohen objected to this judgement, and in early 1950, the court ruled that those who had formally appealed its decision, including Cohen, would be reinstated as respectable members of the community.[8] In the meantime, the Dutch state trial had failed to make any real progress in their investigation of the JR. In May 1950, the trial was dismissed and

Wayne State University Press, 2016), 118. For an overview of the problematic nature of the *Ereraad* and its function, see ibid., 107–136; in 't Veld, *De Joodse Ereraad*, passim.

[4] De Haan, 'An Unresolved Controversy', 121.

[5] Somers, 'David Cohen, een biografische schets' in: *Voorzitter van de Joodse Raad*, 21–22. For the disquiet that was caused, even among critics of the Joodsche Raad, see, for example, Sam de Wolff, 'De Joodse Raad: Wij Richten niet!', newspaper article, 14 November 1947, Inv. No. 13, Archief 181j, NIOD.

[6] In 't Veld, *De Joodse Ereraad*, 66; For the full text of the judgement that was published in the NIW on 19 May 1948, see Knoop, *De Joodsche Raad*, 192–193.

[7] For Cohen's view on the course of events and a description of the situation and atmosphere in the JR office when its members had to produce the list of JR members, see Cohen, *Voorzitter van de Joodse Raad*, 166–171. For the perspective of Mirjam Bolle-Levie, former secretary of the JR on this event, see Interview of Mirjam Bolle-Levie by Johannes Houwink ten Cate, 12 August 1999, Doc. 1 248-1366, M. Bolle-Levie, Inv. No. 1, NIOD; Interview of Mirjam Bolle-Levie by Johannes Houwink ten Cate, 17 September 2003, Doc I 248-A2366, M. Bolle-Levie Inv. No. 2, NIOD.

[8] De Haan, 'An Unresolved Controversy', 125–130.

one year later, Cohen was informed that prosecution was suspended on 'public interest' grounds.[9]

The initial delays and the sudden final verdict of the honour court, combined with the dismissal of charges by the Dutch state, suggest that the JR had stopped being a central issue. There was now a strong focus on rebuilding the country and the Jewish community, which had suffered severe losses: out of around 140,000 Jews who had resided in the Netherlands in May 1940, only 30,000 now remained.[10] Many no longer wanted to be part of the Jewish community and emigrated abroad; the rise of antisemitism and the lack of recognition of the Jews' experiences in Eastern Europe contributed to a sense of trauma experienced by many Jews at this time.[11] The nature of the Jewish communities had drastically changed as well. Those who had survived predominantly belonged to the middle and upper classes, because they had possessed the connections and financial resources that allowed them to go into hiding; the Jewish proletariat had been seriously affected. While pre-war institutions such as the JCC and the Dutch–Israelite religious community re-emerged after the war, Cohen and Asscher (the latter died on 2 May 1950), no longer received the respect of the Jewish communities and were often ignored in public.[12]

In Belgium, where around 66,000 Jews had resided on the eve of the occupation, 18,000 Jews were left in October 1944.[13] The population increased quickly to 30,000 at the end of 1945, in part because Jews returned from exile and transient refugees settled in the country. Fewer than 2,000 Jews returned to Belgium from the places to which they had been deported.[14] Unlike in the Netherlands, there was a generally sympathetic attitude towards the Jews after the war. The physical and mental condition of most of the Jewish population was perilous, which meant that aid organisations had to be quickly reconstituted. In part, the

[9] Houwink ten Cate, 'De justitie en de Joodsche Raad', 162.
[10] Joop Sanders, 'Opbouw en continuïteit na 1945', in Michman, Beem and Michman, *Pinkas*, 216.
[11] Sanders, 'Opbouw en continuïteit', 217; Brasz, 'After the Second World War: From "Jewish Church" to Cultural Minority', 342–346; Dienke Hondius, *Return: Holocaust Survivors and Dutch Anti-Semitism*, transl. David Colmer (Westport, CT/London: Praeger, 2003 [first Dutch ed. 1990]), 75–136; Isaac Lipschits, *De kleine sjoa: Joden in naoorlogs Nederland* (Amsterdam: Mets & Schilt, 2001), passim.
[12] Houwink ten Cate, 'De justitie en de Joodsche Raad', 149.
[13] Steinberg, *L'Étoile et le Fusil: La question juive, 1940–1942*, 85.
[14] Daniel Dratwa, 'Genocide and its Memories: A Preliminary Study on How Belgian Jewry Coped with the Results of the Holocaust', in Michman, *Belgium and the Holocaust: Jews, Belgians, Germans*, 524; Vanden Daelen, *Laten we hun lied verder zingen*, 29–36.

structures of resistance groups such as the CDJ were used as a way to do this.[15] Some of those who had fulfilled a dual role in the resistance and the AJB, including Yvonne Nèvejean and David Ferdman, were involved in the reorganisation of social welfare in Belgium. They were responsible for the institution of the Aid to Jewish War Victims (Aide aux Israélites Victimes de la Guerre), which played a major role in the post-war reconstruction process of the Jewish communities.[16]

The Belgian courts, which initially focused on Belgian political collaborators and on the wartime role of Belgian administrators, were overwhelmed with trial cases in the immediate post-war period. There was little attention for the persecution of the Jews during these trials, as the purges were primarily intended to re-establish the legitimacy of the Belgian government and to improve the level of trust in it.[17] The reluctance to address the issue of the persecution of the Jews materialised during the judicial investigation into the AJB. Afraid that the AJB's legal strategy of cooperation would be linked to the wartime attitude of Belgian government officials, and because the case was considered to be delicate and complex, the military courts were reluctant to carry out an investigation into the Jewish organisation.[18] It was forced to deal with the AJB case in October 1944 after an elaborate complaint by Lazare Liebman, who blamed the organisation for active collaboration with the Germans. However, the trial of the seven members of the organisation's initial central board (Salomon Ullmann, Maurice Benedictus, Alfred Blum, Salomon van den Berg, David Lazare, Nico Workum and Juda Mehlwurm) was not considered a priority by the Belgian courts.

In the meantime, several other investigations were opened, including in local military courts, that enquired into leading members of the AJB's local branches. While the Dutch trials were predominantly centred around the two chairmen, the Belgian court focused more broadly on the entire organisation's board and their local representatives. This reinforces the notion that Asscher and Cohen had been absolute rulers and were considered as such, while the authority of the AJB was spread

---

[15] Dratwa, 'Genocide and its Memories', 524–530; Vanden Daelen, *Laten we hun lied verder zingen*, 44–45.

[16] Dratwa, 'Genocide and its Memories', 524–525.

[17] Nico Wouters, 'The Belgian Trials', in David Bankier and Dan Michman (eds.), *Holocaust and Justice: Representation and Historiography of the Holocaust in Post-War Trials* (Yad Vashem: Jerusalem and New York/Oxford: Berghahn Books, 2010), 222–229. It should be noted that the focus on Belgian collaboration was fed by the belief that German war criminals would be tried by the international community.

[18] Ibid., 232; Vanden Daelen and Wouters, '"The Lesser Evil" of Jewish Collaboration?', 212–213.

among a wider circle of Jewish leaders. The courts' continued reluctance, paired with successful attempts by the defence to gather supporting statements, arguing that the AJB's policy had been similar to that of the Belgian policy of 'the lesser evil', led the military prosecutor to drop all charges. In 1947, the cases against the central AJB leaders were closed.[19]

The absence of moves by the Jewish communities to bring the AJB's leaders to court, as had happened in the Netherlands in the form of an honour court, is remarkable here. Vanden Daelen and Wouters have explained this by pointing to the fragmented nature of the Jewish communities in Belgium; the vast majority of Jews without Belgian citizenship did not want to draw attention to themselves, fearing they would face expulsion.[20] Internal division among former Jewish resistance networks, most notably the communists and the various Zionist factions, might also have played a role.[21]

Since their actions were never genuinely investigated by a court (of honour), and because the Belgian Jewish communities were relatively decentralised, it was easier for the AJB leaders to continue the lives they had lived before the war. The fact that the first AJB chairman Salomon Ullmann remained the Chief Rabbi of Belgium after the liberation of the country and served in this position until he emigrated to Israel in 1957 most significantly highlights the different position of the initial AJB's leadership in the post-war communities compared with the Netherlands.[22]

In France, the Jewish communities had lost nearly one-third of their pre-war population, with around 200,000 Jews residing in the country immediately after the liberation.[23] We have seen that the first leaders of the UGIF-Nord, André Baur, and the UGIF-Sud, Raymond-Raoul Lambert, were arrested, interned and deported. In contrast to the leaders of the JR and AJB, they did not survive the war; both were killed in the gas chambers at Auschwitz. There were other important Jewish leaders in France who also did not survive the war, including twenty-three

---

[19] Donnet, 'Het onderzoek door het militaire gerecht: het geheugen buitenspel gezet', 291–319.

[20] Vanden Daelen and Wouters, '"The Lesser Evil" of Jewish Collaboration?', 212; Donnet, 'Het onderzoek door het militaire gerecht', 318–319.

[21] Donnet, 'Het onderzoek door het militaire gerecht', 316.

[22] For further reading on Ullmann's post-war occupations, see Schreiber, *Dictionnaire Biographique*, 343–344; Vastenhout, 'Filling a Leadership Void', passim.

[23] Séan Hand, 'Introduction' in: Séan Hand and Steven T. Katz (eds.), *Post-Holocaust France and the Jews, 1945–1955* (New York/London: New York University Press, 2015), 3; Annette Wieviorka, 'Les Juifs en France au lendemain de la guerre: état des lieux', *Archives Juives. Revue d'histoire des Juifs de France*, Vol. 1, No. 28 (1995), 5–6.

(out of the sixty) Rabbis who had served as members of the Consistory, Jacques Helbronner, and Léonce Bernheim, a socialist activist and Zionist spokesman. Overall, the religious and associative life of the Jews had severely changed post-war society, not least because many synagogues had been either damaged or destroyed. Moreover, while some community leaders fled from Nazism and never returned to France, others – including many who had held leading roles in Jewish resistance groups – believed there was little future for Jews in France and emigrated elsewhere, including to Palestine.[24]

There was a strong focus on the renewal of the French Jewish communities after the war. The disappointment that many Jews experienced in relation to the active compliance of the Vichy regime, necessitated the reconstruction of Jewish society in such a way that it no longer depended on the state. With a sense of excitement and enthusiasm Jewish organisations, primarily those that sprang from resistance groups such as the CRIF, perceived this moment as an opportunity to create a new future for the Jews in France. They aimed to gain the upper hand in the reshaping of institutions and policies 'in order to create a self-sustaining and independent community'.[25] At the same time, as Daniella Doron has argued, this was only an outward appearance. In the case of child welfare, in particular, communal leaders were worried about the consequences of the war on Jewish society, and there existed an underlying mood of 'crisis, anxiety and pessimism'.[26]

Because there existed a sense of distrust relating to those Jewish organisations and individuals whose wartime conduct was a matter of fierce controversy, a number of Jewish groups, often under communist influence, called for an internal purge of the Jewish community after the liberation. This is indeed what happened, first through the short-lived CUDJF, a resistance organisation whose representatives arrested the UGIF's last chairman Georges Edinger, and second through the CRIF, which instituted an honour court. Both institutions investigated the wartime conduct of the UGIF's employees and the CRIF specifically

---

[24] Jacob Kaplan, 'French Jewry under the Occupation', *American Jewish Yearbook*, No. 47 (1945), 109–110; David Weinberg, 'The Revival of French Jewry in Post-Holocaust France: Challenges and Opportunities', in Hand and Katz, *Post-Holocaust France and the Jews*, 26–27.

[25] Weinberg, 'The Revival of French Jewry', 27. Also see Pierre Birnbaum, *Jewish Destinies: Citizenship, State and Community in Modern France* (New York: Hill and Wang, 2000), 217.

[26] Daniella Doron, *Jewish Youth and Identity in Postwar France: Rebuilding Family and Nation* (Bloomington/Indianapolis: Indiana University Press, 2015), 20.

focused on the Jewish leaders' failure to protect the Jewish children who had lived in the UGIF-Nord home of Neuilly. Initially, the children of the Neuilly home had been evacuated in anticipation of upcoming raids. However, they were brought back because the UGIF leaders, Georges Edinger in particular, feared reprisals. On 25 July 1944, these children were arrested and sent to Drancy, after which they were deported to Auschwitz and murdered upon arrival.[27]

While the legitimacy of the CUDJF was challenged because those investigated claimed to be unfamiliar with the organisation, the CRIF was criticised both by members of the Consistory and by organisations such as the Association of Former Jewish Deportees for failing to make a general evaluation of the UGIF's policies. In the end, the UGIF leadership was held accountable for its failure to remove children from the homes that were overseen by the Germans (many of these children were arrested and deported), but any further investigations were halted, which angered the Jewish press.[28]

The controversy surrounding the UGIF contributed to social disintegration. This was further reinforced by the antagonism between the immigrants and French Jews that had dominated pre-war society and was highlighted again in this period.[29] Above all, we can conclude that few pre-war institutional structures or leaders remained that could facilitate the rebuilding of the Jewish communities in France. The impact of the traditional Jewish leadership, including those who had played leading roles in the UGIF, had largely dwindled, and it played a limited role in the process of reconstruction.

As Annie Kriegel has pointed out, the long list of employees and directors of the UGIF as well as of the Rabbis and Consistorial leaders, who were deported with their families prevents us from discussing the case of the Jewish leaders in terms of resistance or collaboration.[30] Around 6 million Jews lost their lives during the Nazi Holocaust. They died

---

[27] Laffitte, *Juif dans la France allemande*, 323–27; Ibid., 'Between Memory and Lapse of Memory', 675–677; Anne Grynberg, 'Juger l'UGIF (1944–1950)?', in Hélène Harter, Antoine Marès et al. (eds), *Terres promises: Mélanges offerts à André Kaspi* (Paris: Publications de la Sorbonne, 2008), 507–526. For the conclusions of the CRIF investigator on the specific case of the deportation of children, see Comité d'Épuration, Déportation des enfants: conclusions de l'enquêteur, CRIF, MDI 311, Mémorial de la Shoah.

[28] Perego, 'Jurys d'honneur', 149–154; and 'Le Consistoire Central et la création du CRIF', 177.

[29] Perego, 'Jurys d'honneur', 155; Marc Olivier Baruch (ed.), *Une poignée de misérables: L'épuration au sein de la société française après la Seconde Guerre mondiale* (Paris: Fayard, 2003), 537.

[30] Annie Kriegel, 'De la résistance juive' in: *Pardès*, No. 2 (1985), 197.

in gas chambers in Auschwitz, Treblinka, Belzec, Sobibór and Chelmno, or were brutally shot, including during operations in German-annexed Western Poland (Wartheland), the Soviet Union and other sites in Eastern Europe. Still others died as a result of the hardships from which they suffered as a result of German policies; malnourishment, exhaustion (owing to forced labour) and the forced evacuations from concentration camps after the Soviet offensive in summer 1944 (so-called death marches) were among the chief causes. In the Netherlands, around 102,000 Jews perished (c. 75 per cent of the entire Jewish population). In Belgium and France, the number of victims amounted to around 25,000 (c. 40 per cent) and 73,000 (c. 25 per cent) respectively. Even though working for the 'Jewish Councils' provided a temporary exemption from deportation, it did not secure survival. Most of the Jews who worked for either of the organisations, as well as their families, were deported to concentration and extermination camps in the end. In the case of France, the relative number of murdered Jews was even (significantly) higher among those who worked for the UGIF central board.[31]

This comparative study has attempted to provide a balanced understanding of the form and function of the JR, the AJB, the UGIF-Nord and the UGIF-Sud in their respective societies. Even though the literature has paid a good deal of attention to the decisions of the Jewish leaders and their alleged role in the deportation of the Jews from their respective countries, we have seen that how the Jewish representative bodies functioned was in large part decided by their German overseers and by the contexts in which they were forced to operate, and was informed only to a lesser extent by the choices of the Jewish leadership.

Putting these findings into a broader context shows that the actions and decisions of the organisations' leaders, and their impact on the fate of the Jewish communities at large, have been disproportionally scrutinised and evaluated. Instead, we should understand their choices in the context of both long-term socio-cultural factors and the particular nature of German rule at the time each decision was made. Only when these structures are properly investigated is it possible to come closer to a full understanding of the complex situation these Jewish leaders faced.

In terms of dissimilarities, the fact that the JR was established as 'early' as February 1941, and that it was modelled after the *Judenräte* with only local authority in Eastern Europe, made it unique when compared with the AJB, the UGIF-Nord and the UGIF-Sud. Even though the JR formally extended its influence to the entire country eight months

---

[31] Laffitte, *Juif dans la France allemande*, 368.

after it was established and, from then on, resembled its counterparts in Western Europe in terms of geographic jurisdiction, its official status remained unaltered. That is, the JR was not anchored in Dutch law, and it was directly subordinate to the SS and local civil authorities. Despite the fact that there existed institutional rivalry between these authorities, they both firmly worked towards the same goal: the swift removal of Jews from Dutch society. This resulted in substantial pressure on the JR.

By contrast, the AJB, the UGIF-Nord and the UGIF-Sud came into existence (nine months after the JR) after a long period of negotiations between officials of the Military Administration, the SiPo-SD (and Vichy). Through the course of the occupation, these Jewish organisations in Belgium and France were overseen by representatives of each of these institutions, which obstructed a firm grip by the SS on them (as was the case in the Netherlands). Moreover, the interests of these German (and Vichy) authorities that oversaw the AJB, the UGIF-Nord and the UGIF-Sud at times differed, which further destabilised their supervision.

We have seen, for example, that the Military Administration was first and foremost interested in exploiting resources for the German war industry. In order to safeguard the stability that was necessary in order to achieve this aim, its officials were sensitive to the responses of the non-Jewish when anti-Jewish measures were implemented. This ran counter to the desire of the SiPo-SD to carry out the process of discrimination, isolation and deportation of the Jews as quickly as possible. In the case of France, Vichy officials had their own agenda, aiming to maintain as much autonomy over Jewish affairs as they could.

These circumstances affected how much room for manoeuvre the Jewish leaders had. In Belgium, conflicts of interest between the SiPo-SD and the Military Administration and their desire to gain the upper hand not only frequently delayed the decision-making process from the German side, but also meant that the AJB leaders were unsure to which department they ought to address themselves. Since one of the key motivations of the Jewish leaders was to buy time and to delay German policies, they were able to use this ambiguity to their own benefit. In France, the presence of SiPo-SD, the Military Administration and the Vichy regime created a situation that was more complex than that in the Netherlands and Belgium. Particularly in the first phase of the occupation, the Vichy-led CGQJ, which directly supervised the UGIF, was a source of frustration for SS-Hauptsturmführer Theodor Dannecker.

The anti-German outlook of Xavier Vallat and other Vichy officials problematised the relationship with the Germans, which decreased the effectiveness of German rule in France in the earliest part of the occupation. This, in turn, was one of the factors that resulted in more room for manoeuvre for both the UGIF-Nord and the UGIF-Sud. In the Netherlands, the strong presence of the SiPo-SD and the fact that its interests aligned with that of its rival institution, the civil administration, ensured that anti-Jewish regulations, and the mass deportation of Jews, could be accomplished without any real impediments. This made the context in which the JR was forced to act more stringent; there was little room for manoeuvre.

There were also differences in terms of the social structures and communities in which these organisations and their leaders operated. For example, the existence of alternative forms of representation, whether legal or illegal, proved to be major determinants for the course of events. These differences originated in the pre-war period. The social, religious and economic landscapes in the Netherlands, Belgium and France, both before and during the war, were highly diverse. The more uniform Dutch Jewish community made it easier to establish an organisation that represented the Jews in the Netherlands at least to some extent. Even though the leadership of the JR did not represent the large number of poor Jews that resided in the country, we can say that its leadership was emblematic of the development of increasing secularisation and integration into non-Jewish society that broadly characterised Jewish society at large.

In Belgium and France, it was impossible to fulfil any representative function vis-à-vis the strongly divided Jewish communities that resided in the country. In the changing pre-war communities, the traditional power of the Consistories in both countries faded, in Belgium even more strikingly than in France; the vast number of immigrants meant that an effective central leadership was entirely absent. Moreover, either before or shortly after the German invasion, pre-war leaders fled Belgium and France, which further contributed to a decentralisation of the communities in these countries.

The different social foundations on which the JR, the AJB, the UGIF-Nord and the UGIF-Sud were built affected both how far they were accepted by their communities and the way the Jewish leaders perceived their own role. To varying degrees, the positions of the French and Belgian leaders were not as solid as those of their Dutch counterparts. This meant that these leaders did not share the authoritative position of the Dutch leadership. Differences in self-perception and the (lack of) acceptance by the Jewish communities affected the ways the chairmen governed the Jewish organisations. The choices they made in terms of resisting German orders or withdrawing from the boards were also partly informed by these factors.

In Belgium and both French zones, the AJB, the UGIF-Nord and the UGIF-Sud leaders at some point either voluntarily decided to withdraw from their position, or were forced to do so because they refused to follow German regulations. Their withdrawal resulted in a leadership vacuum that was not immediately filled. In the Netherlands, by contrast, two chairmen continued to believe very strongly that their cooperation with the Germans, and receiving minor concessions in return, served the Jewish community best. The fact that they considered themselves to be the most capable representatives of the Jewish community contributed to their determination to remain in place.

The fluctuation in members of the central boards of the AJB, the UGIF-Nord and the UGIF-Sud turned out to work in favour of the Jewish communities in Belgium and France since it not only stalled German tactics, but also contributed more broadly to the Germans losing their grip on these Jewish communities. This was also caused by the fact that the AJB, the UGIF-Nord and the UGIF-Sud were less centralised bodies with comparatively little authority over the communities. This frustrated the Germans as the Jewish organisations were hardly functional in carrying out their anti-Jewish policies. With the exception of some individuals, such as Dannecker and Brunner in France, the SS seems to have lost its interest in using these organisations to facilitate the removal of Jews from Belgium and France during the course of the occupation.

In the Netherlands, the situation was different because of the strong and stable position of Asscher and Cohen (which had its pre-war origins) and the fact that the JR, in contrast to its counterparts, soon became the only major representative organisation the Jews could turn to. The various ways in which the central board members responded to German demands and the effectiveness with which they ruled over the Jewish communities affected the occupying authorities' perceptions about how the Jewish organisations were functioning. Not surprisingly, there was a greater level of satisfaction with the way the JR served German interests.

We have also seen that the 'Jewish Councils' in Western Europe cannot be regarded as uniform bodies. The heterogeneous responses of the organisations' members to increasing anti-Jewish regulations were not always consistent with the official policies they carried out. In the Netherlands, individuals outside the JR's central board, such as Walter Süskind, interpreted their role differently from the organisation's chairmen by engaging in clandestine activities. This stood in contrast to the central orders of the JR's leadership. Similar tendencies can be identified in the other two countries, where the autonomy of individuals working for the Jewish organisations was greater than in the Netherlands.

In Belgium, a clear difference in viewpoint can be identified between Salomon van den Berg and Maurice Benedictus, both members of the AJB's central board. Van den Berg continued to believe in the added value of the AJB in terms of providing social welfare to Belgian Jews. He was a strong proponent of law-abiding action and he resented clandestine activities. During the course of the occupation, when the German Security Police, sometimes aided by local Belgian police forces, increasingly targeted Jews for arrest (including those with Belgian citizenship), van den Berg continued to serve as central board member and local Brussels chair. Benedictus, by contrast, believed that there was nothing more that he could do to serve the interests of the Jews when Nazi policies radicalised, and he resigned from his post and fled abroad in December 1942.

Moreover, we should note that the actions of individual members were not consistent throughout the occupation. Even the Jewish leaders at times acted against the policies they officially propagated and, to varying degrees, were either actively or passively involved in clandestine operations on different levels. The involvement of the central board members of the AJB, the UGIF-Nord and the UGIF-Sud in clandestine activities shows that there was at times a difference between the outward appearance of so-called cooperation with the Germans and the actual activities of the organisations' functionaries. In an inherently complex situation, the Jewish leaders oscillated between cooperation and resistance and the many nuances of behaviour that exist in between. This liminality of human behaviour is inherent to the conduct of individuals and, more specifically, to the conduct of individuals who are forced to function under severe pressure.

The complex interrelations that existed between clandestine activity and the JR, the AJB, the UGIF-Nord and the UGIF-Sud underline their dynamic nature. Neither the German anti-Jewish regulations nor the general conditions of war were factors that could be predetermined. Initially, the Jewish leaders aimed to aid the communities as far as possible while protecting them from the direct threat of the Germans. Their intentions were increasingly frustrated throughout the war as they were forced to deal with, and abide by, increasing anti-Jewish measures and legislations. As a result, while they had mainly started off by attempting to provide social welfare to the Jewish communities at large, the organisations ended up trying to save as many Jews as possible from deportation. This was a gradually evolving process, and the responses of the central board members to it wavered during the course of the war.

While differences have decisively shaped the nature of these Jewish organisations, and affected their day-to-day operations, similarities between them can also be identified. An important similarity between all Jewish representative organisations in Western Europe is that their existence was shaped by local initiatives, ad-hoc decisions and institutional rivalry between the various German (and Vichy) departments. In line with the absence of a clearly defined plan for how the Greater German Reich would be governed, there was no central order outlining the structure, role and tasks of the 'Jewish Councils' in Western Europe.

As a result, their organisation largely depended upon improvisation by individual German (and Vichy) departments and local conditions. As local circumstances differed, the nature of the Jewish organisations changed accordingly. The lack of premeditation shows once again that the rationale behind the establishment of these 'Jewish Councils' was not to make these bodies instrumental in the so-called Final Solution to the Jewish Question. Instead, they were used by the SS or rivalling institutions when they were considered useful and avoided when they were not.

The findings of this study allow us to identify larger patterns of action that were applied by German authorities across the occupied territories. We have seen that ideas concerning the establishment and function of the 'Jewish Councils', formulated by prominent Nazi officials in Berlin, were constantly adapted and improved, often in accordance with local structures and administrators. German (SS) officials used the experience they had gained in one locality to further develop the implementation of the so-called Final Solution to the Jewish Question in other geographic locations. The fact that Theodor Dannecker proposed the establishment of a Jewish *Zwangsvereinigung* in France, and directly referred to previous experience in Germany and the Protectorate of Bohemia and Moravia, shows that previous experience played a major role in determining policies. Similarly, the fact that the JR initially had only local authority can be explained by the fact that the two highest ranking Nazis in the Netherlands, Arthur Seyss-Inquart and Hanns Albin Rauter, had previously observed the establishment of *Judenräte* with only local authority in occupied Poland. Yet it soon became clear that this local model proved impractical in the Netherlands, where Jews were not concentrated in local ghettos. The influence of the JR was then extended to the entire country.

Put together, this study has demonstrated that in order to understand and explain the nature of the Holocaust, and more specifically the way in which anti-Jewish policies were implemented and dealt with by the Jewish communities, it is essential to compare and contrast across the boundaries of the nation-state. The predominant focus on the 'Jewish Councils' within national contexts has obscured aspects that proved important in understanding and explaining why these bodies functioned the way they did. Only by comparing case studies is it possible to determine what factors were distinctive in each locality and how these factors affected the course of events. As a result, comparative studies stimulate multi-perspective approaches towards the subject.

Even though there is an increase in the number of comparative and transnational studies on the Holocaust, language barriers and other practical factors, such as an extensive knowledge of the historiographies of each of the case studies involved, still seem to discourage scholars from engaging in (macro-level) comparative research. Comparative, or transnational, research that draws on a broad range of sources, varying from German source material on the bureaucratic implementation of anti-Jewish policies to ego documents such as diaries and testimonies of the victims, is particularly rare. This obstructs an integrative understanding of the history of the Holocaust. Comparing case studies enables a full understanding of the wide range of (overlooked) factors that were decisive in shaping the histories of the Holocaust across Europe.

Bibliography

Primary Sources

Archival Sources and Interviews

France

American University in Paris (AUP)

University of Southern California (USC) Shoah Foundation, the Visual History Archive
- Noémi Mattis (Perelman), 24 November 1995
- Liliane Klein-Lieber, 21 June 1996

Archives Nationales de Paris (AN)

3W 142	Louis Darquier de Pellepoix, depositions
3W 158	Charles Du Paty de Clam, documentation, interrogations, depositions
3W 336	Xavier Vallat, documentation, inquiries
3W 337	Xavier Vallat, interrogations, documentation
3W 338	Xavier Vallat, Confrontations, depositions
AJ38 6302	Dossier Charles du Paty de Clam
AJ39 6278	Dossier Joseph Antignac
AJ38 1141	Archives of the UGIF
AJ38 5777	Archives of the UGIF, correspondence with the CGQJ

Mémorial de la Shoah, Paris

Centre de Documentation Juive Contemporaine (CDJC) Collection

V	German Embassy
XXIV	État-major allemand en France
XXV	Gestapo France
XXVb	Gestapo France
XXVI	Gestapo France
XXVIII	CGQJ
XLIXa	Gestapo France

LVIII	Fonds de Union Générale des Israélites de France (UGIF)
LXV	Gestapo France
LXXIV	Procès des collaborateurs
LXXVI	État-major allemand en France
XCVI	Commission rogatoire
CCXIII-CCXXI	Fédération des Sociétés Juives de France (FSJF)
CCCLXXIX	CGQJ – Fonds Braun
CDX-CDXXX	Fonds de Union Générale des Israélites de France (UGIF)
CDLXI	Belgique
DLXI	Fonds Anny Latour
DLXV	Fonds de Union Générale des Israélites de France (UGIF)
DCXLVIII-DCXLIX	Fonds de Union Générale des Israélites de France (UGIF)
DCCCXXX	Fonds de Union Générale des Israélites de France (UGIF)
CMXX-CMXXI	Fonds Lucien Lublin
CMXXV	David Diamant
CMXLIII	Fonds Éclaireuses et éclaireurs israélites de France

YIVO Institute for Jewish Research Collection

| MK490 | UGIF records from YIVO |
| MDC | UGIF Zone Sud |

Belgium

Algemeen Rijksarchief (ARA), Brussels

Conseil de Guerre de Liège
  No. 4030/44   Report Grigorijs Garfinkels
  No. 19186/45   Report Noé Nozyce

Centre for Historical Research and Documentation on War and Contemporary Society (CEGESOMA), Brussels

AA 753	Archief R.D. Katz betr. joden in België tijdens de bezetting
AA 1915	Dossier Esta en Maurice Heiber
AA 1196	Interviews met Belgische joden betr. joodse organisaties en verzet
AA MIC/41	Oorlogsarchief Dr. Salomon Ullmann
AB2167	Historique du Comité de Défense des Juifs

Documentatie Oorlogsslachtoffers (DOS), Brussels

Film XIV (R184.Tr50 077)	Marburg Documentation
R497/Tr206.891	Meeting reports AJB Brussels branch
R497/248.745	Meeting reports AJB Brussels branch

R497/Tr146.666   Meeting reports AJB central board
R696/Tr267.125   Salomon Ullmann papers
R.715/Tr248.00   Archives Marcel Blum

Fondation de la Mémoire Contemporaine, Brussels

Interviews
- Fela Perelman-Liwer, 1984/1988/1989
- Irène Rosenzweig-Zmigrod, 1996

Kazerne Dossin, Mechelen

Joods Museum van Deportatie en Verzet (JMDV)-Centre National des Hautes
   Études Juives (CNHEJ), Buber Collection
- Archives of the AJB
JMDV-Musée National de la Résistance (MNR)/Nationaal Museum van de
   Weerstand (NWM)
- Archives of the AJB
N 682.302 Reports of the Foreign Police (Vreemdelingendossiers)
   - A295861, Robert Holzinger
   - A158016, Max Katz
   - 1522381, Noé Nozyce
   - 1160919, Juda (Jules) Mehlwurm
   - A143129, Chaïm Pinchos Perelman
   - 876189, Saül Pinkous
   - A317631, Louis Rosenfeld
   - 1313133, Idel Steinberg
   - 1501782, Oscar Teitelbaum
   - 1550810, Nico David Workum

Krijgsauditoraat, Brussels

- 4030 N 1944   Dossier Grégoire Garfinkels
- 8036/44   Penal files of the AJB leadership
- 54 199/45   Dossier Salomon van den Berg
- NNSE 24 291/46   Dossier David Lazer

The Netherlands

National Archive (NA), The Hague

Centraal Archief voor de Bijzondere Rechtspleging (CABR):
- Abraham Asscher
- David Cohen
- Ferdinand Hugo aus der Fünten
- Albert Conrad Gemmeker
- Wilhelm Harster
- Willy Paul Franz Lages

NIOD, *Amsterdam*

014	Reichskommissar für die besetzten niederländischen Gebiete
020	Generalkommissariat für Verwaltung und Justiz
077	Generalkommissariat für das Sicherheitswesen (Höhere SS- und Polizeiführer Nord-West.
181b	Comité voor Joodsche Vluchtelingen
181d	Coördinatie-Commissie
181j	Prof. Dr. D. Cohen
182	Joodsche Raad voor Amsterdam
244	Europese dagboeken en egodocumenten
250i	Westerbork, Judendurchgangslager
DOC I (248)	Personal Files

- Abraham Asscher
- Mirjam Bolle
- David Cohen
- Wilhelm Harster
- Isaac Kisch
- Gertrude van Tijn
- Wilhelm Zöpf

DOC II	Documenten
KBI	Knipselcollectie personen
KBII	Knipselcollectie zaken
	Fiches Loe de Jong

Joods Museum, Amsterdam

Documents collection

Rijksarchief Noord-Holland, Haarlem

Dossier Joodse Ereraad (39)

Israel

Yad Vashem, Jerusalem

M.19   Joodse Raad, Friesland
O. 29   Belgium Collection
P.7   Mark Yarblum Archive about the French Underground
Film Center

United States of America

United States Holocaust Memorial Museum (USHMM), Washington DC

Film Collection
Oral History Interview Collection

United Kingdom

The Wiener Library, London

Testimony Collection
- Maurice Heiber, 1956
- Irène Zmigrod, 1956
- Roger van Praag, 1956
- Esta Fajerstein, 1956

Printed Primary Sources

Diaries and Memoirs

Berr, H. *Journal: The Diary of a Young Jewish Woman in Occupied Paris*, transl. from the French by D. Bellos. London: Maclehose Press, 2008.

Bloch, P. *Jusqu'au dernier jour. Mémoires*. Paris: Albin Michel, 1983.

Bolle, M. *'Ik zal je beschrijven hoe een dag er hier uit ziet': Dagboekbrieven uit Amsterdam, Westerbork en Bergen-Belsen*. Amsterdam/Antwerp: Uitgeverij Contact, 2005; first ed. 2003.

Cohen, D. *Voorzitter van de Joodse Raad: de herinneringen van David Cohen*, ed. E. Somers. Zutphen: Wallburg Pers, 2010.

Cohen, D. 'Pro Domo' in P. Schrijvers, *Rome, Athene, Jeruzalem: leven en werk van prof. Dr. David Cohen*. Groningen: Historische Uitgeverij, 2000.

Gamzon, D. *Mémoires*. Jerusalem: published by author, 1997.

Gamzon, R. *Les eaux claires, journal 1940–1944*. Paris: Éclaireurs Israélites de France, 1981.

Gorgiel-Sercarz, *Memoirs of a Jewish Daughter*. Tel Aviv: H. Gorgiel–Sercarz, 1990.

Hillesum, E. *Het verstoorde leven: dagboek van Etty Hillesum*. Haarlem: De Haag, 1981.

Kar, J. van de. *Joods Verzet: terugblik op de periode rond de Tweede Wereldoorlog*. Amsterdam: Stadsdrukkerij van Amsterdam, 1981.

Kapel, R. S. *Un rabbin dans la tourmente, 1940–1944*. Paris: CDJC, 1986.

Lambert, R. R. L. *Diary of a Witness 1940–1943: The Ordeal of the Jews of France during the Holocaust*, transl. from the French by I. Best, ed. R. Cohen. Chicago: Ivan R. Dee, 2007; first French ed. 1985, 3–210.

Mechanicus, P. *In dépôt: Dagboek uit Westerbork*. Amsterdam: Van Gennep, 1989; first ed. 1964.

Schnek, G. 'Être jeune en France, 1939–1945' in J.-M. Dereymez (ed.), *Être jeune en Isère, 1939–1945*. Paris: l'Harmattan, 2001, 59–64.

Vallat, X. *Le Nez de Cléopâtre: souvenirs d'un homme de droite, 1919–1945*. Paris: Éditions 'Les Quatre Fils Aymon, 1957.

Other Primary Sources

Allgemeine Übersicht für die Zeit vom 1. December 1941–15. March 1942, 16 March 1942, Brussels, in *Dokumente. Die Endlösung der Judenfrage in Belgien*, S. Klarsfeld and M. Steinberg (eds.) New York: The Beate Klarsfeld Foundation, 1980.

Die Verfolgung und Emordung der europäischen Juden durch das nationalsozialist-ische Deutschland, 1933–1945, Vol. 5: West- und Nordeuropa 1940–März 1942, H. Mayer, K. Happe and M. Peers (eds.) Munich: De Gruyter Oldenbourg Verlag, 2013.

Die Verfolgung und Emordung der europäischen Juden durch das nationalsozial-istische Deutschland, 1933–1945, Vol. 12: West- und Nordeuropa Juni 1942–1945, Happe, K. Lambauer, B. and C. Maier-Wolthausen, eds. Munich: De Gruyter Oldenbourg Verlag, 2015.

Het Joodsche Weekblad: uitgave van den Joodschen Raad voor Amsterdam. The Hague: Omniboek, 1979.

Les Juifs sous l'occupation. Recueil de textes français et allemands. Sarraute, R. and P. Tager, eds. Paris: CDJC, 1982.

Verordnungsblatt des Militärbefehlshabers in Belgien und Nordfrankreich.

Verordnungsblatt für die besetzten Niederländischen Gebiete (VOBL).

Newspaper Articles

Ensel, R. and E. Gans, 'Niet weten van gaskamers verklaart passiviteit niet', *NRC/Handelsblad,* 16 May 2013.

Ensel, R. and E. Gans, 'Over 'Wij weten iets van hun lot', *De Groene Amsterdammer,* 6 February 2013.

Ensel, R. and E. Gans, 'Nivellering in de geschiedenis: wij weten iets van hun lot', *De Groene Amsterdammer,* No. 50, 12 December 2012.

Paxton, R. 'Jews: How Vichy Made It Worse', *New York Review of Books,* No. 6 (2014).

Polak, H. 'Het wetenschappelijk antisemitisme: weerlegging en vertoog', *Volksdagblad voor Gelderland,* 27 December 1938.

Secondary Sources

Aalders, G. *Nazi Looting: The Plunder of Dutch Jewry during the Second World War,* transl. from the Dutch by A. Pomerans. Oxford/New York: Berg, 2004; first Dutch ed. 1999.

Abicht, L. *Geschiedenis van de Joden in de Lage Landen.* Antwerp: Meulenhoff/Manteau, 2006.

Abicht, L. *De Joden van België.* Amsterdam/Antwerp: Atlas, 1994.

Abitbol, M. *Les deux terres promises: Les Juifs de France et le sionisme 1897–1945.* Paris: Perrin, 2010; first French ed.

Adam, U. *Judenpolitik im Dritten Reich.* Düsseldorf: Droste, 1972.

Adler, J. 'The Jews and Vichy: Reflections on French Historiography'. *The Historical Journal,* Vol. 44, No. 4 (2001), 1065–1082.

Adler, J. *The Jews of Paris and the Final Solution: Communal Response and Internal Conflicts, 1940–1944,* transl. from the French. Oxford: Oxford University Press, 1987; first French ed. 1985.

Albert, P. C. *The Modernization of French Jewry: Consistory and Community in the Nineteenth Century.* Hanover, NH: Brandeis University Press, 1977.

Anderl, G., D. Rupnow and A. Wenck, *Die Zentralstelle für Jüdische Auswanderung als Beraubungsinstitution.* Vienna: Oldenbourg, 2004.

Anders, F., K. Stoll and K. Wilke (eds.). *Der Judenrat von Białystok: Dokumente aus dem Archiv des Białystoker Ghettos 1941–1943.* Paderborn: Ferdinand Schöningh, 2010.

Aouate, Y. C. 'La place de l'Algérie dans le projet antijuif de Vichy (octobre 1940–novembre 1942)', *Revue française d'histoire d'outre-mer,* Vol. 80, No. 301 (1993), 599–613.

Arendt, H. *Eichmann in Jerusalem: A Report on the Banality of Evil.* New York: The Viking Press, 1963.

Assan, V. 'Israël William Oualid, juriste, économiste, professeur des universités', *Archives Juives,* Vol. 46, No. 1 (2013), 130–143.

Ayoun, R. 'Les Juifs d'Algérie dans la Tourmente Antisémite du XXe siècle', *Revue Européenne des Études Hébraïques,* No. 1 (1996), 57–99.

Bajohr, F. and A. Löw. *The Holocaust and European Societies: Social Processes and Social Dynamics.* London: Palgrave Macmillan, 2016.

Barkai, M. (ed.), *The Fighting Ghettos.* Philidelphia: Lippinicott, 1962.

Baruch, M. *Servir l'État français. L'administration en France de 1940 à 1944.* Paris: Fayard, 1997.

Bauer, Y. 'Jewish Resistance in the Ukraine and Belarus during the Holocaust', in P. Henry (ed.), *Jewish Resistance against the Nazis.* Washington, DC: The Catholic University of America Press, 2014, 483–503.

Bauer, Y. *The Death of the Shtetl.* New Haven/London: Yale University Press, 2009.

Bauer, Y. *Rethinking the Holocaust.* New Haven/London: Yale University Press, 2001.

Bauer, Y. *American Jewry and the Holocaust: the American Jewish Joint Distribution Committee, 1939–1945.* Detroit, MI: Wayne State University Press, 1981.

Bauer, Y. *The Jewish Emergence from Powerlessness.* London: Macmillan, 1980.

Bauer, Y. 'The Judenräte: Some Conclusions', in Y. Gutman and C. Haft (eds.), *Patterns of Jewish Leadership in Nazi Europe, 1933–1945.* Jerusalem: Yad Vashem, 1980, 393–405.

Bauer, Y. *They Chose Life: Jewish Resistance in the Holocaust.* New York: American Jewish Committee, Institute of Human Relations, 1973.

Bazarov, V. 'HIAS and HICEM in the System of Jewish Relief Organisations in Europe, 1933–1941', *East European Jewish Affairs,* Vol. 39, No. 1 (2009), 69–78.

Bekkenkamp, A. *Leendert Overduin: het levensverhaal van een pastor Pimpernel, 1900–1976.* Enschede: Van de Berg, 2000.

Bensimon D. 'Socio-Demographic Aspects of French Jewry', *European Judaism: A Journal for the New Europe,* Vol. 12, No. 1 (1978), 12–16.

Bensimon D. *Socio-démographie des juifs de France et d'Algérie 1867–1907.* Paris: Publications Orientalistes de France, 1976.

Benz, W. (ed.). *Dimension des Völkermords: die Zahl der jüdischen Opfer des Nationalsozialismus.* Munich: Oldenbourg, 1991.

Bergh, S. van den. *Deportaties: Westerbork, Thersiënstadt, Auschwitz, Gleiwitz.* Bussum: Van Dishoeck, 1945.

Berkley, K. P. L. *Overzicht van het ontstaan, de werkzaamheden en het streven van den Joodsche Raad voor Amsterdam.* Amsterdam: Plastica, 1945.

Berkovitz, J. *The Shaping of Jewish Identity in Nineteenth-Century France.* Detroit, MI: Wayne State University Press, 1989.

Birnbaum, P. *Jewish Destinies: Citizenship, State and Community in Modern France*. New York: Hill and Wang, 2000.

Birnbaum, P. *The Jews of the Republic: A Political History of State Jews in France from Gambetta to Vichy*. Stanford, CA: Stanford University Press, 1996.

Birnbaum, P. and I. Katznelson. *Paths of Emancipation: Jews, States and Citizenship*. Princeton: Princeton University Press, 1995.

Billig, J. *Die 'Endlösung der Judenfrage'. Studie über ihre Grundsätze im III. Reich in Frankreich während der Besatzung*, transl. from the French by E. Schulz. New York: The Beate Klarsfeld Foundation, 1979; first French ed. 1977.

Billig, J. *Le Commissariat général aux questions juives, 1941–1944* (3 volumes). Paris: Éditions du Centre, 1955, 1957 and 1960.

Blom, J. C. H., D. Wertheim, H. Berg et al. (eds.), *Reappraising the History of the Jews in the Netherlands, transl. from the Dutch by D. McKay; this is a revised and updated version of the 2002 publication of this work*. London: The Littman Library of Jewish Civilization in association with Liverpool University Press, 2021.

Blom, J. C. H. 'The Persecution of the Jews in the Netherlands: A Comparative Western European Perspective', *European History Quarterly*, Vol. 19 (1989), 333–351.

Blom, J. C. H. 'De vervolging van de Joden in Nederland in internationaal vergelijkend perspectief', *Gids*, Vols. 6–7, No. 150 (1987), 484–507.

Blom, J. C. H. 'In de ban van de Joodse Raad', in ibid., *In de ban van goed en fout? Wetenschappelijke geschiedschrijving over de bezettingstijd in Nederland*. Bergen: Octavo, 1983, 47–56.

Blumel, A. *Un grand Juif: Léon Meiss*. Paris: Éditions Guy-Victor, 1967.

Boas, H. 'The Persecution and Destruction of Dutch Jewry, 1940–1945', *Yad Vashem Studies* Vol. 6 (1967), 359–374.

Bok, W. 'Vie juive et communauté, une esquisse de leur histoire au vingtième siècle', in *La Grande Synagogue de Bruxelles: Contributions à l'histoire des Juifs de Bruxelles, 1878–1978*. Brussels: Communauté Israélite de Bruxelles, 1978.

Boom, B. van den. *Wij weten niets van hun lot: gewone Nederlanders en de Holocaust*. Amsterdam: Boom, 2012.

Boom, B. van der. *'We leven nog': de stemming in bezet Nederland*. Amsterdam: Boom, 2003.

Boom, B. van der. *Den Haag in de Tweede Wereldoorlog*. The Hague: SeaPress, 1995.

Boterman, F. *Duitse daders: de jodenvervolging en de nazificatie van Nederland, 1940–1945*. Amsterdam: Uitgeverij de Arbeiderspers, 2015.

Botz, G. *Nationalsozialismus in Wien: Machtübernahme, Herrschaftssicherung, Radikalisierung, Kriegsvorbereitung, 1938/1939*. Vienna: Mandelbaum Verlag, 2018.

Braber, B. *This Cannot Happen Here: Integration and Jewish Resistance in the Netherlands, 1940–1945*. Amsterdam: Amsterdam University Press, 2013.

Braber, B. *Zelfs als wij zullen verliezen: Joden in verzet en illegaliteit, 1940–1945*. Amsterdam: Balans, 1990.

Bracher, N. 'Up in Arms: Jewish Resistance against Nazi Germany in France', in P. Henry (ed.), *Jewish Resistance against the Nazis*. Washington, DC: The Catholic University of America Press, 2014, 73–91.

Brachfeld, S. *Ils ont survécu. Le sauvetage des juifs en belgique occupée*. Brussels: Éditions Racine, 2001.

Brachfeld, S. 'Jewish Orphanages in Belgium under the German Occupation', in D. Michman (ed.), *Belgium and the Holocaust: Jews, Belgians, Germans.* Jerusalem: Yad Vashem, 1998, 419–432.

Brachfeld, S. *Ils n'ont pas eu les gosses: l'histoire de plus de 500 enfants juifs dans parents 'fichés à la Gestapo' et placés pendant l'occupation allemande dans les homes de l'Association des Juifs en Belgique, AJB.* Herzliya: Institute for Research on Belgium Judaism, 1989.

Brasz, C. and Y. Kaplan (eds), *Dutch Jews as Perceived by Themselves and by Others: Proceedings of the Eighth International Symposium on the History of the Jews in the Netherlands.* Amsterdam: Brill, 2011.

Brasz, C. 'Dutch Jews as Zionists and Israeli Citizens', in Y. Kaplan and C. Brasz (eds.), *Dutch Jews as Perceived by Themselves and by Others: Proceedings of the Eighth International Symposium on the History of the Jews in the Netherlands.* Leiden/Boston/Cologne: Brill, 2001, 215–234.

Brauman, J., G. Loinger and F. Wattenberg (eds.). *Organisation juive de combat: résistance/sauvetage, France 1940–1945.* Paris: Editions Autrement, 2002.

Brinckman, B. 'Een schakel tussen arbeid en leiding: het Rijksarbeidsambt (1940–1944)', *Bijdragen tot de Geschiedenis van de Tweede Wereldoorlog,* Vol. 12 (1989), 85–161.

Brisaud, A. *La dernière année de Vichy.* Paris: Perrin, 1965.

Bronkhorst, D. *Een tijd van komen. De geschiedenis van vluchtelingen in Nederland.* Amsterdam: Mets, 1990.

Bronzwaer, P. *Maastricht en Luik bezet: een comparatief onderzoek naar vijf aspecten van de Duitse bezetting van Maastricht en Luik tijdens de Tweede Wereldoorlog.* Hilversum: Verloren, 2010.

Bruland, B. 'Norway's Role in the Holocaust: The Destruction of Norway's Jews', in J. Friedman (ed.), *The Routledge history of the Holocaust.* London: Routledge, 2011, 232–247.

Caestecker, F. 'The Reintegration of Jewish Survivors into Belgian Society, 1943–1947', in D. Bankier (ed.), *The Jews are Coming Back: The Return of the Jews to their Countries of Origin after World War II.* New York: Berghahn/ Jerusalem: Yad Vashem, 2005, 72–107.

Caestecker, F. 'Onverbiddelijk maar ook clement. Het Belgische immigratiebeleid en de joodse vlucht uit nazi-Duitsland, maart 1938- augustus 1939', *Bijdragen tot de Eigentijdse Geschiedenis,* Vol. 13/14 (2004), 99–139.

Caestecker, F. *Alien Policy in Belgium, 1840–1940: The Creation of Guest Workers, Refugees and Illegal Aliens.* New York/Oxford: Berghahn Books, 2000.

Caestecker, F. *Ongewenste Gasten: Joodse vluchtelingen en migranten in de dertiger jaren.* Brussels: VUB Press, 1993.

Caron, V. 'The Survival of the Jews in France, 1940–1944', book review, *The Journal of Modern History,* Vol. 92, No. 2 (2020).

Caron, V. 'French Public Opinion and the Jewish Question, 1930–1942: The Role of Middle-Class Professional Organization', in D. Bankier and I. Gutman (eds), *Nazi Europe and the Final Solution.* Jerusalem: Yad Vashem, 2003, 374–410.

Caron, V. *Uneasy Asylum: France and the Jewish Refugee Crisis 1933–1942.* Stanford, CA: Stanford University Press, 1999.

Caron, V. 'The UGIF: The Failure of the Nazis to Establish a Judenrat on the Eastern European Model', in *Working Papers I*. New York: Columbia University Center for Israel and Jewish Studies, 1977.

Ceserani, D. *Eichmann: His Life and Crimes*. London: William Heinemann, 2004.

Chouraqui, A. *Cent Ans D'Histoire: L'Alliance Israélite Universelle et la Renaissance Juive Contemporaine, 1860–1960*. Paris: Presses Universitaires de France, 1965.

Cohen, A. *Persécutions et sauvetages: Juifs et Français sous l'occupation et sous Vichy*. Paris: Éditions du Cerf, 1993.

Cohen, D. *Zwervend en dolend: de Joodse vluchtelingen in Nederland in de jaren 1933–1940, met een inleiding over de jaren 1900–1933*. Haarlem: Bohn, 1955.

Cohen, R. 'Le Consistoire et l'UGIF: La situation trouble des Juifs Français face à Vichy', *Revue d'histoire de la Shoah: Le Consistoire durant la Seconde Guerre Mondiale*, Vol. 169, No. 2 (2000), 28–37.

Cohen, R. *The Burden of Conscience: French Jewish Leadership during the Holocaust*. Bloomington and Indianapolis: Indiana University Press, 1987.

Cohen, R. (ed.) *Diary of a Witness 1940–1943: The Ordeal of the Jews of France during the Holocaust* transl. from the French by I. Best. Chicago: Ivan R. Dee, 2007; first French ed. 1985.

Cohen, R. 'French Jewry's Dilemma on the Orientation of Its Leadership: From Polemics to Conciliation, 1942–1944', *Yad Vashem Studies*, Vol. 14 (1981), 167–204.

Cohen, R. and Z. Szajkowski, 'A Jewish Leader in Vichy France, 1940–1943', *Jewish Social Studies*, Vol. 43, No. 3 (1981), 291–310.

Conway, M. *The Sorrows of Belgium: Liberation and Political Reconstruction, 1944–1947*. Oxford: Oxford University Press, 2012.

Coutois, S., D. Peschanski and A. Rayski, *Le sang de l'étranger: Les immigrés de la MOI dans la Résistance*. Paris: Fayard, 1989.

Croes, M. and P. Tammes, *'Gif laten wij niet voortbestaan': Een onderzoek naar de overlevingskansen van joden in de Nederlandse gemeenten, 1940–1945*. Amsterdam: Aksant, 2006.

Coutau-Bégarie, H. and C. Huan, *Darlan*. Paris: Fayard, 1989.

Cüppers, M. *Walther Rauff: In deutschen Diensten: Vom Naziverbrecher zum BND-Spion*. Darmstadt: WBG Academic, 2013.

Curtis, M. *Verdict on Vichy: Power and Prejudice in the Vichy France Regime*. London: Weidenfeld & Nicholson, 2002.

Daalder, H. *Politiek en historie. Opstellen over Nederlandse politiek en vergelijkende politieke wetenschap*. Amsterdam: Bert Bakker, 2011; first ed. 1990.

Daelen, V. Vanden. and N. Wouters, 'The Absence of a Jewish Honor Court in Postwar Belgium', in L. Jokusch and G. N. Finder (eds.), *Jewish Honor Courts: Revenge, Retribution and Reconciliation after the Holocaust*. Detroit, MI: Wayne State University Press, 2015, 197–224.

Daelen, V. Vanden. *Laten we hun lied verder zingen: de heropbouw van de joodse gemeenschap in Antwerpen na de Tweede Wereldoorlog, 1944–1960*. Amsterdam: Aksant, 2008.

Delarue, J. *Histoire de la Gestapo*. Paris: Fayard, 1987.

Dickschen, B. 'De VJB en het onderwijs', in R. van Doorslaer and J.-Ph. Schreiber (eds.), *De curatoren van het getto: de vereniging van joden in België tijdens de nazi-bezetting*. Tielt: Lannoo, 2004, 182–203.

Diner, D. 'Historisches Verstehen und Gegenrationalität. Der Judenrat als erkenntnistheoretische Warte', in F. Bajohr, W. Johe and U. Lohalm (eds.), *Zivilisations und Barbarei. Die widersprüchlichen Potentiale der Moderne*. Hamburg: Christians, 1991.

Donnet, A. 'Het onderzoek door het militaire gerecht: het geheugen buitenspel gezet', in R. van Doorslaer and J-Ph. Schreiber (eds.), *De curatoren van het getto: de vereniging van de joden in België tijdens de nazi-bezetting*. Tielt: Lannoo, 2004, 291–319.

Doorslaer, R. van. 'Het Belgische Jiddischland. Een politieke geschiedenis van de joodse gemeenschappen in België tussen de twee wereldoorlogen', *Les Cahiers de la Mémoire Contemporaine*, Vol. 11 (2014), 43–66.

Doorslaer, R. van. (ed). *Gewillig België: Overheid en Jodenvervolging tijdens de Tweede Wereldoorlog*. Amsterdam/Antwerp: Meulenhoff and Manteau, 2007.

Doorslaer, R. van. and J-Ph. Schreiber (eds.). *De curatoren van het getto: de vereniging van de joden in België tijdens de nazi-bezetting*. Tielt: Lannoo, 2004.

Doorslaer, R. van. 'Salomon van den Berg of de ondraaglijke mislukking van een joodse politiek van het minste kwaad', in R. van Doorslaer and J-Ph. Schreiber (eds.), *De curatoren van het getto: de vereniging van de joden in België tijdens de nazi-bezetting*. Tielt: Lannoo, 2004, 111–146.

Doorslaer, R. van. 'Jewish Immigration and Communism in Belgium, 1925–1939', in D. Michman (ed.), *Belgium and the Holocaust: Jews, Belgians, Germans* (Jerusalem: Yad Vashem, 1998), 63–82.

Doorslaer, R. van. *Kinderen van het getto: Joodse revolutionairen in België, 1925–1940*. Antwerp/Baarn: Hadewijch, 1995.

Doron, D. *Jewish Youth and Identity in Postwar France: Rebuilding Family and Nation*. Bloomington/Indianapolis: Indiana University Press, 2015.

Drake, D. *Paris at War, 1939–1944*. Cambridge, MA: The Belknap Press of Harvard University Press, 2015.

Drake, D. *French Intellectuals and Politics from the Dreyfus Affair to the Occupation*. Basingstoke: Palgrave Macmillan, 2005.

Dratwa, D. 'The Zionist Kaleidoscope in Belgium', in D. Michman (ed.), *Belgium and the Holocaust: Jews, Belgians, Germans*. Jerusalem: Yad Vashem Studies, 1998, 43–62.

Dratwa, D. 'Genocide and its Memories: A Preliminary Study on How Belgian Jewry Coped with the Results of the Holocaust', in D. Michman (ed.), *Belgium and the Holocaust: Jews, Belgians, Germans*. Jerusalem: Yad Vashem Studies, 1998, 523–557.

Dworzecki, M. 'The Day to Day Stand of the Jews', in I. Gutman and L. Rotkirchen (eds.), *The Catastrophe of European Jewry: Antecedents, History, Reflection*. Jerusalem: Yad Vashem, 1976, 367–399.

Eismann, G. *Hôtel Majestic: Ordre et sécurité en France occupée, 1940–1944*. Paris: Éditions Tallandier, 2010.

Engelking, B. and J. Leociak, *The Warsaw Ghetto: A Guide to A Perished City*, transl. Emma Harris. New Haven/London: Yale University Press, 2009.

Fein, H. *Accounting for Genocide: National Responses and Jewish Victimization during the Holocaust*. New York: Free Press, 1979.

Fenoglio, L. 'On the Use of the Nazi Sources for the Study of Fascist Jewish Policy in the Italian- Occupied Territories: The Case of South-Eastern France, November 1942–July 1943', *Journal of Modern Italian Studies*, Vol. 24, No. 1 (2019), 63–78.

Fenoglio, L. 'Between Protection and Complicity: Guido Lospinoso, Fascist Italy, and the Holocaust in Occupied Southeastern France', *Holocaust and Genocide Studies*, Vol. 33, No. 1 (2019), 90–111.

Fenoglio, L. *Angelo Donati e la 'questione ebraica' nella Francia occupata dall'esercito italiano*. Turin: Silvio, Zamorani, 2013.

Finkel, E. *Ordinary Jews: Choice and Survival during the Holocaust*. Princeton/Oxford: Princeton University Press, 2017.

Fishman, J. and J. S. Fishman, 'On Jewish Survival during the Occupation: The Vision of Jacob van Amerongen', *Studia Rosenthaliana*, Vol. 33, No. 2 (1999), 160–173.

Flim, B. J. *Saving the Children: History of the Organized Effort to Rescue Jewish Children in the Netherlands, 1942–1945*. Bethesda, MD: CDL Press, 2005.

Flim, B. J. *Omdat hun hart sprak: Geschiedenis van de georganiseerde hulp aan Joodse kinderen in Nederland, 1942–1945*. Kampen: Uitgeverij Kok, 1996.

Fogg, S. *Stealing Home: Looting, Restitution, and Reconstructing Jewish Lives in France, 1942–1947*. New York/Oxford: Oxford University Press, 2017.

Fogg, S. *The Politics of Everyday Life in Vichy France: Foreigners, Undesirables and Strangers*. New York/Cambridge: Cambridge University Press, 2009.

Fraser, D. *The Fragility of Law: Constitutional Patriotism and the Jews of Belgium, 1940–1945*. Abingdon: Routledge-Cavendish, 2009.

Fredj, J. 'Le Consistoire Central et la création du CRIF', *Revue d'histoire de la Shoah: Le Consistoire durant la Seconde Guerre Mondiale*, Vol. 169 (2000), 164–180.

Frenk, J. L. 'Le Linké Poalé Zion et la Résistance en Belgique durant la Seconde Guerre mondiale', *Cahiers de la Mémoire Contemporaine/Bijdragen tot de Eigentijdse geschiedenis*, Vol. 12 (2016), 63–98.

Friedl, S. 'Negotiating and Compromising Jewish Leaders' Scope of Action in Tunisia during Nazi Rule (November 1942–May 1943)', in F. Bajohr and A. Löw (eds), *Holocaust and European Societies: Social Processes and Social Dynamics*. London: Palgrave Macmillan, 2016, 225–240.

Friedla, K. *Juden in Breslau/Wrocław 1933–1949: Überlebensstrategieen, Selbstbehauptung und Verfolgungserfahrungen*. Cologne/Weimar/Vienna: Böhlau, 2015.

Friedländer, S. *The Years of Extermination: Nazi Germany and the Jews, 1939–1945*. New York: HarperCollins, 2007.

Friedman, Ph. *Roads to Extinction: Essays on the Holocaust*. New York, Conference on Jewish Social Studies, 1980.

Friedman, Ph. (ed.), *Martyrs and Fighters: The Epic of the Warsaw Ghetto*. New York: Praeger, 1954.

Fuks, L. 'Oost-Joden in Nederland tussen beide Wereldoorlogen', *Studia Rosenthaliana*, Vol. 11, No. 2 (1977), 198–215.

Galen Last, D. van. 'The Netherlands' in B. Moore, *Resistance in Western Europe*. Oxford: Berg, 2000, 189–221.

Gans, E. 'De generaal en zijn adjudant. Piet Schrijvers' biografie van David Cohen', *Biografie Bulletin*, Vol. 10, No. 2 (2000), 146–161.

Garfinkels, B. *Les Belges face à la persécution raciale, 1940–1944.* Brussels: ULB, 1965.

Gatrell, P. and P. Nivet, 'Refugees and Exiles', in J. Winter (ed.), *The Cambridge History of the First World War*, Vol. 3. New York/Cambridge: Cambridge University Press, 2014.

Gérard-Libois, J. and J. Gotovitch, *L'an 40: La Belgique occupée.* Brussels: CRISP, 1972.

Gerritse, T. *Rauter: Himmlers vuist in Nederland.* Amsterdam: Boom, 2018.

Gildea, R. *Fighters in the Shadows: A New History of the French Resistance.* London: Faber & Faber, 2015.

Goldberg, A. 'The History of the Jews in the Ghettos. A Cultural Perspective', in D. Stone (ed.), *The Holocaust and Historical Methodology.* New York/Oxford: Berghahn, 2012, 79–100.

Gotovitch, J. 'Resistance Movements and the "Jewish Question"', in D. Michman (ed.), *Belgium and the Holocaust: Jews, Belgians, Germans.* Jerusalem: Yad Vashem, 1998, 273–285.

Gotovitch, J. *Du rouge au tricolore: les communistes belges de 1939 à 1944: un aspect de l'histoire de la résistance en Belgique.* Brussels: Éditions Labor, 1992.

Goudsmit, S. 'Fragmenten uit het Dagboek van Sam Goudsmit', *Studia Rosenthaliana*, Vol. 4, No. 2 (1970), 232–242.

Graaff, B. de. 'Collaboratie en Verzet : Een Vergelijkend Perspectief', in J. Jonker and A. Kersten (eds.), *Vijftig jaar na de inval: geschiedschrijving en de Tweede Wereldoorlog, bijdragen aan het congres gehouden aan de Vrije Universiteit te Amsterdam op 11 en 11 mei 1990.*'s Gravenhage: SDU Uitgeverij, 1990, 95–108.

Green, N. *The Pletzl of Paris. Jewish Immigrant Workers in the Belle Époque.* New York: Holmes and Meier, 1986.

Griffioen, P. and R. Zeller, *Jodenvervolging in Nederland, Frankrijk en België 1940–1945: overeenkomsten, verschillen, oorzaken.* Amsterdam: Boom, 2011.

Griffioen, P. and R. Zeller, 'Jodenvervolging in Nederland en België tijdens de Tweede Wereldoorlog: Een Vergelijkende Analyse', *Oorlogsdocumentatie '40-'45*, Vol. 8 (1997), 10–63.

Grison, L. 'L'Alliance israélite universelle dans les années noires', *Archives Juives*, Vol. 34, No. 1 (2001), 9–22.

Gross, A. and R. Dearin, *Chaim Perelman.* New York: State University of New York Press, 2003.

Gruner, W. *Die Judenverfolgung im Prokterkorat Böhmen und Mähren: lokale initiativen, zentrale Entscheidungen, jüdische Antworten 1939–1945.* Göttingen: Wallstein Verlag, 2016.

Grynberg, A. 'Juger l'UGIF (1944–1950)?', in H. Harter, A. Marès et al. (eds.), *Terres promises: Mélanges offerts à André Kaspi.* Paris: Publications de la Sorbonne, 2008, 507–526.

Gutman, Y. and S. Bender (eds.). *The Encyclopedia of the Righteous among the Nations: Rescues of Jews during the Holocaust – France.* Jerusalem: Yad Vashem, 2003.

Gutman, Y. *The Jews of Warsaw, 1939–1943: Ghetto, Underground, Revolt.* Bloomington: Indiana University Press, 1982.

Gutman, Y. and C. Haft (eds.). *Patterns of Jewish Leadership in Nazi Europe, 1933–1945: Proceedings of the Third Yad Vashem International Historical Conference – April 1977.* Jerusalem: Yad Vashem, 1979.

Haan, I. de. 'An Unresolved Controversy: The Jewish Honor Court in the Netherlands, 1946–1950', in L. Jokusch and G. N. Finder (eds.), *Jewish Honor Courts: Revenge, Retribution and Reconciliation in Europe and Israel after the Holocaust*. Detroit, MI: Wayne State University Press, 2016.

Hachmeister, L. *Der Gegnerforscher. Die Karriere des SS-Führers Franz Alfred Six*. Munich: Beck, 1998.

Haft, C. *The Bargain and the Bridle. The General Union of the Israélites of France, 1941–1944*. Chicago: Dialog Press, 1985.

Hájková, A. 'The making of a Zentralstelle: Die Eichmann-Männer in Amsterdam', in J. Milotová, U. Rathgeber et al. (eds.), *Theresienstädter Studien und Dokumente. Institut Theresienstädter Initiative*, 2003, 353–381.

Hand, S. and S. T. Katz (eds.). *Post-Holocaust France and the Jews, 1945–1955*. New York/London: New York University Press, 2015.

Happe, K. *Veel valse hoop: de jodenvervolging in Nederland, 1940–1945*, transl. from the German by Fred Reurs. Amsterdam: Uitgeverij Atlas Contact, 2018; first German ed. 2017.

Happe, K. 'The Role of the Jewish Council During the Occupation of the Netherlands', in F. Bajohr and A. Löw (eds.), *The Holocaust and European Societies: Social Processes and Social Dynamics*. London: Palgrave Macmillan, 2016, 207–225.

Harter, H., A. Marès et al. (eds.). *Terres promises: Mélanges offerts à André Kaspi*. Paris: Publications de la Sorbonne, 2008.

Hauff, L. *Zur politischen Rolle von Judenräten, Benjamin Murmelstein in Wien, 1938–1942*. Göttingen: Wallstein Verlag, 2014.

Have, W. ten. *1940: Verwarring en Aanpassing*. Houten: Spectrum; Amsterdam: NIOD, 2015.

Hazan, K and G. Weill, 'l'OSE et le sauvetage des enfants juifs. De l'avant-guerre à l'après-guerre' in J. Sémelin, C. Andrieu and S. Gensburger (eds.), *La résistance aux génocides. De la pluralité des actes de sauvetage*. Paris: Presses de Science Po, 2008, 259–276.

Hensen, M. and S. Jensen, *Denmark and the Holocaust*. Copenhagen: Institute for International Studies, Department for Holocaust and Genocide Studies, 2003.

Herbert, U. *Best: biographische Studien über Radikalismus, Weltanschauung und Vernunft, 1903–1989*. Bonn: Dietz, 1996.

Hershco, T. 'Le Mouvement de la jeunesse sioniste (MJS)', in C. Richet (ed.), *Organisation juive de combat. Résistance/sauvetage, France 1940–1945*. Paris: 2006, 127–131.

Herzberg, A. J. *Kroniek der Jodenvervolging, 1940–1945*. Amsterdam: Meulenhoff, 1978; first ed. 1950.

Hilberg, R. *The Destruction of the European Jews*. London: W. H. Allen, 1961; a revised and updated version of this work was published in 1985.

Hirschfeld, G. *Nazi Rule and Dutch Collaboration: The Netherlands under German Occupation, 1940–1945*, transl. from the German by L. Willmot. Oxford/ New York/Hamburg: Berg, 1988; first German ed. 1984.

Hofmeester, K. 'Antisemitismus in den Niederlanden im 19. und 20. Jahrhundert', in H. Lademacher, R. Loos and S. Groeneveld (eds.), *Ablehnung – Duldung – Anerkennung. Toleranze in den Niederlanden und in Deutschland. Ein historischer und aktueller Vergleich.* Münster/New York: Wachsmann, 2004, 604–630.

Hofmeester, K. 'Image and Self-Image of the Jewish Workers in the Labour Movements in Amsterdam, 1800–1914', in C. Brasz and Y. Kaplan (eds.), *Dutch Jews as Perceived by Themselves and by Others.* Leiden: Brill, 2001, 187–202.

Hondius, D. *Return: Holocaust Survivors and Dutch Anti-Semitism*, transl. from the Dutch by D. Colmer. Westport, CT/London: Praeger, 2003; first Dutch ed. 1990.

Houwink ten Cate, J. 'Der Befehlshaber der SiPo-SD in den besetzten niederländischen Gebiete', in W. Benz, G. Otto and J. Houwink ten Cate (eds.), *Die Bürokratie der Okkupation. Strukturen der Herrschaft und Verwaltung im besetzten Europa.* Berlin: Metropol, 1999, 87–133.

Houwink ten Cate, J. 'De Joodsche Raad voor Amsterdam 1941–1943', in W. Lindwer (ed.), *Het fatale dilemma: De Joodsche Raad voor Amsterdam 1941–1943.* 's Gravenhage SDU Uitgeverij Koninginnegracht, 1995.

Houwink ten Cate, J. 'Heydrich's Security Police and the Amsterdam Jewish Council, February 1941–October 1942', *Dutch Jewish History*, Vol. 3 (1993), 381–393.

Houwink ten Cate, J. 'De justitie en de Joodsche Raad', in E. Jonker and M. van Rossem (eds.), *Geschiedenis en cultuur: achttien opstellen.*'s Gravenhage: SDU, 1990, 149–168.

Houwink ten Cate, J. 'Het jongere deel: Demografische en sociale kenmerken van het jodendom in Nederland tijdens de vervolging', *Jaarboek van het Rijksinstituut voor Oorlogsdocumentatie*, Vol. I (1989), 9–66.

Huiskes, G. and R. van der Koef, *Vluchtelingenkamp Westerbork.* Hooghalen: Herinneringscentrum Kamp Westerbork, 1999.

Hyman, P. *The Jews of Modern France.* Berkeley: University of California Press, 1998.

Hyman, P. *From Dreyfus to Vichy: The Remaking of French Jewry, 1906–1939.* New York: Columbia University Press, 1979.

Jäckel, E. *Frankreich in Hitlers Europa. Die Deutsche Frankreichpolitik im zweiten Weltkrieg.* Stuttgart: Deutsche Verlags-Anstalt, 1966.

Jansen, C. and D. Venema. *De Hoge Raad en de Tweede Wereldoorlog: recht en rechtsbeoefening in de jaren 1930–1950.* Amsterdam: Boom, 2011.

Jokusch, L. and G. N. Finder, *Jewish Honor Courts: Revenge, Retribution and Reconciliation after the Holocaust.* Detroit, MI: Wayne State University Press, 2015.

Joly, L. *L'État contre les juifs: Vichy, les nazis et la persécution antisémite.* Paris: Éditions Grasset, 2018.

Joly, L. *Vichy dans la 'solution finale': histoire du commissariat général aux questions juives, 1941–1944.* Paris: Grasset: 2006.

Joly, L. *Xavier Vallat (1891–1972): Du nationalisme chrétien à l'antisémitisme d'État.* Paris: Grasset, 2001.

Jong, L. de. *Het Koninkrijk der Nederlanden tijdens de Tweede Wereldoorlog.* The Hague: SDU Uitgeverij Koninginnegracht (1969–1991).

Jong, L. de. *De Duitse vijfde kolonne in de Tweede Wereldoorlog*. Amsterdam: Meulenhoff, 1953.

Jonghe, A. de. 'De strijd Himmler-Reeder om de benoeming van een HSSPF te Brussel (1942–1944)', *Bijdragen tot de Geschiedenis van de Tweede Wereldoorlog*, Vol. 3 (1974), 9–81.

Jonghe, A. de. *Hitler en het politieke lot van België (1940–1944). De vestiging van een Zivilverwaltung in België en Noord-Frankrijk: Koningskwestie en bezettingsregime van de kapitulatie tot Berchtesgaden, 28 mei – 19 november 1940*, part 1. Antwerp: De Nederlandsche Boekhandel, 1972.

Kaplan, J. 'French Jewry under the Occupation', *American Jewish Yearbook*, No. 47 (1945), 71–118.

Kaspi, A. (ed.). *Histoire de l'Alliance israélite universelle de 1860 à nos jours* (Paris: Armand Collin, 2010).

Kavanaugh, S. *ORT, the Second World War and the Rehabilitation of Jewish Survivors*. London: Vallentine Mitchell, 2008.

Kershaw, I. *Hitler 1889–1936: Hubris*. London: Allen Lane, 1998.

Kershaw, I. *Hitler 1936–1945: Nemesis*. London: Allen Lane, 2000.

Kieval, H. J. 'Legality and Resistance in Jewish France: The Rescue of Jewish Children', *Proceedings of the American Philosophical Society*, Vol. 124, No. 5 (1980), 339–366.

Kinzel, T. *Im Fokus der Kamera. Fotografien aus dem ghetto Lodz*. Berlin: Metropol, 2021.

Klarsfeld, S. *Vichy-Auschwitz: le rôle de Vichy dans la solution finale de la question juive en France*, 2 Volumes. Paris: Fayard, 1983–1985; reissued in 2001 as Vol. 1 of the series *La Shoah en France*.

Klarsfeld, S. and M. Steinberg (eds.). *Dokumente. Die Endlösung der Judenfrage in Belgien*. New York: The Beate Klarsfeld Foundation, 1980.

Klarsfeld, S. *Le livre des otages: la politique des otages menée par les autorités allemandes d'occupation en France de 1941 à 1943*. Paris: Éditeurs français réunis, 1979.

Klarsfeld, S. *Le mémorial de la déportations des juifs de France*. Paris: Klarsfeld, 1978.

Klee, E. *Das Personenlexikon zum Dritten Reich: wer war was vor und nach 1945*. Frankfurt am Main: Fischer, 2003.

Klein, B. 'The Judenrat', *Jewish Social Studies*, Vol. 22, No. 1 (1960), 27–42.

Knoop, H. *De Joodsche Raad: Het drama van Abraham Asscher en David Cohen*. Amsterdam: Elsevier, 1983.

Knout, D. *Contribution à l'histoire de la resistance juive en France, 1940–1944*. Paris: Éditions du Centre, 1947.

Kok, R. 'Het fotoalbum van de Joodsche Raad voor Amsterdam', in W. Lindwer (ed.), *Het fatale dilemma: De Joodsche Raad voor Amsterdam 1941–1943*. The Hague: SDU Uitgeverij Koninginnegracht, 1995, 171–176.

Kopuit, M. *Dat heeft mijn oog gezien: het leven in oorlogstijd in krantenberichten uit de Joodse pers 1940–1945*. Kampen: Kok, 1990.

Kossmann, E. *The Low Countries 1780–1940*. Oxford: Clarendon Press, 1978.

Krausnick, H. and M. Broszat, *Anatomy of the SS*, transl. from the German by D. Long and M. Jackson. New York: Walker & Co., 1968; first German ed. 1965.

Kriegel, A. 'De la résistance juive', *Pardès*, No. 2 (1985), 191–209.

Kristel, C. *Geschiedschrijving als opdracht: Abel Herzberg, Jacques Presser en Loe de Jong over de jodenvervolging.* Amsterdam: Meulenhoff, 1998.

Kulka, O. D. 'The Reichsvereinigung and the Fate of the German Jews, 1938/9–1943. Continuity or Discontinuity in German-Jewish History in the Third Reich', in A. Paucker (ed.), *Die Juden im nationalsozialistischen Deutschland/The Jews in Nazi Germany, 1933–1945.* Tübingen: J. C. B. Mohr, 1986, 353–364.

Kwiet, K. *Reichskommissariat Niederlande: Versuch und Scheitern nationalsozialistischer Neuordnung.* Stuttgart: Deutsche Verlags-Anstalt, 1968.

Laffitte, M. 'Les Rafles de Janvier 1944 à Bordeaux et les Raisons de l'Aveuglement de l'UGIF', *Revue d'Histoire de la Shoah*, Vol. 203 (2015), 371–385.

Laffitte, M. 'Was the UGIF an Obstacle to the Rescue of Jews?', in J. Sémelin, C. Andrieu et al. (eds), *Resisting Genocide: The Multiple Forms of Rescue.* New York: Columbia University Press, 2011, 395–410.

Laffitte, M. 'L'UGIF face aux mesures antisémites de 1942', *Les Cahiers de la Shoah*, Vol. 9, No. 1 (2007), 123–190.

Laffitte, M. 'l'Association des Juifs en Belgique (AJB): Des notables postiers de la solution finale', *Revue d'Histoire de la Shoah*, Vol. 2, No. 185 (2006), 87–109.

Laffitte, M. *Juif dans la France allemande.* Paris: Éditions Tallandier, 2006.

Laffitte, M. 'L'OSE de 1942 à 1944: Une survie périlleuse sous couvert de l'UGIF', *Revue de la Shoah*, Vol. 2, No. 185 (2006), 65–86.

Laffitte, M. 'L'UGIF, collaboration ou résistance?', *Revue d'histoire de la Shoah*, Vol. 2, No. 185 (2006), 45–65.

Laffitte, M. *Un engrenage fatal: l'UGIF face aux réalités de la Shoah 1941–1944.* Paris: Liana Levy, 2003.

Laffitte, M. 'Between Memory and Lapse of Memory: The First UGIF Board of Directors', in J. K. Roth and E. Maxwell (eds), *Remembering for the Future: The Holocaust in an Age of Genocide.* Basingstoke: Palgrave, 2001, 674–687.

Lagrou, P. *The Legacy of Nazi Occupation: Patriotic Memory and National Recovery in Western Europe, 1945–1965.* Cambridge: Cambridge University Press, 2000.

Lagrou, P. 'Belgium', in B. Moore (ed.), *Resistance in Western Europe.* Oxford: Berg, 2000.

Laloum, J. 'Du culte libéral au travail social: la rue Copernic au tempts des années noires', *Archives Juives*, Vol. 41, No. 1 (2009), 118–132.

Laloum, J. 'L'UGIF et ses maisons d'enfants: l'enlèvement d'une enfant', *Monde Juif*, Vol. 124 (1990), 172–176.

Lambauer, B. *Otto Abetz et les Français, ou, l'envers de la collaboration.* Paris: Fayard, 2001.

Lang, W. de. *De razzia's van 22 en 23 februari 1941 in Amsterdam: Het lot van 389 Joodse mannen.* Amsterdam: Atlas Contact, 2021.

Latour, A. *La resistance juive en France.* Paris: Stock, 1970.

Lawson, T. *Debates on the Holocaust.* Manchester/New York: Manchester University Press, 2010.

Lazare, L. *Rescue as Resistance: How Jewish Organizations Fought the Holocaust in France*, transl. Jeffrey M. Green. New York: Columbia University Press, 1996.

Lee, D. *Pétain's Jewish Children: French Jewish Youth and the Vichy Regime.* Oxford: Oxford University Press, 2014.

Lefenfeld, N. 'Unarmed Combat: Jewish Humanitarian Resistance in France during the Shoah', in P. Henry (ed.), *Jewish Resistance against the Nazis.* Washington, DC: The Catholic University of America Press, 2014, 92–120.

Leff, L. M, *The Archives Thief: The Man Who Salvaged French Jewish History in the Wake of the Holocaust.* Oxford: Oxford University Press, 2018.

Leff, L. M, *Sacred Bonds of Solidarity: The Rise of Jewish Internationalism in Nineteenth-Century France.* Stanford, CA: Stanford University Press, 2006.

Levisse-Touzé, C. *L'Afrique du Nord dans la guerre 1939–1945.* Paris: Albin Michel, 1998.

Lévitte, S. *Le Sionisme: quelques pages de son histoire.* Paris: Éditions des Cahiers Juifs, 1936.

Leymarie, M. and J. Prévotat (eds.). *L'Action française: culture, société, politique.* Villeneuve d'Ascq: Presses universitaires du Septentrion, 2008.

Liebman, M. *Né juif. Une enfance juive pendant la guerre.* Paris and Gembloux: Duculot, 1977.

Limore, Y., 'Rescue of Jews: Between History and Memory', *Humboldt Journal of Social Relations*, Vol. 28, No. 2 (2004), 105–138.

Lindwer, W. *Het fatale dilemma: De Joodsche Raad voor Amsterdam 1941–1943.* The Hague: SDU Uitgeverij Koninginnegracht, 1995.

Lipschits, I. *De kleine sjoa: Joden in naoorlogs Nederland.* Amsterdam: Mets & Schilt, 2001.

Longerich, P. *Holocaust: The Nazi Persecution and Murder of the Jews.* Oxford: Oxford University Press, 2010.

Longerich, P. *Politik der Vernichtung: Eine Gesamtdarstellung der nationalsozialistische Judenverfolgug.* Munich: Piper, 1998.

Löw, A. and A. Zajaczkowska-Drozdz, 'Leadership in the Jewish Councils as a Social Process. The Example of Cracow', in A. Löw and F. Bajohr (eds.), *The Holocaust and European Societies: Social Processes and Social Dynamics.* London: Palgrave Macmillan, 2016, 196–203.

Löw, A. 'Documenting as a "Passion and Obsession": Photographs from the Lodz (Litzmannstadt) Ghetto', *Central European History*, Vol. 48, No. 3 (2015), 387–404.

Lozowick, Y. *Hitler's Bureaucrats. The Nazi Security Police and the Banality of Evil.* London/New York: Continuum, 2002.

Malinovich, N. *French and Jewish: Culture and the Politics of Identity in Early Twentieth-Century France.* Oxford: The Littman Library of Jewish Civilisation, 2008.

Manekin, R. 'Orthodox Jewry in Kraków at the Turn of the Twentieth Century', *Polin: Studies in Polish Jewry*, Vol. 14 (2011), 165–198.

Marcot, F. 'La Résistance dans ses lieux et milieux: des relation d'interdépendance', *La Résistance et les Français. Nouvelles approches. Cahiers de l'Institut d'Histoire du Temps Présent*, No. 37 (1997), 129–146.

Marrus, M. and R. Paxton. *Vichy France and the Jews.* Stanford, CA: Stanford University Press, 2020; this is an updated and revised version of the 1981 publication of this work.

Marrus, M. 'Varieties of Jewish Resistance: Some Categories and Comparisons in Historiographical Perspective', in Y. Gutman (ed.), *Major Changes within the Jewish People in the Wake of the Holocaust*. Jerusalem: Yad Vashem, 1996, 269–300.

Marrus, M. 'Jewish Resistance to the Holocaust', *Journal of Contemporary History*, Vol. 30, No. 1 (1995), 83–110.

Marrus, M. *The Nazi Holocaust: The Victims of the Holocaust*. Toronto: Mecklermedia, 1989.

Marrus, M. 'Jewish Leaders and the Holocaust', *French Historical Studies*, Vol. 15, No. 2 (1987), 316–331.

Marrus, M. and R. Paxton, 'The Nazis and the Jews in Occupied Western Europe, 1940–1944', *The Journal of Modern History*, Vol. 54, No. 4 (1982), 687–714.

Marrus, M. *The Politics of Assimilation. A Study of the French Jewish Community at the Time of the Dreyfus Affair*. Oxford: Clarendon Press, 1971.

Massenge, C. 'De sociale politiek', in R. van Doorslaer and J-Ph. Schreiber (eds.), *De curatoren van het getto: de vereniging van joden in België tijdens de nazi-bezetting*. Tielt: Lannoo, 2004, 215–244.

Mazower, M. *Hitler's Empire: How the Nazis Ruled Europe*. New York: The Penguin Press, 2008.

Meinen, I. *De Shoah in België*, transl. from the German by I. Goerlandt. Antwerp: De Bezige Bij, 2011; first German ed. 2009.

Meinen, I. 'De Duitse bezettingsautoriteiten en de VJB', in R. van Doorslaer and J-Ph. Schreiber (eds.), *De curatoren van het getto: de vereniging van de joden in België tijdens de nazi- bezetting*. Tielt: Lannoo, 2004, 46–70.

Melkman, J. 'De briefwisseling tussen Mr. L. E. Visser en Prof. Dr. D. Cohen', *Studia Rosenthaliana*, Vol. 8, No. 1 (1974), 107–130.

Ménager, C. *Le Sauvetage des Juifs à Paris. Histoire et Mémoire*. Paris: Presses de Sciences Po, 2005.

Meyer, A. *Täter im Verhör: die 'Endlösung der Judenfrage' in Frankreich, 1940–1944*. Darmstadt: Wissenschaftliche Buchgesellschaft, 2005.

Meyer, B. *A Fatal Balancing Act: The Dilemma of the Reich Association of Jews in Germany, 1939–1945*, transl. from the German by W. Templer. New York/ Oxford: Berghahn Books, 2016.

Michel, A. *Les Éclaireurs Israélites de France pendant la Seconde Guerre Mondiale, september 1939 – septembre 1944: action et évolution*. Paris: Éditions des Éclaireurs Israélites de France, 1985.

Michman, D. 'Comparative Research on the Holocaust in Western Europe: Its Achievements, its Limits and a Plea for a More Integrative Approach', *Moreshet Journal for the Study of the Holocaust and Antisemitism*, Vol. 17 (2020), 286–306.

Michman, D. 'Reevaluating the Emergence, Function and Form of the Jewish Councils Phenomenon', in *Ghettos, 1939–1945: New Research and Perspectives on Definition, Daily Life, and Survival: Symposium Presentations*. Washington, DC: Center for Advanced Holocaust Studies, USHMM, 2015, 67–84.

Michman, D. *The Emergence of Jewish Ghettos during the Holocaust*. New York/ Cambridge: Cambridge University Press, 2011.

Michman, D. 'Judenräte, Ghettos, Endlösung: Drei Komponenten einer anti-jüdischen Politik oder Separate Faktoren?', in J. A. Mlynarczyk and J. Böhler (eds.), *Der Judenmord in den eingegliederten polnischen Gebiete, 1939–1945*. Osnabrück: Fibre Verlag, 2010, 167–176.

Michman, D. 'Kontroversen über die Judenräte in der Jüdischen Welt, 1945–2005. Das Ineinandergreifen von öffentlichem Gedächtnis und Geschichtsschreibung', in F. Anders, K. Stoll and K. Wilke (eds.), *Der Judenrat von Białystok. Dokumente aus dem Archiv des Białystoker Ghettos 1941–1943*. Paderborn/Munich/Vienna/Zürich: Ferdinand Schöningh, 2010, 309–317.

Michman, D. 'On the Historical Interpretation of the Judenräte Issue: Between Intentionalism, Functionalism and the Integrationist Approach of the 1990s', in M. Zimmerman (ed.), *On Germans and Jews under de Nazi Regime: Essays by Three Generations of Historians*. Jerusalem: Magness Press, 2006, 385–397.

Michman, D. 'De oprichting van de VJB in internationaal perspectief', in R. van Doorslaer and J-Ph. Schreiber (eds.), *De curatoren van het getto: de vereniging van de joden in België tijdens de nazi-bezetting*. Tielt: Lannoo, 2004, 25–45.

Michman, D. 'Jewish Leadership in Extremis', in D. Stone (ed), *The Historiography of the Holocaust*. New York: Palgrave Macmillan, 2004, 319–340.

Michman, D. 'Why did Heydrich Write "the Schnellbrief"? A Remark on the Reason and on its Significance', *Yad Vashem Studies*, No. 32 (2004), 433–447.

Michman, D. *Holocaust Historiography, A Jewish Perspective: Conceptualizations, Terminology, Approaches and Fundamental Issues*. Portland, OR/London: Vallentine Mitchell, 2003.

Michman, D. 'Why Did So Many of the Jews in Antwerp Perish in the Holocaust?', *Yad Vashem Studies XXX*. Jerusalem: Yad Vashem, 2002, 465–481.

Michman, D (ed.). *Belgium and the Holocaust: Jews, Belgians, Germans*. Jerusalem: Yad Vashem Studies, 1998.

Michman, D. '"Judenräte" und "Judenvereinigungen" unter nationalsozialistischer Herrschaft: Aufbau und Anwendung eines verwaltungsmassigen Konzepts', *Zeitschrift für Geschichtswissenschaft*, Vol. 46, No. 4 (1998), 293–304.

Michman, D. 'Preparing for Occupation? A Nazi *Sicherheitsdienst* Document of Spring 1939 on the Jews of Holland', *Studia Rosenthaliana*, Vol. 31, No. 2 (1998), 173–189.

Michman, D. 'The Zionist Youth Movements in Holland and Belgium and their Activities during the Shoah', in A. Cohen, Y. Cochavi and Y. Gelber (eds), *Zionist Youth Movements during the Shoah*. New York: Lang, 1995, 145–171.

Michman, D. 'Jewish Religious Life under Nazi Domination: Nazi Attitudes and Jewish Problems', *Studies in Religion/Sciences Religieuses*, Vol. 2, No. 22 (1993), 147–165.

Michman, D. 'The Uniqueness of the Joodse Raad in the Western European Context', *Dutch Jewish History*, Vol. 3. (1993), 371–380.

Michman, D. 'De oprichting van de 'Joodsche Raad voor Amsterdam' vanuit een vergelijkend perspectief', in M. de Keizer and N. D. J. Barnouw (eds.), *Derde Jaarboek van het Rijksinstituut voor Oorlogsdocumentatie*. Zutphen: Walburg Pers, 1992, 75–100.

Michman, D. 'Migration versus "Species Hollandia Judaica". The Role of Migration in the Nineteenth and Twentieth Centuries in Preserving Ties between Dutch and World Jewry', *Studia Rosenthaliana*, Vol. 23 (1989), 54–76.

Michman, D. 'Belgium', in I. Gutman (ed.), *Encyclopedia of the Holocaust*. New York: Macmillan, 1990.

Michman, D. *Het Liberale Jodendom in Nederland 1929–1943*. Amsterdam: Van Gennep, 1988.

Michman, D. 'Planning for the Final Solution Against the Background of Developments in Holland in 1941', *Yad Vashem Studies XVII*. Jerusalem: Yad Vashem, 1986, 145–180.

Michman, D. 'Problems of Religious Life in the Netherlands during the Holocaust', in J. Michman (ed.), *Dutch Jewish History : Proceedings of the Symposium on the History of the Jews in the Netherlands*. Jerusalem: Institute for Research on Dutch Jewry, 1984, 379–399.

Michman, D. 'Die jüdische Emigration und die niederländische Reaktion zwischen 1933 und 1940', in K. Dittrich and M. Würzner (eds.), *Die Niederlande und das Deutsche Exil, 1933–1940*. Königstein: Athanäum Verlag, 1982, 73–86.

Michman, J., H. Beem and D. Michman. *Pinkas: Geschiedenis van de joodse gemeenschap in Nederland*. Amsterdam/Antwerp: Uitgeverij Contact, 1999; first ed. 1992.

Michman, J. 'The Controversial Stand of the Joodse Raad in the Netherlands: Lodewijk E. Visser's Struggle', *Yad Vashem Studies*, Vol. 10 (1994), 9–76.

Michman, J. 'The Controversy Surrounding the Jewish Council of Amsterdam. From its Inception to Present Day', in M. Marrus (ed.), *The Nazi Holocaust: Victims of the Holocaust*. Westport, CT/London: Greenwood, 1989, 821–843.

Michman, J. 'Planning for the Final Solution against the Background of Developments in Holland in 1941', *Yad Vashem Studies*, Vol. 17 (1986), 145–180.

Michna, P. 'Visual Representations of modernity in documents from the Łódź Ghetto' in J. Dominic Palmer and D. Brzeziński (eds), *Revisiting Modernity and the Holocaust: Heritage, Dilemmas, Extensions*. Abingdon, Oxon; New York, NY: Routledge, 2022, 88–107.

Michna, P. 'Modernism in the Lodz Ghetto. A Tentative Interpretation of Forgotten Holocaust Documents', *Miejsce (Place)*, Vol. 6 (2020), 81–111.

Middleton-Kaplan, R. 'The Myth of Jewish Passivity', in P. Henry (ed.), *Jewish Resistance against the Nazis*. Washington, DC: The Catholic University of America Press, 2014, 3–26.

Mildt, D. de. *De rechter en de deporteurs*. Hilversum: Uitgeverij Verloren, 2018.

Mlynarczyk, J. A. and J. Böhler (eds.). *Der Judenmord in den eingegliederten polnischen Gebieten, 1939–1945*. Osnabrück: Fibre Verlag, 2010.

Molle, P. van. *Het Belgisch parlement: 1894–1972*. Antwerp: Standaard, 1972.

Monneray, H. (ed.). *La persécution des Juifs en France et dans les autres pays de l'Ouest presentée par la France à Nuremberg: recueil de documents.* Paris: Éditions du Centre, 1947.

Moore, B. 'Integrating Self-Help into the History of Jewish Survival in Western Europe', in N. J. W. Goda (ed.), *Jewish Histories of the Holocaust: New Transnational Approaches.* New York/Oxford: Berghahn Books, 2014, 193–208.

Moore, B. *Survivors: Jewish Self-Help and Rescue in Nazi-Occupied Europe.* Oxford: Oxford University Press, 2010.

Moore, B. (ed.). *Resistance in Western Europe.* Oxford: Berg, 2000.

Moore, B. *Victims and Survivors: The Nazi Persecution of the Jews in the Netherlands 1940–1945.* Oxford: Berg, 1997.

Moore, B. *Refugees from Nazi Germany in the Netherlands, 1933–1940.* Dordrecht/Boston/Lancaster: Martinus Nijhoff, 1986.

Moraal, E. *Als ik morgen niet op transport ga ... kamp Westerbork in beleving en herinnering.* Amsterdam: De Bezige Bij, 2014.

Nefors, P. *Breendonk 1940–1945: de geschiedenis.* Antwerp: Standaard Uitgeverij, 2011; first ed. 2004.

Nicault, C. 'Face au Sionisme, 1887–1940', in A. Kaspi (ed.), *Histoire de l'Alliance Israélite Universelle de 1860 à nos jours.* Paris: Armand Colin, 2010, 189–226.

Nicault, C. 'L'Acculturation des Israélites Français au Sionisme après la Grande Guerre', *Archives Juives*, Vol. 39, No. 1 (2006), 9–28.

Nicault, C. 'L'Utopie sioniste du "nouveau Juif" et la jeunesse juive dans la France de l'après guerre: Contribution à l'histoire de l'Alyah française', *Les Cahiers de la Shoah*, Vol. 5, No. 1 (2001), 105–169.

Nicault, C. *La France et le sionisme, 1897–1948. Une rencontre manquée?* Paris: Calmann-Lévy, 1992.

Ory, P. *Les Collaborateurs, 1940–1945.* Paris: Éditions du Seuil, 1976.

Ousby, I. *Occupation: The Ordeal of France, 1940–1944.* London: Murray, 1997.

Paldiel, M. *Saving One's Own: Jewish Rescuers During the Holocaust.* Lincoln: University of Nebraska Press, 2017.

Paldiel, M. *The Righteous Among the Nations: Rescuers of Jews during the Holocaust.* Jerusalem: Yad Vashem/New York: HarperCollins, 2007.

Paxton, R. *Vichy France: Old Guard and New Order, 1940–1944.* New York: Knopf, 2001; first ed. 1972.

Perego, S. 'Jurys d'honneur: The Stakes and Limits of Purges among Jews in France after Liberation', in L. Jockusch and G. N. Finder (eds.), *Jewish Honor Courts: Revenge, Retribution, and Reconciliation in Europe and Israel after the Holocaust.* Detroit, MI: Wayne State University Press, 2016, 137–164.

Piersma, H. *De drie van Breda: Duitse oorlogsmisdadigers in Nederlandse gevangenschap, 1945–1989.* Amsterdam: Balans, 2005.

Polak, J. A. *Leven en werken van mr. L. E. Visser.* Amsterdam: Athenaeum-Polak & Van Gennep, 1997.

Poliakov, L. *Harvest of Hate. The Nazi Program for the Destruction of the Jews of Europe.* New York: Syracuse University Press, 1954.

Poliakov, L. *La condition des Juifs en France sous l'occupation italienne.* Paris: CDJC, 1946.

Poznanski, R. *Propagandes et persécutions: La Résistance et le 'problème juif'*, *1940–1944*. Paris: Fayard, 2008.

Poznanski, R. 'Union Générale des Israélites de France', in W. Laqueur (ed.), *The Holocaust Encyclopedia*. New Haven/London: Yale University Press, 2001, 653–657.

Poznanski, R. 'Le Consistoire central pendant la Guerre: Bilan et perspectives de recherches', *Revue de la Shoah. Le Monde Juif*, No. 169 (2000), 181–194.

Poznanski, R. 'Reflections on Jewish Resistance and Jewish Resistants in France', *Jewish Social Studies New Series*, Vol. 2, No. 1 (1995), 124–158.

Poznanski, R. *Jews in France During World War II*, transl. from the French by N. Bracher. Waltham, MA: Brandeis University Press, 2001; first French ed. 1994.

Poznanski, R. 'A Methodological Approach to the Study of Jewish Resistance in France', *Yad Vashem Studies*, Vol. 18 (1987), 1–39.

Presser, J. *Ondergang: de vervolging en verdelging van het Nederlandse Jodendom, 1940–1945*. The Hague: Staatsuitgeverij Martinus Nijhoff, 1965.

Puttemans, J. *De bezetter buiten: beknopte historiek van het onafhankelijkheids- front, nationale verzetsbeweging, 1941–1945*. Lier/Almere: NIOBA, 1987.

Rabinovici, D. *Instanzen der Ohnmacht. Wien 1938–1945. Der Weg zum Judenrat*. Frankfurt am Main: Jüdischer Verlag, 2000.

Rajsfus, M. *Des Juifs dans la collaboration: l'UGIF 1941–1944*. Paris: Études et Documentation Internationales, 1980.

Rayski, A. *The Choice of the Jews under Vichy: Between Submission and Resistance*, transl. from the French by W. Sayers. Notre Dame, IN: University of Notre Dame Press, 2005; first French ed. 1992.

Reitlinger, G. *The Final Solution: The Attempts to Exterminate the Jews of Europe, 1939–1945*. New York: Beechurst Press, 1953.

Rodrigue, A. 'Rearticulations of French Jewish Identities after the Dreyfus Affair', *Jewish Social Studies*, Vol. 3, No. 2 (1996), 1–24.

Rodrigue, A. *French Jews, Turkish Jews: The Alliance Israélite Universelle and the Politics of Jewish Schooling in Turkey, 1860–1945*. Bloomington: Indiana University Press, 1990.

Rosenblum, T. 'Een plaatselijk voorbeeld: het comité van Luik', in R. van Doorslaer and J-Ph. Schreiber (eds.), *De curatoren van het getto: de vereniging van de joden in België tijdens de nazi-bezetting*. Tielt: Lannoo, 2004.

Rosengart, L. 'Les maisons de l'OSE: parcours d'une enfance fragmentée', in M. Lemalet (ed.), *Au secours des enfants du siècle*. Paris: Nil, 1993.

Roth, J. K. and E. Maxwell, *Remembering for the Future: The Holocaust in an Age of Genocide*. Basingstoke: Palgrave, 2011.

Rothkirchen, L. *The Jews of Bohemia and Moravia facing the Holocaust*. Jerusalem: Yad Vashem, 2015.

Rozett, R. 'Jewish Resistance', in D. Stone (ed.), *The Historiography of the Holocaust*. Houndmills: Macmillan, 2004, 341–363.

Rubenstein, R. L. 'Grey into Black: the case of Mordecai Chaim Rumkowski', in J. Petropoulos and J. K. Roth (eds.), *Gray Zones: Ambiguity and Compromise in the Holocaust and its Aftermath*. New York: Berghahn Books, 2005, 299–310.

Ryan, D. *The Holocaust and the Jews of Marseille: The Enforcement of Anti-Semitic Policies in Vichy France*. Urbana/Chicago: University of Illinois Press, 1996.

Safrian, H. *Eichmann's Men*, transl. from the German by Ute Stargardt. New York/Cambridge: Cambridge University Press, 2010; first German ed. 1993.

Sanders, J. 'Opbouw en continuïteit na 1945', in D. Michman, H. Beem et al. (eds.), *Pinkas: Geschiedenis van de Joodse gemeenschap in Nederland*. Amsterdam/Antwerp: Uitgeverij Contact, 1999, 216–251.

Sanders, P. *Het Nationaal Steun Fonds: bijdrage tot de geschiedenis van de financiering van het verzet, 1941–1945.*' s Gravenhage: Martinus Nijhoff, 1960.

Saerens, L. 'De Jodenvervolging in België in cijfers', *Bijdragen tot de eigentijdse geschiedenis*, No. 17 (2006), 199–235.

Saerens, L. *Vreemdelingen in een wereldstad: een geschiedenis van Antwerpen en zijn Joodse bevolking (1880–1944)*. Tielt: Lannoo, 2000.

Saerens, L. 'Die Hilfe für Juden in Belgien', in W. Benz and J. Wetzel (eds.), *Solidarität und Hilfe für Juden während der NS-Zeit*, Vol. 2. Berlin: Metropol, 1998, 193–280.

Scheffler, W. *Judenverfolgung im Dritten Reich 1944 bis 1945*. Frankfurt am Main:Bücklergilde Gutenberg, 1961.

Schellekens, M. *Walter Süskind: Hoe een zakenman honderden Joodse kinderen uit handen van de nazi's redde*. Amsterdam: Athenaeum, 2011.

Schenkel, M. *De Twentse paradox: de lotgevallen van de joodse bevolking van Hengelo en Enschede tijdens de Tweede Wereldoorlog*. Zutphen: Walburg Pers, 2003.

Schippers, H. *Westerweel Group: Non-Conformist Resistance against Nazi Germany, A Joint Rescue Effort of Dutch Idealists and Dutch-German Zionists*. Berlin/Boston: De Gruyter Oldenbourg, 2019.

Schleunes, K. A. *The Twisted Road to Auschwitz: Nazi Policy toward German Jews*. Urbana/Chicago: University of Illinois Press, 1970.

Schoentgen, M. 'Luxembourg', in W. Gruner and J. Osterloh (eds.), *The Greater German Reich and the Jews: Nazi Persecution Policies in the Annexed Territories 1935–1945*. New York/Oxford: Berghahn, 2016, 307–311.

Schreiber, J-Ph. 'Tussen traditionele en verplichte gemeenschap', in R. van Doorslaer and J-Ph. Schreiber (eds.), *De vereniging van de Joden in België tijdens de nazi-bezetting*. Tielt: Lanoo, 2004, 71–110.

Schreiber, J-Ph. *Dictionnaire Biographique des Juifs de Belgique: Figures du judaïsme belge XIXe-XXe siècles*. Brussels: Éditions de Boeck Université, 2002.

Schreiber, J-Ph. 'Les Juifs en Belgique: une présence continue depuis le XIIIe siècle', *Cahiers de la Mémoire contemporaine – Bijdragen tot de eigentijdse Herinnering*, Vol. 2 (2000), 13–37.

Schreiber, J-Ph. *Politique et Religion: le consistoire central israélite de Belgique au XIXe siècle*. Brussels: Editions de l'Université de Bruxelles, 1995.

Schrijvers, P. *Rome, Athene, Jeruzalem: leven en werk van prof. dr. David Cohen*. Groningen: Historische Uitgeverij, 2000.

Schwarzfuchs, S. *Aux prises avec Vichy: Histoire politique des Juifs de France, 1940–1944*. Paris: Calmann-Lévy, 1998.

Seberechts, F. 'De Duitse instanties en de anti-Joodse politiek', in R. van Doorslaer, E. Debruyne, F. Seberechts et al. (eds.), *Gewillig België: overheid en jodenvervolging tijdens de Tweede Wereldoorlog*. Amsterdam/Antwerp, Meulenhoff/Manteau, 2007, 271–286.

Seberechts, F. 'De Belgische overheden en de Jodenvervolging, 1940–1942' in: R. van Doorslaer, E. Debruyne, F. Seberechts et al. (eds.), *Gewillig*

België: overheid en jodenvervolging tijdens de Tweede Wereldoorlog. Amsterdam/ Antwerp, Meulenhoff/Manteau, 2007, 253–373.

Seibel, W. *Macht und Moral: Die 'Endlösung der Judenfrage' in Frankreich, 1940– 1944.* Munich: Wilhelm Fink Verlag, 2010.

Sémelin, J. *The Survival of the Jews in France, 1940–1944.* London: Hurst & Company, 2018; revised and updated version of *Persécutions et entraides dans la France occupée: comment 75% des juifs en France ont échappé à la mort.* Paris: Éditions les Arènes-le Seuil, 2013.

Sémelin, J., C. Andrieu and S. Gensburger. *Resisting Genocide: The Multiple Forms of Rescue.* New York: Columbia University Press, 2011.

Sémelin, J. *Unarmed Against Hitler: Civilian Resistance in Europe, 1939–1943.* Westport, CT: Praeger, 1993.

Shabbetai, K. *As Sheep to the Slaughter? The Myth of Cowardice.* Bet Dagan: Keshev Press, 1962.

Shirman, I. 'Een aspekt van de 'Endlösung'. De ekonomische plundering van de joden in België', *Bijdragen tot de Geschiedenis van de Tweede Wereldoorlog*, Vol. 3 (1974), 163–182.

Snijders, K. *Nederlanders in Buchenwald, 1940–1945: een overzicht over de geschiedenis van Nederlandse gevangenen die tijdens de nationaal-socialistische bezetting van 1940–1945 in het concentratiekamp Buchenwald zaten.* Göttingen: Wallstein, 2001.

Sica, E. *Mussolini's Army in the French Riviera: Italy's Occupation of France.* Urbana/Chicago/ Springfield: University of Illinois Press, 2016.

Silberklang, D. *Gates of Tears: The Holocaust in the Lublin District.* Jerusalem: Yad Vashem, 2013.

Somers, E. (ed.) *Voorzitter van de Joodse Raad: de herinneringen van David Cohen.* Zutphen: Wallburg Pers, 2010.

Staal, P. *Roestvrijstaal: speurtocht naar de erfenis van Joodse oorlogswezen.* Delft: Eburon, 2008.

Steinberg, L. 'Jewish Rescue Activities in Belgium and France', in Y. Gutman and E. Zuroff (eds.), *Rescue Attempts during the Holocaust: Proceedings of the Second Yad Vashem International Historical Conference.* Jerusalem: Yad Vashem, 1977, 603–614.

Steinberg, L. *Le comité de défense des Juifs en Belgique, 1942–1944.* Brussels: Éditions de l'Université, 1973.

Steinberg, L. *La Révolte des justes: les juifs contre Hitler, 1933–1945.* Paris: Fayard, 1970.

Steinberg, M. and J. Gotovitch. *Otages de la terreur Nazi: Le Bulgare Anghelhoff en son groupe de Partisans juifs Bruxelles, 1940–1943.* Brussels: Uitgeverij VUBPress, 2007.

Steinberg, M. *La persécution des Juifs en Belgique (1940–1944).* Brussels: Éditions Complexe, 2004.

Steinberg, M. *Un Pays occupé et ses juifs: Belgique entre France et Pays-Bas.* Gerpinnes: Editions Quorum, 1998.

Steinberg, M. 'The Jews in the Years 1940–1944: Three Strategies for Coping with a Tragedy', in D. Michman (ed.), *Belgium and the Holocaust: Jews, Belgians, Germans.* Jerusalem: Yad Vashem Studies, 1998, 347–372.

Steinberg, M. 'The Trap of Legality: The Belgium Jewish Association', in M. Marrus (ed.), *The Nazi Holocaust: The Victims of the Holocaust*. Toronto: Mecklermedia, 1989, 797–820.

Steinberg, M. *L'étoile et le fusil, 3 volumes: La question juive 1940–1942 (Vol. 1), 1942. Les cent jours de la déportation des Juifs de Belgique (Vol. 2), La traque des Juifs, 1942–1944 (Vol. 3)*. Brussels: Vie ouvrière, 1983–1986.

Steur, C. *Theodor Dannecker: ein Funtionär der 'Endlösung'*. Essen: Klartext Verlag, 1997.

Struye, P. and G. Jacquemyns, *La Belgique sous l'Occupation Allemande (1940–1944)*. Brussels: Ceges, Éditions Complexe, 2002.

Suhl, Y. *They Fought Back: The Story of the Jewish Resistance in Nazi Europe*. New York: Crown Publishers, 1967.

Szajkowski, Z. *Analytical Franco-Jewish Gazetteer, 1939–1945*. New York: Shulsinger Brothers, 1966.

Szajkowski, Z. 'The Organization of the "UGIF" in Nazi-Occupied France', *Jewish Social Studies*, Vol. 9, No. 3 (1947), 239–256.

Tammes, P. (ed.), *Oostjoodse Passanten en Blijvers: Aankomst, opvang, transmigratie en vestiging van Joden uit Rusland in Amsterdam en Rotterdam 1882–1914*. Amsterdam: Menasseh ben Israel Instituut, 2013.

Tammes, P. 'Abandoning Judaism: A Life History Perspective on Disaffiliation and Conversion to Christianity among Prewar Amsterdam Jews', *Advances in Life Course Research*, Vol. 17 (2012), 81–92.

Tammes, P. '"Hack, Pack, Sack": Occupational Structure, Status and Mobility of Jews in Amsterdam, 1851–1941', *Journal of Interdisciplinary History*, Vol. 43, No. 1 (2012), 1–26.

Tammes, P. 'Demografische ontwikkeling van joden in Nederland vanaf hun burgerlijke gelijkstelling tot aan de Duitse bezetting', in K. Matthijs, B. van de Putte, J. Kok et al. (eds.), *Leven in de Lage Landen: Historisch-demografisch onderzoek in Vlaanderen en Nederland*. Leuven/Den Haag, Acco: 2010, 239–269.

Tammes, P. 'Jewish Immigrants in the Netherlands during the Nazi Occupation', *The Journal of Interdisciplinary History*, Vol. 37, No. 4 (2007), 543–562.

Trunk, I. *Jewish Responses to Nazi Persecution: Collective and Individual Behavior in Extremis*. New York: Stein and Day, 1979.

Trunk, I. *Judenrat: The Jewish Councils in Eastern Europe under Nazi Occupation*. Lincoln: University of Nebraska Press, 1996; first ed. 1972.

Tuchel, J. 'Heinrich Müller: Prototyp des Schreibtischtäters', H. C. Jasch and C. Kreutzmüller (eds.), *Die Teilnehmer: die Männer der Wannsee-Konferenz*. Berlin: Metropol-Verlag, 2017, 111–128.

Umbreit, H. *Der Militärbefehlshaber in Frankreich*. Boppard am Rhein: Harald Boldt Verlag, 1968.

Unger, M. *Reassessment of the Image of Mordechai Chaim Rumkowski*, transl. N. Greenwood. Jerusalem: Yad Vashem, 2004.

Valk, H. J. *De Rotterdamse Joden tijdens de bezetting*. Rotterdam: s.n., 1955.

Vandepontseele, S. 'De verplichte tewerkstelling van joden in België en Noord-Frankrijk', in R. van Doorslaer and J-Ph. Schreiber (eds.), *De curatoren van het getto: de vereniging van de joden in België tijdens de nazi-bezetting.* Tielt: Lannoo, 2004.

Vastenhout, L. 'Remain or Resign? Jewish Leaders' Dilemmas in the Netherlands and Belgium under Nazi Occupation', *Holocaust and Genocide Studies*, forthcoming.

Vastenhout, L. 'The Jewish Council of Amsterdam: A (More) Useful Tool in the Deportation Process?' in P. Black, M. Raggam-Blesch and M. Windsperger (eds.), *Deportations of the Jewish Population in Territories under Nazi Control. Comparative Perspectives on the Organization of the Path to Annihilation*, Beiträge zur Holocaustforschung des Wiener Wiesenthal Instituts für Holocaust–Studien (VWI), Vol. 9. Vienna: New Academic Press, forthcoming.

Vastenhout, L. 'Filling a Leadership Void: Salomon Ullmann's Position during Nazi Occupation', *Les Cahiers de la Mémoire Contemporaine/Bijdragen tot de Eigentijdse Herinnering*, forthcoming.

Vastenhout, L. 'Female Involvement in the 'Jewish Councils' of the Netherlands and France: Gertrude van Tijn and Juliette Stern', in D. Nešťáková, K. Grosse-Sommer, B. Klacsmann et al. (eds.), *If This is a Woman: Studies on Women and Gender in the Holocaust*. Boston: Academic Studies Press, 2021, 142–160.

Velaers, J. and H. van Goethem. *Leopold III: De koning, het land, de oorlog.* Tielt: Lannoo, 1994.

Veld, N. K. C. in 't. *De Joodse Ereraad.* The Hague: SDU Uitgeverij, 1989.

Verhoeyen, E. *België Bezet, 1940–1944.* Brussels: BRTN Educatieve Uitgaven, 1993.

Vincenot, A. *La France résistance. Histoire de héros ordinaires.* Paris: Les Syrtes, 2004.

Vries, H. de. 'Sie starben wie Fliegen im Herbst', in H. de Vries, A. B. van Keulen-Woudstra and H. Vinckers (eds.), *Mauthausen: 1938–1988.* Bredevoort: Achterland, 2000, 7–18.

Vromen, S. *Hidden Children of the Holocaust: Belgian Nuns and Their Daring Rescue of Young Jews from the Nazis.* New York/Oxford: Oxford University Press, 2008.

Wasserstein, B. *Gertrude van Tijn en het lot van de Nederlandse Joden.* Amsterdam: Nieuw Amsterdam Uitgevers, 2013; this work was published in English as *The Ambiguity of Virtue: Gertrude van Tijn and the Fate of Dutch Jews.* Cambridge, MA: Harvard University Press, 2014.

Weber, E. 'Reflections on the Jews in France', in F. Malino and B. Wasserstein (eds.), *The Jews in Modern France.* Hanover/London: University Press of New England, 1985, 8–27.

Weinberg, D. 'The Revival of French Jewry in Post-Holocaust France: Challenges and Opportunities', in S. Hand and S. T. Katz (eds.), *Post-Holocaust France and the Jews.* New York/London: New York University Press, 2015, 26–37.

Weinberg, D. *A Community on Trial: The Jews of Paris in the 1930s.* Chicago: University of Chicago Press, 1977.

Weisberg, R. *Vichy Law and the Holocaust in France.* Amsterdam: Harwood Academic Publishers, 1996.

Weiss, A. 'Jewish Leadership in Occupied Poland: Postures and Attitudes', *Yad Vashem Studies*, Vol. 12 (1977), 335–365.

Wielek, H. *De oorlog die Hitler won*. Amsterdam: Amsterdamsche Boek- en Courantmij, 1947.

Wieviorka, A. 'Les Juifs en France au lendemain de la guerre: état des lieux', *Archives Juives. Revue d'histoire des Juifs de France*, Vol. 1, No. 28 (1995), 4–22.

Wieviorka, A. *Ils étaient juifs, résistants, communistes*. Paris: Denoël, 1986.

Wieviorka, A. 'l'UGIF n'a jamais été un Judenrat', *Pardès*, Vol. 2 (1985), 191–209.

Wieviorka, A. and M. Laffitte. *À l'intérieur du camp de Drancy*. Paris: Perrin, 2012.

Wieviorka, O. *The Resistance in Western Europe, 1940–1945*, transl. from the French by J. M. Todd. New York: Columbia University Press, 2019; first French ed. 2017.

Wieviorka, O. *The French Resistance*, transl. from the French by J. M. Todd. Cambridge, MA/London: The Belknap Press of Harvard University Press, 2016; first French ed. 2013.

Wieviorka, O. 'France' in B. Moore (ed.), *Resistance in Western Europe*. Oxford: Berg, 2000, 125–155.

Wormser, G. *Français israélites: Une doctrine – une tradition – une époque*. Paris: Éditions de Minuit, 1963.

Wouters, N. 'The Belgian Trials', in D. Bankier and D. Michman (eds.), *Holocaust and Justice: Representation and Historiography of the Holocaust in Post-War Trials*. Jerusalem: Yad Vashem/New York/Oxford: Berghahn Books, 2010, 219–244.

Wouters, N. 'De Jodenvervolging voor de Belgische rechters, 1944–1951', in R. van Doorslaer, E. Debruyne et al. (eds), *Gewillig België: overheid en jodenvervolging tijdens de Tweede Wereldoorlog*. Amsterdam/Antwerp: Meulenhoff/ Manteau, 2007, 801–1029.

Wouters, N. *De Führerstaat: overheid en collaboratie in België, 1940–1944*. Tielt: Lannoo, 2006.

Yagil, L. *Chrétiens et Juifs sous Vichy (1940–1944): sauvetage et désobéissance civile*. Paris: Cerf, 2005.

Yahil, L. 'The Jewish Leadership of France', in Y. Gutman and C. J. Haft (eds), *Patterns of Jewish Leadership in Nazi-Europe, 1933–1945: Proceedings of the Third Yad Vashem International Conference*. Jerusalem: Yad Vashem, 1979, 317–333.

Yahil, L. *The Holocaust: The Fate of European Jewry, 1932–1945*, transl. from the Hebrew by I. Friedman and H. Galai. New York/Oxford: Oxford University Press, 1990.

Zariz, R. 'The Jews of Luxembourg during the Second World War', *Holocaust and Genocide Studies*, Vol. 7, No. 1 (1993), 51–66.

Zee, N. van der. *Om erger te voorkomen: de voorgeschiedenis en uitvoering van de vernietiging van het Nederlandse jodendom tijdens de Tweede Wereldoorlog*. Amsterdam: Meulenhoff, 1997.

Zeitoun, S. 'L'OSE au secours des enfants Juifs', in *Le Sauvetage des Enfants Juifs de France. Actes de Colloque de Guéret – 29 et 30 May 1996*. Guéret: Associations pour la recherche et la sauvegarde de la vérité historique sur la Résistance en Creuse, undated, 93–104.

Zimmerman, M (ed.), *On Germans and Jews under the Nazi Regime: Essays by Three Generations of Historians*. Jerusalem: Magnes Press, 2006.

Zuccotti, S. *The Holocaust, the French and the Jews*. Lincoln University of Nebraska Press, 1999; first ed. 1993.

Unpublished secondary sources

Donnet, A. 'Le procès de l'A. J. B. n'aura pas lieu: Analyse du dossier 8036/44 de l'Auditorat Militaire de Bruxelles', doctoral thesis Katholieke Universiteit Leuven, 1992–1993.

Doorslaer, R. van. 'De kinderen van het getto: Joodse immigratie en communisme in België 1925–1940', doctoral thesis Rijksuniversiteit Gent, 1990.

Douarion, B. le, 'Le Comité "Rue Amelot", 1940–1944 à Paris. Assistance aux Juifs et Sauvetage des Enfants', master's thesis Paris Sorbonne, 1994.

Hofmeester, K. 'De Joodse Raad in de illegale pers: de berichtgeving over de Joodse Raad in zes illegale bladen nader beschouwd', doctoral thesis Universiteit Amsterdam, 1987.

Kieval, H. *'From Social Work to Resistance: Relief and Rescue of Jewish Children in Vichy France'*, BA Harvard University, 1973.

Manekin, R. 'The Growth and Development of Jewish Orthodoxy in Galicia: the "Machsike Hadas" Society 1867-1883', doctoral thesis (in Hebrew) Hebrew University, 2000.

Romijn, P. 'Snel, streng en rechtvaardig: politiek beleid inzake de bestraffing en reclassering van "foute" Nederlanders, 1945–1955', doctoral thesis Rijksuniversiteit Groningen, 1989.

Stamberger, J. 'Jewish Migration and the Making of a Belgian Jewry', doctoral thesis University of Antwerp, 2020.

Index

Visser, Lodewijk Ernst, 9, 54, 55, 66, 98,
    124, 178

Weill, Joseph, 108
Westerbork, 159, 169, 233–238
Wiener, Rabbi Joseph, 28, 46, 117

Yellow star. *See* Jewish star

Zionism
  Belgium, 127
  In society, 26–28, 36, 180, 182, 247
  Of council members, 115–117, 144,
      232
  Effect of, 34

France
  In society, 203, 212–213
  Of council members, 32–33, 45, 105,
      112–113, 221–223
  Netherlands, 24–25, 32, 42–43, 54,
      97, 179
Zionist Youth Movement (Mouvement de
    Jeunesse Sioniste, MJS), 212–213,
    222–224
Zmigrod, Irène, 192, 231
Zöpf, Wilhelm (Willy), 60, 64, 67, 71,
    165
Zuilen (*pillars*), 26
Zwangsvereinigung (compulsory
    organisation), 77, 255

For EU product safety concerns, contact us at Calle de José Abascal, 56–1°, 28003 Madrid, Spain or eugpsr@cambridge.org.

www.ingramcontent.com/pod-product-compliance
Ingram Content Group UK Ltd.
Pitfield, Milton Keynes, MK11 3LW, UK
UKHW020358140625

459647UK00020B/2537